FRED COUPLES

FRED COUPLES

Golf's Reluctant Superstar

Kathlene Bissell

Forewords by
Jim Nantz and Paul Marchand

CB
CONTEMPORARY BOOKS

Library of Congress Cataloging-in-Publication Data

Bissell, Kathlene.
    Fred Couples : golf's reluctant superstar / Kathlene Bissell ;
foreword by Jim Nantz and Paul Marchand.
       p.   cm.
    ISBN 0-8092-2778-9 (cloth)
        0-8092-2485-2 (paper)
     1. Couples, Fred, 1959–   .   2. Golfers—United States—
Biography.
   I. Title.
GV964.C68B57   1999
796.352′092—dc21
[B]   99-17944
                                           CIP

Cover design by Todd Petersen
Front-cover photograph copyright © 1992 Gary Newkirk / Allsport USA
Back-cover photographs: top, copyright © 1996 J. D. Cuban / Allsport USA; bottom,
copyright © 1992 David Cannon / Allsport USA
Author photograph by Zuzana Killam courtesy of the *Jacksonville* (Ill.) *Journal-Courier*
Interior design by Jeanette Wojtyla
Interior photographs courtesy of the author except as noted

Published by Contemporary Books
A division of NTC/Contemporary Publishing Group, Inc.
4255 West Touhy Avenue, Lincolnwood (Chicago), Illinois 60712-1975 U.S.A.
Copyright © 1999 by Kathlene Bissell
Printed in the United States of America
International Standard Book Number: 0-8092-2778-9 (cloth)
                                      0-8092-2485-2 (paper)

00 01 02 03 04 05 LB 21 20 19 18 17 16 15 14 13 12 11 10 9 8 7 6 5 4 3 2 1

This book is dedicated to Violet and Tom Couples,
who were apart only four days during their 46-year marriage.

Contents

Foreword

The first time I saw him, I knew Fred was destined for greatness. We met on August 29, 1977. Coach Dave Williams of the University of Houston welcomed his next class of freshman golfers, who would one day contribute to his growing list of championships. We were all feeling awkward and uneasy about meeting new friends and anxious to find out if our golf games measured up to Houston's unparalleled standards. There were seven of us in all. Everyone seemed a bit edgy except for this quiet, self-assured kid from Seattle. After a brief introduction, Coach immediately put us to the test with a round of golf at Sugar Creek Country Club, a half-hour drive from campus. We all felt some pressure in our attempts to make a positive first impression, and although I didn't play in Fred's group I certainly felt his presence. While I plodded along, hitting numerous pitch-out shots en route to a wayward 81, Fred was bombing tee shots into us with amazing ease, firing an effortless 70, the day's lowest round. I knew then, witnessing that indescribable swing, that I would never beat him in golf.

We had a ball in college. While I was clearly the least-gifted golfer, I also was perhaps the most meticulous one about other issues, such as going to class. It was no accident that by second year, Coach Williams had put me in a four-person suite with Fred, Blaine McCallister, and John Horne. I was always certain of Fred's future, and I wanted to make sure he never lost sight of it. Every time I introduced him to a new friend, it was "This is Fred Couples, he's going to look great someday in a green jacket." By my junior year, I was still living in the suite with the guys, but I'd given up on golf. I began my broadcasting journey at a local radio station and would practice my interviewing skills with my ever-willing roommates. With Fred, the make-believe interview was always set in Augusta's famed Butler Cabin. We would imagine he had just won the Masters, his favorite tournament. Of course, I would pretend that I was sitting across from him as CBS's host. To this day, people think this story makes "good copy" and can't possibly be true, but it is. On April 12, 1992, the interview happened again, only this time we were in the Butler Cabin, not our dorm room, and this time the whole world was watching.

I often get asked what Fred is really like. The truth is, all you have to do is look at him to find the answer. He's kind, he's gentle, and he's still shy. On the golf course, he has always had charisma, and it seems as though he is enveloped in a sense of magic, an aura that was evident that first day of college.

One thing that has led to his enormous popularity is his endearing childlike innocence. Speaking of children, he is completely smitten by them. There is nothing he adores more than his little GiGi and Oliver, and it is so pleasing to see the genuine joy and happiness they have given him along with his wonderful wife, Thais.

Fred is fiercely loyal to friends and family. The world may know him as a great golfer, but I promise you, he's even a better person. The only thing that I would wish for him would be at least one more green jacket. After all, when we were kids, we rehearsed the ceremony more than once.

Jim Nantz

Foreword

I've been a lucky person in so many ways. One is that one of my true heroes in life is also one of my best friends. Because of this friendship, I've logged thousands of miles the last 12 years studying and occasionally offering advice to one of the "handful of most talented golfers in the history of the game." I don't use that phrase without having done my homework. You see, I became fascinated with golf about 30 years ago as a 10-year-old Hoosier. I knew by age 15 that my passion was about figuring out the golf swing. That was when I caught my first glimpse of the pros. My dad was given a couple of Masters badges as a gift, and we made our first trip to Augusta in 1972, not knowing how a golf tournament could leave such a lasting mark on an aspiring junior golfer. Needless to say, the memory of the warm, drizzly April night 20 years later when a few friends and I took turns trying on Fred's new green jacket will proudly be etched right on the surface of my mind forever.

My teenage years were spent on the course, the range, and at night with my head in all the golf books and journals I could get my hands on. After a lot of practice and some good results in junior and school tournaments, I received a golf scholarship to the University of Houston. Because of the great success of Coach Dave Williams in the 1960s and '70s, UH's golf program was chock full of good players during all the years I was there, a real hotbed of young talent. After all the work I'd done trying to figure out this complex game and learning from other good players, I knew immediately that the skinny kid from Seattle who lived across the hall had some very special gifts. His natural talent and freewheeling disposition were a sight to behold, his array of skills immense. Graceful power, soft touch, creative scrambling, cool confidence. His shotmaking seemed to me more like an art form than a sport. Indeed, he was a "player" from the very start.

Now, as a "grown-up" junior player who makes a living as a club professional teaching the game, I have a much more thorough understanding and appreciation of what I was witnessing in those early years back at

UH. And I have watched with pleasure as Fred's star has risen to the very top of professional golf. Along the way he has won over the hearts of so many golf fans. Finally! A book to help illuminate the Fred fascination. On the following pages you can enjoy some insight into all those qualities that make Fred Couples such a compelling sports star. His talent and good looks make a great package. Dig a little deeper and you can't help but admire Fred's quiet strength through all the ups and downs of both golf and life. His humor and humility have been his ever-present personality characteristics. And I would say that in all the years of following Fred around the golf course I have found his authentic style so refreshing. There has always been a real sincerity in Fred's uncomplicated and unaffected nature. While looking so calm and relaxed, Fred performs his skills right out of his soul. And you can't help but root for talent with that kind of honesty. Read on to help quench that thirst for some Fred facts. And in the meantime, Fred, keep playing on. We're pulling for you!

Paul Marchand

Preface

I want to thank Fred Couples for allowing me to write about his life and career. Fred has placed a huge amount of trust in me, particularly since life has thrown him many off-speed pitches. It has been an honor to work on re-creating his story.

As you'll discover, this book could not have been completed without cooperation from his friends, many of whom are his biggest fans. They recall amazing situations that Fred would say are "no big deal," one of his favorite phrases. They remember situations that demonstrate more than one-word descriptions ever could, the kind of person Fred Couples is off the course. And many, like Jim Nantz and Paul Marchand, have been with him through exhilaration and despair. All in all, as they have said, Fred Couples is the kind of guy you can count on and like to call a friend whether he's famous or not.

Jim and Paul have known Fred since their college days when they were all members of the University of Houston golf team. To have them participate with such enthusiasm was more than rewarding. Their perspectives are invaluable because they have seen Fred grow as a person, facing challenges, overcoming difficulties. Their comments and "I was there when" examples add significantly to the overall picture.

Now, to answer the first question people ask me, which is "How did *you* get to write a book on Fred Couples's life?" The easy answer is I asked him. Twice. The first time was in 1992, between Fred's victory at Bay Hill and the Players Championship. I told him he was looking pretty much like a superstar and asked if we could work on a book about his career. He said it wasn't a good time. I didn't realize then exactly what he meant, but by the end of 1992, I understood.

The harder answer is that it took 15 years.

I met Fred about six or seven months after I had started writing about golf. He was practicing after a round at Bay Hill. It was 1984. I asked if I could talk to him at his convenience for a story on mixed-team events. Many people play those at their own clubs and courses, and because Fred had won the J.C. Penney Mixed Team, it made sense to ask him about the best way to approach that kind of competition. He agreed, and we talked in the grill room after he was done practicing. I found Fred was easy to talk to. Direct. Honest. Mentally quick. My impression was that he was sincere in what he said. I have not changed my opinion about him since that initial interview. He is still the same person. He gets pulled in more directions, but he is still the same guy.

About a year later, I accepted a position with a golf and real estate development company in California that, as luck or circumstance would have it, was also one of the companies that Fred represented. Because of that connection, I would see Fred from time to time at events. When I started a television program, he agreed to do instruction and often did interviews for the program. And so, in that way, I had a record—over time—of his thoughts and feelings about the game, what he was trying to do with his career, beginning in 1984 and extending to the present. He knew I had that material and knew we didn't have to cover old ground. Like any busy person, Fred hates to waste time doing the same thing twice. There was a lot I didn't have to ask him, and he knew that, too.

Four years after Fred said it wasn't the right time, he gave this project the nod with the idea that it would be dedicated to his mother, Violet, who died in 1994.

Fred knew I met Violet at the Skins Game in 1992, and he was aware of how highly I regarded her. Violet was a vibrant, warm, friendly, outgoing woman, and other than the late Dinah Shore or Barbara Nicklaus, I had not met anyone who—on first impression—exuded that much charm. I could see the happy part of Fred's personality in her. Violet was exceptional, as many of her friends will attest. Unfortunately, I never saw Violet again. But I have never been able to forget her. So, Violet, wherever you are, and Mr. C, as she called Fred's father, this is for you.

Acknowledgments

From day one, Rob Taylor, my editor at NTC/Contemporary Publishing, understood Fred Couples's special place in golf. Rob spearheaded this project from beginning to end. He was not forced to leap any tall buildings, but he came close on occasion. Without his guidance and interest, and that of Editorial Director John Nolan, this story about the life of one of golf's most popular players would still be untold.

This book is for Violet and Tom Couples and also for the millions of Fred's fans from Riviera to Westchester, Miami to Seattle, Manila to Dubai, who—like many of his friends—view Fred as an exceptional talent. What Marilyn was to a hot summer in New York, Fred is to golf. And that's why everyone wants to know about him.

As *Sports Illustrated*'s Rick Reilly once noted: "Fred Couples is like chocolate. Nearly everybody likes him and most people like him a lot."

Many fans know by now that Fred married Thais Bren in September of 1998. Thais possesses the same warm, wonderful qualities that made Violet Couples one in a million. And that's why Fred couldn't do without her.

My thank-you list is long, but significant. As you read, you'll see where they helped.

Rob Taylor and John Nolan at NTC/Contemporary Publishing.

Thais Bren Couples and Cindy Couples Sparks. Jim Nantz, Paul Marchand, who are well known to many. Ann and Tony Porcello, the late Pete Sobich, and Paul Kaimakis—all of the Seattle area.

Caddies—the most all-encompassing one-word job description anywhere—Joe LaCava and Linn Strickler.

CBS Sports, especially Chuck Will and Lance Barrow. NBC Sports, especially Tommy Roy. The USGA, especially Suzanne Carlson. PGA of America, especially Jamie Roggero, Julius Mason, and Montana Pritchard. The PGA Tour, many people for many things.

John Ashworth, John Bracken, John McClure, and Mark Rolfing, who are Fred's friends and business associates.

Brad Faxon, Raymond Floyd, Jay Haas, Davis Love III, Mark O'Meara, Tom Purtzer, Payne Stewart, and Tom Watson, who are who they are.

Lynn Roach and Ann Nimmer of the Players Group.

Gerald Barton and Chris Cole, Dave Boone of DDB Needham, Helen Casey, Chris Cole, Steve Cole, Ron Drapeau of Odyssey, Steve Dallas, Terry Diehl (formerly of just about everything including the PGA Tour, OCC and ESPN), John Horne, Gordon Johnson, Marquis Mefford, Tim O'Connor (of Palm Beach Polo and Country Club), David and Fred Renker, Marge Ryan, Louise Stone, Tommy Tolles, and Susan Ryan Weeks.

Dick Harmon, of River Oaks Country Club, and Charlie and Judy Epps, who run the Three Amigos.

Librarians at University of North Florida, PNGA, Seattle Public Library, Jacksonville Public Library, fastscripts, Monte Kohler and Janice Niles-Davis (of O'Dea High School), University of Houston Sports Information Department, and Chris Gray and Jerry Fehr from Washington Junior Golf.

Several golf-writing friends who helped with finding facts and providing details here and there: Larry Bohannon, of the *Desert Sun*; Doug Ferguson, of AP; Doc Giffin, who is Arnold Palmer's press secretary; Melanie Hauser; Len Shapiro, of the *Washington Post*; Bev Norwood, of IMG; Craig Smith, of the *Seattle Times*; Garry Smits, of the *Florida Times Union*; Bob Sommers, former editor of *Golf Journal*; and Gary Newkirk, whose photo was chosen for the cover. Gary, thanks as ever, for being in the right place at the right time.

Tournament people and events including Fred Robledo, General Bill Yancey, and Ernie Dunlevie. The Bob Hope Chrysler Classic. The Doral Ryder Open and Judi Janofsky. The FedEx St. Jude Classic. Charlie Brotman and the Kemper Open. Tom Place and the World Cup of Golf. In addition, the tournament media directors at the 150–200 events I have attended since 1984.

Very special thanks to Jaime Diaz, Larry Dorman, Steve Hershey, and Gary Van Sickle—four wonderful writers—for their excellent coverage of golf over the years and, as a bonus, their friendship.

Of special note are the photographers who took me under their collective wings in 1984 to teach me how to shoot golf: Brian Morgan, Tony Roberts, and the late Lawrence Levy.

And last, but certainly not least, Red and Gert Hohmann for helping me along the fairways and out of the rough and teaching me how to play golf in the first place.

FRED COUPLES

1

"Classic Couples"[1]

> *"When I grow up, I want to be just like Arnold Palmer."*
>
> —from a Fred Couples elementary-school paper

Bermuda Dunes Country Club wasn't quite Augusta National, but for Fred Couples, who had recently navigated another heart-stopping, hairpin turn on his E-ticket, roller-coaster-ride called Life, the 1998 Bob Hope Chrysler Classic was as good a place as any for a midcourse correction.

The California desert community where the tournament is played still enjoys the veneer of its celebrity-strewn history, but for Couples, the location meant more than that. For him, it had personal history. It was where he was married. Where he made adult friends. Where he bought his first home. Where he met the rich and famous and became one of them. Where George Brett, Johnny Bench, John Cook, and even Dinah Shore had been neighbors.

When Couples arrived on the Friday before tournament week, he had a fine supporting cast providing positive intangibles. His girlfriend, Thais Bren, accompanied him, and one of his best friends, John McClure, had arrived from Dallas. Couples and McClure had known each other for years. McClure sold him his house in Rancho Mirage in 1984. They had played golf often when McClure worked as assistant project manager at Mission Hills, home of the Dinah Shore tournament. Later, when Couples moved east to the Palm Beach Polo and Country Club and McClure was transferred there to work on real estate development, they resumed their friendship. The two played friendly golf Saturday and Sunday and later called it practice. By Monday, McClure had returned to Dallas and, like the other half of a tag team, caddie Joe LaCava appeared on the doorstep. Ann and Tony Porcello, who had known Couples since he was a youngster, filled out the ranks since they often spent the winter season in Indian Wells.

At the golf course, Couples's Tour friends greeted him for the first time since the fall season. The Hope was the first full-field tournament of the year. La Costa Resort had hosted the Mercedes Championships the week before, but that featured *winners* from 1997, and for only the second time in eight seasons, Couples had not earned a place in the event.

In the pressroom, nationally known writers, including the late Jim Murray from the *Los Angeles Times* and Bob Verdi of *Golf World*, gathered, as did others who had followed Couples's career.

Couples was surrounded by people who had tracked his progress and who wished him well. Yet, at the beginning of the week, not one of his friends, fans, followers, or any member of the working press would have picked Fred Couples to win the arduous, 90-hole Bob Hope tournament. They knew six-hour pro-am rounds would test his patience and torment his tender back. The previous year, TV cameras had even shown him lying down in the fairway, stretching during a round. They knew what he'd been through the last nine months. His father's death. His girlfriend's breast cancer treatments. His professional life had been put on hold while he dealt with Real Life. Even grizzled, cynical journalists hoped he would play decently, handle the questions about his father as best he could. No one expected much from him. Absolutely no one anticipated a victory. Couples was about to prove one more time how unpredictable he could be.

The Bob Hope Chrysler Classic is a stalwart on the PGA Tour, with a glittering 39-year history. It's not the longest-running event. That honor goes to the Western Open, which began in 1899.[2]

The origins of the Bob Hope Chrysler Classic can be traced to the 1959 Thunderbird Invitational, played at Thunderbird Country Club, the first 18-hole, postwar golf course in the desert. In 1960 it became the Palm Springs Golf Classic.

After many requests, Bob Hope finally allowed his name to be used in 1965, bringing the tourney instant prestige, which the touring professionals needed at that time.[3] Hope also attracted a cavalcade of stars, and when the tournament was televised, the stars were put on the host course. It became known as the "A Rotation," the featured location for the Saturday telecast.

The A Rotation is where Arnold Palmer plays. Where President Ford plays. Where Bob Hope, up until a few years ago, played. Where the defending champion plays. It is subject to big galleries, huge demands for autographs, and a general frenzied hubbub that increases each day as the tournament progresses.

Before the 1998 tournament, Couples made a request. He asked that he be allowed to play in the "noncelebrity" field. Because the tournament director understood what Couples had been through in 1997, the request was granted, although ordinarily Couples would be a definite A Rotation player. At that point Couples was like a hermit crab coming out of a too-small, borrowed shell in search of a roomier, more comfortable one. He was Punxsutawney Phil checking for a shadow. He wanted to take a peek, but if he didn't like what he saw, he might well go back into hiding for another six weeks.

And so, playing well out of the limelight in the noncelebrity field, Fred Couples hit his first drive of the year on Wednesday at La Quinta Country Club and went on to post an opening-round 64. He said he putted well, "which you do when you're eight under. If you can do well at this course, then you've got a chance in the tournament. Last year I shot 71 here, so I'm really pleased about today."[4] Andrew Magee, however, fired a first-round 63 at Indian Wells to take the lead.

On Thursday, Bruce "I-never-practice-off-season-and-I-don't-play-much-either-but-I-still-go-to-the-bank" Lietzke followed his first-round 65 with a second 65, this time at Indian Wells. At the end of the day, he was leading by a shot over Magee, who had posted a 68.

In his second round, Couples played at PGA West on the Arnold Palmer course, where he bogeyed four of the last five holes and still managed a 70.

As luck would have it, on Friday Couples played with Don Sutton, who had just been elected into the Baseball Hall of Fame. For Couples, a life-long baseball fan, this was a gift from heaven. They could talk sports. Relax. For Don Sutton, a golf enthusiast and a golf commentator for Turner Sports, playing with Fred Couples was equally exciting. Sutton even brought souvenirs from Cooperstown for Couples and his caddie, Joe LaCava.[5]

They started on the back nine at Bermuda Dunes, and Couples provided fireworks with a stunning eagle at the 18th, finishing with a 66 despite what he called an average back nine. He was four shots back of the leader, Andrew Magee, who couldn't seem to do anything but shoot low.

After the third round, Couples was brought to the interview room. Usually four behind the lead doesn't rate an interview. But it was Fred Couples. It was his first tournament of the year. Everybody in the press corps knew about his off-course problems. Yet, in spite of that, he was in contention.

"I really thought the way I was hitting it, I would play well. I was five under on the front, and the back nine . . ." He paused, as though looking for the right words. "I am just a little golf tired. I just scrambled a little bit. I can't keep it going just yet. As I was just telling someone, tomorrow is obviously a big day. I am playing Indian Wells, and other people are playing courses where you can still shoot six or seven under, but if I play well tomorrow, I think I can keep myself in the tournament. If I don't, it's over. As you know, you need to birdie every other hole to have a shot at this thing.

"I have a lot of goals," he added. "But if I don't win here, I am not going to be in here on Sunday saying my goal is to dedicate this year to playing better. I want to play better. If I practice and play more, I will play better. If I don't, then I will play like I did last year, and I don't plan on doing that."

Strong words for a guy who rarely makes statements: Goals. Playing better. Caring about it. It sounded very much like a wiser, more mature, sensible Fred Couples, not the one who had been accused by Tom Weiskopf seven years earlier of having "no goals in life. Not one."

Meanwhile, Andrew Magee's third-round 64 at the Palmer Course included six birdies on the front nine and two on the back. It could have been lower. He missed two birdie putts inside four feet, but the golf gods also gave him two 25-footers.

"I played probably the best round of golf I've played in two years," Magee claimed afterward. "I hit every fairway and every green." Magee was 21 under par, a new 54-hole tournament record.

On Saturday, the A Rotation put on their show at Bermuda Dunes. Alice Cooper, ponytail tied back. Glenn Frey, singing and swinging. San Francisco 49er Jerry Rice was mobbed by fans. Greg Maddux looked on in agony after a misdirected tee shot. Gerald Ford gave it a thumbs-up when his ball found the short grass instead of spectators.

But Bruce Lietzke, playing at PGA West, fired a course record–tying 62 (David Duval broke the record with a 59 in 1999) to become coleader with Andrew Magee.

Lietzke said afterward in the pressroom at Bermuda Dunes, "I didn't make a putt over fifteen or sixteen feet. I didn't make any oceangoers. I just hit it really, really close a lot."

Many liked Lietzke's chances on Sunday because he had won the Bob Hope in 1981, when Bermuda Dunes was also the host course. Lietzke, a pronounced fader of the ball, added, "For me this golf course plays easier than any of the other ones, for my particular game. But I expect it does for a lot of players." Magee agreed.

After Couples's Saturday round at Indian Wells, Mark Rolfing of NBC interviewed him. He had finished birdie-birdie, and Rolfing asked if it felt good to be back. "I'm looking for a good year, like everyone else," Couples commented. "For me, last year was a struggle. I'm ready for this year. I don't want to say too much more."

Rolfing mentioned Couples's personal problems off the course the previous year, the illness of his girlfriend, the death of his father. Mentioned the effect it might have on his game. It had to be difficult for Rolfing, a friend of Couples, to ask.

Couples answered with typical humility. "I'm just another person who was seeing a woman and who has a father. Both of them were in a little bit of trouble, and my dad passed away. But as a golfer, whether I'm a good player or not, I'm no different. I'm a son. I spent some time with him. I think he's much more comfortable now.

"I learned a lot about myself, and I'll never have another father. But I do have a girlfriend I enjoy being around and love, and she's doing great."[6]

When Sunday dawned, it was another picture-perfect day in the desert, the one place where the Weather Channel is watched only by people who are leaving town.

The players were in threesomes, which happens in final rounds on the West Coast because play has to conclude before prime time television begins on the East Coast.

Lietzke, Magee, and Couples made up the final group.

NBC producer Tommy Roy opened his telecast around Couples, citing the golfer's winless streak since the 1996 Players Championship and his off-course problems. It ended with a small smile from Fred Couples, caught off guard, in the middle of a practice swing.

On the course, players made moves early.

Lietzke started hot with a birdie from six feet on the first and another on the second to go to −27.

Magee make a snake, a 25-footer for birdie on the fourth. On seven, he nearly holed out a 7-iron, leaving himself a six-footer, which he converted to tie at −27.

Couples, meanwhile, had birdied the par-5 first, but gave it back at the third with a three-putt from 40 feet. He birdied the sixth, hitting a wedge to less than 12 feet, and the eighth, a par 5, by getting up and down out of a greenside bunker.

On the ninth, Divine Providence gave Couples an assist as he bounced a shot off NBC walking announcer Roger Maltbie's golf cart and birdied from what everyone but Couples agreed could have been out-of-bounds. The drive just missed going into the cart itself by about two inches, missed the windshield by about another inch, and miraculously ricocheted left through a fairway bunker and into light rough. Couples casually slashed it out and made birdie. He had scraped and lucked and putted his way to −25 by the end of nine, two behind Lietzke and Magee.

At the par-5 13th, Magee's 3-wood shot leaked right into a greenside bunker. Lietzke, perhaps the last player on tour to still use a 3-wood that is actually wood, had 253 yards and smacked what was supposed to be a routine fade. Mysteriously, it didn't cut and ended up in a bunker left of the green.

Couples, in the first cut of rough, had 250 yards to hole, 239 to the front, and he chose a 2-iron. It came to a halt on the fringe. Eagle chance to tie for the lead.

Magee's long bunker shot rolled 20 to 25 feet past the hole.

Lietzke came out closer than Magee, which wasn't saying much.

Couples lined up his eagle putt. It rolled smoothly, but it stopped a foot left of the hole and a bit short.

Magee settled for par.

Couples tapped in for birdie, but he hadn't gained on Lietzke, who also birdied to go −28. Lietzke was the sole leader. Amazingly, it was only his second event in eight months.

At the 14th, both Magee and Lietzke hit wedges that refused to hold the renovated green. It was as if the putting surface had been turned into a trampoline.

Meanwhile, Couples was making his friends and fans crazy again. His drive had landed 78 yards from the hole but was only in bounds by 10 or 12 feet. It was a great angle. That was the good news. The problem was he had a tall eucalyptus between himself and the hole. After looking and walking, pacing and pondering, Couples opened up a wedge and swung hard, shooting the ball up and over the tree and landing it three feet from the pin. The gallery roared enthusiastically. It looked like a typical Fred Couples oops-nearly-OB-oh-well-smash-it-up-there-somehow-three-foot birdie kind of a hole. He slid the putt in on the left edge to go to −27, tied with Magee, just one back of Lietzke.

Lietzke poured in his par putt to stay alone at -28, one shot clear. He looked calm.

All parred the 15th and 16th.

At the par-3, 206-yard 17th, Couples had a long putt that looked into the bottom of the cup on the way by. Couples's disappointed, heart-felt reaction was so dramatic, it made the local paper the following Tuesday in a follow-up story. In the Friday round at Bermuda Dunes, his putt on the 17th had stopped right on the lip. He probably wondered what he had to do to make birdie on the hole.

As the three men approached the 18th tee, it was impossible to tell from his expression whether Couples's back bothered him. He was focusing on the birdie finisher ahead, where his length would give him an advantage.

The 18th at Bermuda Dunes is a par 5 measuring 513 yards. At that distance, and without a strong east wind—which would be a rarity in the desert—it is reachable. However, tall palm trees on the right side of the fairway interfere with the second shot, and water on the right in front of the green adds another dimension, particularly with the Sunday pin placement, which is traditionally on the right side. Eagle is possible, but it takes two perfect shots, the kind Couples had made on Friday. Or a little help from the rules.

The gallery at the 18th at Bermuda Dunes is golf's best backstop. John Cook proved it in 1992 when, in a five-way playoff, he took a drop and holed a chip for eagle and the victory. The ideal play is to hit into or under the bleachers behind the 18th and receive a free drop, since it is a temporary immovable obstruction.

But back on the 18th tee, Bruce Lietzke was no doubt trying to reproduce his performance of 1981, when he won the tournament and went on to have his best year ever.

Of the three, only Couples had made eagle there. Lietzke and Magee had both made birdies in their previous trips.

Couples still had the honor, and he hit a powerful shot that veered slightly left, bounced, and landed in the short cut of rough, leaving him a flier lie and a good angle to the pin. He tossed the driver to Joe LaCava but did not change his expression. The game face was on as Lietzke and Magee played their tee shots.

The threesome walked down the fairway, each warrior preparing for what he hoped would be the championship blow.

Couples waited while the others hit. He went through all his usual motions. He bent and stretched. Reached and twisted. It was a habitual activity, reflex now, and dated to long before he ever had problems with his back.

Lietzke was first from 266 yards. With a mighty slash of his antique persimmon 3-wood, his shot went up over the palm trees, hit the lip of a bunker, and slid onto the bank in front of the green, about five feet above the water. He was safe and dry, but not on the putting surface.

That cracked open the door for Couples and Magee.

Magee tried to cut a 3-wood from 257 yards, but it didn't curve. He yelled at it, imploring it to alter its direction. He bashed the ground in frustration. It was in the grandstand, and he would get a drop, but he was farther away than he liked for a realistic chance at eagle.

Up to the time Couples's second shot was hit, 32 players—less than half the field—had gone for the green that day. Four made it. Four found water and only one made eagle.

He had a decent lie. His drive was about 285, which gave him about 228. It was a 3-wood, a club that Couples can hit just about as far as a driver, if he needs to. The ball was slightly below his feet. He wiggled. He gripped. He looked. Finally he swung and the gallery, filled with many loyal Couples followers, waited eagerly as it arced through the air. When it floated to the putting surface, 20 feet below the hole, they exploded into appreciative applause. He had hit the shot he absolutely needed to hit, forcing Lietzke to scramble for birdie to win. Couples would have a run at eagle.

They walked up the fairway to the clapping and cheering of thousands that lined the hole from the tee to the stands behind the 18th green.

"Couples continues to play with a heavy heart and a bad back," Dick Enberg of NBC said as the three came toward the finish.

Magee took his drop, but he still had 35 to 40 feet of grass to negotiate before landing on the green. He hit it too softly, and it stopped well short of the hole, leaving him a tough birdie putt in a must-make situation.

Lietzke faced an easy uphill pitch. He hit it high, and it ran by the hole about eight feet. He looked unmoved.

Couples scouted his eagle. He would have to go up over a ridge, after which the ball would straighten out a bit. The gallery was hushed as Couples took his cross-handed grip and sent it away, and as everyone watched in anticipation, it stopped less than a foot from the hole. Couples put his hand over his eyes as though to say, "Oh no, so close," then waved his visor to crowds and tapped in for 66. He had birdie and was at −28.

Couples laughed with Lietzke's caddie, juggling the golf ball he now had in his hand.

Magee made an absolutely sensational birdie attempt, particularly under the circumstances, but the ball caught the lip and made a cruel, split-second, 90-degree turn, throwing itself away from the cup. He was done at −27.

Now Lietzke, with his no-practice-no-play philosophy and 46-year-old nerves, faced a must-drop, eight-foot putt to win outright. If he could do it, he would become one of few players to win the same tournament with a short and long putter. He would also elevate his already cult-hero status, causing those who spent hour after hour at the practice range to wonder why they were doing it.

Couples shaded his eyes from the setting sun. The gallery hushed.

Lietzke made a smooth pendulum swing. The ball seemed to take forever to get to the hole, and just when it should have headed down, it made a wiggle and grazed the left edge. Playoff.

There had been six playoffs at Bermuda Dunes in the Bob Hope Chrysler Classic.

"The most memorable tournament, I think, was 1968," General Bill Yancey, former executive secretary of the tournament, recalled. "General Eisenhower was in the VIP stands. We had Air Force and Navy and Marine Corps bands—at least—lined up in the first fairway, and when the last group putted out, they all marched up the 18th fairway playing service songs as a special salute to General Eisenhower. It was a thrilling moment, and I know it brought tears to his eyes. But as luck would have it, the tournament ended in a tie. While all this was happening, Arnold Palmer and Deane Beman were out on the back nine starting a playoff, and I often wonder what would have happened if the playoff had gone all the way back to 18. What would we have done with the bands?"

The 18th at Bermuda Dunes was also the site of Arnold Palmer's last PGA Tour victory, in 1973. And for that reason alone it has special meaning.

Couples and Lietzke went back to the 18th tee. Couples was 4–4 in playoffs. Lietzke was 6–5.

Colorful hot-air balloons floated overhead. Palm fronds waved gaily in the end-of-day breeze that materializes when the light begins to disappear behind the mountains to the west. The crowd rumbled with excitement.

If momentum was a factor, it was in Couples's favor.

Lietkze had the honor. He had been keeping up with Couples most of the day, but his drive sailed up and caught the wind. It was three yards shorter than his earlier effort.

Couples's drive was five yards farther than his had been.

Lietzke would be lucky to reach the green. The wind had already played with his shot pattern once. His 3-wood flew up, and as the gallery murmured and watched and pointed, it dropped short and left of the opening in front of the green. He had taken the water completely out of play, barely missing the palms. The ball nestled up against the first cut of rough.

Again Couples used his 3-wood. After taking his stance, he backed off, brushing away insects hovering around the ball. He approached again and looked at his target. He could see Lietzke's ball, but that was not where he was aiming. He swung and belted it up and over the world and into the Bob Hope Classic blue tarp that covers the base of the bleachers. The ball bounced up near some television cables next to the green, and he would get a free drop. He would be chipping while Lietzke hit a sand wedge. Advantage Couples.

Lietzke's last title had been in 1994 at the only other 90-hole Tour event: Las Vegas. Couples had not won in nearly two years.

Lietzke faced his third. He did not want to leave it short. His wedge was past the hole, about 15 feet. He had needed to be closer for certain birdie.

Couples marked, and, with guidance from a Tour official, determined the proper location for relief. As he listened to the ruling, he put his left hand out and Joe LaCava put the ball in it. Two reflex actions. Neither of them so much as looked at the other in the exchange.

The 94-year-old legend and tournament namesake, Bob Hope, watched the action, Ernie Dunlevie, the founder of Bermuda Dunes, by his side.

Couples's ball was on a slight upslope; he had just under 30 feet. He walked to the pin, wedge in hand, staring at the grass as though instructing blades to make a path for the ball. The sun to the west hit him square in the eye as he prepared to chip for eagle and the outright win. Finally, there was nothing left to do but hit the shot. He paused. Settled. Stroked. It was enough, but not perfect—no John Cook—and it rolled three feet beyond the hole. The gallery erupted with approval, sure of his birdie to come.

For Lietzke, five on this hole twice would be hard to accept. Though the gallery had been quiet before, this time, the 'dink' of his putter hitting the ball was almost deafening. But there was no roar to follow. The ball drifted left and Lietzke tapped in for par, putting the pressure on Couples's broad shoulders.

Couples was three feet away from another victory in a career where short putts had cost him at least one major title.

It was uphill, less than a cup of break. He studied it while new Chryslers floated nonchalantly in the lake below.

The crowd seemed restless and energized, waiting for Couples to finish his routine. Looking at him, it was hard to tell if it was for par or eagle. If it was the first hole or the last. He was maintaining his composure, which he had done through the good shots and the bad shots all week. When the putt was struck, he knew it was in. Couples looked up calmly, smiled, and as the thousands of fans shrieked and shouted their approval, he gave a soft boxer-style air punch. Then he shook Bruce Lietzke's hand. It didn't make up for what he had lost, but it was a great way to begin again.

Roger Maltbie, the roving reporter for NBC grabbed him. "Nineteen ninety-seven was a tough year, but you've gotta feel good about this," he said enthusiastically.

"It feels great," Couples admitted. "I wanted to get out of the house and did not expect to play like this. Bruce and I are buddies, and it was a fun time with Andrew. I'm kind of speechless. I had a lot of patience with myself. Last year was a struggle, and this year I looked forward to playing well, and so far I've accomplished one goal. That's to win a tournament."

Dick Enberg closed with a quote from a person he called a friend of Couples, who described him by saying, "There's no frosting on him. He's all cake."

The friend was Tony Porcello, from Seattle, Washington.

Couples tossed the ball to the gallery gathered at 18 and the ceremonies began.

After the photos, the handshakes, and the congratulations from tournament officials, there was the press conference.

"I love to play golf, to compete," Couples said. "I know I don't always show it. Winning again is important, because I know I have what it takes. This year, if I'm not playing well, I hope to be more of a battler."

And his concluding statement: "When you lose your father, I don't believe any tournament can ease that. I think about my dad."

"This is not the greatest win I have ever had, but it was a great time to win a tournament. A lot of things with me are very important, and winning again was very important."[7]

The 1998 Bob Hope Chrysler Classic had been meaningful on several levels. Fred Couples had opened a new chapter in his life. He had battled self-doubt and heartache and grief and errant shots and overcome the odds and won in his first attempt of the year. In some ways it was the biggest victory of his career.

In tragedy, Couples had journeyed far enough inside his soul to discover the remaining parts of life that were most significant to him. He knew there was nothing he could do to bring his parents back. And, as it turned out, the game his father taught him and the love his mother and father had given him those many years before in Seattle had become his foundation. He would have that always.

2

The Birthing Tee

*"He never hit balls or practiced as a kid. The only
way I could get him to hit was to have a contest."*
— Steve Cole

Seattle is called the Emerald City, because it is perpetually green. Its hill-sides wear a mantle encrusted with nature's gems, an original design of firs and pines and spruces set off by gleaming lakes and streams. The city itself is situated in a sheltered port, the northwest's equivalent of Tampa Bay or San Francisco Bay.

Directly to the west, across Puget Sound, are the Olympic Mountains, tall enough to obscure the distant Pacific. The 7,000-foot-plus peaks stretch for miles along a hook-shaped peninsula that is like a thickened version of Cape Cod, but points toward the Orient instead of Europe. They protect Seattle from downpours that drench the westernmost coast-line, an area called The Hoh, which receives so much precipitation, over 150 inches a year, that it is technically a rain forest. By comparison, Seat-tle, on the protected side, has only 36 inches, 20 inches less than Miami.[1]

The most distinguishing characteristic of the Seattle area is its cloudy skies. The city is draped in a mantle of gray an average of 201 days each year, leading the nation in lack of sunshine.

Into this sometimes misty, often cloudy, occasionally foggy, perpetu-ally green environment, Frederick Steven Couples came into the world on October 3, 1959, the youngest of three children of Tom and Violet Couples. There was a trace of precipitation in the air that day.

Tom was a World War II veteran, an athlete and onetime baseball hopeful, a good-looking man. Violet was the epitome of the organized Donna Reed–June Cleaver–All-American mom who could always be counted on to help her family, whether it was allowing an extra friend to come over at the last minute for dinner or getting a job to help with expenses. She was an effervescent woman, full of energy. Even later in life, when faced with a vicious cancer that would eventually take her from the family she loved, she exuded energy, charm, warmth, and friendliness. Tom was the strong, silent type.

Right off the birthing tee, Fred was like most of us, one of the millions of Heinz 57 variety, mixed-breed American melting pot kids. Assimilated, yet with roots, just like generation after generation that came before him. His father's family name was Coppola—Italian—but it had been changed, just as many other immigrant families' names were changed when they came to the United States, to sound "more American." Violet's maiden name was Sobich, and she had family in Seattle, including a sister and a brother, Fred's Uncle Pete. Violet and Tom were both Catholics and raised their children in the church traditions.

When Fred was born, his older brother Tommy was already ten. Cindy was two. She would be just the right age for arguments. No one in the Couples household thought Fred would become world famous. In fact, if anyone would become a sports legend, the family thought, it might be Tommy, who later played minor-league baseball in the New York Yankees organization.

"Freddie's father worked with the two boys," Uncle Pete remembered about the Couples youngsters. "They were forever playing catch. Both of them had superb eye-hand coordination when they were just little kids. Tom could have been a hell of a big-league player, but the war got in the way. The Second World War."

According to Uncle Pete, Tom Couples "was a very handsome man in his younger years." But in Tom's case, beauty was not just skin deep. "He was as fine a man as you'll ever know. In fact, I would have to say that Tom Couples was one of the three nicest men I have ever known, and I don't know anyone who didn't like him."

"Tom worked a number of jobs," Sobich explained. "When they [Tom and Violet] first got married, financially they didn't have much. He was working two and three jobs. I remember one morning he woke up, and he couldn't remember what job he was supposed to go to that day. He was working at the Seattle Tennis Club, working at the dairy, and working at the Parks Department."

Later on, Tom Couples would do well enough to quit his other two jobs; he remained with the City Parks and Recreation Department until his retirement.

Sobich remembers that Fred's father had illnesses in his younger years. He had back problems, even when he was young. Violet had to work. But the children always had a place to go. As they were growing up, they lived about a half a mile away from their grandmother Sobich.

Cindy Couples Sparks, Fred's sister, shares the strong Italian family features of her father and brothers, but softened in a feminine way. The family jawline is there. Her penetrating eyes are pale brown instead of Fred's pools of burnt umber. Fred and Cindy make identical expressive gestures, have similar speech patterns. She has claimed they also have a similar ability to channel-surf—a trait that they shared with their dad.

When the children were younger, the family lived in an area called Rainier Valley. As a boy, Fred used to play all sports.

"They played hockey in the vacant lot next door between the houses," Cindy explained with a smile. "What they would do was to water down the lot, and it would get slick and muddy, and it was a real mess. I remember that one time they had to hose down the neighbor's house because they got so much mud on it from the hockey."

Fred often cites soccer as another sport he played as a youngster, but he has also said he was "too slow and a little lazy" and so he wasn't really good at it. Slow and lazy would turn out to be perfect for another sport, and a swing that would prove to be a gold mine.

According to Uncle Pete, there was more love than money in the Couples household, but they were able to save enough for family trips and outings. Cindy remembered several different summer excursions:

"We went to Disneyland. We had annual family vacations at Lake Chelan, which is east of Seattle, where the weather is always nice in the summer. We used to stay at a place called Campbell Lodge."

Money for extras also came from Violet who worked as a secretary for the Boeing Union.

Cindy and Fred, like most youngsters, fought frequently. At times they would wrestle on the sofa in the middle of arguments. "It happened all the time, but I can't even remember what about." They never had sibling battles with Tommy. "He was much older," Cindy said. "You know how it is, brothers and sisters wanting the same things and the older brother not wanting us around."

Tommy went to Franklin High School and then to Seattle University, but Cindy and Fred went to Catholic elementary schools and Holy Names Academy (Cindy) and O'Dea (Fred) for high school, "because the schools where we lived were not that good," she recalled. It may also have been Violet's way of being certain her children were raised in what she felt was a proper atmosphere.

When Cindy was in sixth grade and Fred was in fourth, the family moved to Beacon Hill. There have often been stories written that the move affected Fred's baseball, but Cindy doubted it. "What baseball?" she asked, in a Fred-like questioning mode. "PeeWee?"

After the move Fred started to play golf at Jefferson Park. It was two blocks from home.

Uncle Pete explained how it happened. "A friend of mine sold them a new house," he said. "It was his toughest sell ever. Tom Couples was financially very frugal. He was afraid of taking on the bigger mortgage at the time."

"I showed it to Vi and she loved it," "Uncle" Paul Kaimakis, the real estate broker and family friend, explained. "It was one of the hardest deals we ever closed. The sale price was $18,250. It was only $500 out-of-pocket, but his father [Tom's] had built the house he was in. So, eventually, we sold him the house, and what's two blocks away? Jefferson Park Golf Course. Now, if that house had been 25 blocks west or east, Freddie would not be a golfer. Think about that. There is no reason anybody would walk 50 blocks to a course. His career hung on a thread, really."

Fred started playing golf with help from his dad, the baseball player. That's one reason, to this day, Couples's swing resembles a baseball player's motion at bat. He has the same fluid motion, the same powerful release, and the characteristic snap of the wrists at impact. Tilt that swing up to horizontal, and it's a major-league home-run cut.

"I loved golf when I started, and I just think I developed, not the right swing, but the right strength for golf. I'm strong in my hands. My legs are very strong—and when you play out of the rough—you get used to it," he noted about his early years. "I think I was blessed with the right muscles to play."

Another factor that Couples mentioned about his early golf experience is that Jefferson Park had two courses. There was a par-3, or executive-length, course and a standard course. "I learned on the short course," Couples said. "Then, when I got good enough, I went across to the big course. So when I was starting, I never played a course that I couldn't handle, and I think that's important."

The "short course" is also where Couples had his first hole-in-one, at age 10, and the only hole-in-one of his career until after he turned pro. He was with Uncle Paul when it happened.

"The fourth hole is uphill, and you can only see half the flag," Paul Kaimakis explained. "We got to the green, and we could only find one ball. It turned out to be mine, and we couldn't find the other one. And we looked everyplace else, and the only place we hadn't looked was in the cup. Sure enough, we finally looked, and it was his ball. We got so excited. He only had, like, four clubs in his bag. He grabbed the clubs and the ball and threw the bag over his shoulder and said, 'Call my dad, because he'll never believe me' and he ran home. I finished the nine holes and called his dad to confirm it."[2]

Fred tagged along with his older brother's pals, too, as Steve Dallas remembered.

"Fred and I became acquainted because his brother Tom and I played baseball together. We went to the Yankees out of high school and didn't do as well as we thought and both of us went back to Seattle University. I got fed up with baseball, and I quit playing and started playing golf." Dallas is now a golf pro in Arizona. "When I met Fred, he was about 11 or 12 years old, and he really got excited about golf then. I'd been playing for a couple years, and said let's go play golf. I got him a set of clubs, and I helped him a little with his swing," Dallas explained. "I gave him his first driver. It was a George Bayer Jumbo. In fact, he qualified for the Tour with that club, and I always ask him if he's still got that driver. When he took it with him, that was part of me."

To this day Couples credits Steve Dallas as one of the people who helped him get started in golf and who influenced his game when he was beginning.

Still, no one anticipated that Fred would become a successful professional athlete, except, of course, Fred himself. "I remember he wrote one paper in elementary school—you know those things they make you write," Cindy explained. "His was on how he wanted to grow up to be a professional golfer just like Arnold Palmer."

Though Palmer was his hero, it was another golfer's swing he imitated.

"When I was growing up, Tom Weiskopf used to be my favorite player to watch. He's a lot taller, and he's got a lot better swing, but I used to pay a lot of attention to him," Couples said years later.[3]

Uncle Pete said there was steady improvement. By the time Fred was 14 years old he was playing in tournaments.

Fred credits two more individuals, both older, with advancing his skills: Jay Turner and Steve Cole.

Jay Turner, son of noted Washington golfer Hans Turner, lived just six blocks from the Couples home. He and Fred became acquainted through a local event.

"His dad would drive us over [to Jefferson Park], and we'd climb over the fence and play until dark," Turner recalled. "They'd pick us up on the putting green. We had lots of holes in our pants from climbing the fence." There were seven or eight golf holes that they could play without being discovered, and they would loop back and through the woods, staying out of sight.

According to Turner, Jefferson Park had another important feature: good golfers went there. "Most of them were older guys, 10 years older than us. They had a pretty good core contingent. There were 18-, 19-year-olds. Guys who were in their twenties, thirties, pretty good players. Guys like my dad, they let us tag along."

Another Seattle friend, John Bracken, remembers playing junior tournaments with Fred. "We played in Seattle junior tournaments from the time we were 11 or 12. He used to dominate those events. He won by so many strokes, it was a joke. He always kind of carried himself confidently, not in what he said, but the way he looked and played. We just always assumed he was cocky. Once we got to be 13 or 14 and I actually got to know him well, he was shy.

"We'd go to tournaments together. By the time we got to be 16, there was a group of four or five of us. We used to go to the Northwest, go to Western Juniors from age 13 to 17," Bracken said.

Another man was about to enter the mix. Steve Cole, a former city amateur champion, who had recently turned pro, leased the range at Jefferson Park. It was 1975.

"Within the first week Jay Turner came over to introduce himself and said he'd like a job," Cole remembered. "I said sure, because I knew Hans [Jay's father] lived within a couple blocks. Jay said he also had another kid who'd like some work. And that was Fred. He was 15. Jay had said he was a good player, a young kid starting out. I said to bring him in. I could see right away that, Fred had unusual talent. So I brought over other people. Good players. Amateurs. And they would play after school. Fred got a lot of competition. You have to play with better players to get better," he summarized. "I realized the best thing was not to mess with him. I didn't do anything with him in terms of mechanics. But by bringing in good players, it gave him a mark to try to beat, which he did in no time."

Cole, like Steve Dallas, could see that Fred's game was something special. He could also see that Fred was, as Brad Faxon would say years later, a great partner with anybody. As Cole explained it, "I took him to tournaments, played partnerships, pro-ams. We did well. He got some exposure at age 16."

Steve Dallas had also turned pro and at that time was an assistant at Sahalee Country Club, site of the 1998 PGA Championship. "We won several pro-ams in Washington and Oregon. I can remember Freddie as being the guy everybody wanted to be around. He hit the ball a long way, even at 16 and 17, and he was a nice kid. At other tournaments, he would caddie for me. He was learning that way as well as playing good golf as a junior."

Uncle Pete recalled Fred's absences from family life. "At age 15 and 16 he was never around for family events because he was always playing golf somewhere. He started traveling to tournaments then. He was such a good young player that they played with him. He was very fortunate. They were much older."

According to Cole, Fred didn't have a social life. "You know how it is, necking in the backseats of cars. Fred did not do any of that. He never went out. He only had one date in Seattle that I know of, and we joked with him because it turned out she was five years older and had a kid. It was a blind date somebody set him up with."

Fred didn't even bother to get a driver's license when he turned 16, an honor that most United States citizens consider both a national birthright and a near religious experience.

Fred's life was, in short, golf, golf, golf, and more golf, broken up by interludes of baseball, hockey, basketball, soccer, and TV, plus eating and sleeping. No chitchatting on the telephone with girls. No driving hither and yon to see what the other kids were doing, because he didn't drive. Fred was a cute kid without pretense. That's what made everyone like him as a young man, and that's why people like him as an adult. He's a what-you-see-is-what-you-get kind of human being. Sincere. Direct. No fuss. No fanfare. Just Fred.

John Bracken still remembers how he found out that Couples didn't drive.

"We were going to a tournament in Portland in the spring of our senior year in high school. We were about halfway down, and I made some statement to the effect that, 'Hey, I'm getting a little tired.' And he told me to just pull over. No sense getting in a wreck. I took that to mean pull over, and we'll switch, and he'll drive. So about five minutes later, I did.

"I told him to drive the last hour, but he said he couldn't. He said he didn't have a driver's license. So I asked if he left it at home and he said, 'It's not that I didn't *bring* my driver's license. I don't *have* a driver's license.' I remind him of that to this day."

While Couples didn't drive, he did get to his part-time golf course job on time.

Steve Cole indicated Couples was an exceptional employee. "We never had a problem. If he had to do something or couldn't be there, if he didn't cover, somebody else did. Actually a time or two, I was impressed. When bad weather or something happened, he went out of his way to get things done, get equipment in or whatever.

"There was never any BS trying to get away with something or me trying to lay something on him. When Fred says something, I listen. He's got my total respect. There's a brain attached to his mouth. With a lot of people, the brain is not always attached."

Couples has hit many remarkable shots, but Uncle Paul and Uncle Pete said the best shot they ever saw Fred hit was at Twin Lakes in the final match of the Pacific Northwest Golf Association Junior Tournament in 1976. His tee shot on the par-5 15th went right of the fairway in such a bad location that he had to take an unplayable lie.

He was on a 45-degree downslope and could hardly stand up on it, but he hit a 3-wood 220 yards.

"He turned it left to right off that hook lie, on dirt. It was the best shot I've ever seen any player hit under those circumstances. A kid playing in tennis shoes. He curved it around everything. Left was a canyon, and there's an elevated green with trap on the right, trap left, and he made the putt for a birdie," Uncle Pete said.

Couples laughed when reminded of the shot. "It might have been the hole where I won the match. The drive went right against the right side of the mountain. I was playing Dave Wallace in the finals. I had to keep backing up to find a place to drop. I had a 20-footer for birdie."

According to Uncle Pete, when Fred began to enter tournaments, his father would never follow him.

"Tom would always be 100 to 150 yards behind him, under a tree. He didn't want to jinx him," Uncle Pete explained. "Sometimes he might be a couple holes away. Fred's playing 11; he'd be on 14. But he always knew what the score was. He never let Fred know he was there."

Uncle Pete also remembered the first time Fred's mother attended a golf tournament—naturally, to see her son compete. "It was pretty funny. She was dressed up and even wore high heels. She'd never been to a golf tournament before and had no idea. After that, she knew."

The O'Dea High School yearbook mentioned that Fred was one of the key players on the golf team as a freshman in 1974. In fact, they missed competing in the state championships by only a single shot. But in the team photo, the guy in the middle of the bottom row, Fred Couples, isn't even listed by name.

By 1976 all that had changed, and there was a four-by-six photo of the State AA Champion, Fred Couples. He was called the "brightest ray of the team." By this time, the school was glad he was just a junior. He had won the state championship by five strokes.

Under his senior class photo, complete with suit and tie, Couples noted that his future plans were "to go to college to play golf and become a professional golfer or a businessman."

When Fred was a senior in high school, Steve Dallas took him to Pinehurst to caddie at the PGA Tour Qualifying School. "What he got out of it, most of the time, was his perception of what other people were doing. Watching things, getting creative by watching and seeing lots of shots, not just by me, I'm sure, but by others too."

After they returned, Uncle Pete remembered asking Fred to assess his chances of being a pro. "Fred thought about it for a minute and said, 'Yeah, I think I can do it.'"

As usual, it turned out to be the understatement of a lifetime.

Fred began to enter tournaments, and while many have said that his mother's job helped pay for entry fees and flights, Uncle Paul says some of the money came from another source. "I know for a fact that Pete helped out financially with Fred. When Fred was a youngster, they couldn't afford to send him off to play in tournaments. As a teenager going around the country playing in amateur tournaments, that costs money. Money they didn't have."

There is one money-related characteristic of his youth that Couples would carry for his career: he doesn't use a glove. And there is a practical reason. When he was growing up in Seattle, it rained a lot. He didn't have enough money to replace them all the time.

But lack of funds couldn't mask his talent. Fred proved himself at home by winning the Washington State Junior, the BC Junior in his first attempt, and the Seattle City Junior several times.

He and Jay Turner often paired up. "The second year we won the Amateur Best Ball at Ocean Shores, in the first round the wind was just blowing 30 miles per hour steady, right off the ocean," Turner recalled. "Through nine or ten holes we were one under. I'm looking at the card, and we're headed toward the toughest part of the course with long, good holes. I figured we were done. He reels off six birdies in a row. Boom, boom, boom. I thought, 'Oh my God, this is the toughest part' where I figured we would struggle to make par. We won it in 1976 and 1978. We got beat in a playoff in 1977, and he turned pro in 1980."

According to Turner, one of the facets of Couples's game that set him apart from all others was his imagination.

"Today, you see all these sports psychologists talk about visualization. Fred did that when we were kids," Turner said. "At that point in time, golf was very mechanical, but he explained it in terms of feel and vision. It sounded like somebody coming from Mars. He could see certain things, and he could pull off shots a normal guy couldn't even imagine."

Even without constant work on his game, Fred was able to beat most of the players in the area.

"When the weather got crummy in November and December, we'd go to a junior high close by and play basketball. This was maybe when he was 15," Jay Turner recalled. "And he could literally not play golf for two or three months, and then when we started again, it was like he never missed a day."

By the time Fred was a senior in high school, it was clear to everybody in Seattle that he was more than good. But hardly anyone outside the Northwest would listen.

"A lot has changed in the last 20 years," Jay Turner admitted. "At that time, Washington was like Siberia as far as golf was concerned."

Even though Couples had won events in his area, his exposure was limited when compared with others who played in programs of national prominence — like Mark O'Meara, whose high school team had won the state championship in California. Or John Cook, who won the World Juniors in 1974. Or Gary Hallberg, who had won the Illinois Open and Amateur titles. Or Bobby Clampett, who had a stellar amateur career.

But Couples's older friends got busy with a letter-writing campaign to help him find a college scholarship.

"They just didn't scout in this area," Jay Turner explained. "To show you how bad it was, Steve Cole knew the coach at BYU, Karl Tucker. He laughed when Steve Cole told him he had a real good player up here."

Cole remembers several friends of his and his father's writing letters, too. "Mahlon Moe, whose father was a pro at Spokane Country Club and who was an excellent player, participated in three Opens and was a national All-American at New Mexico State, and I wrote letters to colleges. Mahlon knew Fred did not have the academics for the University of Washington, so we went south for better competition. He knew coaches at Arizona State and New Mexico State, BYU. The tone of the letters was pretty much 'We've never done this for anybody, but this kid's got talent.' There was no response. Nobody wanted him."

"Somebody here called Coach Dave Williams of the University of Houston, and he agreed to take a look at him," Turner added.

That somebody was Chris Mitchell of Spokane, who was on the golf team at the University of Houston. "In the course of my first year, Coach Williams asked me if there were any other good players from our area. Of course, Fred was probably the best, and I think that's how he got to Houston." Mitchell had remembered Couples's play in high school. "His senior year in high school, he won the Washington Junior and Washington Amateur at Overlake, shooting a 65 on the last day to win."

Despite the reluctance of most of the schools, Fred Couples did have a few people who knew he had exceptional talent and believed in him. He was better than anyone they had seen. He didn't leave home with everyone having great expectations. The only person with expectations was Fred himself. And he would never tell.

3

Springboard to Success:
Cougar Mania

> *"I had no idea what a college campus was all about. I think my high school had forty people in the graduating class. Then I got to Houston, and getting to class was difficult."*
>
> — Fred Couples

Like most freshmen away from home for the first time, Couples found college a bit unsettling at first. An adjustment this big could be difficult for someone who had not traveled extensively or someone who had lived a sheltered life—like a 17-year-old incoming college freshman who had attended a small Catholic high school.

Of all the Texas cities, Houston is the largest and the most affluent. It is an international metropolis, alive with diverse cultures that converge because of the oil industry. Europeans. Arabs. South Americans. Brits.

Houston is also a technology center. NASA's Mission Control sent astronauts into earth orbit and to the moon and back. But moon shots notwithstanding, business fortunes in Houston still rise and fall with the price of crude.

The monied class moves in circles where private jets are often taken for granted. And when it comes to golf, Houston is a part of the long-standing Texas golf tradition that includes Byron Nelson, the late Ben Hogan, the late Dave Marr, and many others.

In the midst of Houston's redbrick, tree-lined, residential neighborhoods, fine established country clubs like River Oaks and Houston quietly blend into the scenery. On the northwest side of the city, 1956 Masters and PGA Champion Jackie Burke, Jr., developed Champions Golf Club with the late Jimmy Demaret.

For the collegiate golfer, the year-round Texas climate is an important advantage, and it is one reason the University of Houston became a golf powerhouse. However, weather alone did not ensure the Cougars' place in golf history. What brought Houston to prominence was Dave Williams, an engineering professor who accepted the opportunity to become the golf coach in 1952.

As golf coach, Williams found his true niche. He brought more than golf ability to the position. He brought logic and intelligence. That combination allowed him to create one of the most successful golf programs in NCAA history.

After a slow start, Williams fashioned team after team of seemingly unbeatable players, winning his first national championship in 1956 and repeating for the next four years. Many of the players Williams recruited went on to successful careers in professional golf.

Williams had an eye that saw more than a swing. It saw heart and determination, the essential ingredients that separate the wanna-bes from the made-its—the intangibles that eventually built 16 NCAA titles.

In the nonexempt days of the Tour, when golfers had to stay in the top 60 on the money list to secure playing rights for the next season, one in every eight touring professionals had spent at least some time at the University of Houston under Williams's guidance.[1] With more NCAA golf titles than anyone had ever dreamed of creating, Dave Williams was a virtual legend.

Williams had his own scouting system. He discovered golfers nobody else had known, players nobody else considered, kids nobody else bothered to see. Dave Williams, after all, was an engineer by trade, and he knew the value of homework. That's how he found Fred Couples.

By the time Couples was brought to Williams's attention, Houston's golf program already had 13 NCAA championships to its credit.

As CBS television commentator and golf anchor Jim Nantz, a former Houston teammate of Couples, remembered, "When someone told Coach about Fred, the guy said, 'Coach, I've never seen anybody hit it this long, and he's the greatest recovery player I've ever seen in my life.' Coach's answer was 'But can he cheeep and puuuutt?' in his southern drawl. The guy said, 'Better than anybody I've ever seen.'"

At that time, schools were starting to redistribute scholarship money to give more people a chance to play. The team had five full scholarships, and if they were split up, the coach could recruit more players by offering, say, half a scholarship each. The Cougars had 18 players on the team, none on full scholarship.

Fred Couples was offered half a ride. "They'd just graduated four starters. That meant they had room on the team," he noted. He'd have to play his way to a starting position, but that didn't bother him. For Couples, a youngster who was literally unknown outside the Northwest, it was a smart career move, one of several he would make. For Williams, adding Couples to the team was a wonderful decision, because this unknown proved to be much better than anyone else imagined. And he was good in a hurry.

Along with Couples came Blaine McCallister and John Horne—who, according to Nantz, was actually considered the top recruit—and other hopefuls.

"Blaine and Fred and I were roommates as freshmen," John Horne explained. Horne is now a golf professional at Plainview Country Club in Plainview, Texas. "Two seniors lived next door. We shared a bathroom and shower with the end room. We had two bunk beds and one single bed. We were at the very end of the hallway, second room on the left." Room 103, Taub Hall.

Their first day, they teed it up at Sugar Creek Golf Club.

"I was playing in the group ahead of Fred, with Blaine McCallister and John Horne and Joel Gross," Nantz recalled. "I can remember looking over my shoulder and seeing this swing that looked like it was in slow motion, and yet on every hole he was practically hitting into us. I thought, 'This guy's killing it, and it looks like he's barely swinging at it.'"

Nantz remembers that after the round they were all talking about the new guy from Seattle who had just shot two under and wasn't the top recruit. They knew Blaine McCallister of Fort Stockton had won a lot of Texas tournaments, and John Horne, from Plainview, Texas, had shot 10 consecutive rounds in the 60s in competition during the previous summer. Couples was a guy with no press clippings. No "big tournament" victories. Years later, Rick Reilly of *Sports Illustrated* would accuse Couples of being "from nowhere." But boy, could he play.

"As freshmen you do not have a chance to play first semester up until Christmas, unless you are playing good. The exception, of course, was Fred," Horne noted. "We [the team] went to Houston Country Club, and the first time there, Fred shot a 68. He was pretty much the coach's boy after that. Coach wasn't that blind. Fred was just a little better than the rest of us. Before the Christmas holidays, he was already playing in the top five.

"I remember the first time I played with Fred," Horne continued. "It was at Clear Lake Golf Course in Clear Lake, Texas, which is on the way to Galveston. It took me 12 holes to really get a good drive. This is maybe two weeks into the year. I'm already razzing them, you know. Let's see you catch that one. We walked out to the fairway and see the first ball, and it's mine. I had killed it. Twenty yards ahead of me is Blaine, and Fred is past Blaine another 10 yards. That's 30 yards past me, and I thought I hit it a long way. You can't teach anybody to hit a long way just like you can't teach anybody to be seven feet tall."

As freshmen, one foursome was together virtually night and day.

"Blaine and John and Fred and I hit it off right away," Nantz explained. "We were really clingy. We did everything together. We took classes together. We went to games together. Hung out together. Watched *Monday Night Football* together. All that kind of stuff.

"My first year, I didn't room with the other three in room 103. So the game plan was that because there were two seniors in that adjoining room—room 101—when the two seniors left, I remember thinking next year we'll go two and two."

Luckily, Couples had someone around who was planning ahead, because even he admits it wasn't his specialty at that time.

"I had no idea what a college campus was all about," he explained. "I think my high school had 40 people in the graduating class. Then I got to Houston, and getting to class was difficult. Then, when I got to the golf course, that's where I felt the best. That's pretty much what I did for three years."

According to Horne, Nantz even helped Couples make out his class schedules. "Fred wouldn't have known how. Not that's he's stupid. He just wouldn't do it. People think he's out in space, but he knows what's going on at all times."

On the golf course, Couples dominated, but off it, he seemed inexperienced and extremely shy. And he still had no driver's license.

Couples thought Coach Williams put Nantz near the rest of them because he knew Nantz had a sense of responsibility and would take charge.

"Coach had it in his mind that Blaine, John, and I would be the next great Cougar golf team," Couples explained. "His favorite line for Jimmy was 'Boys, this is the next president of the United States. First guy from the University of Houston to be president of the United States.' I didn't know if I was there to play golf or go to school or whatever. I had no clue."

Couples quickly became known for his one-outfit wardrobe. His explanation was that he didn't have very many clothes and made decisions according to the weather. "It was so hot in Texas, and I had these seersucker slacks that were paper thin, and man, I just wore those things every single day."

Unusual habits notwithstanding, Couples made his team debut in the fall of 1977. He finished second in the Al Pryor Intercollegiate in Houston and fourth at Lamar, Pinewood Country Club in Beaumont, Texas.

Paul Marchand, today the head golf professional at Shadow Hawk Golf Club, who would later become Couples's pro coach, was also on the team, a couple of years ahead. "Fred could hit shots other people couldn't even imagine," Marchand recalled. "We used to say that Fred's 3-wood was his chip-out club, because he would hit into the trees and then hit these unbelievable shots to get out and still make par or birdie. Nobody else could hit those kinds of shots."

Couples's freshman year, the golf team won the fall Southwest Conference Championships twoball and fourball events. But they had some fun off the course, too. They had a friend called T.L. who would invent ways to get them into Houston Astros games for free, claiming they worked in the concessions or that it was something they had to do as part of a class.

Of the group, only Nantz was known for actually opening a book. Neither McCallister nor Couples can remember doing much studying, but they do recall playing connect the dots and hangman in the back of class. In English, Couples and McCallister had mulligans because they wrote the truth for an assignment, which was to explain in an essay why they were taking that class. They were taking it at night, they said, because they played golf during the day. The instructor kicked them out.

According to Chris Mitchell, there were "a lot of stories about Fred forgetting he was in school, not making a lot of classes, and Coach telling him he had to show up once in a while. Fred knew when he went to school he really went to play golf. Whether he lasted two or four years, the ultimate goal was not to be in college. It was to play on the - Tour."

While Couples's class attendance may not have set the world ablaze, his on-course record continued strong. In the spring of his freshman year, he was third in the Johnny Maca Intercollegiate at Cedar Lake Country Club in Clear Lake, Texas, and low man on the Cougars' roster at the NCAAs, but the team score was 18th, a disappointment since Houston had won its 13th NCAA golf title a year earlier. Significantly, though, Couples was an All-American for the first time.

The summer between Couples's freshman and sophomore years, he entered tournaments at home and won both the Washington State Amateur and the Washington Open.

In the Washington Open, he beat Don Bies, who at that time was a Tour player from the Seattle area. It is unusual for amateurs to win their state Opens because many pros play. Jack Nicklaus did it in Ohio when he was 16, defeating several Tour notables in the process. Couples did it when he was 18.

Nantz remembered additional details. "When Fred beat Don Bies, Pat Fitzsimons was also a Tour player and finished second or third, but Fred won by four or five shots. There was a $100,000 purse, and I think Don Bies or Pat Fitzsimons got the $20,000, because the top prize passes down to the next guy. Fred was given the maximum allowable for amateurs at that time, which was $300 or $350. I know he gave it all to his mother."

Later that summer, Couples entered the U.S. Amateur but lost in the second round. The Amateur usually coincides with the beginning of school. Couples returned to Houston shortly afterward.

There was about to be a rooming change. As sophomores, Nantz, MacCallister, Couples, and Horne took over the suite that they had coveted as freshmen.

Four guys. Two bedrooms. One shower. History in the making.

"There was a main door between the rooms, and we just kept it open," Horne said. "So it was like a big room with the four of us. Blaine's and Jim's room was always neater than ours, so we hung out and watched TV there."

During a practice round that second season, John Horne saw Couples hit what he described as the most amazing shot of all time. "We were playing Walden on Lake Conroe. We were on a par −5, and I don't know what possessed him, but we were at the 150-yard marker and he said, 'I think I can hit around that tree and knock it on green with a driver.' He pointed to a pine tree in the left rough, 100 yards from the green and way to the left of it. We said, 'You're dreaming.'

"So he takes his driver. Put the ball on a pencil or teed it up way high, and hit the driver 150 yards. The ball went straight up—he's aiming 90 degrees left of the green—and landed on the green, but it was slicing so much, it ran off the green. The second ball he hit sliced around the tree, landed on the green, and stayed on green. It was the most incredible shot I've ever seen."

That was until a few tournaments later at the All-American Intercollegiate at Atascocita. "Paul [Marchand] might have seen this one," Horne noted. "Fred's ball was against a tree in the left rough. He had a backswing, but his left foot was at the base of the tree, so if he followed through, he would break his club. Most people would take an unplayable. Not Fred. What he did was he started taking clubs out of his bag and made practice swings, and at the end of the swing, he'd let go of the club completely. He started with long irons and did the same thing with all his clubs, until he got to the club he intended to use and hit the ball and let go of the club and knocked it on the green and two-putted for par. And here in front of him are all these clubs lying out there. He was picking those clubs up and laughing. He cracked himself up on that one. It was something. A big college tournament. All-American tournament. John Cook. Bobby Clampett. UCLA was there. And he does this in the biggest tournament we've got."

Meanwhile, the Cougar golfers continued their off-course pranks and played a lot of day and night golf on a made-up course that wound around the campus.

"I hate to admit to half of this stuff," Couples said, "but we used to hit balls at the Moody Towers."

Nantz remembered many times that they hit irons around the engineering buildings, but insisted the best practice location was the center of campus, which had a fountain surrounded by "some really good grass. You could get nice tight lies off the grass, and we would hit sand wedges over the fountain and try to stop them before they got to the sidewalk on the other side."

In addition to night golf, they played indoor golf, and as Paul Marchand explained it, "On the golfers' wing of the dorm, there was one window that was broken most of the time. You'd hear it break and go outside, and there'd be nobody in the hallway. The hallway was T-shaped, and people would come walking down the hallway, and we'd be hitting wedges. There were a few close calls. We are lucky that nobody was ever hurt."

Naturally, there was a good reason they were hitting wedges indoors. Rain. When the weather was inclement, they practiced indoors. Twenty-five dollars was the usual charge for broken windows. Eventually, being on tight student budgets, they went to Ping-Pong balls.

Horne said it was a little more aggressive than that. "You have to imagine this really long hall, like in a big hotel or something. We would hit screaming shots down the hall. Fred did not play much of that, but he would egg us on. Not do the actual crime, but he'd say, 'Go ahead. Hit that 2-iron hard as you can down the hall.'

"Now, you're gonna kill somebody if they come out of their room. But if you hit it just right, it would hit the wall at the other end and come back to you. But there was also this window at the other end, so if the shot got too high, it would go through the window."

The fall of 1978 was also the year of Nantz's Big Fib. It was all because of the World Series.

Couples loves baseball so much that his Tour caddie, Joe LaCava, believes that if Couples could do anything or be anybody, he'd want to play center field for the Yankees. Naturally when the Yankees, Couples's favorite team, were playing the Red Sox in a one-game playoff for the American League East title, there was no way he was going to miss it.

"Coach Williams had a rule that we had to play golf every day," Nantz explained. "And you had to turn your scores in every day. You had to hole every putt. If anybody ever conceded a putt, it was grounds for suspension. This one day when Coach started matching up players after class, we feigned illness. Word got to Coach that we were in the room, very sick. He walked into both rooms. We were there in bed, looking like we were gonna die.

"He looked at Fred, and then he came in and looked at me and said, 'I don't know what's going around, but there's no way you boys can play today. Y'all gotta take the day off.'

"This ended up being a very famous baseball game," Nantz said, "known forever as the Bucky Dent game because Bucky Dent hit the home run at Fenway Park to beat the Red Sox. And it was a daytime Monday broadcast. I remember sneaking out of my room—Fred, too—looking down the hall to see if the coast was clear and then looking outside the door of the dorm to see that Coach's car was gone. There was no way we were going to miss that game. I don't think I've ever been so pumped about anything."

Later that year, the golf team decided to play ball. Basketball. "We practiced free throws every day," Nantz explained. "In the contest each person on the team shot 50 free throws. Chris Mitchell hit 49. Mike Klein hit 43. Blaine's memory is not very good because he is starting to change numbers on me," Nantz added. "I hit 39 and he and Fred both hit 38. We hit 207 out of 250 free throws. I'd like to say the second place team was 50 free throws behind us, but that's probably an exaggeration."

When the weather improved, they played golf, too, including some Monday practice rounds at River Oaks. Dick Harmon, head professional there, had spent summers during 1974, 1975, and 1976 in Idaho, where he had become acquainted with Chris Mitchell, who was from Spokane. According to Harmon, it was through Mitchell that Harmon came to know Fred Couples.

Neither Harmon nor Couples knew how important this casual acquaintance would become 10 years later.

As the second year wore on, Nantz came to the disappointing realization that he wasn't good enough to keep up with Blaine and Fred and John. "They just had too much talent. I was getting my head kicked in on the golf course every day." Nantz developed an interest in broadcasting during that second season but remained on the team. He went to the coach and indicated that he wanted to make a change.

"Coach said, 'Jimbo, you could be whatever you want to be. Tv anchor. President. If that's what you want to do, Jimbo, do it. But the main thing is I want you to always be a member of this team. You don't want to be on the golf team, that's fine, but you're staying where you live, and you're a member of the team nevertheless.'"

Nantz became the sports expert, the trivia buff, the answer man, and Williams showed again how smart he was.

"Coach started traveling me with the team," Nantz explained. "I would feed radio reports back home to Houston, and I would act as Coach's assistant. Coach would sit by the scoreboard and watch the matches. He loved to make hands-on contact with his boys at the turn, and he'd always go up and ask a million questions, and all he really wanted to know was what they shot. It was always our favorite thing to imitate him.

" 'Hey, Fred, you're lookin' real good. I like that outfit,' he'd say—and of course it was a team uniform. 'Hey, Fred, red pants look good today. Can I get you anything? You want some chips? Some water? Pencil okay? Good. Good. How about an umbrella? Whaddya shoot?'"

Williams would get the numbers and start calculating.

According to Nantz, if the first guys out were not doing well, he'd hear, "Jimbo, you gotta talk to Fred. You gotta talk to Blaine. These other guys are gonna shoot a hundred."

Nantz knew if they had an off day, it might have been 77 or 78, but to Coach Williams, it was a hundred.

That year Couples really found his footing in collegiate play and was team medalist four times. He tied for first place in the Southwest Conference Championships with SMU's Payne Stewart but eventually lost the title in a playoff.

However, the playoff revealed a few things about Fred Couples's character.

The Southwest Conference rule at that time was that ties would be settled on the scorecards, beginning with the 18th hole and going backward. Couples had birdied the 18th hole, which, according to the rules, gave him the title.

Couples was a sophomore and Stewart was a senior.

"There was a lot of mumbling about it was hardly fair when you're a senior that you don't get a chance to play it off. And you also got a chance to play a Tour event," Nantz recalled.

Payne Stewart also remembered that the scorecard rule was in effect. "If we had done it that way, by the cards, then Fred would have won the championship. But Fred wouldn't do it. He *insisted* on playing off for the title. The first hole was a par 5. I had a five. He had a six."

A berth in the Colonial Tournament also went to the swc champion. So it would be Payne Stewart, not Fred Couples, who had the opportunity to tee it up in Fort Worth with the pros.

Even with a conference championship tie to his credit, Couples didn't get national acclaim.

"At that time, the top guys were John Cook, Mark O'Meara, Bobby Clampett, Gary Hallberg. They got all the attention," according to Paul Marchand.

The last tournament of the year was the NCAA. "I remember at the NCAA in North Carolina, Bermuda Run," Nantz recalled, "Mark O'Meara played for Long Beach State, and he made it as an individual. He was staying across the hall from us. He'd played John Cook in the U.S. Amateur, and we thought they were like superstars. O'Meara was a big-time guy we'd read about and seen on TV when he played the Amateur."

Interestingly enough, what O'Meara remembered was that "Houston was a bigger school. Fred's record was probably better than mine."

Nantz also remembered a special event at Bermuda Run. "On the eve of the NCAA tournament, they held a long-drive contest. They also wanted to have an NCAA straight-driving champion. One player represented each school. They contested it on the 10th tee, playing into a driving rain. They lined the fairway down the middle. Each player attempted to hit three balls in the fairway. They had some formula, using the ones that were closest to the line plus flat out one longest drive.

"Fred won both competitions. His longest was 318 yards into rain and wind with no roll. He also won the straight drive, and his average was 15 yards longer than the next guy. It was an awesome display. He used an old George Bayer driver."

The driver that Steve Dallas had given him years before.

As radio reporter for the team and unofficial assistant to Coach Williams, Nantz went back and forth between matches the next day.

"I was walking with Fred for a while, and in the gallery was a man who was a guest speaker at the banquet on the eve of the tournament. It was Billy Packer.

"What's amazing now is I will be calling my 14th [in 1999] Final Four with Billy Packer this year. Through my association with Billy, Fred's grown close to the Packer family. Fred travels with me on the road sometimes, to our basketball games, working as a runner or gofer for us. And Billy's youngest son, Brandt, now works for CBS as a broadcast associate."

At Bermuda Run, Houston finished ninth. Couples was again low man for the team, team MVP, and an All-American for the second time.

The summer between their sophomore and junior years, Nantz got a job with a radio station. Couples did something else. He played in an event that gave him a preview of what he could become—the 1979 U.S. Open. Not only did he make the cut, but he finished as low amateur at Inverness in Toledo. The tournament was eventually won by Hale Irwin, his second Open of three, but it pitted Couples against the best in the world. While his scores of 76-74-80-72, 302 were not earth-shattering, it was still a good measuring stick. And he held up exceptionally well, finishing in a tie for 48th with professionals Greg Norman and George Burns.

"Fred got a medal," Nantz recalled. "I still remember Jim McKay mentioning it."

But the question is, how good would he have been if not for the 80 in the third round?

"In the third round he was paired with Lee Trevino," Nantz said. That was when he shot 80. "I had never heard Fred describe himself as being as nervous as when he came back and told us all about that round. Lee Trevino was such a superstar at that time."

As Nantz recalled, Trevino hit first, using a driver. Couples told him, "I leaned over and tried to put the ball on the tee, and my hands were shaking so badly, I had a hard time keeping the ball on the tee. I hit a 3-wood and really ripped it right down the middle. It was about 40 yards past Trevino, and it relaxed me a little."

Late summer brought the U.S. Amateur, but Couples lost in the second round. Then it was back to Houston.

Couples showed up for junior year with his suitcase and put it immediately on top of his desk. He opened it up but left the clothes neatly folded inside it, putting his golf shoes in the desk drawers. After doing his laundry, he'd repack the suitcase with his clothes. This was his new approach to clothing storage.

"I used to kid him," Nantz quipped, "that he was one zip away from the PGA Tour." Nantz didn't know how right he would turn out to be.

Between golf in the dorm, golf at night, and golf that was actually played on the golf course, something else occurred. Fred Couples met Deborah Morgan.

It has often been written that the two of them met at the Astrodome, or that she saw him at an Astros game and was interested because she thought he was a baseball player, or that they met at a tailgate party for a football game, but it was none of those places and not nearly as glamorous.

Paul Marchand was there. Fred and Deborah actually met in the UH dining hall. "All athletes ate at the same place in the quadrangle. The swimmers, tennis players, and golfers were in the old dorm area, football players and basketball players were in the new dorms. Deborah was on the tennis team. She was in the middle of everything. They hit it off right away. They went to all the football games."

Couples remarked that he didn't say anything to her at all. He just stared. He was incredibly shy for a college junior. According to Nantz, Couples was so bashful, sometimes he would go out with one of the guys and the guy's girlfriend as the third.

"We'd never met anybody like Deborah. This blonde from California, and she was not a wacky Valley Girl," John Horne admitted. They all thought she was older but somehow was still in school. She was, in fact, six years older.

"We were all kind of excited for him, because as far as we knew Fred had never been on a date in his life," Nantz said. "We heard he had a date once back home. None of us had ever seen that side of him. In two years at college, Fred never had a date or a girlfriend."

As the relationship with Deborah Morgan blossomed, the legend of Fred Couples's golf shots also grew. Nantz's favorite came during a tournament in Tyler, Texas.

"Fred had driven through the dogleg of a fairway. He was 270 yards and out-of-bounds on a hole that was—measuring down the center of the fairway—just over 400 yards long," Nantz explained. "But if you measured over the towering pines and cut the dogleg, it was a little over 300 yards, maybe 310. Fred had to go back to the tee. On the way, he must have decided he could reach it if he took that route, if he cut the corner and went over the trees. Of course, he didn't bother to mention this to anyone. He just took out a golf pencil, which he substituted for a tee, and gave it a rip, landing the ball on the green, 20 feet from the hole."

Couples proceeded to drain the putt for par.

Later in their junior year, Nantz became the public address announcer for University of Houston basketball, and eventually advanced to host the college basketball coach's show. By the spring of 1980, he was a weekend sports anchor at the local CBS affiliate, KHOU, which was the fourth-largest television market in the country. Not bad for a college junior.

"I remember finals week, just week shy of my 21st birthday going to the cafeteria with your tray and you were on TV the night before, you feel like a superstar. I say that in jest."

Nantz's transition to broadcasting added a new dimension to his friendships with the other guys because he became the one they had to stump with sports trivia. They would stay up until all hours trying to ask Nantz a question he couldn't answer, which is probably one reason why to this day he is unflappable on the air.

They would also pretend to be the local news team. "Jimmy was the sports guy," Couples recalled, "and I think Blaine would do the weather. I guess I started the whole thing off. It was an absolute riot, because Jimmy knew everything. Players, stats, and the whole blow-by-blow. For us, it was just something to pass the time, but it was something that Jimmy was into. He was so good at it even then. He'd always say that one day he would interview me at Augusta, because that was our big thing."

"It is true that I used to introduce Fred at all the campus parties as the future Masters champion," Nantz said. "It was the one tournament he really dreamed about playing in and wanted to win. The stories about us practicing interviewing are true. I used to have a tape recorder with a microphone attached, and I'd practice by interviewing all the guys. I told them that when they won tournaments they'd be interviewed by the media, so it would be good practice for them, too.

"I always felt that one day Fred would win at Augusta," Nantz emphasized. "We used to tell him all the time, 'You could win the green jacket. You'd look *great* in the green jacket.'"

Couples showed a marked improvement in his play in the 1980 season. He had five first places: Lamar Intercollegiate, Kingwood, The Woodlands, Les Bolstad, and Morris Williams. He finished second in the Southwest Conference Championships to teammate Ray Barr, and was team medalist in the NCAAs with an eighth-place finish overall. Again, he was team MVP.

Over the summer, Couples again entered the U.S. Amateur, which was held at the Country Club of North Carolina. There he beat Don Bliss, John Slaughter, and Jay Don Blake. Then he faced Jim Holtgrieve in the quarterfinals.

"In those days," Nantz explained, "if you made it to the semifinals, you got an invitation to the Masters. Now only the Amateur champion goes."

Couples lost to Holtgrieve and his dreams of playing at Augusta were shattered. Holtgrieve lost to Hal Sutton, who would become the U.S. Amateur champion in 1980.

For all his vision, even Nantz could not predict what Couples would do next. Nor could he know that the two of them would continue to cross paths at decisive points in their lives for the next two decades.

One thing was certain. Couples would soon prove what NASA's Mission Control already knew. You could go anywhere in the world from Houston.

4

Turning Pro:
Sure. Why Not?

*"Fred was there, staying in his truck. We were—
both of us—we did not have much money."*
—Mark O'Meara

Some people plan their life to the smallest detail. Looking at Fred Couples's life objectively, it would be hard to accuse him of doing that. Even he admits his first career move was made in haste.

After the 1980 U.S. Amateur, Couples took a side trip to L.A. to visit Deborah Morgan before continuing on to Houston. In L.A., he learned about a golf tournament called the Queen Mary Open. Couples, who'd won the Washington Open as an amateur, figured he'd play.

"When I got to the tournament," he said about what would become a defining moment in his life, "they told me I couldn't play unless I was a pro."

He thought about it, but not for long.

"It was an overnight decision," Couples explained.

The "overnight decision" came after a phone call to Steve Dallas, the man who had helped him learn the game.

"It was a spur-of-the-moment thing," Dallas recollected. "He called, and really didn't know if it was the right thing. Fred was heading back to college for his senior year, and he just asked me what he should do. I remember saying that this might be the time you need to give it a try."

But Dallas didn't really know what Fred was considering.

Jim Nantz recalled that "the day he lost in the U.S. Amateur he was supposed to start school. His match with Holtgrieve overlapped the first day of class. We expected him back in the dormitory the next day."

When Couples didn't show, they figured maybe he was staying over an extra day. More days passed. No Fred.

Couples entered the Queen Mary tournament as a pro and finished eighth. It was the kind of boost his confidence needed after the defeat in the Amateur. "I made $2,000, which was great," he said of his pro debut. "Then I had an opportunity to apply to the Qualifying School." He had earned $1,800 in the tournament proper and another couple hundred in the pro-am. That was the good news. The bad news was his family's reaction to it.

He had not shown up at school and had not called home. Violet and Tom Couples were getting desperate, trying to locate their younger son. As any parent would do, Mrs. Couples began calling people, starting with Jim Nantz.

"It was a week, two weeks. When she called I would say, 'No, Mrs. Couples, he's not here. We haven't seen him.' Obviously, they were quite concerned."

According to Nantz, Fred ended up calling his parents from California, and, as the story goes, his dad was so angry Fred had left school a year early to turn pro that he hung up the phone on his son. "I've never talked to Fred about it, but I know that's the case," Nantz said.

"If Fred had beaten Holtgrieve to advance to the next round of the U.S. Amateur he would have received an invitation to the Masters, and he would have come back to Houston for his senior year. No doubt he would never have given up an invitation to go to Augusta. I believe this is when Deborah helped convince him to turn pro," Nantz concluded. "He was young and in love."

Violet Couples also called Steve Dallas. He said recently that he had been confused about getting the call.

"I thought since he didn't say anything to Violet or Tom that he decided against going pro," Dallas explained. "Now I think maybe he just went to Palm Springs."

Dallas remembers trying to be a friend to Couples. "I always felt he and I had some special bond at that time in his life. I thought maybe it was important to him, and I was somehow important to him. I don't know if I always gave the right advice, but I tried. When he got out of school, he was having a tough time trying to find sponsors. I wished I'd had enough to be his backer."

As Couples was making his breakthrough on the links, his girlfriend, Deborah Morgan, was in the process of moving to Palm Springs, where she had been hired by Fred Renker' to be the tennis pro and run the tennis program at the Indian Wells Racquet Club.

Couples, meanwhile, was practicing for the PGA Tour Qualifying School, one of golf's most pressure-packed events. Another player who was getting ready for the Q-School was southern Californian Mark O'Meara. O'Meara and Fred eventually wound up sharing a room.

"I recall the first stage at Crystal Air, kind of due east from Los Angeles, in the high desert." O'Meara was there with a friend who wasn't doing well. "Fred was there, staying in his truck. We did not have much money. My friend and I said that's ridiculous. We decided to take the mattresses off the beds, and Fred stayed with us. It was not that big a deal," O'Meara explained. "My friend missed the cut, so Freddie and I shared. We both qualified."

Fort Washington, in Fresno, was where the final stage of the Q-School was held. Again, O'Meara and Couples found themselves paired up, this time on the course.

"It was the fall of 1980, and the final round, we were playing together, playing pretty well," said O'Meara. "I was playing better, and it looked like I was going to make the cut. He's right on the cut.

"I remember him standing on the 18th tee saying it's not like Point O' Woods, which is a much longer hole. This 18th was kind of a short hole. He hit a 1-iron and then had a wedge or 9-iron, which he thinned to the back edge, chipped eight feet.

"I thought he had to make the putt to make it through the Q-School. The composure he had was typical. Vintage Freddie."

Couples laughed and admitted O'Meara was right. "I was the 25th guy out of 25 spots." After getting through Q-School it hit him: "'Now I've done this. This is what I have to do,' I said at the time. When I was in college, I can honestly say I never thought I'd be on the PGA Tour."

It was an inauspicious start to what would later be a glorious career.

Although Couples's dad was upset that he had left college, Uncle Pete Sobich provided some much-needed support. He brought more than words of encouragement. Uncle Pete worked out a way for Fred to survive financially.

"When Freddie decided to turn pro, there were people who wanted to back him," Sobich explained. "But they wanted a piece of the action. So a friend of mine in a brokerage firm and I guaranteed him $30,000 the first year. We told him, 'All you gotta do is pay us back when you win.' We never took a penny from Fred for anything. I feel that we gave him a good opportunity to own himself." So from his first season on, Fred Couples has been a hundred percent his own man.

His Tour debut in Phoenix proved that just when things look good, they can get worse, as Uncle Pete Sobich revealed. "I remember when he went to his first tournament. We were on vacation, and naturally we were interested in watching him on television. But on the way to the tournament, he was listening to a football game, and he reaches over to tune the radio and he sideswiped a vacation trailer. You know he never drove much. He called his mother. So his mother flies to Phoenix to get him out of this mess. She took him back to Palm Springs. He was not hurt too seriously. He wrecked his car."

Also early in 1981, problems began to develop at the Indian Wells Racquet Club with Deborah. According to David Renker, "She was in the middle of several altercations with members. Her general behavior was a problem."

To everyone's surprise, Couples stayed with her.

By the time the Los Angeles Open rolled around, Couples, who had not made a cut, had called in reinforcements. Steve Cole from Seattle became his caddie.

"I caddied for him from the L.A. Open through Congressional in June," said Cole. "Having been his boss at one time . . . to be a caddie—it was not going to last. I did it for the experience."

During that five-month period Cole was impressed with Couples's ability to be aggressive. "When he was ready to play, he could really shoot a low number. People don't understand that you can't play day after day aggressively. You have to play conservatively—Jack Nicklaus style—in most cases. But when Fred wanted to unleash, he could play spectacular golf, better than his peers."

According to Cole, the strength of Couples's game early on was his play with the driver and the long irons. "If he had an ugly shot, it might be a short iron." Still those who have seen Couples work miracles with the sand wedge or hole out from the fringe can attest to his great touch.

It was a struggle for Couples to make a cut, and he did not succeed until Bay Hill. "I finished about 21st place. It was nerve-racking, because it was my first chance to make two or three thousand dollars," he admitted. Next he played at Inverrary and then at Doral, where he finished 20th. Things were beginning to look up. A friend boosted his confidence by telling him he was good enough to succeed.

A few weeks later, the words of encouragement proved prophetic. Couples was fifth in New Orleans, and for the first time he thought he might have a chance to stay out on tour. But he was not satisfied. "I was playing well and finishing well, but not scoring well. I realized it was tough, but I could do it and handle it." He had made $12,000.

Back in Palm Springs, things were not going as well for Deborah at the tennis club. David Renker recalled, "At the end of May my dad let her go, and it was a major battle with her. When she got in and the season got going, she was demanding and loud, and the membership didn't care for her."

Deborah had a place to go. She joined Fred out on Tour.

At the Kemper Open, which would become the site of Couples's first victory two years later, Steve Cole remembered that it was Deborah who did all the demonstrative things. "I could never quite figure her out. The way she dressed and acted was opposite of the typical wife of successful golfers, which is supposed to be more like a Barbara Nicklaus. But I lived with them for a couple of weeks in Palm Springs and had a great time. She's emotional, but she treated me fine all the time.

"When I left for the season at Congressional, she invited me for drinks. She had Fred's credit card in her hand, and she ordered all the expensive hors d'oeuvres. I was driving out next morning and asked, 'Where's Fred? That's his credit card.' And she just said, 'So what' — in a nice way — 'he can afford it. We'll just use it.' But what struck me as funny was her concern about Fred. She kept asking, "Is Fred going to make it? Is he going to make it?' She was genuinely concerned about that."

Whether it was having Deborah with him, or improved confidence that comes with better finishes, Couples's game was on the upswing. "At Hartford, I finished second, and at Pensacola, third," he recalled.

Linn Strickler, who was Curtis Strange's caddie at the time, remembered being paired with Couples at the Hartford tournament. "It was the sixth hole, a par 5, where I really noticed his game," Strickler explained. "Curtis and Fuzzy had just hit 3-woods off the tee, 20 yards short of the water. There was a pretty good wind blowing. Freddie had made bogey on the previous hole, so he was last up. He hit this 1-iron 240 into the wind, and one-bounces it into water. It was like it was shot out of a cannon. I'd never seen a shot like that. Unbelievable, his power."

Couples's own summary of his first year on the Tour was characteristically short and sweet. "I finished in the top 60. I felt like I was good enough." He finished 53 on the money list and was in contention for Rookie of the Year honors. The placement of the finish was more important than the voting, because at that time, which was before the all-exempt Tour, players had to finish in the top 60 or go back to Q-School.

Voting for Rookie of the Year in 1981 was done before the season was over, and former U.S. Amateur champion Mark O'Meara led all rookies by a few thousand dollars. By the season finale, Couples had overtaken O'Meara on the money list, but O'Meara received the most ballots.

John Horne thinks losing the Rookie of the Year Award had a positive impact on Couples's career, because "Fred said something like he felt that he was not getting any respect. I think it upset him to the point that it helped him. It's always incredible to me that they have shadowed each other all these years. Career money is similar. They've won a similar number of tournaments. O'Meara kills everybody at Pebble. Fred kills everybody in L.A."[2] Some competitions last a lifetime.

Still, Couples was encouraged by his progress. Statistically, he finished second in driving distance.

With his playing rights for the next season guaranteed, Couples decided it was time to make his relationship with Deborah more permanent. They were married December 5, 1981.

"I remember when we heard they were getting married we were in shock," David Renker said. "We thought he was so easygoing and friendly and she was so hyper and completely opposite. It didn't seem like the best match in the world. She always wanted to be the center of attention."

Steve Dallas attended the wedding at a church in Palm Springs. "She was the only girl he ever dated," he said. "I remember driving down. The reception was an indoor-outdoor affair. It seemed lavish at the time." Again Couples had gone against his family's feelings. They were against the marriage.

As far as Fred's career was concerned, however, there were few complaints. Uncle Pete proclaimed the first year as a pro a success. "If I remember correctly, he made about $70,000. And in side money, another thirty or forty thousand. And religiously, every week, if he won a little money, from Titleist or whatever, he would send a check to Mike Foster or his secretary at the brokerage firm. If Fred needed money, they would draw money out of that, and his mother would put it into his checking account. And that's how Freddie survived the first year. And he really came out of the box never in debt to anybody."

Couples began his second season his own man.

"The next year was easier because I knew the courses, got accustomed to the Tour," Couples admitted. "I wasn't in the pro-ams before. I saw them as a practice round, an opportunity to play the courses. Before, I played practice like it was the tournament."

While this statement seems obvious, it is significant. The routine of the first-year touring professional is an adventure. In each new city, there's an opportunity to get lost between the airport and the hotel, between a hotel and a new restaurant, between the hotel and the golf course. There are legions of horror stories about clubs being stolen, caddies that disappear overnight, food poisoning. Name your all-time worst travel story, and it's probably happened twice to a Tour rookie.

Often the accommodations a newcomer can afford aren't the luxury brand. Those players on the lower end of the money list share rooms to keep expenses down. The rookies are saving as much money as they can, because they know it might be a while before they make a good finish, never mind win a tournament. It's nothing but a big money drain, $2,000 to $3,000 to $4,000 a week, and up. And that's the low end, traveling without anyone else.

To the rookie, each golf course is new. The veterans, meanwhile, have played it for years. They know the greens. They know the bunkers. They know the prevailing winds. They know what clothes to pack for the weather. They may even be staying with friends who live on the course. If they're in the top echelon from the previous year, they even have a free car to drive.

A rookie doesn't have those advantages. He's on his own every week for as many weeks as he can play. The first year, when he needs help the most, he gets the least. The situation breeds survivors. It also breeds friendships. Jay Haas remembered how he met Fred Couples.

"The first time I met Fred was at Fort Worth. A friend of Tom Purtzer's was with the Hyatt hotel chain and got us this suite to stay in with three or four different rooms. Tom knew Fred a little bit, and it might have been his first or second year on tour, so he came up to the room. And I'd heard of Fred Couples and didn't know him at all, so I didn't know what to think at first," Haas explained. "We spent two hours playing cards, some silly game we made up as we went along. I thought Fred was one of the funniest guys I'd ever been around. He just had a way with words that was a lot of fun. Since that day we've been close. I just think Fred's easy to be around. Especially one-on-one. There's really no pressure. You don't feel like you have to entertain Fred or anything like that."

Tom Purtzer added to the story. "He never made a hotel reservation. He'd just show up. And he's such a good guy, you'd just take him in. Nobody cared."

Both Haas and Purtzer remembered their own starts and knew how difficult it could be.

Steve Cole was on the bag for a couple of tournaments during that second season and recalled some unforgettable rounds. "I remember at L.A. we started on the back nine, and he bogeys one of the first three holes and still shot a 64. He had that ability to be aggressive for the day. He could sense it and wasn't timid when things were going right."

In 1982 Couples also became friends with Gay Brewer, former Masters champion. They worked a little on Couples's swing technique. Brewer, like Couples, is primarily self-taught.

"He said that there are five fundamentals to the golf game," Couples explained. "The grip, the stance, the takeaway, the follow-through, and the head movement. He said no one has all five. If they did, they'd be the

perfect golfer. Most Tour players have three. Snead and Littler are supposed to have the best, maybe four of the five." Couples said that he
couldn't change his swing, so he modified his grip.

Late in 1982 Couples captured the attention of the field at the PGA
Championship, played at Southern Hills in Tulsa, on Saturday by shooting a 29 on the back side, a new nine-hole record. He added a 66 on Sunday to vault himself into third place. He became a near contender.

John Bracken, Couples's junior golf buddy, was on the bag that week.
"I was finishing up summer school [at Arkansas], and I was 90 miles from
Tulsa. He called to see if I wanted to caddie for him.

"Fred birdied five of the last six holes to shoot that 29, and it's still tied
for the nine-hole PGA Championship record. He didn't have a putt outside
five feet until he got to 18, and I said, 'Why don't you make this 20-footer.
You haven't had a putt outside of six feet, and I've never seen six birdies
in a row.' And he looks at me—and I don't know if it was just contending or what, but he said, 'What are you talking about? How many have I
made?' And he drilled the 20-footer.

"He was two behind Raymond [Floyd] coming into the last two holes
on Sunday. Fred used to have a habit of pushing the envelope. On the
17th, now he'd take a 4-iron and lay up. But then, he was trying to be a
foot from laying up. And he took a 1-iron out and blocked it, and instead
of laying up, he one-skipped it over that water on 17, if you can imagine.
The ball had no business being dry. He pushed it, and the water's a little
shorter on the right, but it wasn't anywhere near where he wanted to hit
it. Hopped it over the water. He made about $26,000, and it was his
biggest check at the time."

Couples's best finishes for the year were the third at the PGA and a tie
for seventh at Sea Pines [Harbour Town]. He entered 28 tournaments and
made the cut in 10 of them, for a total of $77,606. He was eighth in driving distance, averaging 268.7 yards in the wooden driver era. Miraculously, he was again 53rd on the money list and earned the right to go on
to 1983, the year that would really mark the beginning of his career as we
know it.

In December, John Horne attempted Qualifying School and stayed
with Fred and Deborah in Palm Springs. "It was when they lived below
Bob Hope's house. It was hilarious to listen to them argue. I would sit and
listen to them in awe.

"One day he and I and another guy were playing cards on the floor of
the condo. She poured a glass of wine on his back during an argument.
I don't know what it was exactly, but I remember he was brushing her off
and she wanted to do something. He did not have a problem expressing

a thought if he got mad. I was trying not to laugh. Fred can be hilarious without cracking a smile. I think he could be a stand-up comic. He's got these lines popping off to her, and she's popping back to him, and she poured the wine on him and he never even flinched. After she walked off, he got up and changed shirts. They could get after it. Then everything's great the next day."

Horne also remembered that Fred bought Deborah a red Corvette for their anniversary. "I drove it once or twice when I was out there."

At the start of 1983, Couples's level of play was greatly improved.

According to Cole, who was on the bag in Tucson, "He hit some of the greatest shots I ever saw and occasionally the worst. He was in contention. We were on the first par 5 on the back nine. He hit a long true tee shot and then with his 3-wood hit the biggest, highest, pull hook that could be hit by a human being. It took a couple bounces over some trees into no-man's-land, bounced and rolled, and my eyes fixed on a couple of white stakes. He looked at me and said, 'Is it out?' and stuck his hand out for the new golf ball.

"Mike Donald was on the tee behind us, waiting to hit. Afterward he said he couldn't believe anybody could actually hit out-of-bounds from there. After that, he hit the next 3-wood, made bogey, and lost the tournament by a shot or two."

When the Tour moved to Florida, Couples was third at Inverrary. Though things were going well, change was in the air. Curtis Strange and caddie Linn Strickler had a mutual parting of the ways. Couples snagged him at Bay Hill.

"Sure, I knew who he was," Strickler said. "He had posted some great scores by then. When he shot 29 on the back nine at Southern Hills, we all thought, 'Who's this guy?'"

Couples's legendary shyness left him, as it sometimes does when there is something he has to go out and get for himself. Strickler remembered it as a complete surprise. "All of a sudden out of the blue he comes up to me and says, 'I'm Fred Couples. You want to come to work for me?'" Strickler asked if he could work the Masters, but Couples already had someone for that tournament.

This was to be Couples's first year at Augusta, and he recalled just how he felt. "I remember people talking about Magnolia Lane. It was spectacular. The first time I was there, it was when the flowers were out. It was beautiful. It's my favorite tournament.

"I was nervous as heck on the first tee. I'd never seen the course except on TV, and it actually looks nothing like that. And I thought the first tee shot was pretty scary."

In his first outing at the Masters, Couples finished tied for 32nd with rounds of 73-68-81-73. The Masters cut was low 44 players and ties, and 49 advanced. It was a Masters plagued by bad weather, but Couples never forgot it.

Seve Ballesteros won the tournament in the final round on Monday. The green jacket was slipped onto Seve's waiting shoulders by the defending champion, Craig Stadler.

Strickler picked up the bag four weeks later at the Houston Open, where Couples finished sixth. "I told him as a joke in the first few weeks, 'You gotta win quick or you're gonna get paired with Mark Lye and Tim Simpson for the rest of your career. So let's get a win here.' No offense to Lye or Simpson." The fact was a winner got paired with other winners. It was a better attitude and atmosphere.

With that comment, Linn Strickler may have given Fred the necessary boost. It may have been the first time that anybody told Couples he *could* win, not just be good enough to hang on. Deborah was worried about whether or not he would "make it." His family had concerns about whether he was good enough. Even he confessed to having doubts. But Linn Strickler saw what Steve Dallas saw and what anybody with eyes and a knowledge of the golf game would have seen if they just paid attention. Fred Couples was about to be somebody. It was just a matter of time. Strickler was gonna get his guy in gear.

The breakthrough came about a month later, June 5, at the Kemper Open, which was then held at Congressional Country Club. Strickler does not remember any special change in play from Houston to Kemper to indicate Couples was on the verge. As Strickler explained it, "The way he played golf at the time was 'Here's a par 4, give me the driver.' His course management was not that good."

But when it came to distance, he was unlike the rest. "Seven-irons were 150 for other guys. He knew he was stronger, maybe an 8-iron. I'd give him a 9-iron sometimes. He said he'd played golf his whole life over the green. He just hit the ball farther than most people. He was the Tiger Woods of that time, longer than anybody when he wanted to be."

According to Strickler, "Kemper, the way it happened, it was kind of ridiculous." He was being kind.

Couples was tied for the lead on Saturday night with Scott Simpson.

Deborah, certain it was Fred's time to win, had flown in from Palm Springs to cheer him on. She was vocal in the gallery, having fun. She thanked a spectator for getting his head in the way of an errant tee shot on the 15th.

Couples and Strickler tried to concentrate on the golf. "Two in the last group shooting 77s. The other guy shooting 76. We only made one birdie all day, on the first hole," Strickler recalled, shaking his head.

Couples agreed. "I started matching shots with the other guys. I was giving strokes away."

On the 18th green, more nervous than he had ever been in his life and playing like it, Couples faced a 30-foot putt. As though someone had him by the throat when the blade hit the ball, he left it 10 feet short. The second putt had to seem like light-years in distance. Skip the raps on Couples's putting. He did it.

Simpson missed a four-footer for birdie, and the playoff began.

"You can do it, Freddie. You can win it!" Deborah cheered from the gallery.

Thomas Boswell of the *Washington Post* described it as "one of the longest, most complexly theatrical and most ludicrous days of full-retreat golf in the history of the PGA Tour."

The round had taken so long that the last group—Couples, T. C. Chen, and Simpson—finished nearly an hour behind the group in front of them. "Ben Wright [CBS announcer] deemed it the longest day in golf history," Strickler said. "I remember seeing the tape and Wright said something like 'See those ducks? They were mere eggs at the beginning of the day.'"

Instead of an outright victory for Chen, Simpson, or Couples, they tied with Barry Jaeckel, who had believed his day was over and had been in the bar, and Gil Morgan, who had packed his clubs in the car and was leaving.

As the five-way playoff began, the John 3:16 guy in the rainbow wig shouted "Praise the Lord" after every tee shot. No doubt the crowd presumed he was praying for the day to end, but he added to the comedic value of the finish.

Jaeckel was eliminated on the first hole—no doubt a consequence of his long wait in the bar. Reportedly, he shouted in jest for another beer, then hit his drive left into the trees. The others went to the second extra hole, led by John 3:16, his multicolored hair, and religious inspiration.

In the midst of this madness, on the 16th, a 211-yard par 3, Couples hit a career 5-iron that he says was two feet and Strickler calls closer to one. "I felt like crying," Couples admitted. "I've never hit a shot that amounted to so much. I'm just glad it [the putt] was that close and no farther." It was a sure birdie. His putt dropped, sealing the victory.

"And," Strickler recounted his eyewitness report, "that was when Deborah felt safe to jump all over him. You could see me there. And Greg Rita, Gil's caddie at the time. I'm going to go for the tailgate handshake, and it's hold on, here she comes. Then Fred sees her. Fred starts digging his heels in, like it's a buried bunker shot, and she hits him doing about 10 miles per hour. Any other man of weaker frame would have gone over. It was hilarious."

Strickler calls it the "Straddle Jump," an event that catapulted both Fred and Deborah into golf history forever.

Tom Boswell described it: "As Couples saw his putt disappear into the cup, his wife came running. Over the rough, through the traps, and into her husband's arms came blond, blue-eyed Deborah Morgan-Couples, tennis professional, in her little blue dress and her white cowboy hat. The flying four-limb embrace she whipped on her husband was enough to make a moose take a tranquilizer."[3]

Not to be outdone, Dave Kindred wrote:

"An hour later, during a gangsome playoff that looked like Saturday morning at the Elks Club, Couples would win his first pro golf tournament and reap the rewards of a $72,000 check and a priceless embrace from his shy, retiring wife, Deborah, who carried her cowboy hat, platinum hair, electric-blue minidress, four turquoise bracelets, and 10 red-paint toenails through a sand trap at 173 mph to leap into her hubby's arms.

"'Babycakes, I lovya,' demure Deborah Couples said."[4]

Fifteen years and a divorce later, people still remember that tournament because it was so opposite the kind of behavior anyone expects in golf, or anywhere else, for that matter. To say the least, Deborah could be characterized as uninhibited.

In the post-round press conference, Couples summed it up more succinctly and without the superlatives.

"It was a long day," he noted. "Every shot felt like the toughest shot of the year. When I bogeyed the 15th, I felt like I'd lost all chance. I felt like crying on 17 [also a bogey]. It's just a lot of pressure. The people know it, and you know it, and they'll let you know it. When I quit college to turn pro, my parents didn't think it was too good a move. Now I gotta call 'em and see what they say."

The victory at the Kemper Open carried with it a two-year exemption for play on the Tour. Couples also got good pairings. The Kemper win put him into the top 20 for earnings at the midyear point.

The rest of Couples's 1983 season progressed favorably. He placed eighth at Westchester, seventh at the Buick Open.

The PGA Championship that year was at Riviera. Couples gave Linn Strickler a week off and called on his friend John Bracken. Bracken believed Couples's superstitious side led to the request. "I think he said to himself after Southern Hills, which was his best finish except for Kemper, that he wanted me to caddie. Maybe I helped him get relaxed. I told my boss I would need that week off."

Bracken remembered playing practice rounds with "Calvin Pete, Rex Caldwell—those bell bottom pants with no back pockets." But it wasn't a third. It was a tie for 23rd.

Couples's last good tournament of the season was at the Texas Open, where he was ninth. He finished 19th on the money list with earnings of just over $200,000. He had entered 30 tournaments and made the cut in 23 of them, more than twice the number of cuts in 1982, a substantial improvement. He had seven top 10 finishes, had a stroke average of 71.4, was fourth in birdies, was sixth in number of eagles, and was eighth in driving distance.

At least he knew he'd finally found his calling and felt vindicated for the decision he'd made when he turned pro.

5

The 1984 TPC and the Curse of the 10-Year Exemption

"Mannerisms. Freddie's got some of the best. He's a caddie that can play."

— Linn Strickler

For Fred Couples 1984 was the year that defined his talent. Naturally, it didn't start off that way. In fact, at the Bob Hope, right in his backyard, he finished in a tie for 50th.

Yet caddie Linn Strickler still looked forward to work. "It was like a joy for me, because we discussed every club," Strickler said.

Between the two of them, there was enough dry humor to compete with the desert weather.

The comedic deadpan remarks were a constant in Couples's personality. "In Palm Springs it was 'Where do I aim this one, Linn. At the palm tree?'—and there's a million palm trees. He does that just to get a rise out of people."

Strickler said Couples liked to play with the gallery, too. But he never told them what the game was. "If people were crowding and he was taking a practice swing, he could make it go one inch from their nose. He knows exactly what he's doing. That's what makes him so beautiful."

But humorous interludes or not, that spring of 1984 Couples had only two top 10 finishes. At Bay Hill, two weeks before the Tournament Players Championship, he shot 80 on Sunday and tied for 60th. In his two previous visits to the Stadium Course at Sawgrass, where the TPC was played, Couples had left town early. His best score on the course had been a 79. His record there was so bad that he and Deborah had already decided there was no reason for her to make the trip since more than likely he would be home on the weekend.

His Wednesday practice round was an 80.

In 1984, this was no average golf course. In its confines lived vicious denizens of the North Florida swamp that gobbled golf balls faster than players could tee them up. For a while, it even had goats chomping on the grass instead of mowers. That was until the alligators started going after the goats, thereby diminishing the herd's ability to keep the turf at the proper height.¹ It was, and is, as Gary McCord is fond of saying, a dark and evil place. It is the course where Jerry Pate, after winning in 1982, tossed former PGA Tour Commissioner Deane Beman and course designer Pete Dye into the lake to the left of the final hole and then dove in himself, sort of a backstroke victory lap.

They say it's been softened since then, but softened is a comparative term. People still sit behind the island 17th tee and make dollar bets to see whether a player's ball will hit the green and hold. For spectators, it's a wonderful place to drink beer and watch other people suffer. Sure the crowd moans sympathetically when balls hit the wooden bulkheads and splash into the water. Or when they take a big hop on the back of the green and slither into the drink, past the alligator's nose. But on a warm sunny Saturday or Sunday, it's hard to find a good seat. It's so much fun, they sell skyboxes around it. It's the S&M course of the PGA Tour.

As the tournament began in 1984, Tom Watson commented on the changes made in the first two years: "The word isn't *easier*. It's *fairer*."

The first day, winds howled. Gusts were in the 35–40-mile-per-hour range. Jim Thorpe led with a 68. There were 12 other players under par, including John Mahaffey with a 69. At the island 17th, 64 golf balls found the water, a new record. It surpassed the old mark by 12. One even belonged to Mahaffey, who described the par-3 17th as one of the "best par 5s on the course." Couples managed a 71.

On Friday, with a prediction of more wind, the officials gave the course an easier setup, they said. But the wind didn't arrive, and the field got lucky. Five shots were holed for eagle two, and another eight eagles were made on par 5s. Watson made six birdies in a row. Scores under 70 were common. But only one man had a 64. Fred Couples. The guy who'd shot over 160 in the first two rounds in his two previous attempts at the TPC. It was better than good. It was a course record.

As Strickler told it, "We bogeyed the first hole, and he slammed his putter in his bag and said, 'That's to show you yesterday was a fluke.' And he proceeds to make eight birdies and an eagle the rest of the day and bogeyed 18 to shoot 64."

Nothing like a little Italian temper to get the score down.

Couples bettered the previous course record by two shots. He birdied the second hole, a par 5, and holed out a sand shot from 88 yards at the short par-4 fourth. He sank putts of 10 and 20 feet at seven and eight, making the turn at 32, four under par. On the back, he birdied 10 from 20 feet, 11 from four feet, 13—the often-overlooked "other" treacherous par 3—from 20 feet, the 15th from 12 feet, and the 16th, a par 5, with two putts after reaching the green with driver, two-iron. He had the lead by two over Thorpe.

Deborah decided to fly in for the weekend, and she cheered every shot. Again people took note of the contrast in their personalities.

Saturday came and went with Couples making three bogeys on the front but enough birdies to finish with 71. He finished two ahead of the field, and he said he was looking forward to playing with Watson and Seve Ballesteros, the swashbuckling Spaniard who had already won the Masters twice. Writers noted that Couples was unemotional and said his big interest that day was rushing to the nearest television set to watch Houston play Virginia in the NCAA basketball tournament.

Strickler says otherwise.

"On Sunday he was nervous as a cat on a griddle," Strickler explained. "They're announcing on the first tee: 'Out of Kansas City, Missouri, winner of five British Opens, etc., etc., Tom Watson. From Santander, Spain, winner of the 1980 and 1983 Masters and the 1979 British Open, Severiano Ballesteros.' Together they'd won three of the last five Masters, four of the last seven British Opens. 'And here's Fred Couples, winner of the Kemper Open.' He moved so fast, if you see the tape. He was moving 100-miles per hour. He told me all day, 'All I want to do is get out of these guys' way.'"

Dan Jenkins, who was still writing for *Sports Illustrated* then, called Couples "the odds-on favorite to collapse in the final round."

"It was one of the toughest last days he'd had up to then. Hits a 1-iron on the first hole and hooked it into the left trees," Strickler said, shaking his head.

Couples scrambled out for par. Watson was not so lucky, but birdied the second to pull even. Then Couples also birdied. Ballesteros failed to take advantage of the par 5.

Meanwhile, Lee Trevino, playing in the group ahead of them, was making a move. Trevino had been spending more time in the TV tower for NBC than playing or practicing, and he was loose. Nobody expected him to do well. He birdied the second and third.

Couples three-putted number four and his lead was cut to one over Trevino and Ballesteros. But he birdied five.

"He was in the bunker on seven, that par 4," Strickler added, "and hit his second shot into the right trap." Bogey.

"On eight the pin is six yards over the trap. We get to the tee, and Herman is dancing because Trevino makes a 25-footer to tie for the lead, and we haven't made a par lately," Strickler continued.

"Seve's first. He hits 3-wood and misses left of the green. Watson pops up, short of the green. Freddie sees all this stuff. He takes a 2-iron and *stands* on this thing. It carries the trap and goes just short of the hole [two feet]. He taps in for birdie. After eight we had a one-shot lead.

"On nine he launched another one. His approach was six feet, and now it's a two-shot lead."

Watson and Ballesteros, the two favorites, had not mounted a charge. It was the surprising Trevino, with a blazing 32 on the front, who held on for the back nine.

On 10 Watson said Couples hit "one of the two best shots I've seen him make."

Couples had hit his tee ball left into a waste bunker.

"He had to hit a big hook out of it. It was a beautiful shot, a big old hook around a tree," Watson said with a grin of admiration—this from someone who has made his share of miracle shots.

Strickler added, "It was a 40-yard hook with a 9-iron, a mile in the air, and he landed it eight feet from the jar. Fred had a slice stance, a downslope. Watson and Ballesteros, they both missed the green with 9-irons from the fairway. To hit a balloon hook, one of those reroute jobs [Strickler gestured, waggling hands and arms in the air]—you can't talk to that shot. Everybody's goin', 'You've *got* to be kidding me!' It was unbelievable. He was lucky as hell. He's charmed. Like the Masters on 12 with the ball hanging on the shelf. Somebody likes him up there."

Up ahead, Trevino birdied the 12th, from about 15 feet. But Couples one-upped him with a birdie of his own from about 10.

"We were watching the guy we had to beat right ahead of us— Trevino," Strickler said solemnly, cagey veteran that he is.

"Fred made birdie on 13, then got in the waste bunker on 14. Bogey. Went in the really deep grass on side. It was against the wind that day. At that time pars were working for us," Strickler said with a sigh.

"I wanted him to get to 18 with a two-shot lead. We finally got to 17— did not make birdie on 16 [the par 5]—and on 17 he pushes this 8-iron thing right over the sand trap. 'Is it going to hang on?' I'm asking myself. And it lands right of the flag and stays on green. I'm at the Gatorade cooler watching and hoping and knowing how close it was. So once it was on the green, I said, 'We got it. If Trevino's going to birdie the 18th hole, fine. There ain't no way you're making a six on 18. We're shooting for a five and getting out.'"

The 8-iron on the 17th landed five or six feet behind the pin, between the pin and the bulkhead, perilously close to the water. The pin, which had to be no more than 12 or 15 paces from the right side of the green, was not Couples's real target.

"I didn't even look where the flag was," Couples said afterward. "I just aimed for the middle of the green. The only reason it landed near the hole was that I pushed the shot."

On the 18th Couples hit a 1-iron off the tee. Watson recalled the second shot. "He hit a great shot on the final hole. He had pushed his tee shot into the right rough and then hit a 7-iron 200 yards up onto the green."

Couples admitted he had considered aiming into the gallery, knowing he'd get a drop. But instead he hit the green, leaving himself 25 feet. He three-putted for the title, the money, and the 10-year exemption.

"He hit only four fairways," Strickler added in amazement.

Afterward, Couples said simply, "Winning here was something I never thought would happen. My biggest satisfaction is winning this tournament against this field. My biggest accomplishment this week was beating the course."

Five years later, when asked to reflect on that victory and what it meant to him at the time, he said, "The TPC I will never forget, because I had never played a good round of golf there in my life."

Steve Hershey predicted good things for Couples's future in his follow-up article for USA *Today.* "The feeling of many PGA Tour players is that Fred Couples could become one of the dominant players on the tour."[2]

Trevino also envisioned big things. "Fred's going to be a player to be contended with every week now," he said.

A few weeks later, at Augusta, Couples's humor surfaced again, according to caddie Strickler. "He's over the ball on the ninth fairway and asks, 'Where do I aim this, Linn. At the white visor?' I look up and there's, like five hundred white visors. I say, 'Go to the 35th one from the right.'" He tied for 10th.

Couples skipped the two Texas tournaments and entered the Memorial, where he proceeded to shoot 75–80. He claimed to be unconcerned.

"If I miss five straight cuts, then I might worry about it," he said prior to defending at Kemper the following week. "I certainly didn't expect to do well after taking so much time off. We all have to take time off, and when you do, sometimes it takes a while to get back in the groove."[3]

Besides, he was still number three on the money list. "The only thing I'm doing well at all is driving. I'm hitting the ball straight, but you have to hit a lot of long irons here [Congressional]."[4]

In addition, he cited the move into his new house. "I've been moving furniture. When I go home, I like to do things with Debbie. I don't like to play at all. It's easy to go hit balls for 20 minutes, but then you run into everybody at the pro shop, and you're there two hours."[5]

He was ninth at Winged Foot for the U.S. Open and fourth at the British Open, which was held at St. Andrews. It was his first experience there, and he would grow to enjoy it.

Strickler remembered with particular fondness the eagle on the 18th hole at St. Andrews. "He's got 110 over the Valley of Sin. He's got an 8-iron out. I took the club out of his hand. I said, 'No way in life! If you hit 8-iron you're going to put it in Cruden Bay, the original 19th hole of golf. If you catch this thing, it's going to go over the world. It'll hit on the back fringe and roll over.'

"So he says okay and hits 9-iron and doesn't think it's enough. It hit the back edge and gave a slow trickle. It must have taken 45 seconds. People are going, 'Aahhh, aahhh.' It was something. It was the longest prolonged ovation I had ever heard in golf. When it finally went in, I looked at him and said, 'Eight-iron, huh?'

"We played it four under for the week. Langer finished third. Watson hit on road on the 17th and lost to Seve." But the joke of the tournament was that Couples had forgotten his passport en route, and had to fly back from Chicago to California to get it.

Then, inexplicably, in his best year ever, he packed it in for six weeks and sat out 15 of the last 27 events and still finished in seventh place on the money list, making over $330,000. He managed a 20th-place finish at the PGA Championship. Perhaps Couples had climbed a mountain and needed a little time to enjoy the scenery before discovering that there's a mountain next door that's even higher and more interesting.

His victory at the TPC earned him a feature in *Sports Illustrated* by Jaime Diaz, who called him a "fresh-faced slugger" and alluded to Couples's distaste for talking about himself by writing, "Trying to get Couples to say something even marginally brash about his remarkable game is like waiting around a par 3 for someone to score a hole-in-one."

As Couples pointed out in the article, he'd seen other guys "say how great they were playing, and now they aren't up there anymore. I'm an everyday person and I just want to keep an even keel."

If he only knew what lay ahead.

There's a world of wisdom in the caddie ranks. They see a lot, hear a lot, know a lot, and pretty much keep their mouths shut. But there was a noticeable difference with Couples, and it had to do with his wife. "After he won the TPC, Deborah started coming out less and less," Strickler said. To understand the significance of that, it's important to understand that she was extraordinarily important to him for a lot of reasons.

Over the years, Couples had had a series of support systems that worked. As a youngster, his family was there, especially his mother. As a teen, golf friends took him where he needed to go and encouraged him to get better. In college, Jim Nantz, by Couples's own admission, got him to class. And after he decided to turn pro, Deborah kept him organized. When she wasn't there for him all the time, it had to affect his play. She once said, "He thinks of me as his good-luck charm. That's why he wants me to come out."

A few former Tour players have remarked that when things are good at home, it's easy to play good golf. What they mean is that there's some kind of a comfortable personal environment that allows them the mental freedom to go out and do their best. Whether it's having close family members or a wife or close friends, it's important to have that support system to count on, no matter what.

Is it a lot to ask of a wife or of parents? Sure. But that's part of the deal. The spouse of a successful athlete—man or woman—is second fiddle. But to the continued success of the athlete, that support is essential. It helps spur them to higher goals. When the support system goes, so does the athlete's performance.

Deborah wanted to do something else. For a time, she entered a few professional events on the women's tennis tour. She bought another house in Newport Beach, considering it an investment. But she spent less time at golf events. To compound the problem, there was the life Deborah was fashioning for them. It was better than anybody's wildest dream. To use a Couples-like understatement, it was better than the movies, because it was real.

Deborah and Fred moved out of the condo in Palm Springs and into a house-size condo in a world-class resort: Mission Hills Country Club, in neighboring Rancho Mirage. George Brett lived in the neighborhood, as did Johnny Bench. Dinah Shore lived on the ninth hole of one of the golf courses.

The Coachella Valley, comprised of communities from Palm Springs to Indio, is where Frank Sinatra flew the flag on a street named after him, where President Ford went to retire and play golf, where actor Bill Devane keeps polo ponies, plays golf, and runs a restaurant, where Robert Wagner often drops in on weekends, where Bob Hope has a home on the hillside. It is not at all like living in an ordinary community, city, or town someplace else in the U.S. It is not at all like the life that most people have.

And who wouldn't want to rub elbows with celebrities? Even Couples, faced with the opportunity to play golf with baseball greats, found the attraction irresistible. He played numerous home matches with George Brett, and the two became friends.

"He would write little notes at the beginning of the year for me," Couples explained, "and set goals—where I want to finish on the money list, and what tournament he thinks I should win.

"George liked to find out what was going on in golf, and I always asked about Kirk Gibson or Bret Saberhagen and all that. I think it's probably like that with every athlete or with businesspeople."

Couples was getting his first taste of success, and after years of lacking the best in life, he now had it everywhere. He had to learn how to deal with it and maintain it, and the learning was difficult.

In March of 1985, at the Honda Classic, he was in contention all the way. He led the first round with a course-record nine-under-par 63.

The second day, he and Curtis Strange shared the lead at 131. When the third round was completed, Couples and Strange were still deadlocked at 15 under.

Then, on Sunday, playing in the final group, he skied to a final-round 78, with a ball in the water on the 10th. He and Strange disagreed on where the ball had entered the hazard, forcing Couples to replay the ball from the tee. He finished fourth, furious with himself for playing his way out of the lead and failing to recover.

At the end of the month, Couples again finished fourth, this time at the Panasonic Las Vegas Invitational, again behind winner Curtis Strange, who would go on to take the money title and set a new record for money won in a single season. But this time, he had not been the tournament leader as he had been at the Honda.

In 1985, his performance in the majors slipped compared to 1984. He was 10th at the Masters, 39th at the U.S. Open, did not play in the British Open, and came back for a sixth place at the PGA. He made just over $170,000. That's a lot of cash, but nothing compared to his potential. Even with pro-ams on Mondays, the life of luxury takes a consistent infusion of funds.

In retrospect, maybe the best thing about 1985 was his renewed friendship with Jim Nantz, who had gone from Houston to being the television anchor in Salt Lake City, Utah. Unwittingly, Couples was about to do something for his college friend, payback for the days Nantz looked after him.

"In August of that year, I auditioned for CBS Sports. The following week Fred just happened to be playing a tournament in Salt Lake City, a junior-senior event called The ShootOut at Jeremy Ranch. Needless to say, I was feeling some anxiety, the audition had gone well, and I had been told I was now one of two finalists for the position at CBS. The week he was there, he watched me anchor some broadcasts at KSL-TV, and I sought his advice on how to handle the enormity of this once-in-a-lifetime career opportunity. He said something that was simple, yet insightful, into how he handles pressure: 'Just treat it like it's not a big deal.'"

The visit is still fresh in Couples's mind.

"I remember it like it was yesterday," Couples said. "I watched Jimmy do the news in Salt Lake City, and I was laughing so hard I almost wet my pants. It was just like in the dorm rooms, and he was always so good. It was just so cool, you know? I'd never seen anyone do the news before . . . for real. Anyway, to me this CBS audition would have been like getting an exemption to the Masters when you're 25 years old—you know, what do you do? You give it a shot and, obviously, Jimmy went and knocked them dead."

For Nantz, having an old friend around during a time of change took the edge off the pressure. As Nantz said about what was happening in his life, "Of course, it was a big deal. The big break to go to the network is something everyone in television dreams about, and CBS was interviewing me to become the next host of the college football studio show. I knew that could lead to basketball, golf, and all kinds of other experiences. Fred's words gave me a quiet confidence. It helped.

"Two weeks later, after more interviews and auditions, and interviews with the top brass, I became the youngest full-time broadcaster in CBS Sports history at age 26."

Nantz not only got the job, he was slowly and carefully being groomed as Pat Summerall's replacement. He got that job sooner than he expected.

Nineteen eighty-five was a less-than-remarkable year for Couples, but it should not have been anything to really worry about. His place on the money list dipped from seventh at the end of 1984 to 38th at the end of 1985. He played in 26 events and made the cut in 23. He just didn't light up the course often enough to make it count at the bank the way he had in 1984. To say it didn't begin to bother him would be wrong. But he didn't improve, and the beginning of the next year was worse. There were other forces at work. Several sources reported problems in his marriage.

Even caddie Linn Strickler noticed. "It seemed like that was the time he and Deborah were figuring out their match was not made in heaven. That was my interpretation. He started to [complain] at me, but I was doing the same job. He damn sure couldn't yell at her. He could be the best player in the world, but I knew there was no way in the world I could hang on to the job. I initiated him to the Tour. I feel like that. What Deborah was doing was upsetting his life."

Couples was not known as a club thrower. According to Strickler, his idea of showing anger might be to take the wrong exit ramp out of a bunker. "You have to rake a bunch [when Couples is angry]. He asks, 'Where have you been,' and I say, 'Raking your mess for the last five minutes.'"

When Strickler worked for him, he said Couples was a real stay-in kind of guy. "You can't, after dinner or room service, pry Freddie out at night for a dance or whatever."

And it's not as though Couples was searching. He really wanted Deborah to be with him, even though there were plenty of women interested. Strickler continued, "He was not scared of women, but he could have had any girl around and probably didn't know it. Didn't *know* it. I mean, I was doing great. I'm getting these numbers passed to me. I mean, I've got a pocketful of matchbooks. I'm saying, 'Oh yeah. Oh yeah. He'll call ya' — knowing that wasn't the case. 'But if you want some good stories, I'm available.' You know, I was a young man at that time, too. That was before AIDS and all that. We weren't exactly flower children, but there was plenty of motivation."

Strickler also pointed out some of the facts of caddie life. "There's no excuses needed [for ending their player-caddie relationship]. It was just time for a change. We spend more daylight hours together than they do with their wives. It's easy to figure out why, if things aren't working, you're the first to go."

Their last tournament as a pair was the 1986 L.A. Open. "Curtis [Strange] hired me back, so I won the first tournament back with Curtis, and he says, 'See what you've been missing?'"

There were other rumors that were less pleasant, and those who tell the tales have requested anonymity. For example, Deborah told one man, "When I go out, I leave my wedding ring in the soap dish . . . the idea being if it fell down the drain, so what."

Deborah was called promiscuous, and much, much worse.

One source, when reminded of how Couples always described his wife as being tired of having him hang around the house and sending him out to play, had this reply: "And *he* got tired of waking up in the morning and finding out she wasn't home yet. That can get a little tiring, too."

But others, like John Horne and Uncle Pete, remember how much Deborah did for Fred when he was first starting out.

Life was clearly becoming uncomfortable for Couples on many levels. When he said at the 1986 Western Open that if he won he might quit golf altogether, he really meant it. Few knew he was concerned about being able to keep up payments on the houses at Mission Hills Country Club and Newport Beach. California real estate prices being what they are, his slide down the money list and his worries over the expense of maintaining, furnishing, and keeping two good-size homes contributed to his dismal performance on the course. He had just finished digging himself out of a financial hole, and now it looked as though he was being sucked back into it.

Then, to top it off, the press started to accuse him of not caring about his golf game, particularly after the Western Open comments. He took six weeks off after the PGA, citing his dislike for playing in hot weather, which didn't make sense to people who knew he had played collegiate golf in Houston and lived in the severe desert heat of southern California. Couples said, "There wasn't much sense in beating my brains out when I knew I wasn't going to win." He was not a walking endorsement for Tony Robbins.

"He never got accused of trying too hard," Strickler said. "He always looked so laid-back. But knowing deep down how he was, [I knew] that was his shield against failure." He said that for people to say Couples didn't care was absurd. "Like not being a good putter. You can't risk . . . you can't bear the consequence of not performing well or you won't ever have a chance. A lot of people can't choke because they never give themselves a chance to choke." In other words, it's hard to have the guts to make a mistake — like hitting a ball into the woods at the wrong time or missing a four-foot putt that you would ordinarily make — in public.

"Mannerisms," Strickler added. "Freddie's got some of the best. He's a caddie that can play. He was supposed to be as good then as he is now. With that 10-year exemption, he could have taken that and gone right to the top."

But it didn't happen.

His place on the money list dipped from seventh at the end of 1984 to 38th at the end of 1985 and all the way to 76th in 1986. At the 1986 Masters, his finish was even lower, tied for 31st. He missed the cut at the U.S. Open, and finished 46th at the British Open and 36th at the PGA.

In *Golf Magazine*, he made the list of players who hit the best trouble shots. Larry Mize recalled pairings with him at Phoenix and at the Bob Hope tournament and said, "Freddie can make birdies from the boondocks."

And Johnny Miller added that Couples was "blessed with the talent to see shots, to invent and improvise. Because he's a wristy player, he can move his hands at high speeds and get lots of spin."

Raymond Floyd, in a quote that was little noticed by those who would later begin to criticize Couples's attitude, noted that he was "so competitive he's going to pull the shot off."

But being noted for trouble is not where you want to be if you are a rising young star. Being known for victories, for good play, for scoring—that's the reputation a player wants. Unfortunately, trouble summarized the state of his career at the end of 1986.

The 10-year exemption, the privilege that formerly came with winning the U.S. Open, the PGA Championship, the Players Championship, or the World Series of Golf, can be anything but a blessing.[6] Look what it did to Nick Price in 1983. To Bob Tway in 1985. To Ian Baker-Finch. To Mike Reid. To Roger Maltbie. To Sandy Lyle. To Hal Sutton. And even to Curtis Strange, although Curtis is so tough, it took two U.S. Opens to get to him.

It's hard, after reaching a plateau, to go even higher. And when things are crumbling all around, and there's no direction, it's hard to figure out how to right the ship—if, in fact, it can be righted. The 10-year exemption curse is so hard to overcome that only a few can mount the charge that it takes. Tom Watson. Jack Nicklaus. Arnold Palmer. Raymond Floyd. Hale Irwin. There aren't many who can shrug it off. The seductive siren of years of success stares people right square in the face, saying "Take me, I'm yours." But the siren, like all netherworld things, is elusive. And worse yet, fickle.

Yet the fates that were dispensing trouble would eventually show the way out. A couple of friends talked Couples into staying with his game. One offered to buy one of Couples's houses if he couldn't keep up with the payments. By luck, by accident, and through old friends, he found his golf game again. As Strickler said, the golf gods did like him.

6

Practice Almost Makes Perfect

"My God, he's the James Dean of golf."
—John Ashworth

During the summer of 1986, while his golf game was in shambles, Fred Couples managed to have some fun with a new hobby, thanks to Jay Haas. It was during that time that Haas introduced him to Mustangs. The cars, not the horses.

Haas hosted a charity Skins Game in Greenville, South Carolina, for the Children's Cancer Center and invited Curtis Strange, Peter Jacobsen, and Couples to play in it.

"Fred said he wanted a '65 or '66 fastback," Haas recalled. Haas knew one that was for sale. "We went to see it, and Fred said if he won enough in the Skins Game he was going to buy it. He won $8,500 and bought the car, and ended up staying eight days at my house. We drove it around. Got new tires."

At that point, Couples probably needed a diversion. He had said publicly that he was considering throwing in the towel. He seemed to be adrift. He wanted to get better, but he wasn't exactly sure how to do it.

At the PGA Championship, which was held at Inverness in Toledo, he got lucky. Not as lucky as Bob Tway did with his chip-in to beat Greg Norman, but lucky in another way. Couples accidentally reunited with an old friend, someone he knew from Houston: Dick Harmon.

Dick Harmon is one of the sons of 1948 Masters champion Claude Harmon, who mentored many accomplished players, including the late Dave Marr, who went on to win the 1965 PGA Championship, Jack Burke, Jr., who won the 1956 Masters, and Mike Souchak.

The Harmon sons,[1] although they did not have green jacket talent, are all golf professionals and learned the game under their father's guidance.

They have the eye that can see a swing, analyze it, take it apart, and put it back together. Equally important, they also know what not to touch.

"At the time I saw Fred at the PGA, I was teaching Lanny Wadkins, who was Player of the Year in 1985," Harmon noted. "If I could handle Lanny Wadkins, I thought I could handle Fred."

One of Couples's college friends, Paul Marchand, was about to join the mix.

"At that time, I was an assistant to Dick at River Oaks," Marchand explained. "When Dick saw Fred at the PGA Championship, he said something like 'Why don't you come down to Houston and stay. Paul's there. I'm there. Come down and practice and work on your game.' He just planted the seed."

Couples had never been known to study, analyze, or work on his swing. In fact, he had an aversion to it, and according to Marchand, he disliked watching himself on video.

Whether it was the frustration of knowing he could shoot low numbers but not win as often as he'd like, or thinking maybe it was time to just try something new, or knowing Paul Marchand, an old friend, would at least understand him, Couples was ready for a change at the end of 1986.

Couples's first visit to Harmon was the following February, after he won the pro-am portion of the AT&T with George Brett and finished fifth in the tournament overall, then had a sixth in Hawaii. Somewhere in the realms of his private psyche, Couples was starting to want more.

"The first time Dick and I talked about Fred," Marchand said, "I told him he wasn't going to believe this guy. What he can do. The way he hits it. The sound it makes. The way he plays the short game, the way he drives it.

"Dick said that he'd seen some good players and noted that Couples was not exactly lighting up the Tour. Then, after coming in from the tee the first day watching Fred, Dick said, 'I see what you mean.'"

After the warm-up of the first session, Couples said, "Well, tell me something. What am I going to do? Tell me to work on something."

That convinced Harmon and Marchand that Couples was serious. They developed a game plan based on Couples's style of play.

"I recall I told him that he was too close to the ball and too upright," Harmon said. "It was hard for him to hit the ball consistently one way or the other. And if he could get away from the ball, it would let his swing flatten out. I think I told him his basic shot should be a fade."

"Good players want to miss in one direction. With a fade, Fred knew where the ball wasn't going. He has played pretty much a fade from then on. He has a shorter swing. He went from being too loose at the back to being more consistent."

Marchand recalls similar conversations, but he elaborated:

"Fred has incredible flexibility and range. His build promotes that. He's almost a freak of nature. He also has incredible strength and incredible reactions. Put all that talent together, and he has a very special physical package.

"His looseness tends to make his swing slow. Most people would like to be slow and loose and be able to hit balls from the inside. But his can get too slow. On the range, Dick would watch and I'd watch. Fred would hit four or five shots, and we'd get him on video. That was a big deal, to get him to watch video.

"So for him to get just a little bit of structure, to think, 'This is what I do now, and this is what I'm trying to do'—just that little bit of self-knowledge and the idea that maybe he could know things and it wasn't going to throw him way off, I think that kind of helped him elevate to a higher level. And I think part of it was also being friends before, at Houston."

As a teaching pro, it takes a special kind of confidence and courage to work with a Tour pro who can beat you nine times out of ten on the course and say, "Try this." You have to see the problem, understand what to do to correct it, and explain it simply without destroying the good things the player is already doing.

Couples decided to trust his friends.

There had been many people who had tinkered with their swings, with mixed results. As an amateur, Couples lived under the shadow of Mark O'Meara and Bobby Clampett. According to the experts, over-analysis caused the end of Clampett's competitive golf career. Though O'Meara won at the end of 1984 and then twice in 1985, he'd gotten there by slowly and painstakingly rebuilding his entire swing under the watchful eye of Hank Haney.[2] This was the price of understanding and tweaking the swing? Who needed it?

For Couples, knowing Clampett's experience and what O'Meara had been through, it had to be difficult to consider a swing change. Couples knew himself, his body, his game. He was reluctant to mess up something he at least understood. And he was a 10-year exemption ahead of a lot of guys.

After the first practice session Couples played in Los Angeles, and he finished 17th. The visit in Houston hadn't ruined him, after all.

When Couples headed east for the Florida swing, he and Deborah rented a place at Palm Beach Polo and Country Club for several weeks. The club had been purchased in October of 1986 by the real estate company Couples represented. It was fairly convenient, under 90 minutes to Doral and 20 minutes closer to the Honda Classic in Fort Lauderdale. As a Florida base, it even worked for Bay Hill week in Orlando, saving a costly, time-consuming, and energy-draining trip back to the West Coast. Besides, Deborah liked it.

The polo season, which had begun in late December, was well under way. Even though Fred was playing relatively well at Doral, Deborah had decided she didn't want to drive down to the tournament on Sunday. One of the executives at the Polo Club got her a ticket for the polo match that afternoon. According to all reports, she loved it instantly.

Meanwhile at Doral, Fred finished sixth. It was looking—briefly—as though he was truly on the comeback trail. Then he tied for 61st at Bay Hill and missed the cut at the TPC for the second year in a row. Worse yet, he was not invited to the Masters because he hadn't won in the previous year and his 10-year exemption didn't count there.

Two weeks after the Masters was the Houston Open. Fred and Deborah arrived a week early so he could work on his game with Marchand and Harmon again.

Marchand recalled, "We were on the tee at River Oaks Sunday afternoon, and Fred asked me to remind him to call the tournament and commit by five o'clock." He had seen his picture in the newspaper that morning and wasn't sure he'd entered.

"And sure enough, I didn't think of it, and he didn't think of it. It was about 5:30 he remembered, and he called the Tour from my apartment. He told them he was here and was double-checking. And they told him he wasn't in, and they were sorry, but it was a hard-and-fast rule, and there wasn't anything he could do or anybody he could call. It was the first time it had happened to him.

"Fred went back in the room and put the pillow over his head in the bed and stuck his head out and said, 'You know, for the next 30 seconds I'm going to feel like a complete idiot, but then I'll be okay.'"

So he stayed another week, and as things turned out that error might have been one of the biggest blessings of his career.

Years later, Couples would say of this time that if there was anything he could do over it would be "to have a little more faith in somebody helping me with my golf game. I have an unusual grip and a different swing. I have a lot of rhythm in my swing, and I've improved my swing a lot, but the last five or six years that I've worked with Dick Harmon and Paul Marchand—and some other people, but mostly those guys— have really revamped my game to where I have a lot of confidence."

He added that he had spent several days with the two club pros hitting what he claimed to be "more balls than I had ever hit in my life." It was a new leaf for the guy whose work ethic was not considered the best on the Tour. In fact, Couples's propensity to skip practice was so well-known that Steve Hershey of USA *Today* wrote that practice was "something he enjoyed as much as a root canal."

But this time there was a difference. "The practice was fun," Couples commented, "because I usually don't do it. I wouldn't do anything that Tom Kite wouldn't do, but for me it was a chore [before]. They [Harmon and Marchand] told me a couple of things, and I actually started hitting the ball better. So I thought if that could help a little bit, then if I could spend some time with them. . . ."

He was in the midst of an early career crisis, one that other players have had. The ones that push through it, last on the Tour. The ones that don't, go home, some never to return.

Tour pros don't want a 10-page discourse on swing theory. They want answers now that will work today and, they hope, tomorrow. From Dick Harmon and Paul Marchand, two people Couples knew and trusted, he got what was really the first substantive help ever with his swing.

From the time he had started playing, no one had really wanted to touch Couples's style. It was unusual, but it worked better than the swings of most players, even without any so-called educated eyes working on it. Having the courage to listen to someone else about his golf game was a big step for him. He had never needed to, because most of the time he could beat at least half of the world's best on sheer ability and little or no practice. So, he thought, why practice? But now, he wanted to beat that other half.

From the session in Houston, Couples went to Las Vegas, where he finished eighth, with only four bogeys on his card for the entire 90 holes of the tournament. But it would be the next week, at the Byron Nelson Golf Classic when he would see encouraging results.

The Byron Nelson is held at the TPC at Las Colinas, the posh Four Seasons Resort in Irving, Texas, just west of Dallas. The high-rise luxury hotel on MacArthur Boulevard has balconies that overlook the course. Guests enjoy beautiful sports facilities, including indoor tennis and racquetball, a health and fitness center, and, of course, a swimming pool.

The first round of the tournament, Couples came in with a 65, tied with Gary Hallberg and Gary Krueger. They were one stroke behind leaders Payne Stewart and Greg Norman. Then, as the rules say, outside agencies arrived.

Thunderstorms are so predictable during the Byron Nelson that homeowners in the Dallas metropolitan area fertilize their lawns the week before the tournament. To no one's surprise, Friday play was interrupted by rain, thunder, and lightning shortly after two-thirty in the afternoon.

At day's end, there were still 20 players out on the course. They finished up Saturday morning, at which point Couples was tied with Norman at 132, one back of the leaders, Ben Crenshaw, Bob Lohr, Tom Byrum, and Donnie Hammond.

It was a week of records. The second round produced the lowest lead ever for that event at −9. It was also a record cut for the tournament at −1, 139.

Saturday, thunderstorms took a holiday, but it was Texas hot and humid, and play was slow. Couples, resurrecting his performance from the 1984 TPC, posted a 64 and took the lead over Mark Calcavecchia by two. He was on tournament-record pace for three rounds at −14. Norman had slipped to −11.

With Couples in contention, Paul Marchand and his wife, Judi, discussed the idea of Paul traveling to Dallas for the final round. "This is going to sound ridiculous, I know," Paul admitted more than 10 years later, "but at that time, we actually had a long discussion about whether or not we could afford the $75 for the round-trip ticket."

By the back nine, Couples had let his lead slip away. He was one stroke behind playing partner Bob Lohr, who was at −14. A herd was giving chase. Calcavecchia and Hammond were tied with Couples at −13. Norman had posted only one birdie, yet he was two back at −12.

Calcavecchia finished early in a blaze of birdies at 14, 15, 16, and 17. He wound up at −14, with a six-under round of 64. All he could do was wait and hope.

At the 14th, Couples was losing gas. He hit into the trees and gallery behind the green, then scrambled to save par, remaining one behind.

Lohr missed the green with his second as well as his par-saving putt, falling out of the lead and into a tie with Couples and Hammond.

Couples's drive on 15 went into the right rough. He recovered in spectacular style, hitting an 8-iron to six feet. His birdie putt hung on the lip, taunting him. A quarter inch equals a drive.

Norman had chili-dipped his third shot at the par-5 16th, a costly error. Then he missed an eight-footer for par and fell to −11. Barring miracles, he was done.

Hammond also butchered the hole, leaving a ball in the greenside bunker, and went to −12. He was in reverse with the accelerator to the floor.

It was up to Couples and Lohr to catch Calcavecchia. They had about the same distance to the green on the 16th. Couples stood all over a 1-iron that found the front fringe, then chipped to three feet and made his birdie to tie for the lead, −14.

"I needed that birdie at the 16th," he said later, "because I knew it would be tough getting one at 17 or 18."

Lohr pared and remained one back.

On the 17th, Couples's 4-iron to the 220-yard par 3 landed just six feet from the pin, giving him a chance at the outright lead. But he missed the putt. Then he faced the 415-yard uphill final hole needing four to force a playoff, birdie for the outright win.

Again Couples's drive found the rough. This time it was left. He recovered with an 8-iron from 155 to the back fringe, leaving himself a treacherous downhill 25-foot putt as the only avenue to outright victory. He lagged to a foot from the hole, making the par putt easy.

Playoff. This time it was a two-man contest with someone just as long but very tough and dangerously streaky: Mark Calcavecchia.

Calc had just come off his best year ever and followed with a victory at the 1987 Honda Classic. He was battle-scarred and determined, a fierce competitor with a stare that burns holes in the grass.

Couples carded a final-round 70, missing fairways to both sides. That day he was struggling.

The playoff started at 16, the 554-yard par 5.

Couples's drive was a near disaster, almost out of bounds. "I was standing right there where the ball hit," Marchand recalled. "The reports said four inches, and I don't think it was four inches. I think it was on the line. If any part of the ball is in bounds, it's in bounds. And I think it was that close."

An official from the PGA Tour staff ruled the ball in play.

"He whipped out an iron and just killed it," Marchand noted about Couples's second shot. But it didn't quite make the green.

Calc, who had hit a 265-yard drive into the fairway, found the bunker with his second. He blasted out to two feet for a sure birdie. Couples pitched to five feet and made it. They went on to the 17th, where they both scrambled for pars.

As though reading the same playbook, both men found the right rough with their drives on the 18th. It was the best angle to the green, but they wanted to be in the fairway.

Calc hit first, from about 148, but between the flier lie and adrenaline, his 9-iron found the rough over the green.

Couples, with only 130 yards, reached the green but was below the pin 25 to 30 feet.

Calc's chip, sitting high on the grass, skidded out of control and rolled past the hole all the way to the opposite fringe, leaving him about the same-length par putt that Couples faced for birdie.

"It was a very fluffy lie, and I just hit a bad chip," Calcavecchia admitted.

With Couples's two putts, his comeback was officially under way.

Not much was made of Couples's accuracy problems, although his failure to find the fairways almost cost him the tournament. Of the five he hit on Sunday, only one of them was on the back nine.

"Obviously, I struggled," he said in USA Today. "I was hitting the ball well on the front, but all of a sudden the fairway looked a foot wide, and I couldn't hit them. But I got some good lies in the rough, hit good iron shots, and made some good putts for pars."

Deborah was there for the victory, and a photo of the two of them appeared in USA Today in the Monday edition. Paul Marchand stayed for dinner. It was an important week for all of them.

Afterward, Couples noted that earlier in the season "the furthest thing from my mind was winning a tournament." Knowing the background makes that statement all the more powerful. But his play at the Hope and in Phoenix and at the AT&T put him in a better frame of mind. "I was playing better and having fun again," he had said.

Though Couples would, characteristically, never make a point of it, he began working more on his game with Harmon and Marchand. He admitted as much to Steve Hershey of USA Today and added, "that's unusual, but I don't want to go through three months of barely making the cut again." He said he was upping his playing schedule to 30 events.

"Another story at the time," Dick Harmon recalled, "was that he [Couples] represented a real estate company, and he had their logo on his shirt. But on Friday or Saturday, he had worn a River Oaks visor. The company saw he was on television and had FedExed a stock of visors to him. But he didn't wear them. He said there was no way he could take the visor off. He said it was like a lucky horseshoe. Boy did he catch heat for that, but it was not a big deal to him."

"It will be fun going to tournaments now that I'm playing well," Couples added after the victory. "Golf isn't a lot of fun when I'm playing mediocre. Last year I'd get to a tournament, and by Friday, I was ready to move on. If I played bad, I didn't go to the range and try to work it out. It was really a wasted year."

Then, as a stopgap, he added, "But if I don't do well at Colonial, I don't really care." Well, he really did care, but he just didn't want to let people know how much. Later on, he would become more honest about his efforts, but sometimes, in the hype, people would forget to listen.

He was up and down the rest of the year. Seventh at the U.S. Open, 40th at the British Open, and smart enough to miss the cut and leave town early at the PGA which was contested in the worst possible heat and humidity imaginable at PGA National in West Palm Beach, Florida. However, the tournament provided an additional opportunity for Fred and Deborah to visit Palm Beach Polo and Country Club.

With Fred's newly enhanced bankroll, Deborah was in an acquisition mode. She became interested in owning a place.

Deborah understood what the polo set in the Palm Beaches meant. It meant money. Lots of money. Status—or at least notoriety—that she would never have in Palm Springs but might be able to achieve as the wife of a Tour player back east at a country club with a wealthy membership. In Palm Springs, she could never top a Delores Hope or Barbara Sinatra. But in the Palm Beaches, well, just look at Lily or Roxanne Pulitzer. If all Deborah wanted to do was play polo, she could have done that in Indio, at Eldorado Polo Club or Empire Polo Club, just 25 minutes from their place at Mission Hills Country Club. It wasn't just the sport. It was the ambiance.

The fact was, Deborah liked it, and that was enough for Fred. It was worth a try.

By December 1987 another residence was added to the Couples portfolio of homes: a place in Las Casitas, Spanish-style condo units on the east side of the property.

For the year, Couples entered 27 events and was in the money 21 times. He had nine top 10 finishes and had moved up on the money list again, this time to 19th, not even counting a midpack finish in his visit to the two-year-old event in Kapalua, Hawaii.[3]

Couples's stroke average had started to fall, finally, and was down to 70.41, a good sign indeed. It was a forecast of things to come.

With homes on two coasts, there were many exciting changes and new opportunities. One was with an upstart company called Ashworth, after the designer and cofounder, John Ashworth. And in less than five years, it changed the entire golf clothing industry.

To understand the significance of Ashworth clothing, one first has to look back at golf photographs of the mid-1980s when polyester was still king and golf clothes were the butt of jokes. All that was about to disappear.

The Look came about in 1987, then made its Tour debut in 1988. But the idea had been in John Ashworth's head for much longer.

Ashworth went to the University of Arizona and was on the golf team there. After college, he held a number of jobs, including being an assistant pro and caddying for Mark Wiebe, before becoming involved in retailing with Gerald Montiel.

Ashworth had always had a special fashion sense, and after several false starts in other golf-related business ideas, he suggested to Montiel while they were driving down the I-5 freeway outside LaJolla that there was a niche market for a new kind of golf apparel.

As Ashworth pointed out, "Mainstream America was way past that terrible polyester and plaid pants look, but the golf world was stuck. Nobody was willing to change. Year after year, it was the same old regurgitation. Even in college. They had these stupid uniforms. A hundred percent polyester. Tight fitting. Terrible colors. I think that's one reason my golf career faded out. I wanted to look cool."

Ashworth was a 27-year-old with an idea and a sense of fashion. He thought there was a market for different golf apparel, and he wanted some Tour players to wear the clothes. "From the get-go, for me it was Fred Couples and John Cook," Ashworth explained. "Not just one guy. A split personality. They had to have the right attitude. Nonchalant. Young. Good attitude. Good looking. In my mind, it was always Fred and John.

"I grew up with John playing golf a few years ahead of me. I looked up to him. He was a California kind of guy. Had the Porsche. Winning Cal State Amateur. The U.S. Amateur. Had the long hair back when that was in. All his great accomplishments always stuck with me.

"And when I was in college, we played a couple of events against Houston, although I never played with Fred. He was their number one, playing our number one. And I remember watching him play and thinking, 'That guy is the coolest.' He had his shirttail out. He was cruising down the fairway. I thought, 'My God, he's the James Dean of golf.'

"He'd only won a couple of events, but he had the charisma. Before we had a stitch of clothing, I went to Newport and sat down with Fred and Deborah and told them what we were going to do. I think I had a pair of pants and sketches, and I explained to them the 100 percent cotton, loose fitting and so forth. He did not have a clothing company deal and said, 'Hey, sounds great to me. Let's go for it.'"

Because Ashworth was short on money and big on ideas, he made Cook and Couples partners in the company and paid them in stock. "We really liked them and respected them and wanted them to be part of the whole deal," Ashworth said.

It was the end of 1987, and John Ashworth, former junior golfer, former assistant golf pro, former caddie, former retail buyer, began designing. Every new look, every collection, he did with Cook and Couples in mind.

"I wanted to make sure those guys looked good and felt good. And what was great was that they both started playing really good golf after that," Ashworth added.

Today Couples, according to Ashworth, is one of the largest stockholders in the company. He is on the board as a nonvoting member.

Ashworth characterizes Couples's business sense as "sneaky good. He's a dumb-as-a-fox kind of guy. He comes off happy-go-lucky, and he is. But underneath it, he is really shrewd and a lot more sensitive than he lets on."

The original shirts were "pretty ordinary" by today's standards, in Ashworth's words. But even in solids and basic stripes, they broke the mold. As Ashworth himself described the look more than 10 years ago, "it's street-active," which to John Ashworth meant that he could play golf and then go someplace for dinner or a beer without people laughing at his clothes. It was a look that was casual, sporty, yet cool.

What Ashworth's company did was bring down the hard-collar style of men's golf shirts to the softer banded ones so prominent today. He changed the shirt sleeves to be cuffed instead of straight hemmed. He added designs to the cuffs and the collars. He gave people room to move in place of restrictive, skintight shirts. He brought down an industry that had been chained to polyester and silhouettes of tight-fitting garments. He brought back cotton because it was more comfortable. He sought fabrics that were thick and rich, not skimpy and shrinky.

The Look made its debut at the beginning of 1988 when the West Coast swing began. And from that point on, everyone wanted to know what John Cook and Fred Couples were wearing.[4]

While Fred Couples was making fashion news, his wife was taking up a new sport: polo.

Contrary to previous reports, Deborah Couples had not ridden before this season. She learned it from the ground up. She was athletic, had great courage. She practiced hard. She opted for the double whammy: private lessons and group polo clinics. With her unstoppable energy and prodigious athletic ability, she became good enough to play in matches.

It is no easy feat to ride a pony full-throttle down the field, bumping and jostling with seven other players, all swinging mallets and chasing a four-inch white ball. Lesser people have been maimed in the process. But Deborah loved it. She loved the action. She loved the excitement.

She also loved the social aspects, the moneyed crowd, the parties, the balls, the festivities. And, because Fred was such a terrific golfer and a personable guy, she was accepted by members, by the athletes, and by others involved in the sport.

The polo players loved golf. And no one was more popular on the course than Fred. Ever the sports enthusiast, he could appreciate their exceptional skills. Further, he at first backed Deborah's interest in learning this new game. He said if he was doing what he wanted to do, why did it matter to other people if she did what she wanted to do?

Their place at Las Casitas was, according to Fred's description, small. During that winter, Deborah set her sights on what she would later call The Hacienda, which was a farm on Palm Beach Point near the Polo Club. She bought. She gutted. She began decorating, and according to those who saw the before and after, did an admirable job. She announced herself as an interior designer/tennis pro, taking out her own ad in the polo program in a subsequent season. She had an idea that people would want to pay to spend a weekend playing golf and tennis with Fred and Deborah at the Polo Club.

That winter season, Deborah had to have been doubly busy. After Fred's 1987 victory at the Byron Nelson, he began 1988 in the Tournament of Champions at the sumptuous La Costa Resort and Spa in Carlsbad, California. Deborah attended. La Costa was long a favorite of wives, girl-friends, and families, because the spa gave them virtual carte blanche to facials, massages, herbal wraps, and fitness rooms for the entire week. It was a wonderful way to kick off the golf season.

Couples finished 16th there, then went on to the Palm Springs area for the Bob Hope tournament, where he finished 12th while staying at his place in Rancho Mirage.

The next week, he lost a playoff in Phoenix to Sandy Lyle. Lyle won with a bogey after three extra holes. Couples put a ball in the water. People would ask him about that tournament for years afterward.

Two weeks later, in San Diego, he led the first day with a 63 on the north course at Torrey Pines. At the end of three rounds he was just two shots out of the lead, but he finished in a tie for 10th.

Couples followed that with his worst finish ever in Los Angeles, 41st. Then he returned home to Florida, just in time for pre-arrival festivities for H.R.H. The Prince of Wales. All of Palm Beach was abuzz.

Prince Charles's team, Windsor Park, was to play Palm Beach as one of several events to benefit the Masai Mara wildlife preservation in Africa. The princely weekend was March 6, the Sunday of the Doral tournament. There were parties, luncheons, balls, galas.

While the match was being played, Fred Couples was an hour and a half south, at Doral, playing the final round of a golf tournament. He finished in a tie for 19th.

The royalty departed, leaving everyone with memories of the occasion, photos of the events, and newspaper clippings to fill scrapbooks. While others recounted the glitz and glitter over coffee and lunch, Fred drove to Fort Lauderdale and finished ninth in the Honda Classic. After a week of rest, he was 23rd at The Players Championship, then finished up the first quarter of the year with his best finish ever at the Masters, a tie for fifth behind the victorious Scot, Sandy Lyle. He was fourth at Hilton Head behind eventual winner Greg Norman.

He had six top 10 finishes in 13 events, not bad for a guy who had nearly given up golf 18 months earlier. It's just that everyone on the Tour was about to be steamrolled—again—by Curtis Strange.

Strange had played the first four months of 1988 as if he was MIA, with a 12th at the Bob Hope as his best finish from January through the Masters. Suddenly he woke up and won in Houston, then again four weeks later at the Memorial. And he followed that by winning his first major three weeks later in an unforgettable, 18-hole, unsmiling, junkyard-dog playoff with Nick Faldo at The Country Club in Brookline.

Couples, meantime, had slipped to 30-plus place in Las Vegas and Houston, but he made an adequate defense at the Byron Nelson, finishing 10th. After a week of rest, he was 15th at the Memorial and 16th at the Kemper, then slid again at Westchester to 30th while preparing for the U.S. Open at Brookline, where he finished 10th. He was playing a lot, having good finishes but no victories.

Seve Ballesteros won the British Open at Royal Lytham. Couples, continuing his love for European courses, tied for fourth. Between them were a pair of Nicks: Price in second and Faldo in third.

Couples returned to the States and bounced up to third at the Buick Open.

Jeff Sluman won the PGA Championship at Oak Tree, with Paul Azinger second. Though Couples was top 10 in the other three majors, he did not play well enough to make it to the weekend at the PGA.

Jay Haas remembered needling him during a practice round. "We were on the first par 3 on the back side, and Fred's getting ready to tee up the ball, and I started pawing at the ground and making these horse sounds. And he's in the middle of his swing and he went ahead and hit the ball, but he was laughing at the same time. Deborah had gotten into polo, and so we were kind of giving him grief about it."

After mid-August, Couples played only three events, the B.C. Open, where he finished 6th; the Pensacola tournament, where he closed with a 69 to finish tied for 21st; and his last outing for the year, at Pebble Beach in the Nabisco Championships, the season ender for those who had finished in the top 30. He finished seventh there and took home $68,000.

Even without a victory, he earned $50,000 more than he had the previous year. He made more cuts than ever, but most important, he finished in the top 10, ten times. He was learning to give himself a chance, making his way up the leader board. By year's end he had missed only one cut out of the 27 events he played.

His scoring average had come down again—even with his expanded playing schedule—this time to 69.76, nine places behind Chip Beck, who won the Vardon Trophy with an average of 69.46. He won $489,822 for the season, finishing 21st on the money list.

At home in West Palm Beach, where he and Deborah were spending more and more time, people recognized him on the practice tee.

He was unaware that the owners of the club did not extend signing privileges to Deborah, although they did to some other players' wives. There was a reason for it. They feared she would spend their money as casually as she spent Fred's. They could see trouble coming and didn't want any part of it.

7

The Rocky Road of Samuel Ryder, Part I

"There is no bigger burden than great potential."
—Snoopy

By the end of 1988, everyone pretty much ignored Fred Couples, and that continued for about a year. Then, in September of 1989, the world jumped all over him for not being the U.S. hero at the Ryder Cup. Probably because it looked as if he could be, and by the end of the day on Sunday, we needed one.

The year actually started very well. Couples contended just about every time he teed it up, but was unable to find the winner's circle. Mostly, he was being consistent.

At the Doral, his scores of 69-69 the first two days seemed unremarkable compared to Bill Glasson's Friday score of seven under, but Couples was still only two off the lead. However, Glasson didn't falter. Couples held on for second.

Steve Hershey of USA *Today* suggested that maybe Fred was indifferent, not unflappable. Hershey was frustrated watching him. It had been eight years, and he thought it was time Couples did what the insiders thought Couples should be able to do: win about six tournaments a year, easy. The insiders, of course, were not on the back tees every Thursday. They were writing about it. After Doral, Hershey penned:

> If ever a player was due to win, it's Couples. After his first round of the year, he led the Bob Hope Chrysler Classic with 65. He stayed in contention until the end, falling a shot shy of a three-way playoff won by Steve Jones. The following week at Phoenix, he had

three rounds of 68 or better and tied for 16th. He played in the final group at Los Angeles, but shot 71 and finished seventh. After three more sub-70 rounds at San Diego, he closed with a 71 to tie for 12th.

Doral's second place check of $140,000 boosted his earnings to $240,140 this year, but he's still searching for that strong finishing round.[1]

Worse yet, the two started talking four-footers. "On Thursday and Friday, I just step up to putts and hit 'em," Couples said later in the same article. "If they go in, great. Then on Saturday and Sunday I start to press."[2]

Hershey once said about Greg Norman when he shot a 66 on Thursday, "Doesn't he know it's not Sunday?" referring to Norman's habit of coming in with a hot round on Sunday either to pressure the leaders or win. Maybe Hershey should have suggested to Couples to pretend it was Thursday or Friday when he got to the greens. But at least Hershey was paying attention. Nobody else was.

Couples, for his part, kept going to the bank. A 13th at Bay Hill. Fourth place at the Players Championship. Sixteenth in Houston. Eleventh at the Masters, with a final-round 67. Third with a final-round 65 at Hilton Head. Fifteenth in Greensboro. Sixteenth at the Memorial. Fifth at Westchester. He finished 21st at Oak Hill in Rochester, New York, at the U.S. Open, where Curtis Strange became the first repeat winner since Ben Hogan in 1950 and 1951.

At the British Open, Couples finally made his second headline of the year, for shooting a 68 at Royal Troon along with six others in the first-round. The media pretty much ignored the actual first-round leader, Wayne Stephens. It's known as the "Unknown Leads Open" story, which is traditional for both the U.S. and British Opens.

Couples attributed part of his first-round success to playing with Nick Faldo and watching his course management. He was following his own pattern. Back at the range at Jefferson Park, he learned to get better by playing with better players, seeing what he could learn from them.

In the end, it would be Mark Calcavecchia's year to beat Greg Norman and Wayne Grady in their four-hole playoff when Norman, leading the playoff on the last hole, drove into the bunker, the only place he could lose the tournament, then hit it short of the green and put his third over the green, and out-of-bounds. Calcavecchia hit a magnificent 5-iron to seven feet and made birdie to prove beyond a shadow of a doubt that he deserved to win it. Couples finished sixth, making birdies on the last four holes to come back from a disastrous 40 on the front side.

Back at home the last week of July, Couples turned in a lackluster performance compared to the rest of his year. He missed the cut at the PGA and the International. He was definitely headed in the wrong direction. Just in time for the Ryder Cup.

In 1987 for the second time in a row, the European team had won the Ryder Cup. So, in the fall of 1989, it was essential for the U.S. team to get the damn Cup back. They went into the matches, held at the Belfry, a 7–4 favorite to win.

Raymond Floyd, a tough competitor with a stellar career that included two PGA Championships, a Masters, and a U.S. Open, had been selected captain. Leading a squad composed of six first-time Ryder Cup players, he selected Tom Watson and Lanny Wadkins, two other well-known tough guys, to whip the newcomers into shape. The rookies included Paul Azinger, Chip Beck, Mark Calcavecchia—coming off his best year ever with a victory in the British Open—Fred Couples, and Ken Green.

Despite Couples's middle-of-the-pack finishes going into the competition, Paul Marchand thought he was ready. "I can remember Dick [Harmon] was trying to tell Fred what to expect because he had been to Muirfield in 1987. He said Fred wasn't going to believe the way people yell. Fred said that he'd heard people yell at a tournament before. And Dick went on about how Fred wasn't going to believe the pressure on some of these shots. Match play with all this on the table."

As it turned out, Harmon was right. In a story for *Golf Magazine* a year afterward, Couples described how he felt that week:

> To tell you the truth, I really didn't think about it too much until Deborah and I got over there. Then we were seated at this dinner and Ray Floyd was giving this speech like General Patton. When he said he was about to introduce the 12 best players in the world, suddenly it hit me—my knees went weak. If I'd been asked to stand up and hit a ball right then, hell there's no way I could have done it.[3]

Couples had never considered himself one of the best players in the world. He just didn't know he was that good.

Europe had one rookie on their team: Ronan Rafferty of Northern Ireland. Everybody else had played at least once. Tony Jacklin, the captain, had been on seven Ryder Cups teams himself, and was repeating as their leader for the fourth time. He'd found a winning ingredient, and the Europeans didn't want to let him go. He also had what the sportswriter

Dan Jenkins might call "serious depth," with Bernard Langer, Nick Faldo, Jose Maria Olazabal, Seve Ballesteros, and Ian Woosnam on his side.

The Belfry was a venue the European players knew well, because they played it each year. U.S. players saw it only during the Ryder Cup. However, many commentators mentioned that the course is much more like U.S. courses than most other tournament sites in Europe.

Raymond Floyd leaned heavily on his veterans the first day, pairing them with the newcomers to ease their nerves and show them the ropes. As Johnny Pott, veteran of three Ryder Cups, once said: "You have no idea what nervous means until you are standing on the first tee and the announcer says, 'And now playing for the United States . . .'"

Couples sat out the morning foursomes, which saw the United States take an early 3–1 lead.

In the afternoon fourball matches, nothing Floyd tried worked. The U.S. team went down in flames. In addition to Ballesteros/Olazabal and Faldo/Woosnam victories, Howard Clark and Mark James battled Fred Couples and Lanny Wadkins for a 3 and 2 victory, but they had to chip in twice to do it. It was Couples's first outing. Later, he admitted he'd felt awful about that match, saying that if he'd played decently they would have won it.

After day one, the United States was behind, 3 to 5.

When Sunday dawned, the European team was not going out just to play 12 singles matches. It was for mother and country and continent. It was playing for honor and to avenge all past wrongs in the history of the Western world. If Tony Jacklin was any kind of captain, that is most likely what he told them. They were the underdogs. They were the poor cousins (except for Ballesteros and by now Faldo). They needed only five points to keep the Cup in Europe, because, according to the rules, a tie meant that the country who won the Cup last keeps it.

The U.S. team was faced with a distinct uphill battle. They needed 7½ points, in some combination of the 12 singles matches, to defeat Europe. A tie was worth half a point. The teams split the first six matches.

Couples drew Christy O'Connor, Jr., who had last appeared in Ryder Cup play in 1975. At the 15th, he was 1-up on O'Connor. But O'Connor found inner strength and birdied the 16th to draw even. At the 17th, Couples missed a putt, but so did O'Connor, and then it came down to the final hole. Couples outdrove O'Connor by 70 yards and looked like he had a chance to wedge up and birdie. At least that's what everyone expected. But Christy O'Connor, Jr., at that point 0–3–0 lifetime in Ryder Cup matches, hit the shot of his career, a screaming 2-iron to two feet from the pin. Joyous shouts went up from the greenside crowd and the partisan throngs that had gathered along the fairway.

Now Couples, standing in the fairway, had to hit into certain birdie range just to tie. Pressure? You bet your Maxfli. He pushed his 9-iron wide of the green. He chipped up to five feet, and at that point stuck out his hand to congratulate Christy O' Connor, Jr.

Three months later, he said:

"I guess I blanked. Everything was running through my head. My mind was going crazy. It was the most I'd ever concentrated on golf . . . and where had it gotten me? From where I stood, it looked like I had to hole out to have a chance . . . I was absolutely devastated. If I'd lost the U.S. Open on the final hole, I'd shrug and say forget it and go on. All day that final day I saw red on the scoreboard. It looked for a while like we might even sweep them. For some reason, I couldn't get over the feeling that I'd let everyone down. It was the low point of my career.[4]

So much for not caring.

Watson secured his 3 and 1 victory over Sam Torrance, but when Ken Green was defeated by Jose Maria Canizares, it was all over. The rest of the matches were won by the U.S. team, but the Europeans retained the Ryder Cup for another two years.

To say that the U.S. squad was heartbroken is an understatement. Usually, PGA Tour players don't cry. But at the Belfry tears of disappointment flowed from more than one source, among them Fred Couples.

A news photo of Couples and Calcavecchia at the closing ceremonies revealed their mood of deep dejection.

Tom Watson was spirited in defense of the team. "There is disappointment, no question about that, because we feel we were unlucky not to have won. They hit the ball into the cup from off the green about seven times during the weekend."

Payne Stewart showed some attitude about it. "The way I figure it, they got lucky and tied us."

Ray Floyd said simply that "a tie is not a loss."

In the only other Ryder Cup tie, in 1969, the final day concluded with a singles match between Jack Nicklaus and Tony Jacklin. In what the PGA of America calls one of the most memorable moments of sportsmanship, Nicklaus, who at the time was playing in his first Ryder Cup, made his own four-foot putt and then conceded Jacklin's putt of two feet.

Somehow 20 years later, for the 1989 U.S. Ryder Cup team, a tie was a whole lot like kissing 12 sisters.

Couples was said by several sources to have asked Raymond Floyd during the flight back to the States when and how points started counting for the next Ryder Cup. Raymond Floyd gave him more than a summary of how to get on the team. He also gave him direction and a little "fatherly" advice, although Floyd was closer to the age of an older brother.

"One thing I told Fred after he felt the burden of the Ryder Cup on his shoulders—and I don't know if I ever convinced him—is that it was a team effort and we were all a part of the team. We were 13," Floyd explained nearly a decade later. "I told him that this experience would make him a better player, that he would now be able to go on to the next level and that he'd learned something from this. I told him it would make him a better player because he'd been through he toughest thing he could ever go through."

In terms of golf, Floyd would prove to be right.

"I think one of the real turning points of Fred's career was when he lost in the singles at the Belfry to Christy O'Connor on the last hole," Paul Marchand said about the whole experience. "It just killed him. He didn't realize what the Ryder Cup was going to feel like."

According to Marchand, that is also the time Raymond Floyd first took an interest in Couples. "I remember hearing the story of Fred coming back on the Concorde," Marchand recalled. "Raymond said when he heard Fred ask him when you start making points for the next time, he knew Fred was going to be okay. Raymond and Tom took a special interest in Fred because they saw him as an up-and-coming kid who had a lot of talent. They seemed to say that all that nonchalance is fine, but you've got to realize what you're capable of doing. They were really supportive of him when he lost. What Raymond and Tom said was 'Keep your style, but go out there with a purpose and realize that you have the ability to do great things, and so on. It meant something to him that those guys would say that. I don't think he talked a lot about it, but if you knew him, you could see it."

There was PGA Tour golf played after the Ryder Cup. At the Walt Disney event, Couples, thanks to a second-round 65, was two back at the beginning of the final round, but on Sunday, he could not manage to pull ahead of eventual winner Tim Simpson.

The next week, Couples had an excellent chance at the Nabisco Championships (now called the Tour Championship), held at Harbour Town Golf Links on Hilton Head Island. The last-place winner at that time received $40,000. First place often determined the leading money winner for the year. At that time only the PGA of America awarded Player of the Year honors, which is determined by the number of high finishes in Tour events, bonus points for the majors, scoring average, and place on the money list. Tom Kite, who had won two tournaments in 1989, the Players Championship and Arnold Palmer's at Bay Hill, was a contender for leading money winner, as was Curtis Strange, who had won his second U.S. Open. Payne Stewart, the PGA Champion, was also near the top. But Couples, with a victory at the Nabisco Championships, and $450,000 plus a $175,000 bonus, could have pulled into the number-one position. A long shot, but a chance. Going into the tournament, Tom Kite was only about $150,000 ahead of him on the money list, and Couples had not won an event that year.

The first-round lead was held by Donnie Hammond, with a six-under-par 65. Mark O'Meara and Greg Norman were two back at 67.

The Friday weather included strong gusty winds, and most scores went up. Tom Kite's was the exception. He posted a 65, vaulted to the top, and was four strokes ahead of O'Meara and Hammond. Norman fired a 74 and fell into the pack.

Couples had begun 69-74. Sixteen of the 30 players were over par, and Couples, like everyone else, wondered what Kite had eaten for breakfast to skate around in 65.

On Saturday, Wayne Levi emerged with a course-record-equaling 63, shooting 30-33 to go to -8. He was one up on Hammond and three ahead of Kite. Couples carded a 67 and found himself one stroke behind Kite, who had a disappointing 74. Kite and Couples would be paired on Sunday.

Deborah came up for the final round.

Sunday dawned beautifully. Harbour Town Golf Links demands accuracy on just about every shot. The greens, which are the smallest of the courses played each year on the Tour, are protected either by grass knolls, bunkers, trees, or some other noxious device, thanks to the creativity of Pete and Alice Dye. Tall coastal pines line the fairways. Harbour Town, one of Dye's early creations, was helped to national prominence when Arnold Palmer won the first professional tournament played there in 1969.

Shortly after Kite and Couples teed off, Deborah appeared in the crowd, dressed nicely for the occasion. She was a bit nervous for Fred as the round began and occasionally chatted with people in the gallery. Ahead on the course, no one had posted a low number. Fred seemed to be playing along quite well—that is, until the fifth hole. Needing a truly good tee shot, he put the guide on it and let one go into the right woods. It rattled around in the trees. The gallery, packed with Fred fans and

Kite fans, gasped and moaned. Then they murmured, "Where is it? Where is it?" in low hushed tones. Deborah began cursing. She used about every combination of four-letter words known on the planet, and she was loud about it. It was a remarkable display of temper, and would have made sense if it had come from Fred. Inside, he may have been fuming, but she was the one making noise.

Whether he could hear Deborah as she expletive-deleted her way down the golf hole is something that will remain one of golf's mysteries. But he would have to have been deaf or blocking out the gallery not to.

As the day wore on, Tom Kite, who had struggled early, regained his composure and actually seemed to pick up steam. Meanwhile, Couples, for whatever reason, struggled. But he was not the only one.

The low round of the day, a 66, was turned in by Payne Stewart, who was a stroke behind Couples at the start.

Couples finished at par for the round, in a tie for seventh. Kite, his playing companion, had equaled Stewart's total, and the two of them headed for a playoff that Kite eventually won. The first-place money, $450,000 plus the bonus of $175,000, put Kite just over $1.3 million in prize money for the year, and he became the leading money winner and the PGA Tour Player of the Year. Stewart collected a hefty $270,000 and jumped his winnings for the year to just over $1.2 million, second on the money list. Couples collected $82,500 for his seventh-place finish.

At year's end, Couples was 11th on the money list with $693,944, had improved his scoring average to sixth on the PGA Tour at 69.71, had nine top 10 finishes in 24 starts, and had missed only two cuts. He was second in all-around stats on the Tour. He was becoming a contender.

8

Hogan's Alley Becomes Couples's Colosseum

"Ten birdies in 18 holes is not golf. It's Murder One."
—Jim Murray

The 1990 season started out like a roller-coaster ride for Fred Couples. There was no trip to La Costa for the Tournament of Champions. The Bob Hope was a disappointing 54th-place finish. Then—boom—Phoenix was a third, with three rounds in the 60s; AT&T at Pebble Beach, he fell to a disappointing 46th with a final-round 77. A week off and then San Diego, where he had a chance to win until his second shot at the 18th found Devlin's billabong and he slid to fourth.

Finally, at one of his favorite courses, Lady Luck smiled. Riviera. The Los Angeles Open.

Riviera, designed by George Thomas and William Bell in 1925, is a 35-36, par-71 track located just west of Los Angeles in an area called Pacific Palisades. It is squeezed into a ravine that is bordered on the north and south sides by cliffs that are at least six stories high.

Riviera was built before gimmicks, except for the sixth hole, a surprising 170-yard par 3 that sports a small pot bunker in the middle of the green. Sand in a velvet paradise. Riviera has no memorable water hazards. No island greens. No plateaued fairways. No windmills. No clown's mouths. It's hard enough as is.

Out-of-bounds affects play on the 7th, 8th, 12th, and 13th holes. And there are other places where the vegetation—vines, shrubs and the dreaded aloe-like California ice plant—is so overgrown that finding a ball in it could be impossible.

Huge eucalyptus trees line the fairways, framing the holes, catching the not-so-perfect drive in their strange and fragrant limbs. Unlike the florist variety, these have gray-green, scythelike leaves, shaped like a willow, but three times the size. The wiry kikuyu grass grabs the clubhead and twists it.

It is a distinct and challenging golf course characterized by small greens and beautiful, old-style bunkers that look as though they are waves of sand ready to break over the grass.

Riviera became known as Hogan's Alley after Ben Hogan won the L.A. Open back-to-back in 1947 and 1948, then the U.S. Open, held there in 1948. Riviera was the site of Hogan's comeback in 1950, where he finished in a tie with Sam Snead but lost in the playoff.

Couples began the week by winning the individual pro-am on Tuesday—worth $10,000, and certainly enough to put him in a good frame of mind. Joe LaCava, a cousin of Ken Green's, was his new caddie. They'd worked together for about four weeks.

After the first round a virtual unknown, Michael Allen, headed the leader board, with a hot eight-under-par 63, followed by Rocco Mediate at 65 and Peter Jacobsen at 66. Couples was five back of the lead with a 68, three under par for the course, which is 71. The weather was Hollywood perfect.

The second day Allen posted a 68, good enough to set a tournament record of −11 for 36 holes. Mediate was one back, and Couples, with a 67, hadn't done a disappearing act.

Friday evening, Couples, who was staying with his father-in-law in the L.A. area, planned to attend a hockey game. It was an odd way to tune up for what would become one of his lowest competitive rounds ever,[1] but who was to argue.

On Saturday, Couples at 135, began four back of the leader. Again the weather was idyllic, 78 degrees and sunny, with a five- to ten-mile-per-hour breeze. He absolutely cruised through the front nine and turned in 30 strokes, a bogey, and six birdies.

At the 12th, he hit his wedge to two feet, a sensational shot on the deceptive par-4. Unbelievably, he missed the putt,[2] but he was still at −14 and was the leader.

At the 13th, another of Riveria's testing par-4s, Couples hit an 8-iron to five feet. He was hitting heat-seeking missiles, not golf balls. This time he made the putt and went to −15.

Couples stiffed a 6-iron to five feet at the 180-yard, par-3 14th, but he could not convert. Another short one that got away. He was still −15.

He played a merely average 15th hole. Driver, 8-iron to the fringe, chip to six inches, and tap-in for par. Either the noose was tightening, or he realized what a good round he had going and got a little crazy.

His high-lob 7-iron at the 16th, a beautiful but dangerous 168-yard par-3, surrounded by a nasty necklace of bunkers, rolled 30 feet past the hole. He made par.

The 17th, a 578-yard par-5 took away the Couples length advantage because of the strategic positioning of the small green, set to the left of the fairway and guarded by overhanging trees and bunkers. It demands three shots. Couples's wedge let him down. He was 15 feet from the hole and did not make the putt.

At the 18th, Couples unleashed a perfect drive to choruses of "You da man" and "Fred-deee, Fred-deee, Fred-deee," the L.A. mantra.

Ahead in the fairway at the 18th, Couples studied his approach as he waited for playing partner Hal Sutton to smooth a 5-iron. There were cheers as Sutton's ball landed six feet from the pin.

Then Couples, 156 yards out, selected a 7-iron, and in what must have been for him one of the most thrilling moments of his career, he hit a shot that landed less than two feet from the cup. The crowd went absolutely ballistic.

It was here that, as the television cameras followed him up to the green, he said hello to Deborah, who was at home in Florida.

Couples's tap-in was a formality. He was leading at −16, a tournament record, and he had tied the course record of 62, which was set by Larry Mize in 1985.

Rocco Mediate and Gil Morgan were tied, two shots behind.

"Every time I looked up, the ball was going where I looked," Couples said after the round. "It was ridiculous." It included 10 birdies and a bogey, a 30 on the front (par 35), and two back-nine putts that were makable for birdie—one a two-footer—that he missed. If he'd made the putt on 12 and the one at 14, it could have easily been a 60.

Jim Murray wrote:

> Fred Couples took the Riviera course at the Nissan L.A. Open Saturday and shook it like a dog shakes a rag doll. He went after it like a fighter whose man is on the ropes, glassy-eyed and bleeding. It was caveman golf. Not for the squeamish. . . .[3]

Sunday was every bit as nice a day as Saturday. But what would it be like at the end? That had to be on Fred Couples's mind. He knew he'd been the butt of snide remarks written by members of the press. And even after shooting the lowest number of his career on Saturday, he knew the media would be all over him if he could not win on Sunday. It would be a huge challenge, but at least it was on a course he loved in a city where the crowd had adopted him as one of their own.

The Sunday front nine was not spectacular. In fact, it could be described as nervous golf.

Couples heard someone in the gallery say, "Yeah, he can shoot a 62 any time he wants." He knew everyone was watching and probably expecting more than he was sure he could deliver.

At the first tee, "I wanted to make darn sure I hit a good drive on the first hole, and I did. I didn't hit a very good second shot, but [I got up and down and] made an eight-foot putt for birdie. It was nice to birdie that hole [a 501-yard downhill par-5], because making par there certainly doesn't set the tone. It's a very birdie-able hole."

The second hole is long and the green is small and slightly elevated from the fairway. Tough to hit. It is a par-4 460, slight dogleg right. There he made an unexpected 20-footer for birdie.

A birdie-birdie start on Sunday at Riviera is nothing to sneeze at.

Couples made what he thought was a pretty good putt from off the green at the third, but it did not find the cup.

He was solid on the fourth through the eighth. Then, on the ninth, by his own admission, "I let one get away. That was just bad timing." His approach sailed past the pin on the sharply sloped surface. He missed the birdie attempt, then missed the par.

"It seemed like every time I did something good, I'd do something bad. I played really edgy golf on the front nine," he added. So much so that he lost his lead.

The 10th is a short hole with a severe dogleg right. Sometimes in practice rounds players will try to drive it because it is only 311 yards and slightly downhill. But the dogleg is so severe and the green is so small that trying to drive it is an invitation to disaster. Couples mishit a wedge and didn't even find the green with his ball. But he made a par-saving putt, one he needed.

"It was kind of a nice turnaround to make a putt at 10 after hitting an iron too far right and having it skip off the green," he said. "Making a six- or seven-footer for par, you know, to par that hole making a putt like that is not what you want to do, but it was nice to finally do something good. The putt on 10 was a big putt. When I sank it . . . I felt the tension leave."

At that point, he and Gil Morgan were tied.

"I just knew I was going to have to beat him and start playing better," Couples added matter-of-factly.

Morgan had already won this tournament twice.

By the time they reached the 11th green, Morgan had gone 64 holes without a bogey. There his streak ended. He missed a foot-and-a-half putt and gave Couples the lead alone.

"I don't know if that was a letdown. I'm sure he would have loved not to make bogey," Couples admitted afterward.

At the 12th, it was Couples in the lead at −16, with both Morgan and Mediate one back at −15. Then, as though making up for the miss on 11, Morgan birdied the 12th to tie again. The crowds went crazy. Couples's attempt for birdie was no good.

Morgan knew he was capable of good rounds at Riviera, but the fates had someone else in mind this particular Sunday.

Morgan had the honor at 13. He took aim and then hit his worst shot of the week at the worst possible moment. The ball took flight and headed for a grove of eucalyptus trees on the left, and he watched horrified as the marshal pointed out-of-bounds. Mediate and Couples both split the center of the fairway. Morgan then reteed it down the left side.

Morgan's miscue made the entire group skittish. Mediate's 6-iron hit the center of the green. Couples ended up 30 feet away in two, while Morgan was 40 feet in four. All were extremely aware of the out-of-bounds still lurking 15 feet to the left of the green.

Couples later said, "I thought, 'Don't hit wedge. Don't hit wedge.' So I hit 9-iron and went 30 feet past. I was actually trying to lag and rolled it five or six feet by. I just went to sleep on that putt."

Uncharacteristically, Morgan then committed the unpardonable sin of leaving his putt short. However, with what he went through on the hole, it's a miracle he didn't run screaming into the trees. He finished with a double and dropped to −14.

After the round Morgan said, "The out-of-bounds on 13 was the most significant shot. I was trying to hit a hook, so I can't be too upset. Under stress, my tendency is to hit hooks, and sometimes, to compensate, I block one out to the right. If it hadn't hit a tree, though, it would have been fine."

So it was Couples at −16, Mediate at −15, and now Morgan at −14. All still had chances, even Morgan, although his psyche had to be temporarily damaged.

At the 14th, a 180-yard par-3, Couples, Morgan, and Mediate all parred.

Mediate said he "played really good until I drove down on 15. I tried to hit it too hard, and I pulled it." He hit the limb of another tree with his second and ended up with bogey to fall to −14 with Morgan.

Couples, looking calm on the exterior, spanked one into the center, parred, and now had a two-shot lead with three to play. He knew the next three holes were difficult under the best conditions, let alone while trying to come from behind.

At the 16th, Couples was first up. The 170-yard hole is virtually all carry to a green that is only 20 yards deep, and half that distance wide on the front tongue. The ball landed and stopped 10 feet from the pin. The crowd went nuts, and Couples smiled. Morgan's shot fell into the bunker, and Mediate had a long putt.

Mediate lagged. Morgan, showing he wasn't done yet, nearly holed the bunker shot.

Then it was Couples's turn. He tapped the downhill slider and waited, staring at it as it rolled down, and as it found the bottom of the cup for birdie, he raised his arm exuberantly. For the usually emotionless-looking Couples, it was a lot of body language. It was a three-shot lead. He was a virtual lock.

Now at −17, he doubted anyone else could go eagle-birdie or vice versa on those two final holes, so as Linn Strickler had said years before during the final round of the 1984 TPC, "pars were working." It was completely his tournament to win. He just had to get it to the barn.

He put his drive in the fairway on the 17th, and played it as the three-shot par 5 that it was. No cute stuff this Sunday. His third shot actually struck Mediate's ball, which was already on the green. Morgan was on the fringe. Couples's birdie attempt from 15 feet was no good.

Morgan then studied his situation, pulled the trigger, and holed out from the edge of the green. He gained a shot to go to −15, but realistically, it was too late unless Couples bogeyed the final hole and Morgan could birdie.

The crowd, like a giant amoeba, surrounded the golfers from behind the 18th tee, all along the right side of the quarter-mile-long, uphill hole, five to ten deep, where it folded into the immense gathering, thousands of fans packed around the natural bowl of the green.

Morgan and Couples both hit good drives. Mediate was on the right side of the fairway.

Morgan took a swipe at it and knocked it inside 15 feet, giving him the birdie chance he needed if Couples faltered. Mediate faded a shot and it landed inside Morgan's, about 10 feet from the cup.

Couples finally took his stance in the fairway. A voice from the gallery broke his concentration, and he backed away—that was probably the smartest thing he did all day.

As soon as he struck the shot, the gallery sucked in air and held on to it, finally letting it out in an explosion of joy when the ball hit the putting surface birdie distance from the hole.

Mediate gave his assessment of the situation. "It was fun. These people out here are crazy. They'll yell and scream, and coming up 18 you couldn't even hear. It was just excellent. I love it. And then, just when you're about to hit it, immediate quiet. Maybe a few noises here and there, but it's amazing to me."

When Morgan and Mediate both missed their birdie attempts, center stage belonged to Couples. The thousands gathered along the slopes that surround the 18th at Riviera were so still, it was eerie. Couples took the putter back. The metal touched the ball audibly, and as soon as the blade sent it rolling toward the hole, thousands of voices rose in a thunderous roar of approval. Birdie and victory. Couples raised his hands to the heavens. Finally, he'd had the Sunday lead and he'd won. And he'd done it with birdies on two of the final three holes.

Demons be gone.

At the post-round press conference Couples assessed the victory:

"I'm thrilled to death to win. I hope I don't have to wait another two and a half years to go through this. I look at ease, but I was very nervous out there. I like to win, obviously."

He said he and his caddie, Joe LaCava, had discovered a new pre-shot routine the previous week in San Diego that helped him in L.A. "I usually stand behind the ball and walk up to it and not take any practice swings. At San Diego, I would just walk up to the ball and hit it. Now [this week] I would take two practice swings looking down the fairway, not picturing where the ball was going to go, just to relieve the tension. Then I would walk up to the ball and take another practice swing. When I stood up to the drive, my body and muscles were loose and I felt great.

"The putt at 18, I was thinking, 'Make it. You know those are the easiest putts you can have.' I was thinking how I could lag it down there if Gil would have made it. But once he missed, I had a two-stroke lead. I just felt I could make it. Obviously it was nice to finish with a birdie.

"I'm used to playing near the lead, but I'm not used to winning, and that's the bottom line."

The tournament may have been over, but the ride was just beginning.

He was asked about all his past "failures." Phoenix. The Ryder Cup. The week before in San Diego. The can't-win mentality. And he handled them.

"Yeah, I haven't won a lot of tournaments, but I don't consider myself a loser. I think I do well."

He was asked if this victory got rid of the can't-win tag, and he said he thought he did that at the Byron Nelson two years earlier. "I take golf hard sometimes, and if I don't happen to have it, I'm mad walking up the hill at 18, but once I get in the locker room, get my shoes, and go to the car, it's fine. I think I've learned that you have to take it in stride."

He admitted that winning in L.A. was a "big help because if I hadn't won today, it would have been tough to swallow, but tough on me because everyone's saying you did it again, you did it again."

To give some idea of what the media regularly put Couples through in those days, here are some excerpts from *Golf World* written by Gary Van Sickle:

Stop me if you've heard this one. Fred Couples stands on the 13th tee. It's a warm, wonderful Sunday afternoon. Couples is tied for the lead in a big tournament, in this case, the Nissan Los Angeles Open. He's in position to win.

'There's a swing and a whoosh. He watches with his usual disinterested stare as a pull-hooked drive veers down the left side. He hears the ball connect solidly with one of Riviera CC's stately eucalyptus trees, and he watches it carom left and bounce out-of-bounds by a few feet.

You've heard this one before? Just another one of Fred Couples's 50 ways to leave a leader board, like that drive that bounced off a fan's backside and dribbled into the water on the last hole when he was about to win in Phoenix; that near-shank from the fairway with a 9-iron that cost him a bogey and his match at last fall's Ryder Cup; that second shot that splashed in front of the 18th green the last round when he still had a chance in San Diego last week?

Nope. You haven't heard this one before. At least not lately.

This time, the drive that went out-of-bounds was struck by Gil Morgan, not Couples.[4]

In the Monday USA *Today*, Couples was quoted in Steve Hershey's report saying, "I know all about a loser's label. It's hard to take at times. I may look casual, but I'm trying as hard as I can, and it hurts when you don't win."[5]

He also said that the shot he would remember the most was the one to the 18th on Saturday, which landed inside two feet for the birdie and 62. "That was more fun. Today I had a knot in my stomach for four and a half hours. I may not look nervous, but I was."

And so it went. But with this week, this tournament, the critics finally softened, because it was a sixty-bleeping-two at Riviera, because he made birdies on two of the last three holes. Also because on Sunday, Fred Couples stood up to the challenges and walked off the 18th the champion.

After L.A. and the spring of 1990, Couples's trend of being a contender continued. Just about every time he teed it up, he was on a leader board. Sure he had the occasional bad tournament, but more and more, his name was in the top 10 or top 5. Yet the winner's trophy eluded him just as he reached for it. It was the worst kind of tease.

The next week, at Doral, Couples was in contention after the first round, just two shots off the pace. Jim Gallagher, Jr., led, but Steve Hershey wrote about Couples. He figured after L.A., with the record-tying 62 and the absolute crush of Fred Fans lining Riviera's fairways and screaming and yelling for Couples, people wanted to read about him. Couples had become the flavor of the month.

At Doral after the first round, Couples was with nine other guys at 67. He hit an amazing 16 greens in regulation and had no bogeys. Greg Norman, starting his real season, made a triple on the 398-yard third hole but still shot a 68.

"I'm paying a lot more attention now that I'm playing well," Couples said to Hershey after the first day in south Florida. "In the past, I've tended to fall asleep sometimes, make a bad swing, and cost myself a couple of strokes. The way I'm playing, I don't want to get off track, so I'm concentrating. I feel if I do, I can hit the ball where I'm looking."

It might have helped that he went home every night, an hour and a half up the turnpike to West Palm Beach. It might have helped that he'd finished second on the Blue Monster the previous year. It might have helped that he'd once had a 64 on the course. But it was starting to look as if Couples would eventually shoot a 64 or lower on every course he played.

He wasn't resting on his laurels, though. "I don't want to have a letdown. That tournament is over," he said.

The second day, Couples matched his first-round score, and he and Paul Azinger were tied atop the leader board at 134. The weather stayed pleasant, and both Azinger and Couples shot 70s the third round. It was beginning to look as if the only thing they didn't do was call ahead to see what color outfit the other was going to wear. When the day concluded, they were both at 12 under, looking solid for the final round.

Then on Sunday, Greg Norman, who had gotten out on the wrong side of the bed on Friday, shooting an indifferent 73, suddenly came to life. He started the day seven back at 211. He wasn't exactly ignored when he began, but he was not what the in-the-know crowd would call a serious contender. But the other Greg Norman showed up. This was not the double-bogeying, drive-in-the-bunkering Greg Norman. It was the Greg Norman who, periodically on Sundays, miraculously shoots a 62 that half the world misses because he's so far back in the pack that he's nearly nine holes ahead of the leaders.

In this instance, Norman caused comparative choking in the rest of the field. It was as though six guys needed a Heimlich and couldn't find a friend anywhere to hug them. All had to watch Norman's name and score while they played. Couples fired a disappointing 72, 10 shots higher than Norman's round.

Three others tied, but no one could better Norman's mark. A four-way playoff ensued with Norman, Azinger, Calcavecchia, and Simpson.

Norman made quick but exciting work of it, going for the green on the par 5 in two, missing the putting surface to look as if he would tie the hole, and then miraculously chipping for eagle to win. Couples, meanwhile, steamed up the turnpike to his home at the Polo Club. If it was any consolation, just as it had been Curtis Strange's year in 1985, this would become Greg Norman's year. But on Sunday, when he'd just blown a chance to win his second PGA Tour event in a row, it didn't make him feel much better.

Couples won the pro-am at the Honda the next week with another—guess what—64 but slipped to 38th for the tournament. He missed the cut at the Players and watched the following week as Greg Norman lost at Bay Hill when Robert Gamez holed out from the fairway. For Norman, at least this time it wasn't a major.

In Houston, Couples contended again and finished in a tie for third. It looked as though his game was peaking in time for the Masters.

9

Major Disappointments, Minor Windfalls

"I'm past the stage of saying this is a learning experience."

—Fred Couples

After his hot streak during the winter, Couples continued his newly redis-covered enthusiasm and dedication toward his game. He asked Paul Marchand to go with him to Augusta. In fact, Marchand was supposed to have gone the year before.

"Fred invited me in 1989, and I couldn't go because I was in the running for the head professional job at Houston Country Club. I actually got it Masters week, and I would tell people I felt like I'd just won the Masters," Marchand explained about the career boost.

Couples wasn't the only one of Marchand's "students" at Augusta. Another was Mike Donald.

"Fred had introduced me, and Mike and I worked together in 1989 a little bit toward the end of the year," Marchand recalled.

Whatever Marchand and Donald worked on stuck for a while, because Donald shot a 64 on Thursday and was leading the Masters after the first round. John Huston was two back at 66, Peter Jacobsen at 67. Couples played like—well, like the wrong Fred Couples. He opened with a 74. Ten strokes higher than his friend Mike Donald.

As the week progressed, however, the tournament story was veteran Raymond Floyd, who led after the second and third rounds and during much of the fourth. At the time, Floyd was the oldest player to have won a U.S. Open. He was nearing his debut on the senior circuit, but he was still Raymond Floyd and a real threat to win. No one counted him out, especially with a lead.

"One thing I learned from Raymond," Couples would say a year or so later, "was when you get a lead, try to get more of a lead."

At the beginning of the final day, Floyd was two ahead of Huston, three ahead of Nick Faldo, and five in front of Jack Nicklaus. Even in 1990, everybody remembered what Nicklaus had done in 1986. Although a repeat of that year was unlikely, Jack Nicklaus was still Jack Nicklaus, and the world knew he didn't get all those majors by accident.

Floyd stayed ahead of the field most of the last day—that is, until Faldo, with six holes to play, birdied the 13th and 15th, par 5s, and then the par-3 16th. Faldo headed for the clubhouse and waited.

Floyd held on until 17, where he bogeyed to fall into a tie with Faldo.

With a par for Floyd at the 18th, the playoff began. It took Faldo two holes to become only the second Masters champion to win back-to-back titles.

Couples, who started the last round nearly 10 strokes off the lead, finished well, bouncing back from the opening-round 74 with a 69-72-69 to capture fifth place, one behind Lanny Wadkins and John Huston and one ahead of Jack Nicklaus. For Nicklaus, playing Augusta is like drinking from the fountain of youth. He still routinely beats men half his age.

Donald's scores skied. He finished with an 82-77-76, 47th place.

Couples played at Hilton Head the next week. He did not outduel Pete Dye's imagination and tied for 42nd. However, he bounced back the following week in Greensboro with a fourth and was a fixture on the leader board in the second, third, and fourth rounds.

Couples next unpacked his bags at the Memorial. It was a cold day in May, but the Seattle-native, wearing a ski cap, cruised his way through 37-miles-per-hour winds and 50-degree temperatures, posting a first-round 69, three shots ahead of the next best score. The average score that day was 78.8.

Six years earlier, it was a course he said he dreaded playing because of the difficulty, and because he said he always seemed to hook it into the trees on the par-5 15th. It was so bad that day that Mark McCumber had a seven, eight, and nine on his back nine, scoring 49. Jeff Sluman withdrew before finishing his first nine and already had a 46. A lot of amateurs can identify with scores like that, but for the pros, well, enough is enough. Hal Sutton four-putted the first hole. Donnie Hammond replaced his ball on the first green only to have the wind blow it away, 25 feet down the slope. And the first green is relatively protected.

Couples mentioned that his best round ever at Muirfield was a—guess the number—64, which he shot in 1987. "But this felt better," he added. "There were a lot of times today when I felt like I had a wedge in my hand

and wasn't even thinking birdie. All I wanted to do was get the ball on the green."[1]

Miraculously, he had birdies on the 13th, where a 12-foot putt dropped, and at the often treacherous par-5 fifth and the par-4 ninth. He made a 20-footer at the par-4 17th.

"The 16th was playing 189 yards, and I hit a 9-iron into the back bunker. That's how hard the wind was blowing. I usually hit a 9-iron 135 yards,"[2] Couples explained.

He skipped practice. Really, who needed more of that weather? But he said he was looking forward to the next day, thanking his lucky bounces for the 69. "It's great to have a 69," he said, "because if we don't get any rain, the greens will get even harder, and this course will be twice as hard."

Couples's prediction turned out to be right. The 69 was good to have. He held on to his lead through the second round. But on Saturday the rains did come. Players started. They stopped. They waited. They started. Stopped. Waited. Finally, Greg Norman finished with a 69 and was in the clubhouse waiting as Couples and playing partner Don Pooley tried to get home.

At the 18th tee, Couples was tied with Norman and had simply to par in to go to the final round as coleader. Then the fates struck again. Couples hit a drive that both he and Pooley said landed in the fairway. But when they got to the fairway, they couldn't find it. The marshals said they didn't see it. Everyone looked for the five minutes allowed under the Rules of Golf. The ball was declared lost in a nearby water hazard, and Couples had to take a penalty and drop another ball.

"I didn't think it reached the creek [on the left side of the hole]," Pooley said later. "I saw it hit near the fairway. But if it didn't go in the water, I don't know where else it could've gone."

Couples had 170 yards to an uphill green that is hard to hold under the best of circumstances. The green doesn't have one elephant buried under the surface. It has a herd. And sometimes players swear that they move during putts. Couples pulled his 5-iron and then, from the left side of the green, chipped 12 feet past the hole, two-putting for double bogey, tying him for third with Pooley, Brad Faxon, and Mark Brooks.

"It was a long day," he said afterward. "Maybe I lost some concentration. I've got to work on that."

But in the end concentration had nothing to do with it. The rains came. Sunday's round was washed out, and Greg Norman was declared the winner before he even teed off.

Five weeks later, Couples arrived at Medinah for the U.S. Open with a good attitude. But equally significant, he had a new agent, Lynn Roach. Roach, formerly with Advantage International, had broken away, taking a prize possession in Fred Couples. Roach would prove to be good for Couples, and after a time, Couples's success would springboard Roach's new business.

At Medinah, Deborah speculated and spoke to a few people in the gallery, waiting for Roach to arrive.

"Everybody has to go through Lynn now," she announced to people who worked for the company that owned Palm Beach Polo. However, none of the group she was speaking to actually had anything to do with Couples's agreements with the company. "Tell them that," she added, and turned on her heel, taking Roach to her side without bothering to introduce "Fred's new agent" to anyone.

Caddie "Squeeky" Medlin[3] was also in Couples's gallery. Six months earlier he and Couples had parted ways after a more than two-year relationship. That week Squeek was without a bag, but he watched his old boss play anyway. "Wish I still caddied for him," Squeeky confessed. "He's a great guy." Squeeky introduced people to his fiancée, Diane, who was from just outside Columbus, Ohio.

For Fred Couples, Medinah was an early ticket home. He missed the cut.

For Mike Donald, Medinah was the pinnacle of his career. Paul Marchand played what he called a small part in the success.

"Mike and I worked together in 1990 two weeks before the Open," Marchand recalled. "Then he had this tournament [the Open], and he had about a year and a half afterward, and then just started going wheew, downhill. I enjoyed working with Mike."

For Donald, it was almost the Great American Dream. Except Hale Irwin had experienced a vision of his own, and he turned into Donald's worst nightmare.

At Medinah, Irwin, age 45, became the oldest U.S. Open champion in history. What made the week more unusual was that Irwin had been given a special exemption by the USGA that year. Stranger yet, at his post-round press conference, he admitted that earlier in the week he'd actually had a dream that he would win the tournament. It was as though he was destined to win that championship, no matter what.

The next week, Irwin won again at Westchester. Couples repeated his missed cut, and what had been a spectacular winter looked as if it might be turning into a long, hot, slow summer.

In July, at the Old Course at St. Andrews, where Couples had played his first British Open in 1984, the weather was nearly perfect the first three days. It was the lowest cut in Open history at 143. Finally, it turned "British-like" cloudy and somewhat windy on Sunday.

In the end, Nick Faldo, with major number two for the year, held the claret jug high. Payne Stewart was second. Greg Norman finished sixth in a tie with fellow Australian Ian Baker-Finch. Couples finished down the list in a tie for 20th.

In August, as the players packed their bags and prepared for the final major, headlines about discrimination in golf were shrieking from every sports page and golf publication. It was a controversy that had begun in June and gained momentum as the PGA Championship approached.

Hall Thompson, founder of Shoal Creek Country Club in Birmingham, Alabama, site of the PGA Championship, had been quoted as saying that the all-white golf club would not be pressured into accepting black members.

Protests were planned. Sponsors began to pull out of the event.

Thompson's comment had revealed the real truth about golf. No one bothered to ask if Shoal Creek had Asian members or Jewish members, or Hispanic members or female members or Native American members, but in looking back, it is quite probable that Shoal Creek, like many private clubs then, and even now, had white, male members, period. All this was more or less taken for granted until Thompson opened his mouth and began the accidental, rapid-pace integration of the sport. In less than six weeks, Hall Thompson did for golf what Rosa Parks had done for the civil rights movement. It was called the Shoal Creek Incident, and it had the most far-reaching effect on golf since Walter Hagen opened the club-houses of the country to the golf pros.

The situation was so bad that the commercial time purchases for the tournament were canceled. As Steve Hershey reported in *USA Today*. "Civil Rights groups threatened to picket the then all-white club during the PGA Championship, sponsors pulled their ads from the television coverage and three of golf's governing bodies rewrote their rules for selection of tournament sites."[4]

After six weeks of headlines, Shoal Creek integrated its membership in order to hold the PGA Championship that August. Louis Willie, a businessman from Birmingham, was made an honorary member.

As the *USA Today* story noted, it wasn't just the tournament that was affected. All the U.S. organizations in golf changed their policies. The USGA. The LPGA. The PGA Tour. Politics had nothing to do with it. It was a bottom-line decision.[5] If change did not come, there would be no corporate support for golf. It was adapt or die.

Pressure was eventually applied to those clubs hosting PGA and USGA events prior to 1995 to integrate or opt out. Several opted out.

Historically, Shoal Creek was a turning point in golf. In a few years, Cypress Point would no longer be in the rotation at the AT&T Pro-Am. Butler National would no longer host the Western Open. Aronomink Golf Club was slated for 1993 but withdrew. Oak Tree Golf Club would drop out as a 1994 PGA Championship site.[6] Other clubs would also fall away as tournament sites. But wonderfully, and notably, others would take up the slack, including Shinnecock Hills, Olympic (after being subjected to lawsuits long before the Shoal Creek situation), Winged Foot, Champions, Oakland Hills, Oak Hill, The Country Club, and others.

To underestimate this particular tournament in the business and social history of golf would be foolhardy. To fail to mention it would be more than an oversight. However, to say that it had anything to do with the actual outcome of the PGA Championship in 1990 would be a stretch of the imagination. Because when the tee times came at Shoal Creek, the players played golf and left the name-calling to the politicians and writers. They knew color was not a part of the equation. Skill was.

While the atmosphere was tense, the weather was better than most people had expected in Alabama in mid-August.

Before the start, everyone talked about the rough, a vicious, thick Bermuda grass growing faster than kudzu in the heat. Mike Reid, who had finished second to Payne Stewart in 1989 at Kemper Lakes, noted that rain would make it like glue.

"The marshals are using tongue depressors to mark the balls in the rough so they don't lose them," Reid added with his own special sense of humor. "That's appropriate, because when you see it you want to gag."[7]

But after round one, Bobby, brother of Lanny Wadkins, was ahead of the field. One stroke back were Fred Couples and Mark O'Meara. Billy Mayfair and Scott Verplank were two behind.

By the end of round two, there was a new leader in Aussie Wayne Grady, who started with a first-round 72 but fired 67 on Friday, including birdies at the 16th and 17th to give him a one-stroke lead over the seemingly tenacious Fred Couples and new challenger Larry Mize. Mayfair and Chip Beck were two back at 141.

The course was unusually difficult, even for a major, and the cut came high, at seven over par, 151. Seventy-four players went on to the weekend.

No one suspected Grady was about to forge ahead, least of all Grady himself. He'd just come off his best of five years in 1989 with a victory at

Westchester and a near miss at the British Open, where he was in a three-way playoff with Mark Calcavecchia and Greg Norman.

But after three rounds at Shoal Creek, it looked as if Grady was serious. He shot even par and didn't give up anything to the field. At 211, he was now two ahead of Couples and defending champion Payne Stewart. Gil Morgan and Loren Roberts were the only other players in the field under par.

On Sunday Grady started like a Daytona racer with his foot to the floor. He rolled in a 60-foot putt on the first hole for birdie, spiced up the third hole with a 15-footer, again for birdie, and poured on the hot sauce from 30 feet for birdie on the fourth. But in between the brilliant putting, Grady was human. He bogeyed the second and ninth.

Couples made a mini-charge. He birdied the par-5 third hole from a bunker and made birdie on the sixth, the other par 5 on the front. He just wasn't making anything long.

Morgan also birdied the first hole, then bogeyed the fourth, and birdied the sixth and seventh.

At the end of nine holes, Grady was one under for the round, −6 for the tournament. Couples was −5. Gil Morgan, paired with Couples, was −4. Stewart must have been thinking too much about the chance to win the PGA back-to-back because his usually steady play gave way to a front-nine 38. He was virtually a spectator.

Couples parred the 10th while Morgan birdied, rolling a 35-footer to go to −5. They were both one back.

Couples then birdied the 11th and went to −6, and for the first time in his career, he was tied for the lead on the back nine of a major on Sunday.

Grady answered with a birdie of his own, and elevated himself to −7.

Couples birdied the 12th with a 15-foot putt to tie Grady again.

When Grady bogeyed the same hole minutes later, Couples had the lead by himself. Couples had played the first 12 holes of the final round four under par. It was the best he had done in any major in his entire career.

Whether it was the first time in rarefied air, or just wanting it so much, or, as Couples himself said afterward, "pressure," at the 13th Couples three-putted for bogey. The lead was now a tie.

"At 13," he said afterward, "I stroked it good. I thought I'd made it. I hadn't missed a short putt all day, but after that, I started thinking about it."[8]

Doubt, that great crippler of performance on and off the course, crept into the dark recesses of his mind.

He missed four-footers again at 14 and 15, bogeyed both holes and the 16th, and fell from −7 to −3. From the pinnacle to an also-ran in less than an hour.

At the end of the day, it was a tired Wayne Grady who lifted the heavy Wanamaker Trophy, his first major and his second U.S. victory. He could also enjoy the fruits of a 10-year exemption on the U.S. tour, part of the prize for winning the PGA at that time.[9]

Couples was more than disappointed. "At 14, I had a downhill curler and another one at 15. I didn't make any of them. That was the whole round."[10]

Athletes say that part of learning how to win is learning how to deal with the emotional storm that kicks up inside your brain and your body in the heat of competition. They can see victory and get so excited about the result that somehow it gets messed up on the way and someone else ends up with the trophy. Experienced, successful athletes learn to deal with their emotions. They know they have to do all the things between sensing victory and actually winning. Impatience, nerves, and inexperience are all threats to that goal.

Did losing the PGA in 1990 allow Fred Couples to become a better player? Probably it made him mad enough, determined enough, to vow that the next time he had a chance he wouldn't do the same thing. He might do something else, but he would not repeat his performance at Shoal Creek if he could help it.

"I'm past the stage of saying this was a learning experience," he said disgustedly. "It happened so fast, it was sickening."[11]

While Couples was clearly disappointed, it was, as most observers either forgot or failed to mention, the only time he had held the lead on the back nine on Sunday in a major championship in his career. In USA Today one story was on Grady's success but another featured "Couples's Collapse."

Then after a week off, it was the World Series of Golf in Akron, where Couples finished 13th and Jose Maria Olazabal won, shooting a first-round 61 in which he actually missed a couple of three-footers.

In the Tour Championship at Champions Country Club in Houston, the last event of the year, Couples finished in a tie for 22nd and ended up ninth on the money list, his second-best season in official money with over $700,000.

That's when he began his run in what the golf writers have dubbed the Silly Season. They call it the Silly Season because events are made for TV or invitation-only or limited fields, so there is virtually guaranteed money, which is not allowed in PGA Tour events. The big kahuna of the

Silly Season is the Skins Game. However, Couples was not yet on that invitation list.

With his victory in L.A., his excellent finishes during the year, and his place on the money list, Couples was invited to the Asahii Glass Four Tours Championship, held in Japan. In the event he defeated Nick Faldo in his first match, beating him by four shots. He beat Saburo Fujiki in the second round by three shots. Rodger Davis beat Couples by two in the third round, and the final round was canceled because of rain. Australia/New Zealand was declared the winner because their team members had the lowest cumulative scores, even though the U.S. team won the same number of matches.

Next on tap was a year-old event created by IMG around Greg Norman, held at Sherwood Country Club outside Los Angeles in Thousand Oaks. At that time it was called the RMCC Invitational (Ronald McDonald Children's' Charities), but it would later become The Shark Shootout. There was an attempt for a time to call it the Greg Norman Invitational, until it was pointed out that no active PGA Tour players were allowed to have their name on a Tour-sponsored or cosponsored event. The only PGA Tour tournament with a player's name in the title is the GTE Byron Nelson Classic; Nelson is retired from competition.

The Shark Shootout was a limited-field, changing-format, partner event. The first day would be better ball. The second day, modified alternate shot. The third day, scramble.

It was no surprise that several IMG players were involved. Curtis Strange and Mark O'Meara had won the inaugural year. Other players included Arnold Palmer, Peter Jacobsen, and Greg Norman. But it was not exclusively an IMG affair, since players like Gil Morgan, Chi Chi Rodriguez, and, in 1990, Fred Couples were also in the field. Raymond Floyd would be Couples's partner.

The first round Floyd and Couples managed a 64 together and were well behind defending champions Strange and O'Meara, who had combined for a 59.

Bret Saberhagen and his son were in Couples's gallery. Afterward, Couples paused to talk with Saberhagen, and as they chatted, Couples picked up the youngster and carried him around on his shoulders for a few minutes, laughing and joking. As many of his friends had always noted, Couples enjoyed children. He was sometimes more at ease with them than he was with adults. People who saw this side of him often wondered why he and Deborah did not have a family.

In the Saturday round, the hardest format of all, alternate shot, each player hit driver, then one ball was selected and shots were alternated until the ball was holed out.[12] Raymond Floyd was known for his accuracy, not length. Couples was known for his length, not accuracy. The format gave Couples a chance to freewheel it on every tee ball, knowing he had Ray Floyd as a backup. Everyone, including Couples and Floyd, were amazed when Couples and Floyd somehow manufactured a 57. It was absolutely unheard of to shoot that low.

"I can't remember having so much fun on a golf course," Floyd said, which for a veteran of 28 years on the Tour and winner of multiple majors was saying something.[13]

Mark Calcavecchia and Ian Baker-Finch shot a 62 and got waxed. They were playing with Floyd and Couples and had to watch Floyd hole a shot from the sand on two and chip in for eagle on the 11th. Couples made two lengthy birdie putts, a 20-footer at the 13th and a 15-footer at the 14th. Making matters worse, Calc and Baker-Finch went birdie-birdie-birdie at 11, 12, and 13, but lost a shot to Couples and Floyd who played the same holes birdie-eagle-birdie.[14]

Couples was blasting drives that left Raymond Floyd with wedges to the greens.

"I can hit the greens with a wedge, believe me," Floyd said. "When you get to play in the fairway from where Fred was driving the ball, this is an easy game."[15] Floyd had to be salivating as he walked and walked and walked down the fairway before pulling a club to hit. It was reported that Floyd, one of the great stone faces in golf, actually smiled all day.

They were 30 on the front and 27 on the back.

Calcavecchia said it was something to watch. "Fred drove the ball 320 yards down the middle every time except on one hole, and on that hole Raymond stepped up and hit an absolutely perfect drive."[16]

On Sunday the Fat Lady didn't just sing. She yodeled. A capella.

Floyd and Couples actually scored higher on Sunday in the scramble format. But not by much.

"When we started birdie-eagle today, I knew it was over," Floyd said afterwards.[17] They were three under after two holes. At ten Couples hit a 340-plus-yard drive that landed 10 yards in front of the green. Floyd chipped to a few feet and, ho-hum, Couples made the putt for birdie.

"We really wanted to win this thing by ten strokes," Couples said when the round was complete. They skied all the way up to a 61. They won by only five.

However, far more important than the win was the experience of playing golf with Raymond Floyd as a partner.

As Couples himself said, "I learned so much from playing with this man. His intensity on the course, the intensity in his eyes, was something to see. He'd make a joke or two, but as soon as he turned to walk to his ball, the smile disappeared, and he'd get that look in his eyes.

"I sometimes relax on a golf course, and when I do, I can't always focus on the game again.

"Raymond does not have that problem. Maybe from now on, after this experience, I won't have it anymore either."[18]

That lesson was worth more than the shared purse of $250,000 for first place. The pairing of Couples and Floyd would prove to be a valuable asset 10 months later at the Ryder Cup.

But team madness was not over for Couples in 1990. In December, the Team Championship was contested at Binks Forest, in West Palm Beach, Florida. It was a close neighbor to Palm Beach Polo and Country Club, where the event had been played in 1987, '88, and '89.

This time, his compatriot was not Raymond Floyd. It was the newly famous Mike Donald, who was a longtime friend of Couples.

There was silliness off the course, too, according to Jay Haas, car maniac, who had been invited to stay with Couples that week.

One of the Mustangs Couples had at the time was a 1970 Mach I.

"Now I see this car and it's great," Haas said. "I go to look at it. I opened the door and a *snake* crawled out of this car. So I open up the hood and there was a bird's nest in the engine.

"I said, 'Fred, you're not driving this much . . . and there's a snake in your car.' He just said, 'I don't even want to know, just get that car outta here.'"

The same week Couples and Haas decided they'd give two of the vehicles a much-needed drive.

"The '68 GT 500 convertible was automatic. So he took that one," Haas explained. "I took the '68 GT 500 fastback, and we were drag-racing on back roads and the next day the transmission basically fell out."

They decided to leave driving to NASCAR and went to play golf.

After the first round, during a mild, warm South Florida day, it didn't look as if Couples and Donald would do much, since two groups had posted a 60 and they shot 65. But the second day, though the temperatures stayed the same, the Couples/Donald team heated up and turned in a hot round of 60, lower than all others, to share the lead with Brian Claar/Bill Glasson, Greg Bruckner/Kirk Triplett, and Jim Carter/Rocco Mediate, all at −19.

Before the start of the third round of this low-scoring festival, clouds arrived. Couples and Donald donned wind gear and turned in a 63. No one else could handle the conditions better than they did, and they finished Saturday four shots ahead of the field.

In a week that seemed to include all climates, Sunday was again wind-breaker weather, but the clouds had cleared. With Donald making putts and Couples giving his partner credit for coming through in the crunch, they maintained their edge of four for the victory.

Couples had learned lessons in 1990 when he didn't want to, and he had learned others accidentally. Both would pay off handsomely in the next two seasons when his mettle would be tested.

At year's end he was ninth on the money list, second best in his 10-year career. Of the 22 U.S. events he entered, he made the cut in 18 and had a stroke average of 69.97, which was good enough for 8th place. He was 4th in eagles, had throttled back to 13th in driving distance, and was number 25 in greens in regulation.

In addition to his victory at Los Angeles and the second at the PGA, he was third in Phoenix, in Houston, and at the Memorial, fourth in San Diego and Greensboro, fifth at the Masters, and seventh at Doral.

He tasted success early, shooting his lowest competitive round ever. He suffered disappointment in the summer, losing the PGA Championship after taking the lead on the back nine in the final round. And he'd learned great lessons about the ability to concentrate from one of the toughest of the tough guys, Raymond "Mr. Focus" Floyd.

All in all, it was a very successful year, one to build on and remember the next time he had a chance in a major.

10

~m~

Launching Pad

"Great talent. No goals in life. Not one."
—Tom Weiskopf

"He's a waste product, too."
—Fred Couples

Sometimes you want to eat your words. And about two months into 1991 some people had said things they probably wished they could take back.

But as Couples himself has commented often, "there was a lot going on" in 1991.

Right out of the gate, he hit the Tour full strength. It was as though he had figured out what everyone else had known all along. He was good. Very, very good.

At the Tournament of Champions, La Costa, first week of 1991, he was again in contention, finishing the Saturday round just two back of the leader, Tom Kite. But Kite closed with a 69 to stave off all comers, and the best Couples could manage was a 71. Not good enough to win, but good enough for a nice finish.

Fred and Deborah went home, where polo season was in full swing. Deborah was sponsoring a team by now, and she was a patron and a player. Couples's next appearance was at the Bob Hope tournament, the first week of February. Again he played well. By the end of the third round of the 90-hole endurance contest, he was just three back of the leaders, Tim Simpson and Mark O'Meara. In the fourth round he shot a 67, but so did O'Meara.

In the final round, when Fred reached the holes at Indian Wells closest to the television compound, Deborah made an appearance on the course. She was furious because she'd had to disrupt her polo schedule to attend the golf tournament. But Fred had wanted her to be there.

"I am not at all happy about it," she snapped to an employee of the developer he represented. "And if I'm not happy, Fred's not happy. And he might just not be representing people here anymore," she threatened, and stormed off into the maze of gallery.

Members of the press noted that Deborah had made her appearance for the television holes.

Clearly, no matter what articles had been written portraying Fred and Deborah as a happy twosome, there was a strain in the Couples household that seemed to be getting worse. If Deborah and Fred couldn't solve problems as to which was more important, her polo matches or his golf tournaments, it didn't take a brain surgeon to figure out that whatever was going on at home would explode sooner or later. Particularly when she was making noise in public.

At the end of the day, Corey Pavin beat Mark O'Meara with a birdie-chip-in on the first playoff hole.

Deborah's temper or no, Fred finished fifth and won $44,000. A nice check, but not nearly enough to manage a stable of polo ponies, as he would soon discover.

In Los Angeles two weeks later, Couples prepared to defend his title by winning the pro-am. His name seemed permanently nailed to leader boards, but he was not able to match Ben Hogan's, Paul Harney's, or Arnold Palmer's feat of winning in L.A. back-to-back, although only Hogan had won twice in a row at Riviera (1947–48). Couples finished 12th, nowhere close to his performance the previous year. He seemed, well, just a little bit off. Not himself.

It was also the week that the Weiskopf quote broke. That alone could have done it.

In the March issue of *Golf Digest*, Tom Weiskopf had been quoted as saying that Couples had "great talent [but] no goals in life. Not one. He's not as easygoing as people think. You can see that pressure gets to him."

Couples, hurt by the criticism, replied—uncharacteristically—in kind. Steve Hershey of USA *Today* described the situation:

"Told of the former player's comments, Couples seemed stunned. Keeping his voice level, he said: 'He's a waste product, too. What did he do. Quit at 40? He was supposed to have all that talent. How many majors did he win?

"'If he says I have a lousy grip or swing, that's fine. But to read my mind is crazy. It's funny. I always admired him as a player, but I've never even sat down and had a conversation with him. . . .'

"'I have goals. I'd like to play 20–25 years and have fun doing it. But to tell people about specific goals. That's embarrassing.'"[1]

Worse than anything else for Couples must have been that Tom Weiskopf had been the player whose swing he most admired when he was growing up. But Tom Weiskopf didn't know that. And neither did most other people.

Jim Murray of the *Los Angeles Times* came to Couples's defense with a tongue-in-cheek column which he wrote as a letter to Couples on how he could impress Weiskopf. Number one was to throw clubs. Two was to fire his caddy and berate him publicly. Three was that after a poor round, he should blame the greens, the rough, the architect, the greenskeeper, et cetera, and possibly equate the course to a parking lot.

Number seven on the list was to say that majors were overrated, that the Masters was just a putting contest and that it's as hard to win the Kemper Open as the British Open.

Then Murray got positively brutal:

> If things go bad on a round, don't hesitate to pick up and stalk off the course. Say you got a migraine or heard thunder (even if there's not a cloud in the sky). Just remember, Weiskopf once got flu in the sandtrap on No. 2 at Riviera. I think he was lying four at the time and was looking at a double or triple bogey. That'll give you flu every time. Double bogeys are the leading cause of flu on the tour. Tommy just walked out of the trap and into his car and out of there. . . . I see where you had a "twinge" in your back when you shot your 67 Thursday. That's good thinking. Always keep a twinge in reserve. You never know when you'll need it—in a sandtrap, lying four for instance."[2]

It was a classic situation where everybody said things they later wished they hadn't.

In view of *Golf Digest*'s long lead times for stories, Weiskopf's comments were probably a reaction to Couples's performance at the PGA Championship the previous summer or even the 1989 Ryder Cup, when Couples himself admitted that the pressure got to him.

Tom Weiskopf is a complex person with a beautiful golf swing, a gift for course architecture, and a penchant for sincerity that sometimes gets him into trouble. This was one of those times.

By the time the Tour turned east, Couples had gathered up a little over $117,000. He forgot to enter Doral, which Calcavecchia called "plain stupid," but it has happened to many others.

He was uncharacteristically mediocre in the rest of the Florida events, coming in 41st at the Honda Classic and 50th at Bay Hill and then 23rd at the Players Championship.

Couples rested a week, then went to Houston to prepare for the Masters. As in practice. As in working on a goal. He just didn't go around saying, "Hey, folks, come watch me work toward my goal." To be certain, he didn't call Tom Weiskopf.

He and Paul Marchand practiced shots at Houston Country Club that reminded them of shots Couples would need at Augusta National. When nobody was on the golf course, he played holes backward, thinking of critical tee shots at Augusta.

Masters week, Marchand stayed with Couples, but things were not clicking. After a first-round 68, Couples was never under par and had one of his worst finishes ever, a tie for 35th.

Ian Woosnam won, and in the process showed everyone a new way to play the 18th hole. Woosie flew the bunker on the left and hit his drive into the gallery area between the 18th and 9th holes. He took the bunker out of play altogether.

Woosnam's year marked the fourth in a row that the Masters had been won by a non-American player, and the natives were getting restless. Woosie didn't care. He was deliriously happy.

Couples kept playing and finishing in the pack. He seemed to be going sideways. He was 49th at the MCI Heritage at Harbour Town, 33rd at the Byron Nelson. Then, disappointed with his results since the West Coast, he admitted he was going to have to do better.

"I feel like I'd like to go a year and play well and win a couple times," he said. "So far I haven't. Guys like Tom Watson and Ray Floyd and Curtis Strange, a lot of times when they get in contention, they know what to do, and I don't. And therefore, I hit a bad shot. I get baffled or frustrated, and someone else passes me. I can get the lead, but sometimes I can't hold the lead."

He cited a visit to Kansas City to see Tom Watson. "I learned a little bit from him. And I can't ever be as good as he is, but I can learn how to do things like him," Couples added.

He had also made a schedule change, in anticipation of the Ryder Cup.

"It's hard to skip the Memorial and the Colonial and the Kemper, which I always want to play, but there comes a time. I know I'm going to make the Ryder Cup team. I don't usually play that much in September, so I'm looking ahead."

Determination paid off. Couples finished 10th at Westchester, and the next week, at the U.S. Open at Hazeltine, was only three off the lead after two days of play. A third-round score of 75 was disappointing, but he came back with a 70 on the last day to tie with Larry Nelson at 285, a total that was good enough to beat everyone but Scott Simpson and Payne Stewart, who were deadlocked at 282. For the second consecutive year, the U.S. Open went to a playoff.

Neither Simpson, who had won the championship in 1987 at Olympic, nor Stewart, who'd won the PGA in 1989, played subpar golf on Monday. Stewart posted a 75 and Simpson a 77 to hand a second major to Payne Stewart. With a PGA Championship and a U.S. Open Championship, Stewart was again at the top of his form and halfway to being one of four men to have won the four professional majors in their careers.[3]

Couples's crescendo reached another mini-zenith two weeks later, in Memphis.

The weather was annoyingly hot and Deep South humid. It was like playing in a steam bath, fully dressed. A dreadful week when shirts stick to everybody's skin before tee-off and grips are never quite dry. The kind of weather when hair spray gets gooey and deodorant failure happens at about 9 A.M.

Memphis is the tournament where Raymond Floyd had once finished wearing a towel over his head to protect himself from the heat. However, it was a lot like South Florida in the summer.

The scores were as hot as the weather. Rick Fehr and Jim Thorpe jumped out in front on Thursday with 64s. Couples was four back with a 68. On Friday, it was Fuzzy Zoeller's turn to shoot a 64, and he took over the revolving-door lead. Couples was two back. There were seven players between him and Zoeller.

Everybody over par missed the weekend.

On Saturday, Couples's name came up in the low-number lottery, and he fired one of his partial scorchers at the right time. It wasn't a 63 or 64, but a mere 66. However, it jumped him over the field to the top of the leader board, setting what was a 54-hole record.[4] Even with a torrid pace, he was only one stroke better than Peter Persons and Hal Sutton.

On Sunday, Couples didn't dazzle the crowds at first.

Peter Persons did. He birdied the third to tie and then the fourth to go into the lead, but as soon as he reached the ninth, it was as though he suddenly realized he had a chance to win, got a case of nerves, and shook himself out of contention.

Couples made pars, pars, and more pars. Eleven straight. He was playing like Hale Irwin in an Open, not the typical Couples birdie-bogey
parade.

At the 12th, however, he hit a 130-yard pitching wedge from in a fairway bunker to 20 feet. "It was the biggest shot I hit," he said later. Then,
fired up by the wedge play, he rolled the putt in for birdie.

He also got help from Peter Persons, who bogeyed the same hole for a
two-shot swing.

It was time to get more of a lead.

At the 14th, Couples smashed a 5-iron to 20 feet on the water-guarded
monster par 3. The average score for the week on that hole was 3.488. The
14th had already gobbled two of Jay Haas's golf balls, but Couples birdied
it. At that point he started to look for some shade in the 100-plus-degree
temperatures.

Though he was dripping with perspiration, there was no letup in his
game. At the par-5 16th, he landed in a bunker near the green, blasted to
four feet to save yet another birdie, and parred in safely to take the title,
which was his fifth.

Persons floundered, and was dubbed "Missing Persons"[5] in *Golf
World's* recap. He eventually slid to a 74 final round.

Couples's final score of −15 tied the tournament record, which was
held by Tom Kite and John Cook. Cook, of course, went on to shatter that
by 11 strokes a few years later.

Couples not only won the tournament decisively, he had four rounds
in the 60s, a feat no one else accomplished that week. It was a good pattern of consistency, particularly after his less-than-stellar performance in
the spring.

Afterward, Couples took a couple shots at his critics, too, just to show
them he remembered far more than they thought.

"I've been pointed at for a lot of things," he began. "They said I didn't
practice very hard, that I play early in the year and take the rest of the year
off. They say I didn't want to win."[6] It is really too bad this speech wasn't
broadcast someplace.

Those who knew him, knew better. Amazingly, he had never played
the course before that week. He saw it for the first time on Wednesday.

"Having never been here, when I came out for the pro-am, I was
scared to death of the place," he added. "I certainly am glad I came," he
said, pocketing the winner's check.[7]

The next week at the Western Open, he had a chance again, but Lady
Luck was playing left-handed in Chi-town. Even Greg Norman couldn't
charm her into the victory circle.

On Sunday, Norman, Couples, and Russ Cochran were tied at 10 under par playing Cog Hill Golf and Country Club, which had stepped in to replace Butler National. Norman came out of the blocks like a man possessed, and after five holes he had a six-shot lead, which included three birdies and an eagle.

Then, on the back nine, disaster stuck. Norman found himself in vegetation and vexation. He bogeyed five of the last six, including 13, 14, 15, and 16, for one of the most amazing up-and-down rounds of his career.

Afterwards, Norman called it a Jekyl and Hyde round. It was hide all right. He hid the ball in the shrubs twice and another time stashed it in a woman's handbag. His ball was hiding everywhere but the bottom of the cup. Three birdies, an eagle, five bogeys, and more foliage than the local botanical gardens.

By comparison, Couples's 72 looked fairly routine, but the card showed no signs of his own entanglements with plant life and arm-wrestling the bushes.

Neither Couples nor Norman could keep up with the steady play of Cochran, who avoided disaster and shot 69 for his first Tour victory. It was the second lefty win on the Tour for the year. Phil Mickelson had won in Tucson as an amateur.

With Couples's third at the U.S. Open, a first in Memphis, and a near miss in Chicago, he had certainly done what he said he planned to do: resurrect his game. And with great hopes, he went to the British Open.

It was a fascinating play of names and history as the 120th British Open began at Royal Birkdale, site of Johnny Miller's 1976 victory. The oddsmaker Danny Sheridan put Faldo at 7 to 1, followed by Woosnam and Olazabal at 8 to 1, Ballesteros at 10 to 1, and Couples at 30 to 1.

But, as usual, none of those names shot the lowest that week. When the dust cleared, it was the "next Aussie," Ian Baker-Finch, who stole the show. Never known for his length, Baker-Finch birdied five of the first seven holes and took a five-shot lead. He birdied the second, third, and fourth, and was four ahead of the field. Then, at number six, he holed a six-footer, and followed it up with a 15-footer on the seventh. "Every kid in Australia grows up wanting to win the British Open," the new champion said. "To me it's the world championship."

Before that week, Baker-Finch had had one U.S. victory (at Colonial in 1989), five Australian titles, one European tour win, and five Asian triumphs. The 1991 British Open would become his crowning glory.

Couples, who never led at Royal Birkdale, shot a 64 on the final day to vault himself into third-place money, tied with Mark O'Meara. He said that after Baker-Finch's start, everyone else was really playing for second, but he admitted thinking about a 62 or 63 in an effort to catch the Aussie. He had a chance to go that low, but parred two of the par 5s. At the 15th, he chipped to eight feet and missed the birdie putt. At the 17th, a 526-yard par 5, he hit his approach shot into a bunker, made a great recovery to five feet, but missed it.

Couples stayed in Europe for two more weeks, playing the Heineken Dutch Open and the Scandinavian Masters, despite some discomfort in his back. It had been stiff the first morning after he and Deborah arrived, which he attributed to a soft bed. "I just took a pillow and blanket and went on the floor." What perhaps should have been an alarm passed as an offhand comment.

It was said that a highlight of the British Open week for Couples was meeting Prince Charles in the locker room at Royal Birkdale on Saturday, but His Royal Highness had, of course, been to the Polo Club in 1988, the first year Fred and Deborah lived there.

Couples returned Stateside for the PGA Championship at Crooked Stick, just north of Indianapolis, where a young kid named John Daly was about to redefine length, charisma, showmanship, and domination of a golf course. Couples had always been long, but Daly was otherworldly.

Daly flew over all the hazards Pete Dye created, became a poster child for speed of play, and astounded golf fans with his whoop-it-up style as he charged down the 18th fairway to victory.

Couples finished an undistinguished 27th, with a first-round 74 and a third-round 76.

He rested a week, which he needed after the European jaunt. He still had the World Series of Golf ahead of him. Then, in four weeks, was the event he'd been anticipating for two years. Redemption was on his mind. The Ryder Cup loomed before him.

The change from his usual playing schedule, the early-season rest, the vacation in the spring, skipping the events he normally played, it was all part of the plan, the chance he took, saving his energy for the fall. Would it have been the right thing to do? Would it work? Would he tire too soon, playing his way to Kiawah instead of taking to the couch?

The World Series of Golf is a perk for winners. There's no cut. Even finishing last, players this year would get nearly $8,000. There was no serious pressure, but a victory was worth a 10-year exemption. Couples did not need another 10-year exemption. He needed to stay sharp.

Firestone Country Club is noted for its long par 4s, well-bunkered par 3s, greens that require excellent second shots, and heavy rough. In an average year at Firestone, the bluegrass rough is well over the shoe tops of the players.

Couples began the event with a four-over-par 74 on a day when the best score was 66, turned in by Nolan Henke. Even Jose Maria Olazabal, who had shot a 61 the previous year, opened with par. Obviously Firestone's members and course superintendent had taken the 61 personally and, over the winter, decided that wasn't going to happen again.

Payne Stewart, U.S. Open champion, started with a 73. PGA champ John Daly, 80. Baker-Finch was two better than Couples's score with a 72. Masters winner Ian Woosnam was a no-show. It was jet lag he didn't need three weeks before the Ryder Cup. The European players often skip the World Series.

Couples made a steady climb back, posting a 70, then a 69, and finally a 67 to eventually end up in fourth place. Despite the rough start, he actually finished one stroke out of a playoff that featured the trio of Tom Purtzer, Jim Gallagher, Jr., and Davis Love III, who was just coming into his own with three tournament victories, including two at Harbour Town. Love was at the bright-young-star stage instead of the monkey-on-his-back-because-he-hadn't-won-a-major stage.

Purtzer persevered, and after two holes captured the title and, more important for him at that point in his career, the 10-year exemption.

Couples skipped a week and went on to Canada, where, like the bionic man, he played himself onto the leader board one more time. He could never capture the lead, however. At the beginning of the final round, he found himself in a group four shots back of D. A. Weibring.

With four rounds in the 60s, Couples's play and consistency looked good, except that Nick Price came from five shots back and shot six under to Couples's three under, and walked away with the national championship of Canada.

The ebb and flow of a Tour pro's golf game is a peculiar, elusive, and seemingly ethereal intangible. As Hubert Green once said about winning, "You could make a million dollars if you could bottle it." Of course, that was when winning a million dollars wasn't an everyday occurrence in golf. Players scrounge and scrape and miss cuts or play 15 shots off the final score for a few weeks. Then, either through hard work, determination, or the alignment of the stars, they get into a pattern of success instead of a pattern of nonsuccess.

Fred Couples was working on being successful the last week in September. The Ryder Cup had been his goal since 1989, and he would not waver until he saw the gold trophy back in the hands of the U.S. players.

The difficulty is that golf is not like swimming, for instance, where athletes weight-train, swim two-a-day workouts, perhaps run, and then taper, meaning that they do less and rest their bodies, hoping that the hard work done every hour of every day prior to the taper will get them to the finish one one-thousandth of a second before anyone else.

In golf, working hard physically doesn't necessarily translate into great feel on the greens. Or birdies. Or fairways split down the middle, although practice can't hurt that. Strength training might add some distance. But just hitting bucket after bucket after bucket of balls isn't always enough. If it were, Vijay Singh or Tom Kite would win every tournament.

Golf must be finessed, caressed, corralled, because as they say, you never own success in golf, you just borrow it for a while. Fred Couples intended to borrow up to the limit for a week in September.

He tuned up by playing, because he didn't want to go to Kiawah rusty and without the taste of competition still fresh in his mouth. After Canada, he went to the B.C. Open, an event that usually attracts those lower on the money list in any given year, players who are worried about making it into the top 125 for the next season's exemptions, rookies, and guys who just plain like going to Binghamton, New York, in the fall.

Couples's college teammate, Blaine McCallister, led the first round with a smooth 64, which he somehow managed before play was called because of rain and inclement weather. Faxon and Mayfair were one back.

The second-round lead belonged to Faxon with his own 64, a stroke up on McCallister. It looked like a case of "Anything you can do . . ."

In the third round, Faxon maintained control, but by that time, Couples, who had already shot a 66-67-68, was threatening, just one shot back.

Sunday, Faxon and Couples played together in the last group. By the second hole Faxon looked as if he was taking command when he made a two-foot birdie putt after Couples had bogeyed the first.

Then Couples got it going with a birdie at the par-5 third, repeated with a 15-footer for birdie at the fourth, and added a five-footer for birdie at the fifth. They were tied at −14.

For several holes, no one gained an advantage. Then, at the 11th, Faxon bogeyed, giving Couples the lead. He nursed the one-stroke edge until the 17th.

On the 198-yard par 3, Faxon, who fights the hook demon from time to time, sent a 4-iron left of the green next to a fence and made double. Couples blamed the mishit on a nearby train, which he said blocked out all sound and caused a slight delay in play.

"I would not have hit either," Couples said later. "You've got to hear the sound of the ball when you're playing, and with that train going, you couldn't hear a thing. It just threw him off a little."

Nevertheless, with one hole to play and most of the field already finished, Couples was a lock. He was also surprised to win, admitting that he had entered the tournament only as preparation for the Ryder Cup. The previous week he had practiced in Houston.

"The last couple months have been great. I really didn't want to go in next week not playing good this week, and I practiced pretty hard. When I left, the two guys I was working with [Paul Marchand and Dick Harmon] said you're playing well. It sounds funny, but they just said, 'I think you'll win.' And that's kinda weird to say because you know, you don't ever get that impression. I never feel like I'm going to win a tournament come Wednesday night."

But he also said he wasn't thinking about the Ryder Cup while he was playing the B.C. Open. "This week, it was more important than the Ryder Cup," he said, although it is questionable that anyone believed him. At least he was exhibiting some diplomacy.

More important, he had seen steady improvement in his game since March and April. His four rounds in the 60s at the Canadian hadn't been enough, but at the B.C. Open his score of 66-67-68-68 got the job done by three strokes.

"I've played a lot smarter the second half of the year," he noted.

For the first time in his career, Fred Couples had won two regular Tour events in the same season. Counting the two end-of-season partner events, he had won four times in 10 months. He was as close to the top of his game as he had ever been. It was perfect timing.

11

The War by the Shore

"When I was out there on 10, 11, 12 and I kept
hearing that 'USA,' I'm telling you what,
I couldn't breathe. I couldn't swallow.
I couldn't do anything. . . . I could
barely hit the ball."
—Hale Irwin, U.S. Open winner, 1974, 1979, 1990

For Fred Couples, the 1991 Ryder Cup marked his coming of age as a golfer. Though he proved to be one of the heroes of the team, the entire squad shared the spotlight for a while with the golf course itself, because for the first time—and probably last time—a course was built specifically to host the Ryder Cup. The reasons were three-fold, dating back to the 1985 and 1988 PGA Championships.

The Ryder Cup of 1991 was originally slated for PGA West. But after the PGA Championship at Oak Tree turned into an unprecedented financial bonanza in ticket sales and other revenue, the PGA wanted a bigger cut of the action for future events. Specifically, they wanted a new contract for the 1991 Ryder Cup, giving them a bigger percentage of the money. That was part one.

Part two unfolded when European television executives, who wanted a prime-time telecast, pressured PGA officials to move the venue east. They feared the West Coast time zone would kill the European audience. Rights fees were at stake.

Finally, the PGA of America also wondered if the California desert location of PGA West at the end of September, with its expected 100-degree-plus days, might literally kill the galleries, if in fact southern Californians, noted for lax attendance at sporting events, would even show up.

But the owners of PGA West had a contract—a signed deal, dating to 1985. They counteroffered a plan that allowed the PGA to have a bigger portion of the financial pie and move the event east, so long as it was to one of their other golf courses.

PGA West owners had a large portfolio of golf course properties that included Palm Beach Polo and Country Club, Oak Tree Golf Club, and the newly purchased resort at Kiawah Island, South Carolina, where they already planned to build a new course on a 2½-mile stretch of beachfront property. The rest of the trade began to take shape.

The official announcement was put off for months, according to Chris Cole, who was project director at Kiawah Island Resort and became general chairman of the Ryder Cup in 1991. There was a huge amount of speculation in advance of the press conference. Of all days, it was held April 1, 1989.

While it looked like a united front at the announcement, Pete Dye, in his book *Bury Me in a Pot Bunker*, said, "When the PGA officials first visited the site for the course, they almost threw up. There was a vast expanse of nothing where their beloved Ryder Cup was to be played, and they left shaking their heads in bewilderment."

But shaking their heads or quaking in their boots, it was to be a Pete Dye design, complete with all the nightmare features conjured up when his name is mentioned. Dye always says he is simply trying to build courses that "give golfers the same thrill as Hogan had when hitting his 1-iron at Merion." He doesn't mention he's added a ride on Space Mountain in the middle of the backswing.

In addition to the spectacular setting, two features set the course apart. One is natural: the strong wind that blows in different directions throughout the day. The other involved Dye's decision to play sand around the fairways and greens as waste area.

Eventually, Nick Faldo would proclaim the course too difficult for stroke play. Pete Dye had to love that—Faldo, at the top of his game, saying the course was too tough.

But Chris Cole and Pete Dye battled more than the usual construction problems. They also had a little run-in with Hurricane Hugo, a category-four storm that struck the South Carolina coastline at Charleston in September of 1989.

Hugo was an ugly devil. What General Sherman left standing when he marched from Atlanta to the ocean, Hugo knocked down.

Afterward, Dye and his crew had to get construction back on schedule, in record time, starting all over, with no power, a tree mess that looked like mile after mile of giant pick-up sticks, and a golf course project that had been literally blown to bits. According to Dye, this inspired the crews to work harder and longer than any of them ever had in their lives. They were determined to prove the critics and naysayers wrong. Once the power was restored, they put up lights and worked 18-hour "days."[1]

There was limited VIP play starting in May of 1991. On Memorial Day weekend, the course opened to the public.

While many, including Lanny Wadkins, doubted things would be in shape, Couples himself had played the new track and said that it was fabulous but very tough. He also predicted bogeys and doubles would win holes.

After Labor Day, Chris Cole closed the most heavily watched course on the eastern seaboard. He didn't want so much as a twig out of place for the matches.

Golf publications dubbed the contest "The War by the Shore." In as much as the Gulf War had started and—thankfully—ended earlier in the year, for the first time since the Korean conflict it became tasteful to actually wear fatigues. U.S. captain Dave Stockton took advantage and ordered up hats with fatigue hatbands. He would have conjured up Kate Smith to sing the national anthem if he could have.

The Europeans felt they were the world champions in golf. Nick Faldo had gone on record saying he was disappointed that the United States didn't recognize the Europeans as number one because, after all, they'd won the Cup the last three times. That only added fuel to the verbal attacks on both sides.

Stockton's first strategic decisions were the captain's picks: Raymond Floyd and Chip Beck, who at that time was in the prime of his golf career. Beck had been half of the successful Azinger/Beck duo in 1989, and Stockton wanted him back.

Floyd was chosen because of his success with Couples at the Shark Shootout and for his tenacity. It was believed having him there would help Couples play to his potential.

The lineup for the United States was as follows: Paul Azinger, with a victory in the 1991 AT&T; Chip Beck; Mark Calcavecchia, winless in the United States since his British Open, but high on the money list; Hale Irwin, age 46, with a Ryder Cup record of 9–3–½; Raymond Floyd; Wayne Levi, PGA Tour Player of the Year in 1990, winless in 1991, and a Ryder Cup rookie; Mark O'Meara, whose most recent victory was in 1990; Steve Pate, Ryder Cup rookie who won the 1991 Honda Classic; Corey Pavin, with two victories that year; Payne Stewart, the reigning U.S. Open champion; and Lanny Wadkins, age 41, having one of his "on" years, with a victory in Hawaii;[2] and Fred Couples, with two victories that season, most recently the previous Sunday.

The Europeans had their own combination of power. Bernard Gallacher had played on eight Ryder Cup teams in 31 matches, and had a 13–13–5 record. It was thought that he had learned the winning "Jacklin formula" from 1985, '87, and '89.

His picks were Mark James, Jose Maria Olazabal, and Nick Faldo. Faldo at that point was considered one of the top players in the world. It was inconceivable not to have him on the team.

Olazabal had won the International, had been second at the Masters, and was heir apparent to Seve Ballesteros.

Ballesteros at that time had amassed more than 60 victories internationally, including the Masters twice and the British Open three times. He had done for the Europeans what Arnold Palmer had done for the U.S. players. So whatever Seve wanted, Seve got. And Seve wanted Ollie as his partner. Ballesteros also led in Ryder Cup points for Europe that year.

The rest of the European entourage included Ian Woosnam, 1991 Masters champion; Colin Montgomerie, Ryder Cup rookie with a 1991 victory at the Scandinavian Masters; the cagey Bernhard Langer, winner of 30 international events; veteran Sam Torrance, who had played on every Ryder Cup team since 1981; rookies David Gilford, Paul Broadhurst, and David Feherty, the sometimes opera singer; and Steven Richardson, who had won two tournaments that year but was only two years out of Walker Cup play. It was an interesting combination of experience and new talent.

The event began with a collision. On Wednesday evening the caravan taking players and their wives from Kiawah to Charleston for a banquet came to a screeching halt when a police car zigged out in front of the limos, causing two rear-end accidents. Steve Pate, who was in the middle car, was hit at least twice and was questionable for the start of play with a "bruised hip." Stockton wanted to give Pate a chance to play and opted not to call up the 13th man, Tim Simpson.

At the opening ceremonies, despite the animosity that was being cited in the press, the comments by captains, dignitaries, and representatives of the U.S. and European PGA organizations were sportsmanlike but enthusiastic.

Finally, it was made official. The contest would begin the next morning. Couples and the team marched back out past the fluttering flags as thousands who had gathered cheered the teams.

On Friday, dawn broke clear but chilly. The sun gleamed through gnarled branches of the few scrubby, windblown trees to the right of the first tee. It glared directly into the eyes of the players as they peered down the first fairway in search of the ideal landing spot. The air was crisp enough for gloves and warm-up suits. Players wore sweaters or vests.

For each group, the tee announcer called the names and fans cheered. Flags waved from the dune perches. Photographers were at the ready. Even Tour pro Rocco Mediate had joined the press, working as a photographer's assistant.

"Before the tournament started, a big front came through, and the wind went 180 degrees. It blew exactly the opposite direction. It was a totally different course," Paul Marchand recalled. However, it completely leveled the playing field. Everyone was equally unprepared.

The first morning was great for the United States and disastrous for Europe.

In the fourth match, Couples and Raymond Floyd, with his killer stare that was so strong even photo assistant Rocco Mediate was taken aback by its fierce intensity, dispatched Bernhard Langer and Mark James, 2 and 1. The United States had a 3–1 advantage.

Things were looking good for captain Dave Stockton as he roared around the course in a golf cart with sons Ronnie and Dave, Jr., on the back and wife Cathy riding shotgun.

In the afternoon fourball, Couples and Floyd went up against Faldo and Woosnam. Floyd was now in full X-ray vision, and he encouraged Couples, to an astonishingly large 5 and 3 romp.

Zinger and Beck went back at it with teeth bared, and for the second time that day went down to Seve and Ollie, 2 and 1. Their bunny needed new batteries. Or else they needed to start speaking Spanish.

At the end of the day it was 4½ United States to 3½ Europe. Fans from both sides mumbled but kept their flags aloft.

On Saturday, both captains split up combinations where the magic had fizzled. Azinger and O'Meara stepped up to take on Faldo and Gilford in foursomes. The Americans proved to be an awesome team and trounced the Europeans, 7 and 6. Gilford was upset, but Faldo just about had steam coming from his ears. He sat out in the afternoon, hoping his luck would change.

Wadkins and Irwin fileted Torrance and Feherty, 4 and 2. Wadkins was not interested in having his otherwise stellar record of 15–2–2 in Ryder Cup play ruined by anybody.

Stewart and Calcavecchia were then tested by Mark James and rookie Steven Richardson, but they came away 1-up.

Couples and Floyd tried to do the impossible and went up against Ballesteros and Olazabal. Obviously their Spanish was no better than

Zinger's and Beck's, because even Floyd's Superman gaze did not pene-
trate Seve's lead-lined armor. They went down, 3 and 2. Ballesteros and
Olazabal were playing so well at that point, it is doubtful that even God
hitting a 1-iron would have beaten them.

The U.S. team again won three, lost one, and headed into the afternoon with the competition seemingly well in hand.

In the afternoon, Stockton made pairing shifts and gave Floyd a well-
deserved rest. The Europeans finally mounted a charge and won the first
three.

The final group pitted Stewart and Couples against Ballesteros and
Olazabal, which provided more drama at the end of two very long days.
It proved a brutal contest, with no one gaining a big lead. On the 15th,
Couples hit one of the most incredible pressure shots of his career.
Although there was a huge amount of luck involved, it came at the right
time.

Paul Marchand recalled it: "Payne was way left of the hole in trouble,
up on one of the dunes. One of the officials was there, and while Payne
was taking a practice swing, someone said his ball moved. Rather than
debating it, he picked up. So he was out of the hole."

Unfortunately, Couples had put his second shot into a bunker that
stretched from the left edge of the green along the fairway for 80 to 100
yards. Seve was on the green, looking at birdie and playing well enough
to make one.

The crowd, growing sparse and cold in the late-afternoon gusts off the
ocean, watched in anticipation. Couples looked unflappable, as usual. He
studied the situation, then made the swing,

The ball rocketed upward. It was right on line, headed toward the
pin, and even in the stiff breeze it stayed there. Then it shot down right
into the hole, and everyone went absolutely nuts. Couples leapt into the
air at least three feet, and Payne Stewart, club in hand, raised both arms
and jumped as though he might fly down to the fairway.

Deborah ran out from behind the ropes to hug Fred. He looked totally
astonished, and in a millisecond reflex action, grabbed her around the
waist with two hands and heaved her gently about two feet into the air and
six feet backward out of the way. It was one of the most interesting non-
golf events of the matches, but most spectators were so caught up in the
shot that they didn't even notice. Couples was not about to be caught up
in a repeat of the Kemper, certainly not now. Insiders who had heard
rumors about growing tension in the Couples's household just watched
and wondered.

Stewart and Couples linked arms and celebrated all the way to the green. Ballesteros did his best to shut down their enthusiasm by making birdie on the hole.

Golf World called it the best shot that didn't mean anything. But, in fact, it put pressure on Ballesteros to make the putt.

"The 17th hole, over water, late in the day, was cold," Paul Marchand remembered. "The green was lined with people, and I was standing up on the tee, and the wind was blowing in my face, and I was thinking 'I don't know how Fred made a swing.' It was so cold and wet. Olazabal hit up 10 or 15 feet. And Fred started it up and it landed 20 feet or whatever, and I was thinking 'Man, this is pressure.'"

When they finished on the 18th, it was so late that Olazabal was putting almost in the dark. Fans were tired and wind-whipped.

Couples's memory of the round is simplistic—that he holed out but that they halved the match. He had wanted the whole point.

The players on both sides had beaten themselves up on a monster course for two days to an 8–8 tie.

The singles would decide everything.

For Couples, as well as for the entire team, the victory was almost essential. It wasn't for himself that he wanted to win. For a change, it wasn't about the money. As he had pointed out, "The last time I was on the team and we tied, and I lost two matches, it was pretty frustrating because it was really the first time I'd been on a team like that. If I'd have won my match, and we'd won, it would have been like 12 victories for all the other guys."

The Ryder Cup meant enough to make even tough guys like Lanny Wadkins and Mark Calcavecchia cry. Couples himself had shed tears at the Belfry in 1989.

Couples found that he loved conquering his doubts and fears and showing himself that he had what it took. He enjoyed being able to go up against the best players in the world and having a chance to beat them. It was doing something that counted. It was being a part of something that mattered. It was being able to make the shot when he had to. Fred Couples found he derived immense satisfaction from that. He was making more money than he had ever dreamed. He had cars he didn't drive and homes on both coasts. After that, what else was there? There was coming through for your friends. Coming through for your country. Having shoulders big enough to carry the burden. Winning the point that had to be won. He wanted to be successful this week, but not for his bank account. He wanted victory for the team.

On Sunday the sky was bright blue but flagsticks all over the course bent in the wind.

By tee off, the score had changed to 8½ to 8½ because Steve Pate withdrew. By rules of Ryder Cup competition, Bernard Gallacher put a player's name in an envelope and delivered it to Dave Stockton. That player would sit out. Each side would receive a half a point as though the match had been played and halved. For Europe, the player was David Gilford.

The U.S. team now needed to win six points to take the Ryder Cup from Europe. The combination—whole or half points—would not matter. Twelve were at stake.

Stewart, who was down early and still 4-down at 13, took David Feherty to 17 before losing. Floyd was 4-down to Faldo at 11 but came back to push the match all the way to 18 before losing also.

It was Faldo's first singles victory since 1983. Afterward he said, "The golf course is so hard it's unbelievable. In these conditions, I don't know how you could finish with a scorecard."

Floyd said glumly, "You do not want to let a guy trounce you. It's bad for the team. I thought of that."

Couples kept his eye on the scoreboards, adding and subtracting the numbers. But it's not fun when your side isn't ahead. While early matches were finishing, he was on the easternmost tip of the course, at the fifth, where the wind was howling. Both he and Sam Torrance found it impossible to stop the ball on green on the par 3, but Couples clung to his 1-up advantage. It was the only thing he could control, and this time, he intended to do it.

In the third match Mark Calcavecchia carved a 4-up lead over Colin Montgomerie only to lose it on the last four holes to halve his match.

"He looked like he was in shock," Marchand recalled. "He was on the beach hyperventilating and he looked physically ill. It was a real contrast to everybody else."

One source reported that Calcavecchia had been having such a hard time getting air that the on-site medics had given him oxygen.

Johnny Miller of NBC talked about pressure and how it affects people differently. "The right kind of pressure finds diamonds," he said. "But it's hard to putt when you see three golf balls and don't know which one to putt at."

When Calcavecchia finished, it was Europe 11, United States 9.

Next was Corey Pavin, playing like a man three times his size, who captured a 2-up edge on Steven Richardson at six, and maintained it through the 17th for a 2 and 1 victory.

A move to this house on 13th Street in Seattle proved pivotal in Fred Couples's life because Jefferson Park golf course was just two blocks away.

Young Fred Couples and friends would often squeeze through or climb this fence at Jefferson Park to play a few holes.

The 1974 O'Dea High School golf team photo, with Fred Couples kneeling in the middle of the front row. "Led by senior captain Dan Ito and the play of frosh Fred Couples," the team missed a trip to the state championship by just one point. *(Courtesy of O'Dea High School, Seattle, Washington)*

By 1976, Fred Couples, a junior, had won his district meet in a playoff and the state AA championship by five strokes. He was already showing signs of his trademark follow-through.
(Courtesy of O'Dea High School, Seattle, Washington)

This text actually appeared next to Fred Couples's class of 1977 high school yearbook photo:

Fred Couples
St. George Parish. Honor Roll 1,2; intramurals 1, 2; golf 1, 2, 3, 4; soccer 1.
Future plans: To go to college to play golf and become a professional golfer or a businessman.

(Courtesy of O'Dea High School, Seattle, Washington)

1978 SOUTHWEST CONFERENCE GOLF CHAMPIONS
Standing: CHRIS MITCHELL, TERRY SNODGRASS, FRED COUPLES, MIKE KLEIN, CAPTAIN JOHN STARK AND KALUA MAKALENA inserted on left side

TEAM SET SOUTHWEST CONFERENCE RECORD OF 866 for 54 holes... at Briarwood Country Club, Tyler, Texas. TERRY SNODGRASS WON INDIVIDUAL CHAMPIONSHIP AND MIKE KLEIN AND FRED COUPLES TIED FOR THIRD PLACE INDIVIDUALLY.

Kalua Makalena

As a freshman at the University of Houston, Fred Couples was part of the team that set the Southwest Conference record for the lowest team score in a 54-hole event. *(Courtesy of University of Houston Sports Information)*

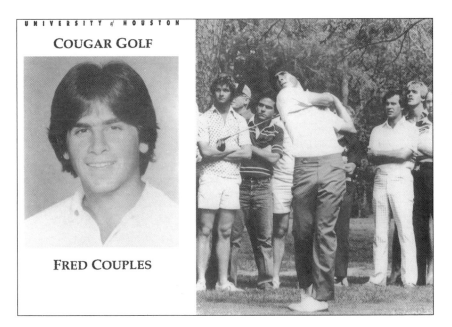

COUGAR GOLF

FRED COUPLES

Under the watchful eye of teammate Paul Marchand (in light pants) Fred Couples plays a shot in a college tournament. Marchand still spends many hours in the same pose as Couples's instructor today. *(Courtesy of University of Houston Sports Information)*

Couples at the Memorial Tournament in 1984, two months after his victory at the TPC.

The 1989 Ryder Cup team. Left to right: Curtis Strange, Mark O'Meara, Fred Couples, Ken Green, Paul Azinger, Tom Kite, Mark Calcavecchia, captain Raymond Floyd, Lanny Wadkins, Chip Beck, Payne Stewart, and Tom Watson. *(Courtesy of the PGA of America)*

Fred Couples held the final-round lead in a major for the first time at the PGA Championship in 1990. But putts like this one wouldn't fall on the back nine, and Wayne Grady eventually won the tournament. *(Copyright © 1990 Richard Dole/PGA of America)*

The late Micah Mefford
and his favorite golfer,
Fred Couples, in 1991
(Courtesy of Marquis Mefford)

Fred Couples holes
out from a bunker on
the 15th on Saturday
in the 1991 Ryder
Cup. This clutch
shot helped Fred and
partner Payne
Stewart halve their
important match
against Seve
Ballesteros and Jose
Maria Olazabal.
*(Courtesy of Jim
Moriarity/PGA of
America)*

An elated Fred Couples clutches the Ryder Cup following the U.S. victory in 1991. Hale Irwin, who won the deciding match, sits next to Couples. *(Copyright © 1991 Steven J. Gilbert/PGA of America)*

The demanding par-3 12th hole at Augusta National has helped define many a Masters Tournament, but never like it did for Fred Couples in 1992. His tee shot landed on the tightly mowed bank, but instead of rolling into Rae's Creek it stuck just above the waterline. Couples made a deft chip to save par and preserve his lead en route to winning his first major. He later called the shot "the biggest break of my career." *(Copyright © 1992 David Cannon/Allsport USA)*

Fred dons the Augusta National Golf Club's official green jacket at the awards ceremony. *(Copyright © 1992 David Cannon/ Allsport* USA*)*

Mickey Mantle was a fan of Fred's and the feeling was mutual. Here he posed for a picture at Preston Trail in Dallas. Left to right: David Frost, Lanny Wadkins, Mickey Mantle, Fred Couples, Preston Trail head pro Gordon Johnson, and John McClure. *(Courtesy of Bill Hooten, Dallas, Texas)*

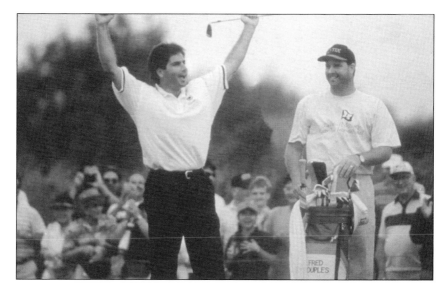

Fred celebrates after making a hole-in-one at Kapalua in 1994 as caddie Joe
LaCava looks on. It was his first as a professional.
(Courtesy of Kapalua International)

Fred Couples holds the
Kapalua International
trophy next to tournament
founder and NBC course
reporter Mark Rolfing in
1994. *(Courtesy of Kapalua
International)*

Couples shares a moment with friend Peter Jacobsen on Sunday at the 1995 Ryder Cup Matches. *(Courtesy of Montana Pritchard/PGA of America)*

Fred was happy to be chosen as a captain's pick by Lanny Wadkins in the 1995 Ryder Cup.
(Courtesy of Montana Pritchard/PGA of America)

Fred Couples makes an eagle on the par-5 16th hole to put maximum pressure on the field at the Players Championship 1996. He went on to win by four strokes. *(Copyright © 1996 J. D. Cuban/Allsport USA)*

"Fred's Back." This double-entendre ad appeared after Couples won the Players Championship in 1996. *(Copyright © Ashworth, Inc., 1996, photo by Barry Grimes)*

Couples salutes his friends and fans at the Fred Couples Invitational in Seattle. *(Copyright © 1997 Rob Perry/courtesy Greater Seattle Golf Events)*

Couples kids with Jim Nantz at the Fred Couples Invitational. *(Courtesy of Greater Seattle Golf Events)*

Fred stands alongside his golf hero, Arnold Palmer, at the most recent Fred Couples Invitational in 1997. *(Copyright © 1997 Rob Perry/Greater Seattle Golf Events)*

John Bracken (left), a friend of Fred's since they were teens, now runs his charity tournament in Seattle. On the right is Fred's agent and friend Lynn Roach. *(Courtesy of John Bracken)*

Couples stretches while he and caddie Joe LaCava contemplate a club selection on the 15th tee at the U.S. Open at the Olympic Club in 1998.

Fred and caddie Joe LaCava in 1994 *(Copyright © Ashworth, Inc., 1994, photo by Barry Grimes)*

The playful side of Fred Couples is captured in this Ashworth advertisement. *(Copyright © Ashworth, Inc., 1996, photo by Barry Grimes)*

With a dramatic birdie on the first playoff hole at the 1998 Bob Hope Chrysler Classic, Fred put a difficult year behind him and captured his first PGA Tour victory in nearly two years. *(Copyright © 1998 Jon Ferry/Allsport USA)*

Fred's fans are always out in force, like these two at the
1998 World Series of Golf.
(Courtesy of the author/Jason [left] and Landon [right] Weber)

On September 12,
1998, Thais Bren
and Fred Couples,
surrounded by
family and friends,
were married in a
ceremony held at
their home in Los
Angeles. It was a
beautiful start to a
new way of life.
*(Courtesy of Thais
Couples)*

Europe 11, United States 10.

The green at 17 was temporarily awash in celebration. Stockton hugged Pavin. Finally, everyone remembered there were players on the tee and quickly scurried off to await the next twosome.

Wayne Levi had held on to Ballesteros for as long as he could. His mission had been to keep Ballesteros occupied, away from the rest of the team. With a short putt for par, Ballesteros finally ended it 3 and 2 at the 16th.

Europe 12, United States 10.

Unfortunately, Ballesteros was now free to rally the troops. Europe was just two points away from keeping the Ryder Cup. The Concorde had already buzzed the course.

Up ahead, the Azinger/Olazabal match, which had been more exciting than a Wild West shoot-out, was concluding. If it had been held in the Roman Colosseum, this match would have been to the death.

After six holes, four had been won with birdies — by Zinger at one, by Ollie at two and three. Then Zinger won the fourth with a bogey and the sixth with a birdie. At the 7th Azinger went 1-up, briefly.

When they approached the 17th, they had gone through 12 lead changes and were tied again. When they left it, Azinger was −1 up, but the score didn't reflect a miracle shot Olazabal had hit out of a waste bunker, a downhill lie in a footprint.

At the final green Olazabal stared at a seven-footer, uphill, a straight putt that he would probably make nine times out of ten. But he missed it and conceded Zinger's putt. It was a huge point.

Europe 12, United States 11. And counting.

Azinger and Stewart, close friends, fishing buddies, hugged like kids. Azinger's smile was impossible to ignore.

A TV reporter asked for a comment, and Azinger remarked, "Raymond Floyd said to me the other day, 'I've won four major championships and never felt the last day in any of those majors the pressure you feel in Ryder Cup.' And it is overwhelming." He kissed his wife, Toni.

Each side gained a point in the next two matches. Beck beat Woosnam with an astonishing 3-wood to the 17th green. And on the same hole, O'Meara fell victim to the coastal winds with two balls in the water. It was Europe 13, United States 12.

What looked like a U.S. lock an hour earlier was past serious to critical.

It was Couples's turn to bring home a much-needed point. By now some had seen beyond the casual veneer of Couples's demeanor and thought it no surprise that he was 1-up early in his match with Sam Torrance. Couples also knew that this was Torrance's sixth Ryder Cup, that

Sam Torrance had walked up the 18th fairway in 1985 with tears in his eyes, knowing his point would win the Ryder Cup for Europe. After the fifth hole, Couples won two more on the front and was 3-up before the turn.

He remembered Floyd's words of advice at the Shark Shootout: *Get more of a lead*. He added another point and was still 4-up through 11. At the 12th, playing downwind, he won again, to go 5-up with six to play. It looked like a body-slam victory. Then he lost the 13th and the treacherous 14th, and fell back to 3-up.

At the 15th, his second shot landed on the right side of the green and bounced completely over it. But fortunately for Couples, Torrance had his own problems and was eight feet from the hole in three.

The unspoken fear was a repeat of the Calcavecchia match. Could Couples get this one all the way to the barn? If Torrance took the point, they would win the matches. Nobody on the U.S. side could give ground now.

Torrance pulled his putt and made bogey. Couples, who had been in two bunkers, also made bogey, and they halved the hole. He was still 3-up with three to play. Torrance was dormie and would have to win a hole to advance. Couples was a near lock, but Calcavecchia had been a lock.

At the 16th Couples, with his length, was sure to have the advantage. He wanted to close it out there.

When they reached the green, Torrance was 20 feet away for par. Couples was closer. Courageously, Torrance, wielding his long putter, made the putt. But, quieting his nerves, Couples tapped in to halve the hole, win the match, and secure the 13th point for the team, 3 and 2.

Europe 13, United States 13—two matches remained.

Deborah ran out to greet Fred, but he was busy hugging Payne Stewart. Everyone patted Couples. He was instantly snagged for an interview. "I got off to a good start," he said quite simply, and then asked for a scoring update. When he was told that it was now tied at 13, he replied with a determined look, "It looks like another push, and we don't need that." He was very solemn. He excused himself to be with the team.

Couples had gone 3–1–1 in his matches, the best of all 12 players on the U.S. side, yet his concern was for the team.

Lanny Wadkins took a lead early and by the 10th, he was 3-up on Mark James. At the 13th Lanny Wadkins bogeyed, but he miracle-birdied the practically impossible 14th to go back 3-up. He lost 15. Two up; three to play.

At the 16th, Wadkins was looking to call in whatever heat-seeking missile he could conjure to close out his match. He was 165 yards into the

wind. Taking little time, as is his habit, he caught one clean, and it
zoomed like an angry hornet over the green to the right.

James's second shot was in a waste area. The ball had been moved by
a spectator. Ballesteros showed up to protect European interests. Wadkins
made it clear the players could handle it. After all the discussion, James
faced an ugly downhill shot from a waste bunker. He chunked it, a hard
shot made infinitely more difficult by the pressure.

Lanny Wadkins again demonstrated his ability to deliver by lagging to
four inches to close out Mark James.

It was now United States 14, Europe 13.

Wadkins sighed with relief and received a huge hug from his wife,
Penny, and various teammates. An announcer approached him.

"It was tough. I don't know that I've ever worked harder. . . . There's
nobody I'd rather have back there than Hale." He choked back tears. He
knew the score and what his point had meant to the team. He was so overcome, that he could not speak.

In the end it came down to The Match, that tenacious seesaw affair
between Hale Irwin and Bernhard Langer. It is a story that will be retold
as long as the Ryder Cup is played. Irwin went up early but was never
ahead by more than two. Langer found the will to come back. Even the
fans were nervous at the conclusion.

The Match went to 18 all square. Irwin needed a tie, at least. But
Langer needed an outright win.

Irwin pulled his tee shot left into the crowd. Miraculously, it hit Kathy
Jorden, a PGA of America media relations manager, in the back and
bounced out onto the edge of the fairway. She was probably the difference
in the matches.

Neither player landed on the green; Irwin was 70 feet away. As he
struck his mile long chip, he looked physically ill because it was 20 feet
short. On the sidelines, Raymond Floyd and Lanny Wadkins looked nau-
seated.

Up on the green, Irwin was in more pain than any healthy human
could imagine. The wait was agonizing. The best he could do was to get
it to a foot and a half. He tossed the hot potato pressure back to Langer,
who had a six-foot putt for par.

Fred Couples sat to Stockton's left, and Deborah sat to Fred's left. As
Langer readied himself, Stockton put his head down, momentarily unable
to watch.

It was downhill, downgrain, a wiggle-wobbler for the championship of
the Western world and two years of bragging rights. When it was a foot
from the hole, Langer lifted his chin to the sky and screamed in agony,
as though a spike had been driven through his heart. A miss.

The crowd surrounding the green was in such an uproar—half with joy, half in despair—that no one heard him.

The United States won its precious half point and the rights to the Ryder Cup for the next two years. United States 14½, Europe 13½.

Couples disappeared to a quieter spot with Roger Maltbie of NBC who asked about the ghosts of 1989.

"They're out of there," Couples replied. He grinned like a newborn, but even in his joy, he was respectful of the other players. "Hale obviously played a hell of a match. To be in that situation, I would not want it. As far as Bernard is concerned, they both hit great shots."

He hadn't had a chance to see the other team members, but said, "It's a great feeling. Two years ago was my first time. It was pretty nerve-wracking. It was a little better this time, and it's great to finally bring this thing back."

The stern look, the game face was gone, replaced by jubilation. He wasn't running around with a bottle of champagne like Payne Stewart, but for Couples, this smile was one of accomplishment and relief.

At the closing ceremony, Vice President Dan Quayle spoke, as did a variety of other dignitaries. The players on the U.S. team passed the Ryder Cup back and forth, up and down the row, so that each would be able to say he held it at least for a little while. They would all receive replicas, but this was their chance to actually hold the Ryder Cup itself. After all, this was what they had come to win.

Sitting at the very end of the row of U.S. players was Fred Couples. Because he had suffered such agony at the Belfry in 1989, and because he had gone 3–1–1, better than anyone else on the team that year, they let him hold the Ryder Cup for the rest of the ceremony. He was still smiling. He just couldn't help it.

In the pressroom Dave Stockton made remarks and then passed the microphone to Couples, saying he knew the event had been on Couples's mind for two years.

"Obviously this has been the highlight of my career," Couples said. "Winning a tournament is great. But playing with the 12 guys, and the captain, it's just great. . . ." He had to stop because he was starting to cry. Then he continued, shifting his focus to a teammate.

"It's a pressure-packed deal, and I give a lot of credit to Hale. His was the last match. From the third hole on, I knew it was going to be within a point, and he knew that from the first hole. There's more pressure here than you can even imagine. You get people screaming 'U.S.A.' and rooting for you, and it's a weird experience."

Irwin said it was one of the more remarkable and thrilling single events in his career.

Chris Cole remembered the post-match celebration that took place in a hospitality tent. "Many of the players went, including Fred. Woosie went in also. We had a replica of the Statue of Liberty right by the stage. Woosie got a beer and was laughing and climbed up on the Statue of Liberty and toasted the Americans. The people were hollering and screaming. It was rowdy fun."

"I've never been so tired," Paul Marchand said, referring to the end of the day after the 1991 Ryder Cup win. "I slept on the floor." Couples and Marchand were so drained, they did not get up until between 1 and 2 P.M. the next afternoon.

"Fred was pretty much a different guy after that," Marchand said. "He really found himself."

He was the new and improved Fred Couples. And now there was no stopping him, because he was no longer afraid to go to the top. Even if he didn't say it, he was pretty sure he belonged up there somewhere. He was about to see just how far he could go.

12

—⁓⁓—

Masters of the Lynx

*"Fred had the first offset, cavity-back set to win the
Masters. Everything prior to that was forged."*
—Dave Boone, formerly with Lynx

After the Ryder Cup, things changed for Fred Couples in several areas.
For one, his agent, Lynn Roach, began the process of finding a club contract suitable for his "star" client. Couples had been with Wilson, Ping,
and most recently Tommy Armour, but his newfound status as one of the
heroes of the Ryder Cup gave him extra leverage in the bidding wars for
a new contract.

While negotiations took place, Couples was playing at the Tour Championship in Pinehurst, where PGA of America Player of the Year honors
would be decided.

The PGA of America award was done on points. The PGA Tour's award
was a ballot by the players, and the results would not be revealed until the
following January at the Tournament of Champions.

The PGA of America awards points for winning the majors, winning
regular events, scoring average, and position on the money list. Going into
the Tour Championship, Couples could have edged out Corey Pavin for
that honor by capturing the $216,000 first-place check if Pavin finished
something like 25th, because that would have given Couples the money
title. He could also have tied Pavin if he had finished second on the
money list.

While the first scenario wasn't a realistic expectation, most people felt
Couples had enough game to have a chance, so much so that PGA of
America officials asked him to tape an acceptance message before the
tournament was finished. His facial expression and body language
revealed that he thought it was ridiculous, but he said nothing and com-
plied with their requests.

On Pinehurst No. 2, Couples's first two rounds of 72-73 were average, but on Saturday he fired a 66 and jumped over everyone in the field except Craig Stadler and Russ Cochran, who were three strokes ahead of him at 208.

On Sunday Couples couldn't find the magic, and technically, on points, would not surpass Pavin. However, there was something else important at stake that week. The Vardon Trophy, for low scoring average for the year. Since the award's inception in 1937, the Vardon Trophy has been won by all the modern greats of the game: Sam Snead, Byron Nelson, Ben Hogan, Arnold Palmer, Jack Nicklaus, Billy Casper, Lee Trevino, Tom Watson, and more.

Though Couples played poorly on Sunday, "I told myself just don't shoot 100 and lose the Vardon Trophy."

He didn't. With the lowest scoring average for the season, 69.59, he proved he was one of the most consistent performers and top competitors on the Tour."

After the Tour Championship, Steve Hershey decided to write about the upcoming vote for Tour Player of the Year. He asked a variety of players who they thought should win it.

Paul Azinger said that if Pavin won the money title and no one won more tournaments, then it rightfully belonged to Pavin. Davis Love III agreed. O'Meara said nobody dominated, but that money was a factor, although he personally didn't believe that money should be the dominating factor.

Hershey did his own tabulations and came up with places in the majors: Pavin was T22, T8, missed cut, and T32. Couples was T35, T3, T3, T27.

Then he added the Ryder Cup, with Pavin 1–2 but winning a crucial match on Sunday, and Couples, at 3–1–1, dominating. Hershey then cast a vote for Couples, although his didn't count.[1] Of course, all the players read Hershey, and so if they were looking for an excuse to vote against the stats, that might have caused enough conversation to do it. The winner's name, however, would still remain in the envelope until January.

When the official season concluded, the media turned to discussions of the year-end flurry of club switching. Players who have improved their market value by winning multiple tournaments or majors hope to fatten their bank balance by changing clubs. The odd thing was that club changes were sometimes the ruination of a perfectly good career.

Tim Simpson, a Ping devotee, had been sixth and eighth in money, then changed to Pro Gear and fell to 85th. He said that it was hard to turn down the money. "It was the biggest mistake I ever made," he said about the switch.[2]

As they say, some guys can play with a broomstick. Couples seemed to be one of them. He laughed and shrugged his shoulders when he was asked if the money was really big enough to cause a change that could end up hurting somebody's game. Couples is just one of those players who wouldn't ever use a club that he didn't like, that he didn't feel was right for his game.

However, Couples did not seem to have difficulty switching manufacturers of irons. He once said he'd been with several different equipment companies and that they had all been wonderful in the way they treated him. Now he was rumored to be changing to Lynx. He did say unequivocally, "I would never change my driver or my putter. For me that's the whole ball of wax."[3]

When it comes to golf clubs, never use never—if for no other reason than that no club is indestructible.

Dave Boone, who was with Lynx for about ten years, was the force behind signing Couples. Yet his memories went back to 1981, when the two of them met for the first time in a golf shop in Palm Desert. He was a Daiwa salesman calling on a customer at Desert Horizons Country Club.

"Fred walked into the shop. We started talking. He looked at the club I had and asked if he could hit it," Boone explained. "Now, the funny thing is, you know how in the desert people are dressed to the hilt. Well, he had on running shoes with the laces untied, shorts, and his shirt was hanging out. He had that long, Dutch Boy hairdo.

"When I watched him hit the ball, I was amazed at his flexibility. He had stocky legs, and he held the club differently than I'd ever seen a good player hold it. I wondered if, under the gun, could he keep it under control, if he had finesse around the greens, which, in fact he did. He had a lot of power."

Boone ran into Couples from time to time, and actually tried to get Daiwa interested in signing Couples, but it didn't materialize.

In 1986 Boone moved from Daiwa to Lynx. And some time after that he met up with Couples again at a pro-am.

During the round Couples looked at the Lynx product, and Boone asked if he might be interested in endorsing them. When Couples said he might be, Boone asked about his deal with Tommy Armour and found out it was a series of one-year contracts for three years. Boone said he'd like to talk to Couples in the last year of the contract.

According to Boone, Lynx was at a crossroads. They needed to do something special to stay competitive.

At that time TaylorMade was a huge force in the industry, having achieved great success with their metal-wood line, which was created by company founder Gary Adams. Callaway was still a relatively new company. A year earlier they had introduced the original Bertha at the formerly small, West Coast PGA Show and had not yet gone public.

Many companies relied heavily on promotions with Tour pros, but Lynx never had a history of utilizing tour professionals to endorse their clubs.

Boone laid out a budget to sign Fred and to properly leverage him and give validation and credibility to Lynx.

Although the new contract did not begin until 1992, Lynx wanted to waste no time, so they started working with Couples on a new club design late in 1991.

Whether it's the "arrow or the Indian" is always a topic for discussion. In Couples's case, his talent speaks volumes. If everyone hit the same driver, the same iron, the same wedge, his talent would still rise to the top. But a talented player, given a choice, selects equipment that improves his performance and his level of confidence.

The week after the Tour Championship, *Golfweek* reported the pending Lynx deal as a heavy rumor and estimated it at between $1 million and $1.2 million a year, which would have eclipsed two-time U.S. Open Champion Curtis Strange's annual deal with Maruman. No one would give exact figures or talk about the possible change, citing the Tommy Armour contract that ran through the end of 1991.

Rick Papreck, then vice president of sales for Tommy Armour, said if the Lynx deal numbers were correct it was crazy, but that's how it was in golf. And this was before Tiger Woods raised the endorsement-money bar to stratospheric levels.

Signing Couples was a big step for Lynx, with estimated annual sales of just over $16 million at a time, when Callaway's sales topped $132 million.

Boone explained some of the inside conversations.

"There was a fair amount of up-front work with Fred, explaining how we would use him. We had specific television and print ad campaigns featuring him. We explained there was a major commitment in industrial manufacturing and the company position to utilize a multimillion-dollar casting facility. We had additional personnel and financial commitment from the parent company. It gave Lynx credibility," Boone added.

What it gave Couples was a five-year deal.

Boone started working on the fun stuff: the design for a set of irons. "We asked him what was important to him. We watched him hit shots and noticed that, to him, ball flight was a key."

Working on the first set of irons was what Boone has called one of the greatest golf-equipment stories of all time.

"I think, from a personal point of view, how we developed a set, compared to how others did it, and how fast we did it, and when we delivered them and what the results were, was pretty amazing," Boone added.

Boone had shown Couples the entire clubmaking process: drawings, master-making, from that point through getting a club.

When it came time to make Couples's clubs, Boone would fly to Couples's location, wherever he was, and Couples would inspect them and make suggestions.

"There were little subtleties," Boone explained. "The transition of the offset. The profile shape. It took about a month and a half to get the masters the way he liked them. Then, once you get masters, there's not much you can do but complete them. You have to make the molds. Typically, this is an eight-week project. We did it in six weeks. The interesting thing about it is that we were using automated molds that took three times longer to make. In the normal process, it might take 12 weeks. We cut it in half," he noted.

Once the molds were done, it started to look like a movie script. A courier drove them from Valencia to Dayton, Nevada, where a crew was waiting to put molds on the wax-injection machine. Then the crew injected 50 sets and started them through the casting process. Meanwhile, Boone had spoken to Couples and they agreed that, if the process finished in time, Boone would meet up with him wherever he was.

"We thought that he could hit them, and then we could tweak them for the new year, 1992," Boone added.

After casting with a custom alloy, the clubs were cooled, broken out of the molds. Then they were heat treated, which allows lofts and lies to be adjusted without stressing the material. The clubheads were sent off to a waiting plane and flown to the Ontario, California, airport.

"I picked them up at 7 P.M.," Boone recalled. "Immediately I delivered the box to Lynx, which was in City of Industry. There was a full crew waiting to polish and grind them to weight. We had shafts and grips selected, precut and ready for assembly. They ground and polished the heads to Fred's exact specs—one and a half degrees upright, and a D 3.75 to D 4.0 swing weight."

After an all-nighter, the crew finished the following morning. The glue was still wet.

Couples was a last-minute addition to the field at the Johnnie Walker World Championship, so Boone climbed onto a plane and headed for Jamaica. By the time Boone arrived, it was Thursday evening and the first round was already completed.

"Friday morning I went to the locker room," Boone said. "They had several of the world's greatest players there: Seve Ballesteros. Greg Norman. Steve Elkington. Davis Love III.

"Davis saw me and said, 'Hey, he's got Fred's new clubs. Let me see them.' So he pulls out the 7-iron. And then he wanted to see the 5. Then Elkington and Norman pulled one out.

"Then Fred showed up and asked, 'Dave, where are my new clubs? Everybody's got one. Who's got the 7-iron? Joe, I've got to play these.'

The rest is history. Couples went on to win the tournament. He didn't mention the new clubs, but he did say he was proud of shooting a low round on Sunday and beating a field that included the world's best players at that time: Faldo, Langer, Norman, Woosnam, Stewart, Baker-Finch, and Ballesteros, to name but a few.

In the final round, Couples started birdie, par, par, eagle, and needed only six putts on his way to a front-nine 30. On the 10th, he birdied again, to go up by two. Bernhard Langer, Couples's closest competitor, bogeyed ten and gave Couples a three-shot cushion that he held through the finish, carding a 66, five under par, the lowest score in the field that day. No one else finished under par. The money, $525,000, wasn't bad either.

"I think I've learned to play with pressure a lot better recently," Couples said of the victory. "I have more confidence and am more in control, not spraying the ball all over the place."[4]

The new, confident Fred Couples had just had his coming-out party.

Those who like to know the inside stuff on equipment may be interested in Boone's comments on Couples's equipment preferences.

"What interested him was what the shaft had to do for a lower ball flight. There were a couple things visually, a straight leading edge, the first score line close to it. What was different in his swing versus others were things like how he hits the ball. He slaps at it, he always told me. His release through the ball is different, plus he hits it low on the clubface and toward the toe.

"The weight distribution, size, loft of the blade, the placement of score lines and center of gravity, those were important."

"The nice thing about Fred is he likes player-improvement golf clubs," Boone added. "It allowed us to move the center of gravity toward the center of the clubface. Most Tour players want it closer to the hosel. But Fred's clubs had good solid feel and were very forgiving."

Signing a Tour player with the skill of a Fred Couples who would hit an off-the-rack iron, a club that Mr. Average Golfer could also hit with success, was really a bonus.

Next they went to work on the Boom Boom driver.

"At the time, Fred had a persimmon MacGregor M45.[5] He had some problems with it because it kept coming apart. He spent as much time trying to keep it repaired as hitting it," Boone explained. "Fred and I had some discussion about metal woods, and he even told the press that he'd probably never hit a metal wood. The problem was he wasn't able to work the ball, hit right-to-left or left-to-right shots that he likes to hit.

"Typical metal woods, if you hit left, they go left. If you hit right, they go right. It is difficult to spin the ball with them. With center hits, the ball would shoot up. If you want to cut around a corner, like on a wood club, you're not able to replicate that shot. If we could do it, if we could develop one, he said he would give it consideration," Boone explained.

The Lynx facility could now cast thin-walled metal woods. They worked with Bob Bush at True Temper using the Iron Byron robot to identify shapes for metal woods to enable Couples to hit the kind of shots he wanted to hit.

"Finally, what was critical at the time was wall thickness. Mid- or oversize heads had to have .125 wall thickness in heat-treated 17/4 stainless," Boone said, getting technical. "Putting that together, we designed a shape and showed it to Fred. He thought it looked pretty good. It was similar to a traditional head."

Two months before the Tour Championship in 1992, Boone met with Couples to test prototypes. He was hitting high fliers with them, according to Boone. They went back to the drawing board.

Their idea was to name the driver Boom Boom to capitalize on Couples's nickname and allow the company to compete with Big Bertha.

Finally, they got one that worked.

"He hit shots on range with it, put it in the bag at the Tour Championship [in 1992] when he was five shots out of last place at the end of the second round, and shot back-to-back 66s, I think, and went from last to fifth. He used the whole set," Boone recalled.

"The Boom Boom woods were 9-degree and 10½-degree drivers, and 13- and 16-degree 5- and 7-woods. We had a strong ad campaign with a screaming golf ball, one of the most famous ads in golf. We got a fair amount of market share quickly with that. The only thing that prevented it from being more successful in wood sales was our ability to manufacture," Boone said.

Couples's driver at the time was a Boom Boom with a 43½-inch shaft, a graphite Unifiber PT plus shaft. It had a 9-degree loft. This was the end of 1992.

The Lynx irons were successful, and the Boom Boom metal woods were successful. According to Boone, competition now caused Lynx to expand to oversize irons, which were becoming the latest rage in the industry.

Just when it looked as if Lynx was turning the corner, there were problems at the parent company, Zurn. Their stock was taking a beating. They were basically an industrial energy and plumbing company, with a specialty in water purification. The situation at Lynx, with the investments the company had to make to manufacture the new products, was not helping.

Ron Drapeau, CFO at Zurn, was brought in to run Lynx during that time. He was a financial guy with a mission to fix it or sell it. He moved to southern California in April and started working on production controls in both their foundry and finishing operations.

Drapeau met Couples for the first time in the summer of 1993 at a sales meeting at Lake Tahoe.

"When Fred came into the room, he electrified it," Drapeau said. "I never saw John Kennedy in person, but Fred had the same kind of thing. A certain personal charm. It was unbelievable.

"Then a couple guys talked, and Fred got up and talked, and what struck me was how emotional he is, how passionate he is. You rarely see that side of him on television.

"He mentioned how much his game had improved, how he was greeted by a sales rep in every city, and how warm he felt to be connected with a company that had made such a big investment in him.

"He was going through difficult times with Deborah and said something like 'This last year has been the best year of my life,' and then he broke down," Drapeau went on. "There were probably 70 people in the room, and I think everybody had a tear in their eye. It was very emotional."

Drapeau came to feel that Couples believed strongly in the product. "He was interested in what we were doing and why it was not more successful, when, in his opinion, the product was as good or better [than the competitors']."

By 1994, according to Drapeau, the production snags had been ironed out.

"In order to take Lynx to a level-one company—we were viewed as level two, along with Daiwa, Cleveland, and some others in terms of irons, and nowhere with woods—we had decided we needed a new product with technology in it," Drapeau explained.

Their answer was the Black Cat, the design for which was drawn up with help from Couples and Boone.

"I made a trip to Fred's home in Dallas with clay models and reviewed with him the concept of stability weighting, weight of the club, the need for help for the average golfer, and got his input on design," Drapeau explained. That was when Couples became more involved in the actual design of the clubs. Before that he was what Drapeau viewed as only an endorser of them.

They tried several designs, including an undercut cavity, but as Boone noted, Callaway beat them to market. They worked with several outside toolmaking people before ending up with a patented way to create the club they wanted.

"If you are making oversize golf clubs, you are working with the same amount of metal but a thinner face. It has a drum effect, a different sound and feel, and that's how we developed the elastomer ring,"[6] Boone continued. "The effect of a thicker top line and an elastomer ring was to move the center of gravity further away from the axis of the shaft, which created oscillation. To reduce oscillation and stabilize the club, we created the flare shaft. It was new—our own technology. Unifiber came up with a sample shaft in three days. The flare shaft is now standard in the industry."

By 1994 the golf-equipment business was quite competitive. Callaway had become a dominant force. Cobra was vaulting into the sales charts, thanks to a deal between the company's founder, Tom Crow, and fellow Aussie, Greg Norman.

"Callaway and Cobra were taking market share, and we wanted to get into position to be a strong fifth or sixth, and eventually third or fourth. We were among the leaders. We knew we had design expertise. It was a matter of getting it made in 90 days, soup to nuts," Boone noted.

According to Boone, toolmakers wanted two years because of the complexity of the Black Cat design, which required 13 masters and 13 different elastomer rings, one for the back of each club.

"We had to do the metal part first and then make masters of the rings," Boone said. "The first ones turned out to be no good, but we used them for reference and gave them to computer cad-cam experts, who designed elastomers to fit the castings."

It used up a lot of precious time. The fluctuations in cavities from club to club, say 5-iron to 6-iron, were small, .003 to .005 inch, too small to be seen by the naked eye. Then the clubmakers had problems joining the shaft and clubhead. They worked with adhesive experts and invested in a thermal-setting robotic device that didn't work.

"When we introduced them at La Costa during a press outing, five heads came off," Boone remembered. They brought in some aerospace experts, hired a guy who glued helicopter rotors together, found an epoxy expert, and examined all processes. It was discovered that assembly had to be done in a controlled environment. Each shaft had to be perfectly clean, uncontaminated by materials. Nothing could be touched by hand. Once they did that, the adhesive problems were solved.

Clean rooms. Tolerances into the thousandths. New shafts. Adhesive experts who glue helicopter rotors. This helps to explain why high-tech golf clubs are not inexpensive.

Lynx ran another ad campaign for Black Cats, and within eight months had $42 million dollars in sales. It was a far cry from the company sales of $16 million of two or three years earlier.

"We introduced Black Cat in January of 1995, and through 1995 took Lynx market share from 3 percent to 8 percent. We increased distribution to about 3,500 green grass accounts and 1,500 off-course. That was a significant increase in outlets," Drapeau stated.

"Fred put the long irons in his bag, the 3-4-5 Black Cat, and he still had Parallax scoring clubs," Drapeau recalled. "Fred also was still playing Boom Boom metal woods. I think the second time his back went out at Doral and he was out for quite a period of time, he came back and was hitting Boom Boom sideways at the L.A. Open [1995] and went to Bertha because it was easier to hit."

Rather than slowing creativity and innovation, Drapeau encouraged his company to develop yet another club design. "We felt we had good success with the Black Cat irons and decided to bring out Black Cat woods in 1996. And they were an interesting story in that the reaction to them got the company profitable. Lynx turned a profit for the first six months of 1996."

But then a new company direction emerged with the retirement of George Schoefield, CEO of Zurn. Bob Womack took over the reins in 1996.

"Bob wanted to restructure Zurn," Drapeau explained. "He decided that the company should not be in the golf business any longer."

An investment banking firm, Bankers Trust, was hired to sell the golf business and brought three potential buyers, but none of those transactions were concluded.

Drapeau found an opportunity to sell the foundry and got board approval to conclude the deal. That made the Lynx property considerably more valuable, because Lynx no longer had to support the cost of the foundry operations and could purchase castings from outside suppliers, as others in the industry were doing.

"Over dinner one evening, as a guest of CoastCast, I met Joe Leach and Ed White. From there, things changed quickly. Joe Leach was a partner at Bear Stearns. Ed White was a partner in his own accounting firm. They were from L.A. and both members at Bel-Air," Drapeau recalled. The dinner was in May of 1996.

"By the time I got to work the next morning, Joe was on the phone and had interest in buying Lynx. He had a group of high-profile investors, some celebrities—either sports or entertainment—who were very interested and excited about golf. They began negotiating with the company, and it concluded in July of 1996.

"Then they went on a road trip in June to L.A., San Francisco, Toronto, and Montreal to raise money, and all the money was raised for equity. There was no debt. And they did have a number of high-profile individuals as founders. Rick Dees. Jim Lampley. John Elway. Patrick Roy. Some put up a substantial amount, some a little. It was a private offering, but they were able to raise $28 million dollars and were oversubscribed in the offering by 10 percent. It was done through [Paul] Little and Associates.

"Ed White became chairman of the company. The board had 20 people on it. Allen Paulsen [owner of the racehorse Cigar and head of the aircraft company Gulfstream] at that time was a member of the board. They had a large board, a lot of individuals who were successful in their own right. They now owned a golf company," Drapeau added.

Drapeau was unable to get a clear view of his role from Ed White. "We could not get that sorted out. He wanted to run it, so it didn't make sense for me to hang around and get paid for being asset manager. I resigned and decided to go forward." About a year later, Ron Drapeau became president of Odyssey Golf after it was purchased by Callaway.

Bruce Burroughs, who was an inventor and one of the founding investors, was named president of Lynx but left after a short time. Ed White resigned. They brought in Dave Schaefer from Cobra. He resigned in the summer of 1998 when financial difficulties at the company, which had gone through a series of leadership changes, mounted to a perilous point.

Still, Drapeau remembers his days at Lynx fondly. He enjoyed his relationship with Couples and remembers seeking his opinion on several different matters. He asked about signing Ernie Els and feels that Couples's association with the company was what brought Els on board. He believed that Michelle McGann was also influenced by Couples's involvement in Lynx. And when asked about Gil Morgan, Drapeau recalled, Couples's response was that Morgan was precisely the kind of person and player they needed. If they could get Morgan, they should.

And, to top it off, Couples continued to be extraordinarily friendly to Drapeau's family, even after Drapeau left Lynx.

"To give you an example, I played in the pro-am of his first Skins Game, which was a carryover, after I had left the company. Then, my kids had gone over with friends to watch the Bob Hope and stopped at an In and Out Burger in Palm Springs on the way home. Fred came in with Tawnya [his former fiancee] and Joe LaCava. The kids sat down inside someplace and Fred finished before they did. He came over and talked with the kids, went out of his way to say hello."

At U.S. Open week, not quite two years after the buyout, strong rumors circulated that the company was in jeopardy. It was clear that the revolving door of management changes plus the downward spiral in the overall equipment market had put Lynx in financial peril.

Part of the problem may have been a reflection of the golf industry at that time. Even Callaway's business was affected by the decline in the Asian markets. However, the overwhelming majority of Lynx sales were coming from the United States.

In July 1998, David Schaefer had resigned as president of the company. Gil Morgan severed his representation agreement because the company had made it clear it would not be able to pay him. Six members of the board of directors had resigned. Couples's percentage of Lynx, according to the 1997 annual report, was 5.4 percent. If sales had reached $40 million a year, he would have received a 2 percent royalty on sales above that number. Sales reached just over $32 million, and still the company was having trouble.

Bankruptcy was declared July 26, 1998. Within six weeks, TearDrop made an offer to buy the company for $8 million, a fraction of what Zurn was paid. They were outbid by Golfsmith. But at the Tour Championship, Couples was wearing an Armour cap and subsequently re-signed with Tommy Armour. According to reports in *Golfweek*, Armour was to pay Couples between $300,000 and $350,000 and Lynx would pay him $500,000.[7]

Now other parties entered the picture, the price escalated, and a bidding war broke out at the U.S. Bankruptcy Court in San Diego. There TearDrop upped its offer to $9 million. Golfsmith went to $9.4. TearDrop upped to $9.44. Golfsmith countered with $9.5. There were eleven bids until it ended in Golfsmith's favor at $10.25 million, $8.35 million in cash and the rest in agreement to cover Lynx's product warranties and returns. The TearDrop offer had been a combination of $.5 million cash, $3.5 million of preferred stock, and options to purchase 20,000 shares of common stock.

As of today, Couples is representing TearDrop and Tommy Armour equipment. Golfsmith has the Lynx brand and products. Gil Morgan has had great success on the senior circuit and is now with Wright Golf. Ernie Els is with TaylorMade. Dave Boone is advising DDB Needham on golf marketing. Ron Drapeau is president of Odyssey Golf. All in all, it was a classic case of the whole being greater than the sum of the parts. Or to use a baseball analogy, like the Florida Marlins the year after they won the World Series. Sometimes when key players are gone, it's hard to get to the top of the league.

13

You Da Man

*"The reason I never answer the phone is because
there might be someone on the other end."*
— Fred Couples

With all due respect to sportswriter Rick Reilly, by the end of 1992
you could paper a very large living room with press clippings about Fred
Couples.[1]

The announcement for PGA Tour Player of the Year came in January;
Couples was selected for the honor. He said it meant a lot to him because
the players had voted. But it was close, 69–68 over Corey Pavin. Only a
fool would gloat after a one-point victory. Obviously, the Tour players
weren't overwhelmingly convinced one way or the other. Sensibly, nobody
asked Couples or Pavin who got their vote.

Characteristically long on sincerity and short on words, his entire
acceptance speech was a paragraph:

"I really don't want to talk about myself. I want to talk about what the
PGA Tour means to me. It means hanging out with my buddies. I don't do
much else but sleep and eat, and because of all of my friends, they voted
me number one. Thanks a lot."

On the other hand, sometimes banquets get long, and players, at least,
appreciate brevity.

Couples looked and sounded as if he intended to make his position
near the top of the charts a permanent one. He was asked what kind of
player he'd like to be and he said he wanted to play well, have people recognize him, and to have respect from the guys on tour, "like I respect guys
like Tom Watson and Ray Floyd." He said he hoped to be playing when
he was 40 and hoped his game was still good enough to be competitive.
He wanted the public to see a good guy, even if he didn't tell jokes all day
long or smile and laugh a lot.

And to show that he really was paying attention, he cited recent achievements like Ryder Cup victories and his three single-event wins the previous year, and he mentioned the two team titles he'd won at the end of the 1990 season. He was seeing it as five or six "wins" in a 12- to 15-month period.

He ducked questions about being number one that were being asked by people who had not noticed him in previous years. He did say that before the Ryder Cup and the Johnnie Walker he didn't feel like he was one of the better players in the world, but that after his finishes at the end of 1991, he felt he could stay with them. He finally felt as if he belonged.

The smallest bit of confidence cannot be overlooked as the difference between creating great success and struggling with mediocrity. On a playing field where first place in the Vardon Trophy race is 69.59 and 50th place is 70.70, it is the little things that matter. The difference between one place and the next sounds small. It looks small. It reads small. But that's how difficult it is to compete at his level.

When the week ended, Couples was a shot out of a playoff. He had one last chance on Sunday; a 12-foot putt on the 18th green could have put him into extra holes with Steve Elkington and Brad Faxon. But it was not to be. He managed a 72-70-68-70, 280. His third-place finish was identical to the start of his 1991 season.

He looked forward to playing in the Bob Hope the next week. "I like the courses and I don't mind playing with the amateurs," he said about the tournament. He still had a residence at Mission Hills, so it would be a week at home. He headed for the desert with his spirits high.

At the Bob Hope, Couples played well. He shot 68-67-69-64-69 and missed a short putt on the 18th at Bermuda Dunes to finish one shot out of a five-way playoff that was eventually won by John Cook. In reality, his score was second best. But because of the playoff, he got sixth-place money, which he shared with David Peoples.

It was like finishing second twice without ever finishing second.

He took three weeks off, then played in Tucson, tying for 16th, skipped three weeks, then teed up at Torrey Pines in San Diego. The wet weather in California made the fairways and greens unusually lush at this beautiful, cliffside course.

Though most people expected Couples to contend, he stated that he was using San Diego to tune up for Riviera. Couples was below par each round, but the other scores were so low that his 67-69-71 was good for only 25th place.

In San Diego, Steve Pate shot a 67 to overtake the field and win the tournament for the second time. He also became the third member of the

1991 Ryder Cup team to find the victory circle. Mark Calcavecchia had scored in Phoenix. Mark O'Meara at Pebble Beach.

Then it was on to the L.A. Open. Riviera. Fred Couples. Soft pretzels. Long, hard hikes up the heartbreak hill cartpath behind the 18th. Barrancas. Eucalyptus. Ball-eating trees. Record rounds. Ashworth debuts. Fairways with Fred-ee fans. You Da Man.

By now Riviera Country Club held many memories for Fred Couples. But this year it would catapult him to even greater heights, silencing his remaining doubters.

What a difference a year made. Tom Weiskopf was in the pro-am, played and made the cut, and the comments from the previous season were not mentioned.

The Thursday lead belonged to Wayne Levi, with a hot 64. But even at that low number, five guys were one stroke back: Keith Clearwater, Buddy Gardner, Doug Tewell, Chris Tucker, and Tom Sieckmann. Couples meandered his way to a 68.

The second day was a photocopy in the weather department, but this time Davis Love III scored an even lower round, shooting a 63.

Couples had a 67 but was four strokes behind Love.

Saturday, Couples played superbly. For a time, it looked as though he might match his 62 from the 1990 tournament.

Davis Love III, Tom Sieckmann, and Sandy Lyle were in the last group. Playing one group in front were Couples, Bob Estes, and Rocco Mediate, who must have felt trapped in a Couples déjà vu experience.

Couples began the day with determination. He birdied the downhill par 5 and improved his standing from −7 to −8.

At the seventh, the 406-yard par 4, he drained a 12-footer to go to −9. At the eighth, he holed out a sand wedge from about 85 yards to eagle and go to −10. And at the ninth, he made a 12-footer to go to −11.

Rocco Mediate, who had witnessed Couples's victory in 1990, must have wanted to walk off the course and donate his clubs to Couples's banker.

Playing one group back, Love was on a birdie roll of his own. He made four more after the first and was at −17 and in charge.

There was no way Love could have missed Couples's birdie from seven feet at the 12th to go to −13 or the Couples friendly gallery. Yet Love still had a commanding four-stroke lead.

Couples was six under on his round to that point, but Love's lead looked insurmountable. There was no logical reason for what happened next. It was like golf's version of the whoopie cushion.

Davis Love III, in the middle of an astonishing round of golf, teed off at the 12th and hit it into the right rough. The green ahead was small, about 35 yards deep and about half that wide. The hole, at 413, wasn't a serious challenge for someone with his length. Love tried to fade a shot from the right rough to the green, and it got tangled up in a ball-eating tree and was flung into the barranca just short of the green. There was no penalty stroke, because being in the barranca was penalty enough.

Love barely advanced his third shot. His fourth got out but was short of the green. His breath had to be hot enough to scorch every blade of kikuyu grass underfoot. He chipped to 10 feet and compounded the error by two-putting. He fell from −17 to −14 and invited a group back into the tournament.

Couples was at −13, just one back, tied with Tom Sieckmann.

When Couples and caddy Joe LaCava checked the leader board, they must have thought they needed an eye exam. Players like Davis Love don't triple-bogey par-4 holes without water.

Couples gave one back at the 13th, playing almost as badly as Love had played the 12th. Drive to the service road, chip out to the fairway, bad pitch to the fringe, and two-putt for bogey.

Couples regrouped. He fired an average shot into the 14th, then made a spectacular 20-foot putt for birdie to go back to −13. He parred 15.

Couples stood on the tee at the 16th, a 160-yard, devilish par 3, and rifled a 7-iron to six inches. How his ball stayed out of the hole is a mystery. The gallery, always Fred-friendly in L.A., shocked the hillsides with enthusiastic cheers. A sneeze-in for birdie to go to −14 and a tie for the lead.

While Couples's gallery applauded their hero, Love, who could see what was happening at the hole ahead, bogeyed again. He had lost the seemingly unbeatable edge.

Couples missed a short putt at the 17th and two-putted for par on the 18th, posting a 64 that could have been a 62. His play hadn't been that far from his record performance.

Afterward, he admitted he had thought about the 62 when he was over the putt at the 17th. "I got a little ahead of myself thinking about what I did two years ago, and I just flinched at it. But I can't think about that, because it was probably my best round of the year."

Couples admitted that they were all laughing at the start of the Saturday round—Love was so far ahead, they thought there might not be any hope to catch him. That showed how competitive Fred Couples had become—enough to be seven shots back at the beginning of a round and give it everything he had in an effort to catch up. Seven under anywhere is a great score. And to shoot seven under when you need to is amazing.

Saturday had been exciting, but what would happen on Sunday when two handsome brutes took their long-hitting games to Riviera? Anything was possible. 62s. 82s. With these two, you never knew. And that's what made it interesting.

Though the weather turned a bit cloudy and cool, it was not unpleasant, at least until Couples teed off on the first hole. It was as though the wrong Fred Couples had returned. He hit his tee shot out-of-bounds and dropped two vital strokes on the 501-yard par-5 first hole. He was now at −12, a shot behind Davis Love. For Couples fans, the only saving grace was that Love didn't birdie it, which he should have been able to do given his length.

On the second, a 460-yard par 4, Couples got one of the two strokes back with a birdie to go to −13.

At the fourth, a beautifully bunkered, long par 3, Love made a 25-footer for birdie to take the lead for the second time in four holes. Couples could manage only a par.

The scores stayed that way until the 10th, where Love hit an awesome sand wedge to two feet and made birdie to go up by two strokes.

But Couples, now more mature, remembered the advice Tom Watson had given him the previous year: *Think about every shot on the last nine holes.* He made birdie on the 561-yard par-5 11th, just as he was supposed to do. He went to −14, now just one back because Love had parred.

At the 12th, both Couples and Love came away with pars. It's a wonder Love didn't leave a keg of dynamite in the barranca as he passed it.

Meanwhile, Rocco Mediate and Sandy Lyle had played their way into a tie with Couples. And there were so many cheering, chatting, clapping, boisterous, enthusiastic fans that it was suffocatingly close. The only open spaces the rest of the way would be the golf holes themselves. If a spot wasn't taken, it was out-of-bounds, roped off for TV, or ice plant.

The 13th, a 420-yard par 4, with out-of-bounds left, was the kind of hole that had ruined rounds for Couples in the past. It had Couples's full attention on the tee. After he hit his drive, cheers echoed in the canyons. The ball came to rest in the rough.

Love was not so lucky. He pulled his left and it hit a tree. His second skidded through the bunker and onto the fringe.

Couples, seizing the opportunity, hit a 135-yard approach to three feet and the gallery exploded. Sure birdie. Sure tie.

Up ahead at the par-3 14th, Sandy Lyle had missed the green right and dropped to −13.

Coming out of the coarse kikuyu grass, Love chipped 12 feet past the hole and did not make his par putt. Couples, with birdie, was now at −15, a precarious one-stroke advantage.

Couples and Love made their way through the sea of humanity and popped through the crowd at the 14th tee. There were people on every patch of grass except where the CBS tower stood.

They were noisy until Couples chose a 7-iron, wiped his grip, and took his stance. Then it was eerily quiet until the smack of the ball. They moaned. He'd missed the green right and long.

Love would be next to try the 180-yard shot. He also selected a 7-iron and hit exactly as he needed to, inside 12 feet and left of the hole.

From the fringe, Couples chipped to a foot and marked.

Love stalked it, finally took his stance, and to the delight and wonder of the thousands surrounding the hole, poured it in to even the contest once more at −15.

There had been five lead changes since number one.

The 15th, second in difficulty for the week, was a par for both.

They went to the 16th, the 168-yard par 3 with the necklace of deep bunkers surrounding it. Love hit first, a spectacular 7-iron to about six feet. The ground reverberated with cheers. Couples tried to do better but could manage only a shot 12 feet from the hole. Each had a makable putt. Love's was a realistic birdie, but the break shoved it left. Couples two-putted. They were still deadlocked.

Both players launched drives at 17, with Couples landing about 15 yards past Love. Still neither golfer could go for it in two.

Couples's third shot landed inside 12 feet, the magic distance of the day. It was an excellent shot—that is, until Davis Love hit his wedge from 76 yards and landed within six feet. Cheers were deafening as the two approached the green. The air was electric with anticipation. People crowded the perimeter of the green, believing it to be a sure birdie for Love.

Couples let his putt go and hoped, as the gallery began its crescendo. It missed by an inch.

Then it was Love's turn to make the putt that could win the tournament. He looked, he paced. The crowd strained to see. He stroked it, and it looked good, but it just missed the right edge. Now he knew playoff was a real possibility, except for the fact that he was playing against Fred Couples, who had been known to fire near hole-outs at the 18th at Riviera.

Love hit a superb tee shot up the hill and right into the middle of the 18th fairway. Couples followed with a long smash that ended up a little farther right than he would have liked, but also in the fairway.

The late Jim Murray once told a story that because he was a member at Riviera, people often asked him what he hit from the top of the hill on the 18th. He said first of all, they were silly enough to assume he could get to the top of the hill with his tee shot. But once on the hill, he quipped, "I usually tell them, 3-wood, 5-iron, a chip, and three putts."

Love had 182 yards to the hole. Selecting a 7-iron, he hit what he believed would be the shot, but it came up 20 to 25 feet short.

Couples had better luck with his, and landed about 15 feet away. He had a chance to finish it off there.

The gallery cheered and television made the most of the exciting finish with two such charming, long-hitting players. The players waved, acknowledging the thousands and the viewers at home, all of whom had gathered to see if one player could make birdie and secure the victory.

Love, who had twice the distance to the hole as Couples, lagged a long one up to within two feet. Instead of marking and waiting, he decided to continue, pressuring Couples to make par. Love also knew that Couples had a makable putt. Should it go in, Love's would be impossible with all the commotion. Love's nerves were so taut that he backed off the two-footer once. When it dropped, he walked toward the edge of the green, where he was greeted by his daughter.

Couples was the only man left on the course. His gallery, throngs of the Fred Faithful, waited eagerly, hoping their guy would win again on the 18th and bring another exciting Los Angeles Open to a close. But Couples also took two to get down. Playoff.

The 10th tee at Riviera is just a few paces below the 18th green, and so after the signing of scorecards, it was a short walk to the first playoff hole. Couples had drawn number one and would tee off first. They shook hands.

Both men placed their shots well on the 311-yard par 4. No one contending tries to drive it, because of the angular placement of the small, well-guarded green. Couples had 95 left and hit first. The ball-striking skill that he had needed to close out Love in regulation suddenly appeared, and his wedge landed just four feet from the pin. The crowd exploded with excited energy.

Love also used a sand wedge from 88 yards and split the distance, landing just two feet from the cup. The gallery that had been at 18 swarmed into the flat. Couples and Love tied the hole with birdies and went on to the second playoff hole, the par-3 14th.

Both used the same club, 6-irons, one more than in regulation. Couples still had the honor. He knew he had to improve on the shot he'd hit earlier, and he got his wish. Ten feet.

The pressure went back to Love. He took a practice swing, then stared at the hole with his squinty-eyed look and made a swing that he hoped would equal his previous attempt there. It was not to be. Love was 30 feet.

With the severe slope of the green, he might as well have been in a different county.

As many people as could squeeze around the par-3 were there to witness what might be the final shot. Sardines have more room.

As soon as Love struck the putt, he knew that it was too firm. It galloped eight feet past the hole. Couples, who watched his friend's agony, also knew this was the opening he needed. He studied. Paced. Kneeled down for the best read of the green. As Couples struck the ball and watched it curve ever closer to the small dark hole, the crowd began its crescendo, and when it dropped all present exploded in jubilation. Love congratulated Couples. It could easily have gone the other way.

Couples had sealed the victory, seemingly casually. But inside he was not casual. It had taken concentration and effort. He had played the Sunday round one shot higher than he needed to get the job done.

In the pressroom, Love was asked if Couples's fans were a problem or if the noisy larger crowd was a distraction.

"The noise didn't bother me," Love said. "It was the people who were verbally pulling against me that bothered me. Not that it made me play bad, but it was just upsetting that people would come to a golf tournament and pull against somebody. . . outwardly.

"I told Fred on about the third hole. He could have run there and tapped it in, but he said, 'I'll mark it,' and I knew what he was doing is letting Tom [Sieckmann] and me putt out before he putted so everybody wouldn't run off."

This was Couples's "home turf," even though he lived 3,000 miles away. But Love also enjoyed the walk up the 18th.

"That was the greatest thing ever," Love said. "You know Freddie's a good friend of mine, and I'm happy for him that people like him that much, and that he can play under that kind of pressure. I told my brother that this is a great warm-up for us if we're ever playing with Freddie in the Masters or the U.S. Open coming down the last stretch of holes. I'm gonna have to get used to it. . . . I can't be mad at Freddie because people like him."

Then Couples came to the interview chair. He was asked about the playoff, and he said he felt relaxed. "It's easier to be in a playoff than it is on 16, 17, or 18. You might be able to make a mistake [and stay in it], whereas on the 18th hole, if I make a mistake and bogey it, Davis wins. So it's a different pressure."

He was asked about the crowd pulling for him, and he had a wonderful answer. "You know, I remember playing at the Byron Nelson with Ben Crenshaw, and it is irritating to hear everybody scream 'Hook 'em, Horns,' and 'Get 'em, Texas,' while you're playing, but it's not like they're rooting against me. It's just that they have a guy from an area that they really root for."

Jaime Diaz, who was then writing for the *New York Times*, penned an interesting phrase that summarized the change Diaz had seen in Couples since the end of 1983: "Couples, who earlier in his career seemed mentally fragile in pressure situations, has come to be considered a steely competitor underneath his almost nonchalant exterior."[2]

That is what had escaped most people, except Raymond Floyd and perhaps Tom Watson, since Couples appeared on the professional scene. He is and has always been a "steely competitor." He may have needed some guidance, which he got from Floyd and Watson, and some confidence, which he got by proving to himself that he could beat players who were ranked number one or two or three in the world. He may have looked casual, but there is nothing casual about Couples's desire to win and the effort he expends to do it.

"When I won in 1990, it was a great relief, because I hadn't won in so long [two and a half years]. This time I felt I would play well," he said.[3] He added that in Davis Love, he could see himself a few years before. He felt Love would soon go on to win many more times. And, of course, he was right about that.

Make no mistake. At this point, Couples—at least in L.A.—was Da Man. He was also the fourth member of the 1991 Ryder Cup to find the victory circle in 1992, and the Tour season was only two months old.

Tom Weiskopf made the cut and finished 67-70-74-72, 283 and in a tie for 62nd, which wasn't bad for someone who would turn 50 and be eligible for the Senior Tour in November of that year.

Couples packed up for Florida and a few weeks of playing at home. He could have taken a rest, but he didn't.

The following week, playing at Doral, he commuted each day, a trip that without traffic took about an hour and 20 minutes. He had home cooking, his own bed, and no suitcases. A practice range at home that he could use when he felt like it. Polo season was in full swing, so Deborah divided time between her matches and his golf.

The flight east had done nothing to cool down his play. The weather was sunny with typical Doral winds, and Couples tied for the first-round lead with a 66. Steve Elkington, Loren Roberts, and Mike Smith posted the same number. Raymond Floyd was one of seven players a stroke back at 67.

The big story already that week was Raymond Floyd. His house had just burned to the ground. Floyd was traveling, but his family had been there. Flames burst forth at night, and though his wife Maria and his children were unhurt, it was both frightening and devastating. Television reports showed the red and orange conflagration in and around what had once been their home. Floyd looked tough, but inside he had to be feeling the kind of vulnerability anyone feels when confronted with a disaster of that magnitude.

Friday, Floyd took the lead on his own with a second 67. Couples and Keith Clearwater were one back.

Amazingly, Floyd shot an identical score on the third day. He was playing like a man possessed and his total was 201, a three-shot edge over Larry Nelson and Couples. The weather was holding.

On Sunday, Couples again had a chance for the victory. But he could not get a putt to drop on the 16th or 17th, although he had birdie opportunities. He hit an errant tee shot on the 18th, and what should have been a par at worst turned out to be a bogey, the only one he made in the tournament.

In an extremely emotional finish, Raymond Floyd, uncertain of Couples's score until he walked to the green on the final hole, won the Doral Ryder Open by two strokes at age 49. His most recent victories had been in 1986, when he had won the Disney tournament and the U.S. Open, becoming, at that time, the oldest winner of the event.[4]

Floyd said afterward that this particular victory meant a lot for many reasons. "My kids saw me win when they were very young. My little girl, Christina, is now 12. She was seven when I won the U.S. Open. I think she remembers that. My boys are old enough and they saw me win in 1986, but they didn't see me when I played in my prime, when I was winning two or three tournaments a year.

"They have had two big weeks here. . . . With a house fire and their dad winning a golf tournament, they have been through a lot."

Couples was disappointed with his finish, but he considered Floyd's victory remarkable. "There are probably a lot of things going through his mind. A lot of people asking him questions about his home. Can a guy that age win again?" Couples added that he thought Floyd played younger than his age. "He is not a 49-year-old man. He plays a heavy schedule. I would like to make the cut when I am 49 or 50, and this guy has won a tournament."

He added that he knew if he didn't play his best, Floyd could beat him.

Floyd became the fifth member of the 1991 Ryder Cup team to win in 1992. He was also one of the first to anoint Couples with new status, when, during the postvictory press conference, he said, "I knew starting out that Freddie is the best player in the world right now. He has been the past year and a half." This, from Raymond Floyd, was high praise indeed.

Couples had four rounds in the 60s. But it wasn't good enough to win that week. So, now it was on to the Honda Classic in Fort Lauderdale.

Floyd was in the field. Couples was commuting, this time with a shorter drive on the identical road.

Advance coverage in USA *Today* focused on Couples. His worst finish that year had been San Diego, which was 25th place. He'd won, had a second at Doral and third at La Costa, and had already pocketed $405,612. He'd shot in the 60s in 18 of 24 rounds he'd played. It was hard not to list him as a favorite.

At Westin Hills Country Club, the sunny weather from Doral was replaced by windy, chilly, and overcast conditions on Thursday. Raymond Floyd continued his good play and was in the lead with a 66, tied with Mike Donald and Keith Clearwater. Couples was three back.

On Friday, the weather was worse, with light rain and—for south Florida—cold temperatures. In the afternoon the skies cleared, but the wind was still gusty. Floyd hung on at −10, leading Corey Pavin and John Riegger by a shot. Couples improved and was three back. Even in the difficult weather, the cut was one under par.

On Saturday, Couples arrived with the good stuff. He came in with a stunning 65, which would have been the low round except that Mark Brooks shot a course-record 64. Couples, however, had the lead outright at 202, and Brooks was one back.

Sunday was finally warm and sunny. Deborah drove down for the final round, and as the writers went out to watch play develop, Larry Dorman asked her what she'd been feeding Fred at home to cause him to play so well.

"Low fat, high carbs," she answered with an enthusiastic smile.

As play turned to the back nine, Jaime Diaz (then of the *New York Times*) mentioned to a friend of Couples that with the way he was playing people were going to expect more detailed answers out of him. Not only that, they were going to expect him to start talking issues, answering questions like those ordinarily posed to Arnold Palmer, Jack Nicklaus, Tom Watson, and Raymond Floyd. They were going to expect him to become more statesmanlike. This from a guy who disliked answering the phone and was just now coming out of what was considered a near-terminal case of shyness.

It was another way of saying the spotlight would be on him. It was a gentlemanly warning that Couples was now fair game. Diaz, who had been following him since 1984, must have felt Couples needed a heads-up to be ready for what was sure to be a media onslaught.

After 12 holes, Couples was three ahead of the field, but at the end of regulation it was another playoff, forced when Corey Pavin made what may have been the shot of the year. Standing 136 yards from the pin on the 18th, he holed a miraculous 8-iron to tie for the lead.

"I was just watching it" Pavin said about the shot. "The thing just never left the pin. Then all of a sudden it just disappeared, and I heard a little *clunk*, and just held my breath for a second. It was just great! I thought either Mark or Freddie would birdie 18, I really did. So I was expecting a playoff."

Couples hit a pitching wedge from 118 yards on the 18th and nearly holed out his shot, which would have won the tournament outright. But as they say, golf is a game of inches.

The playoff began as the sun was sinking in the west. It started on the 10th, which they tied, and then continued to the 18th. After playing the 18th for the second time that day, Couples said he felt that "from 120 yards in Corey has the advantage. He definitely has the advantage on the greens."

Couples's putt was on the same line as Pavin's, but farther out. Pavin watched with great interest as Couples's ball stopped short of the hole.

Pavin said, "I saw Freddie's putt. His putt helped me quite a bit. He was about six or seven feet right of me, but it was close enough to give me a good idea. The winning putt broke about two inches outside the cup." It was a 15-footer.

Corey Pavin became the sixth member of the 1991 Ryder Cup team to win a tournament in 1992.

The same week, in the March 16 issue of *Sports Illustrated*, Rick Reilly took it to Couples. He was critical of Couples's off-course behavior, on the one hand, and then said that Couples was the envy of just about everyone in golf. Reilly always seemed to have a split personality where Couples was concerned: amazed at his talent, but critical of him for not doing more.

Reilly had quoted Couples as saying he didn't read and didn't know how, although he added that Couples was "only half-kidding."[5] But Couples was playing his own game. Why chat up a guy who wants to rake you over the coals half the time? Just let him think whatever he wants, because even if you tell him how you feel, he doesn't pay any attention. If Couples had been interested primarily in self-promotion, he would have said any headline is a good headline.

The Monday after the tournament, Couples responded privately to Jaime Diaz's warning to be prepared for questions on bigger issues, indicating he wasn't comfortable doing that. But he understood. He knew things were changing and he would have to be ready. If only he could have known how ready he would have to be.

However, there wasn't much time for introspection. Couples was about to launch an assault on Arnold Palmer's winter home at Bay Hill. His golf had been really good for nearly a year. But he was about to become ridiculously outstanding.

Bay Hill was weather hell. The week began with 30-mile-per-hour winds, and on Thursday there was intermittent rain—everything from a sprinkle to a downpour—and a 41-minute delay, shortly after noon. Then it cleared, but the wind returned.

Couples shot a smooth 67 and led Mark Brooks, John Huston, Gary McCord, Larry Nelson, and Fuzzy Zoeller by one shot. It looked pretty much like a typical week with a tightly-packed field.

By Friday, under sunny skies with some wind still present, Couples increased his lead and, with a 69, was three shots up on Huston, Nelson, and Mike Harwood, an Aussie.

Then, on Saturday came the golf explosion.

He eagled the fourth, then birdied the sixth from nine feet.

At the eighth, he sunk an eight-footer for birdie. On 11, a birdie from 20 feet. On 13 he hit it close, three feet, and made it. On 15, he sunk a 15-foot birdie from the back fringe. At 16, he just missed a long eagle but converted the birdie putt. At the par-3 17th, it was a four-footer for birdie.

Bay Hill is not an easy course. Couples had never done particularly well there, but on that Saturday he posted a nine-under-par 63. And he missed making birdie on the 12th, a par 5. Amazingly, it was a shot higher than the course record of 62, held by Greg Norman and Andy Bean.

Deborah was on the sidelines cheering on the good shots.

Fred compared it to the low-scoring fest at Riviera in 1990. The amazing thing was that he wasn't being pushed by the field. *Awesome* was an overused adjective that day.

James Achenbach, in his report for *Golfweek* shortly thereafter, asked interesting questions. The first one was "Why can't Couples come up with the kind of lively quotes uttered by his wife?" The second one was "How did Couples's wife Deborah manage to play in a polo match at noon Sunday in Palm Beach and still make it to Bay Hill by the time her husband was playing the ninth hole?"[6]

To answer the first question is to be more knowledgeable than the great and powerful Oz. The second one, however, is easy. Deborah arranged for Greg Norman's helicopter to pick her up. It could have been anyone's helicopter, but it happened to be Norman's, which would have made more sense if Norman had been at Bay Hill on the weekend. Presumably Fred's check at Bay Hill could easily pay for the fuel. Expensive? Sure. But Couples indulged his wife. He supported the polo she loved to play. Everything is relative. Compared to keeping a polo pony, a helicopter trip was nothing.

Sunday turned out to be a seesaw round for Fred Couples. He had birdied and bogeyed his way through 11 holes without improving his position.

Then, on 12, a par 5, he finally made a move, hit a 4-iron to the rough on the left, then put his next shot three feet, made birdie, and went to −18.

Gene Sauers, the closest man to Couples, had fallen to −10. After parring the 14th and 15th holes, Couples was eight shots up on him with three holes to play.

Only a lightning strike could have kept Couples from winning the tournament at that point. He could have crawled in, playing with one club. Any club. Even his putter would have done it. Saying he had a substantial lead is like saying Warren Buffett has money.

On the 16th, Couples was in the fairway and practiced a swing or two with the 3-iron that he'd selected for the 209-yard shot, then slashed away. Deborah started clapping her approval. The ball went right where it was supposed to go — the middle of the green. He made a 20-foot eagle lag and tapped in, making his 13th birdie on the par 5s out of 16 opportunities for the week.

At the 17th tee, Couples had a momentary swing lapse and found the bunker, but he shrugged it off with a recovery to three feet and saved par.

So, now nine shots ahead of his nearest competitor, Fred Couples stood on the 18th tee at the home course of his boyhood golf idol, knowing full well that there was nothing, save an act of God, that could keep him from winning. What a wonderful feeling that had to be. Imagine blasting a home run in Yankee Stadium the way Babe Ruth did. Taking a swing at Ali and having him duck.

No wonder Couples had been smiling most of the back nine.

"When I grow up, I want to be a professional golfer like Arnold Palmer," he had written more than 20 years earlier.

Well, maybe he wasn't just like Arnold, but winning the King's tournament—and not by a stroke, but by a landslide—had to be a very special day in the life of Frederick Steven Couples.

He walloped the drive, smiled as he walked down the fairway to where it landed and, now on autopilot, hit his second to eight feet. He wasn't just walking down the fairway after it. He was running. Then walking. Then running. It might be the fastest Couples has moved to anything but the sofa and the remote control at the start of baseball season.

Then he went into the winning stride. He waved, took off his visor, and drank in the applause. Two putts for par.

He wasn't a lock when the day started, but he probably knew he had a darn good chance. Would he have scored lower if Sauers or someone else in the field had pulled a Greg Norman and come in with a 64 or 65 or 66? Maybe. As it was, he didn't need to. And how would it have been later if he'd been able to muster another 63 or 64 or 65 or 66 and waxed the field by 14 or 15? Five players tied for third, and they were 12 shots back.[7]

He said afterward he was embarrassed about all the attention as it was. "The players are coming up to me, kidding me, asking me what my problems are and saying one of these days I'll have a good round,"[8] he said.

No wonder. He was averaging $88,000 per event played in 1992. He had won over $700,000, and it wasn't even April. He'd been 1–2–2–1 for his last four tournaments. He had the longest string of making cuts, 26. He had held the lead after nine of his last 14 rounds. He'd been over par only once since the beginning of the year.[9] Jaime Diaz, in one of his reports in the *New York Times*, said Couples was coming close to dominance, more than anybody had since Tom Watson in the 1980s. And the Sony ranking system had just put him at number one in the world.

Not a bad month.

Those who hadn't paid attention to Fred Couples the last six months had just had their wake-up call.

His press conference topics were beginning to change a little bit, as Diaz had suggested they might. His answers sounded more confident because, honestly, he had reason to be confident. "I won the Vardon last year, which was, besides the Ryder Cup and winning, probably the neatest thing I've done. So this year, I'm paying attention to that," he said, referring to his winning the 1991 scoring title.

He thought it was "neater" to have won Arnold Palmer's tournament than being number one in the Sony rankings. "It's just nice because when you see these people, they come up, and you've won their tournament, and they are legends," he said.

Despite the rankings, he didn't consider himself the best player in the world, although he said he might be the best player on tour for the last four weeks. "It sounds funny, but I'm trying to win another tournament and see if I can get nine. Two years ago, I thought I might never win another tournament, the way I played. And now I seem to be a little better, and so I'd like to win another tournament or two and see how good I can get," he explained.

Then came the question about winning a major. The best-player-not-to-have-won-a-major monkey that hopped from player to player to player until they got it off their back was now hovering over him, getting ready to pounce and grow to the size of a 400-pound gorilla. It was the question that in the early spring of 1992 still hounded Tom Kite.

Couples gave them the best answer he could at the time. He wanted to deflect the pressure a little. He said, "If I don't ever win a major, I hope that I won't ever worry about thinking that I wasn't that good a player."

He was asked about pressure and replied, "The stronger person you are, the better off you are, and I think that's why Tom Watson, Jack Nicklaus win so many, because they beat people before they tee off. . . . I don't see anyone winning two majors in a year, let alone think about winning all four of them."

Given a crystal ball to see into 1998, Couples might have been surprised.

He also mentioned the growing pressure of time, and people wanting him to do this and that, and how hard it was becoming to spend time with friends.

The last question was about the upcoming Masters in Augusta. "The whole thing for me there is putting, and I have never really putted that bad there, and I've never really putted great for four days. So if I can get the pace of the greens and get the ball in the right spots, and do all that kind of stuff, I should be all right. . . . If I continue to play like this, I don't see why I can't play just as good there as Bay Hill or Doral or anywhere else," he said.

The next Thursday at the Players Championship, he opened with his worst round since the pro-am in San Diego, a 73. His second round equaled his worst score since San Diego, a 71. He made the cut, which was exactly at even par. It looked as if Fred Couples had run out of steam. He'd played seven weeks in a row. He'd been on such a roll since the middle of February that it was hard to imagine that he would ever go a day in his life that would be over 68 or 69 or 70, tops. But there it was. He was human, after all.

That is, until Saturday, when, in sunny but cool weather, he teed off early and came in with a scorching 63. Again.

He broke his own course record of 64, which he shot in 1984. It was two years before Greg Norman's 63, which Norman posted in what was a year of record scoring and record good weather and record absence of wind.

In one stretch, on holes seven through ten, Couples went birdie-birdie-eagle-birdie.

But he teed off so early that most everyone, including a national television audience, missed it.

He birdied the second hole, making a 15-foot putt. At the fourth, he hit a wedge to three feet for a birdie. At seven, he converted another 12-to-15-footer. At eight, he hit a 5-iron 20 feet past the hole on the par 3 and made the downhill putt for two.

"On nine, laid it up, I think 102 yards, and made a pitching wedge for eagle," he explained, and that was when he began thinking about the record.

At ten, his 8-iron landed eight feet, and he birdied. On 12, the short par 4, his sand wedge was friendly with the pin, six or seven feet, and he drained it for another.

He even bogeyed the 15th. At the 16th, which had been kind to him on many occasions and would be again, he chipped to a foot and added another birdie to the scorecard. On the 18th, he hit 3-wood followed up with 9-iron to four feet.

"That was about as nervous as I've been in a while," he said," because I really wanted to make it to shoot 63. I kinda shook it in."

He admitted that he was thinking as he was playing about the computer terminals in the locker room and imagining all his friends saying "What the hell is going on? Now he's eight under. I knew there would be a few guys laughing about it."

Deborah had come up for the weekend, and they planned to have lunch and watch some basketball. He said there were so many people out at night, he liked to relax and stay at home.

Jaime Diaz noted that Couples's scoring average was 67.75 in his last four tournaments. More than two strokes lower than his Vardon Trophy average for the previous year.

"Fred is so hot, he's wearing asbestos shorts," Nick Faldo quipped.

On Sunday, Couples shot his worst round of the year to date, a 74. He finished in a tie for 13th.

Davis Love III, with the L.A. Open experience behind him and with his own near-hometown fans cheering boisterously, went on to shoot a final-round 67, winning his biggest tournament to date.

Couples packed for Houston and a last minute tune-up for the Masters with Dick Harmon and Paul Marchand.

"He was on the crest of a wave. If I recall correctly, his last 17 events, he was 186 under par and had made some unearthly amount of money," Marchand said later.

Harmon remembered that week in a different way:

"Fred loves children. I remember in 1992, when he played so well, the week before Augusta he went to the Final Four, and came back Saturday. Sunday it rained all day, so we could not practice. He spent most of the day watching TV on the couch or in the bedroom with the [Harmon's] kids, looking at their baseball cards. He gave them this great lecture. He asked the boys how school was going, and they said it wasn't so good. He told them that he didn't like it very much either, but he had to do it, so he just buckled down and made sure he did it. He told them it was something you have to put up with.

"And when you have Fred Couples sitting in the bedroom looking at your baseball cards, the kids are going to listen," Harmon explained. "People like him because he's soft. Not a macho man. He's humble. He does not have a lot of ego. What you see is what you get."

In a week, he would have a little more.

By Monday, Couples and Marchand were in Augusta.

14

The Masters

"Just shoot your badge number two more times and you'll win it."

—Jim Nantz said to Fred Couples on Friday evening. Couples's badge was number 70.

Fred Couples drove up Magnolia Lane number one in the world rankings. The question was how would he leave it.

To everyone watching from the outside, Couples was literally on top. Number one on the money list. Two victories and two seconds in the season to date.

Yet the press doubted his heart in the majors, and sports pages were ripe with stories of foreign domination. Larry Mize had been the last American player to don a green jacket, with a hole-out, playoff chip at the 11th that had ripped holes in Greg Norman's heart five seasons earlier. The question the press asked in 1992 was Can *any* American player win Bobby Jones's tournament?

As Couples took his clubs out of the trunk, he carried with him the hopes of a country.

While the writers secretly pined for a U.S. champion, they still doubted the homegrown players. Couples particularly. Most felt that he didn't have the spine, the guts, the determination, the intangibles to win any major. They remembered his missed opportunity at the 1990 PGA Championship. They said he couldn't complete a sentence, so how could he win this week. They looked at Augusta's greens. They looked at the rankings. They looked at the record books. They wondered which foreign player would win.

They remembered three weeks earlier, when Couples had been asked about Augusta in his post-victory press conference at Bay Hill. His low-key response: "I would just like to play good next week."

But because he'd had a spectacular first quarter, they were not going to let him off the hook. They expected him to win one soon. They were disappointed that, with his skill, he hadn't strolled leisurely, accidentally, noncommittally into a major title already. They were in his corner, but he wouldn't deliver. Frustration was rampant. They were ready to sew the buttons on the green jacket themselves and deliver it on a plate if he would just stay out of the woods and make the damned putts for them. They wanted him to be America's Hero at Augusta.

They kept trying to get him to say things like, "Yeah, I think I'm ready to win a major, and I'm pointing toward Augusta." But he was far too smart and too attuned to his own needs to play their game. He knew the golf gods were capricious, and that tempting them might ruin his chances. Unfortunately, most of his sensible Bay Hill comments were left out of the reporting. It didn't fit the image of the guy who was more consumed by his TV remote than his putter. It did fit the personality of someone who knows himself, isn't egocentric, and doesn't want to be thought of that way. Someone who understands the competition and plans accordingly. Someone who hasn't been able to do what he wants to do, but is trying not to put more pressure on himself.

When asked to name a favorite to win, Couples picked Tom Kite, who, for the first time since most could recall, was not even among the invitees. It wasn't a non-answer, but it was close to that.

He was playing with them. Again.

The weekend before the tournament, Couples and Blaine McCallister had gone to the NCAA Final Four in Minneapolis, where they worked as runners for CBS announcers Jim Nantz and Billy Packer.

"They had headsets and listened to commentary, and every once in a while they would run to the pressroom and bring us stats, or to the press food area and bring us popcorn and Coke," Nantz said. "We were on for a five-hour block, and when we do that we almost need somebody to go to the bathroom for us because we can't leave that set area. I think it was Mitch Albom of the *Detroit Free Press* who said he never would have believed his own eyes when he saw Fred Couples juggling two giant popcorns and two Cokes and bringing them to me and Billy Packer. It was interesting. One week before the Masters."

When Couples showed up on Monday, he was wearing an Indiana baseball cap that he got at the Final Four.

"Fred said he was overwhelmed at the number of people who came up to him at Augusta saying they'd seen him at the NCAA tournament. We had taken a few cutaway shots of Fred and Blaine sitting at the runner's table," Nantz explained. In Augusta, Nantz would be in the Butler Cabin, conducting interviews as he had done for CBS since 1989.

Couples had rented a house, and as the week wore on, it would fill up with his entourage: John and Dallene Bracken and Deborah.

"In 1990, '91, and '92, I stayed with Fred," Marchand explained. "In 1992, he was on top of the world. It was mind-boggling to me that he would be the first guy out in the morning, and he would go out and get the newspaper. Fred would read these articles about himself. Number-one player in the world on the Sony rankings. The expectation just kills you at Augusta, and anxiety is no good there. The anxiety had to be so great, knowing that he was playing the best he had ever played, and the number of times guys that had come in playing well early in the year and then not won. Knowing in his mind, 'If I'm ever going to win, this is probably the time.'"

"There was no doubt in my mind he was going to win that week," Nantz said solemnly. But even as the week wore on, he would not tell viewers ahead of time how he felt or how important the tournament was to Couples. He didn't want to curse it.

"Deborah showed up in the middle of the night on Tuesday," Marchand said. "I answered the door at three or four in the morning. She said, 'Don't wake Fred up. I'm not supposed to be here.' I thought, 'What the heck is going on here?' It was weird as far as that was going. He was handling it. I just really didn't want to know all of it, because things were going so well and Fred was playing so good. To me, it didn't seem to me like he was under a big strain, but you could tell things were not right."

Deborah, when asked about the full house, said, "Don't get me started."[1]

Marchand interpreted this as a defense mechanism: she was Fred's wife and yet there were all kinds of other people at the house.

The week progressed routinely. In the Par-3 Tournament, a seldom-discussed but much-enjoyed Wednesday tradition, players tried their hands at making miracle shots on the short course that no one ever sees during telecasts. The water-laden, beautifully scenic holes crisscross a ravine behind and below the row of "cottages" behind the number 10 tee. In fact, this "little Masters" is so popular and so much fun for the crowds that officials had to stop beer sales in concession stands near the layout to keep the crowd from becoming rowdy and "un–Augusta-like."

Since its inception, no one who has won the Par-3 has ever won the Masters in the same year. It's now considered a jinx to win it. Davis Love III, despite his own wonderful winter season, would carry the Par-3 albatross this year, with a five-under-par 22. Love said later that if he really believed in the jinx, he would have hit it in the water on the last hole.

On Wednesday night, the Golf Writers Association honored Fred as their 1991 Player of the Year. Couples did not attend, but Deborah did and made an acceptance speech for him.[2]

When Thursday dawned, it was none too soon for Couples. After all the preparation, "you get anxious to start the tournament," he said afterward.

Nature was smiling. The sun shone. Azaleas and dogwood bloomed. All was right with the world. It looked like there was a chance for U.S. players as veteran Lanny Wadkins brought home a 65 and the first-round lead on the strength of four birdies in a row, starting at the 11th, the beginning of treacherous Amen Corner.

Jeff Sluman, who at the time had only one U.S. title to his name, the 1988 PGA Championship, tied Wadkins with a birdie-birdie jump-start to his round.

Couples was four back, with a 69 that was remarkable because of a shot from the trees.

Joe LaCava remembered the former as one of the best shots he has ever seen Couples hit.

"On the fifth hole, he hit it left into the trees. There's really nowhere to go. You really need to chip out. But he kept looking up, and looking up and he saw an opening in the top of these tall pines about the size of one of those big truck tires. I could tell that's what he was looking at because it was the only space I could see. I backed off, thinking, 'I don't know what he's going to do.' He took an 8-iron and hit it right through this little opening, up on the green. It was just incredible for him to hit it through this little space and then cut it to the green."

Friday would prove to be important in a different way.

Unlike the early rounds of most other tournaments, the Masters repairs groups according to score at the end of each day. So even though Wadkins and Sluman were in the final group, others garnered the spotlight on day two.

The weather was still cooperating, and diminutive Ian Woosnam, the defending champion, was thinking about adding another green jacket to his wardrobe. He started with a resurrected putting stroke and a 20-foot birdie putt, which he said let him concentrate on the rest of his game. The only bogey on his card was at the ninth, when he pushed a drive into the trees behind an electrical box. Though he received a drop, he couldn't get to the green in two, causing him to drop a shot to par.

Australian Craig Parry, nicknamed Popeye for his large forearms, had his hands full trying to keep his driver under control. He'd even driven into a trash container on the par-5 15th and had to lay up. But rubbish or not, he managed to wedge it to 12 feet and sink his birdie. Parry's 15th club was Andy Prodger, one of Nick Faldo's former caddies.

Woosnam and Parry set the pace for the second round with a pair of 66s and came in tied at nine-under, 135.

It was looking pretty much like another foreign invasion, except that, playing late in the day, Fred Couples caught fire on the middle holes. Beginning with the 180-yard, par-3 sixth, a nearly impossible green to land and hold, Couples almost scored the first ace of his professional career.

"It flew in the hole and seemed to stick there for a second, then it popped out," he explained afterwards.[3] It was a seven-iron.

But Couples fought furiously, taking strokes from Augusta National at seven, eight, nine, and ten. At this rate, even Nick Price's course record of 63 appeared in jeopardy. When Couples birdied the 13th, it looked as if the wind was filling his sails and he was about to breeze through to a Sunday triumph.

Then he had an attack of ordinary mortalitis, that disease that lives in every golfer. At the 14th green, the one that Gary McCord once described as harder to hold than a shot to the hood of a car, Couples backed a wedge off the putting surface and followed it with an amateur mistake. He hit it fat, and finally ended his misery with a double, almost erasing the brilliant play on earlier holes. Just to give the press something to remember, he three-putted the 16th, but he limped in with no further injuries, carding a 67, which would turn out to be his low round for the tournament. Even though he'd endured the double and the three-putt, Couples was still just one stroke back.

Wadkins, meanwhile, was on his way to a fuming 75, and Sluman was not much better, carding a 74.

The dark horse became Raymond Floyd, who at age 49 wasn't certain he was ready to plunge headfirst into the Senior Tour. Floyd had last won the Masters 16 years earlier, when Couples was still in high school, and in 1990 he lost a green jacket playoff to Nick Faldo.

Floyd was a closer, and he had already beaten age and fire once that year. Like everyone else in the world, Floyd knew Jack Nicklaus won his Miracle Masters at age 46.

Sixty-three players made the cut at 145 (+1), the top 44 and ties and all players within 10 shots of the lead.

Couples went to the Butler Cabin on Friday for an interview with Jim Nantz. As Nantz explained, that situation is awkward for both of them because of their close friendship. "We don't really know how to look at each other," Nantz added. "I'm supposed to be an interviewer and he's supposed to be the subject, and we are really pals. I know what's in his mind, but I've got to go through the whole procedure of asking questions.

"On the way out, I said if he could shoot his badge number twice, he'd win it," Nantz recalled. Couples's badge number was 70. There was no need for them to say much more because both knew what the tournament meant. Both knew that if Couples won it, Nantz would conduct the green jacket ceremony, the ritual they had joked and kidded about—and yet rehearsed—15 years earlier at the University of Houston.

Couples spent the evening watching the Foreman fight, which would prove to be a good tune-up for a course that delivers one-two punches as well as any.

As though annoyed with herself for providing such weather perfection for two days, Mother Nature revealed her petulant side on Saturday, ushering in severe thunderstorms that suspended action for nearly two hours.

When play resumed, Woosnam and Parry, in the last group, came back to the fourth hole. Woosie made a double immediately. Parry followed suit. At the fifth Woosnam snap-hooked his drive, and his ball was completely unplayable in the woods to the left. He returned, grumbling, to the tee. Reportedly, he was so deep in the vegetation that leaves were still attached to his clothing as he replayed his drive.[4] A double on that hole seemed to finish him. He fell out of the lead and was never in serious contention again. Parry remained steady, the foreign threat.

After the delay, Raymond Floyd played like a man half his age but with the wisdom of many seasons at Augusta National. Paired with Couples, he stuck a shot close at the seventh, only to be outdone when Couples's shot flew into the cup and squirted out two feet away. Greenside robbery. At that point, they took the lead together. But it didn't last long because Couples hit driver, 2-iron at the 535-yard, par-5 eighth, chipped to five feet, and made birdie. His lead evaporated at the ninth when he spun his wedge off the green, a fatal mistake, and was lucky to make bogey. They were tied once again.

Play continued until 7:50 and was called for darkness. There were six players left on the course, including Couples, Floyd, and Parry. That left no real leader on Saturday night. It also meant no one had to attempt sleep on a lead going into Sunday.

That evening the Couples entourage ate dinner at Dick Harmon's rented house. One of the guests, sports psychologist Bob Rotella, asked

Couples what he would think about when he teed off the next morning. Couples replied, "I'm going to think about the best shot I ever hit on that hole and make a swing." Rotella told Couples that in that case he'd be OK.

Couples, Marchand, and caddie Joe LaCava all got up early the next morning to warm up and be ready for the completion of the third round. At 8:15 on Sunday morning, they returned to the course along with the other five players who had been stranded in darkness the previous evening. It was sunny and bright, as though the weather transgressions of the day before had been forgiven.

Couples managed to birdie the 15th with a 4-iron and two putts, and the 16th with a 7-iron to 15 feet. It was looking like luck was on his side. He called 17 a good par. The 18th, however, was a bit of an adventure.

"I remember he was in the trees on the right on 18, and hit a good shot out into the right bunker," Marchand said. "Then he hit a beautiful sand shot and made par. Joe LaCava told me later that was the tournament, that up and down at 18, Fred not feeling like he'd left one out there. It was a great par save."

Couples finished with a 69, one shot better than Nantz had suggested.

Then he met briefly with the press and, in true Couples style, declared that he was off to take a nap. If no one in the pressroom moaned aloud, it was a miracle.

Parry also carded a 69 and was a stroke ahead of Couples. Floyd had come in one shot behind Couples, with a third-round 71. Sluman was back, in a way, with a 71. Ian Baker-Finch, who had not fully cooled from his victory in the British Open, was one behind Floyd at 207.

After lunch, the warriors would begin the final battle. Who would have the courage to wear something that went with green or at least did not clash with it? Would the early-morning play and the layoff hurt the leaders? Which Fred Couples would tee off? The post–Ryder Cup, L.A. Open—and Bay Hill—winning, low-scoring, blazing-putting, miracle-shotmaking Fred Couples, or the three-putting, jaw-clenching, woods-seeking Fred Couples? The pressroom was aflutter with anticipation and pressure of deadlines. There was enough adrenaline everywhere to go to the moon and back. Eighteen holes. Four or so hours. Thousands of cups of coffee and soft drinks, and hundreds of green-wrapped sandwiches later, they'd know whose shoulders the green jacket would grace.

After "the nap," Couples, Marchand, and LaCava went back to the course for the final round.

"We got there early to avoid traffic," Marchand recalled, "and we were out there hitting balls, too early, and Fred was working up a sweat. He was loosened up, and there was still quite a bit of time before the tee-off. He asked, 'What are we doing here this early?'"

At that point, Couples put down some range balls and started trying to hit bad shots. The ropes for the range had been moved back so that the players were close to the spectators. Couples started hitting shanks. Then he hit a few fat shots. And he followed that up with a couple of really big sweeping hooks.

"You could hear the people reacting to the shots, not realizing that he was hitting them on purpose, and Fred was getting a kick out of that," Marchand explained about that incident. "That was his way of working off the tension of the moment."

It would be a day of surprises, starting with Mark Calcavecchia, who had proclaimed that his only goal on Sunday was not to finish last. Starting on the 13th, he fired off six consecutive birdies to finish with a record back-nine score of 29 and the low score of the day, a 65. If nothing else, he proved the course could be had.

But while Calc was lighting up the back side, the real drama was ready to unfold on the front.

Craig Parry, ahead by one when the final round began, widened his lead to three strokes when he birdied the second hole, a par 5, while Couples pull-hooked a drive left into the azaleas and was forced to take an unplayable that led to bogey. It looked like the wrong Fred Couples had shown up and that the foreigners would win another U.S. major.

"Sure enough," Marchand admitted, "the first two holes—and it didn't have anything particularly to do with nerves, he hit big hooks off the tee, and I thought, 'This is not good.'"

Then, just as unpredictably, Parry three-putted the next three holes while Couples birdied the third by landing a 9-iron a foot from the cup. Later Parry complained about noise in the gallery. But Couples would respond that it was just typical gallery noise and that people were dropping beverage cups in his backswing, too.[5] Couples cited noise on the tenth tee, just after he had taken the lead. As the saying goes, when the concentration goes, players can hear butterfly wings.

Raymond Floyd, playing in the group ahead, had a rough start, making bogey on the first, but he followed it up with three straight pars and then birdied the sixth and eighth to take the lead for the first time at −11. Floyd has always been a great front-runner.

Couples, now one stroke behind Floyd, was able to watch the cagey veteran as the day progressed.

Couples gave the fans a thrill at the seventh, saving par with a magnificent shot from the greenside bunker to three feet. Then he birdied the par-5 eighth, to go to −11, and the treacherous ninth, making it pay for the bogey on Saturday. As he left nine, Couples was −12, one up on Raymond Floyd.

Floyd was about to make things easier, committing an uncharacteristic error, a three-putt from 30 feet on the 10th. Couples's 10th hole wasn't pretty, but he managed a clutch one-putt par and got the job done.

They turned to Amen Corner, where tournaments have been won and lost with the bounce of the ball or the change in the wind. Couples had a two-shot lead, but the 11th through the 13th at Augusta National have ruined many a Masters for the greatest of players. This time the par-3 12th would be the turning point.

As Ken Venturi always explained it for television viewers, the wind swirls in the valley, and the flags seldom flutter on both 11 and 12 at the same time. Hogan had told him to wait to hit his tee shot on 12 until the flag at 11 dropped, because that meant the wind would soon blow toward the 12th. Even with that guidance, the green is a small and shallow target, fronted by water, backed by bunkers, and shrouded with stories of doom. A two-stroke lead could be wiped away with a puff of wind, causing a perfectly struck shot to plummet into Rae's Creek or to bury in a back bunker. It had happened time and time again.

Strategically, the 11th green is open to the 12th hole. Golfers finishing on 11 can see the action on 12, and vice versa. So as Couples parred the 11th and headed for the 12th tee, he watched Floyd make bogey on the 12th. Floyd's tee shot had missed the putting surface and landed in the back left bunker. His sand wedge came out eight feet short of the pin, and putting downhill, one of the best clutch putters in the world watched his attempt roll a foot by the hole. It was an error that would prove irreparable.

Couples was now up by three on the tee of one of the most nerve-racking holes in golf. The closet containing the green jackets opened just enough for him to peek inside. But Couples also knew Floyd had the two par 5s in front of him as well as more inner strength than half of the field combined. Anything could happen with six holes to play. Curtis Strange had lost it on the 13th, trying to cross Rae's Creek.

"On the 12th hole, that was as nervous as I've ever been. I felt if I could get past 12, okay," Couples said afterward, "I knew I was going to win." He stretched and twitched—as is his habit—talked it over with caddy Joe LaCava, and settled on an 8-iron to the 155-yard, beautifully adorned torture chamber. A ball in the water would automatically cost two shots. He knew he couldn't afford that with Floyd still on the course. He rubbed the grip of the club with a towel to make sure there was no moisture. He needed perfect contact between hand and club. Perfect concentration. A perfect shot.

Later he would describe the swing as a battle between what he intended to do and what he wanted to do. Although he said he never looked at the flag, and that his intent was to hit someplace in the middle of the green, on that particular day he admitted that there "was something in my body that swings to where the pin is, and I blocked the shot to the right.'"[6]

The ball hit the bank and started to trickle back down the slope. The crowd moaned. The ball slowed, and then for perhaps the first time in Masters history,[7] it stopped two feet from the waterline, perched there like a rogue dandelion that had suddenly sprouted in the midst of a perfect Augusta National fairway. There was a hush, as everyone, Couples included, watched and prayed that gravity would not drag it down. That the wind would not gust and knock it into the water. That a bird would not swoop down for a look at the lie and cause it to sink into oblivion.

It was like a replay of Floyd's shot from Friday—except that this one stayed up.

"I don't know how it stayed dry," Couples said afterward. "It was probably the biggest break of my life. I had a perfect lie on the bank, so it was an easy shot."

He pitched to two feet, then turned and looked down into the creek, reached in with his wedge, and hauled out a ball that was not so lucky. He balanced it for a moment on the blade of the sand wedge, as if to ask, Why me? Then, almost casually, he rolled it back into the depths of oblivion, turned his back on Rae's Creek, made par, and headed for the homestretch.

"There was a reason that ball stayed up," Nantz explained. "Because the weather halted play on Saturday, they had to finish the third round on Sunday. Because of that, they didn't have a chance to mow the bank in front of the green on Sunday between the rounds. It was muddy after the rain, and the mowers could have gotten stuck and made a mess in front of the green, and they elected not to cut it."

Others say otherwise, and whether it was an act of God or an act of maintenance or an act of vanity or some combination of the three, the ball stayed dry when no golf ball should have.

The rest should have been easy, but of course, it wasn't. Couples's tee shot at 13 landed behind a tree and forced him to lay up short of Rae's Creek, which snakes in front of the green. If nothing else, it took the decision away from him, and he had to be satisfied with par. Floyd had also made par at 13 instead of the anticipated birdie.

However, Floyd wasn't about to let him off without a fight. To prove it, he chipped in for birdie at the 14th to pull one stroke closer, a less-than-gentle reminder that the day wasn't over.

Couples followed with an answer of his own. He hit driver, 9-iron to eight feet, and made a birdie himself.

The 15th was another test. Floyd lipped out an eagle putt but made birdie and picked up a much-needed shot. He was still two back of Couples with three to go.

It looked as if Floyd's wish had been granted when Couples's drive at 15 landed behind some pines, making him choose between a lay-up shot or a flaming hook around the trees to the green. This time Couples chose the latter and hit one of his famous creative trouble shots, a power hook that landed safely and rolled over the left edge of the green. All that effort and chance resulted in par instead of the birdie he wanted. Still, he was ahead, and later he would say that having Raymond Floyd, a trusted friend and confidant, in front of him was actually a calming influence.[8] He recalled the advice that Floyd had offered, which was to make birdies on the par 5s and be patient, and that at the end of the day it was making each shot count and not giving up that won tournaments.

There were still three difficult holes to complete. The 16th, always tough, succumbed with a par. Couples ran a putt five feet by on the 17th and was faced with a tough come-back for his four.

"You have no idea how tough that putt is," Floyd remarked[9] when Couples's ball found the bottom of the cup on 17. Floyd had three-putted that same green to fall into a tie with Faldo in 1990.

On the 18th, when it should have been so easy, Couples made it look hard. With two shots to spare, his drive went into the front left-hand fairway bunker. Except for the trees, it was the worst possible location. Though bogey would still win, the rule was that anything was possible at any time at Augusta National.

"I remember that really well," LaCava explained. "Normally I'm pretty positive and confident in Fred's ability. When he hit it in the bunker, for some reason bad thoughts came to mind instead of good thoughts. Normally, I get good thoughts. But there, I'm thinking 'Okay, if we hit in the lip and it comes back in a footprint, who knows what we might make if we can't get it out of there. Three putt, end up tying Raymond.'

"I don't know what made me think of all those bad things, and just as I was thinking those things Fred said, 'Bunker?'

"And I said, 'Yes.'

"And he said, 'No problem.'

"And I said, to myself, 'Wow.' It's not like he was trying to calm me down, it was almost like he knew what I was thinking, but he was so confident it was like, 'No problem.' Neat exchange."

So America's Hero hit a 7-iron up over the outstretched lip of the cavernous bunker, safely to the putting surface, 30 feet from the pin. Both of them knew a four-putt was out of the question. A three-putt would still win it by a stroke.

"The walk up to the green," LaCava continued, "he was in the bunker, and I had to rake it, so I got to watch it from behind. He got to go by himself, and it was his deal. So it was great for me to watch everything happen that way.

"He was very excited," LaCava added. "We've had a few special moments like that. Obviously that's number one, his favorite tournament and the one he wants to win the most."

"Walking up the 18th, I was just staring at the people," Couples recalled. "It was just a great feeling. I was very tired, and I was telling my caddie 'I can't believe how tired I am.' It's over, and I was thinking that I just got through 71 holes, and now I have hit it in the bunker, and I got through this last hole and it's over and we won." Fred-speak at its best.

Floyd, who had been waiting in the Jones cabin to see if there was a playoff, rushed to the 18th green, past waiting photographers, ignoring, for the moment, the questions of reporters. He wanted to be on hand to congratulate Couples for being victorious in the tournament that all the players had known Couples could win.

Couples finished his "routine" par, then gave Deborah a brief hug. But the most emotional TV shot came when he and Ray Floyd embraced behind the 18th green.

"Fred has a game that can win this tournament as much as Jack Nicklaus and Arnold Palmer. His game is perfect for this place," Floyd remarked. "If I didn't win, I wanted him to win it. . . . I'm not disappointed at all. There's no disappointment. This is one more plateau. He will become known as a great player."[10]

Deborah, whose comment earlier in the week registered something less than pleasure, was also overcome with emotion. "That moment will stand still," she said to reporters while waiting for her husband to take the interview stand inside the press room. "It's something I'm going to remember for the rest of my life. It was overwhelming."[11]

Meanwhile, Nantz was in the Butler Cabin waiting. It was a day predicted by Nantz and others at the University of Houston after meeting the kid from Seattle with no national amateur ranking but the most fluid swing anybody had every seen.

"We had practiced it a hundred times, 12 . . . 15 years earlier," Nantz explained. "The last question I asked him, I wanted to bring in the names of all the guys at Houston. I knew I was going to personalize it. I said, 'I can't help but think back to our days at the University of Houston and Taub Hall and guys like John Horne, Blaine McCallister, Paul Marchand . . . walking with you every step of the way. And Fred's looking over and he said, 'Oh, no. Here we go.' And I said, 'Even I said someday you're gonna wear the green jacket.'

"It demanded a response, that statement," Nantz added. "We used to always talk about it. Fred wouldn't allow himself to get emotional, and he wouldn't go there. And that's why he wouldn't look at me. He just said, 'I always figured it was the best tournament I had a chance to win, and it was a course I always loved.' He didn't really put any true emotion into it, because he was dodging it, fighting his instincts that were telling him to cry.

"I said, 'Mr. Stephens, time for the green jacket.'

"Mr. Stephens said, 'Ian, as defending champion, would you please . . .'"

Ian Woosnam slipped the jacket onto Couples's waiting shoulders, passing the torch to the new Masters champion.

"Then," Nantz continued, "Ian said, 'Sure. Good job, Freddie. And you still owe me $20 from earlier in the week.'

"They'd played a practice round earlier in the week. And Ian put the jacket on Fred, and the jacket sleeves were short on him—about four inches or so—and I said, 'It's a perfect fit.' And Fred started to say 'Not really.' And I just kept on talking, because my voice was quivering as it was.

"I just said, 'Fred Couples, the Masters champion. For all of us, good night.' That's what I meant by perfect fit."

On camera, both of them fought to hold back tears. "He couldn't look at me," Nantz said, remembering the moment as if it happened yesterday. "I knew he would lose it. Somehow we got through the interview.

"Then I stood up, and I thought we were still on camera. Frank [Chirkinian] rolled credits, which he should have done, and the two of us [Fred and Jim] just stood there and hugged and bawled for a minute, and we weren't worrying about it or thinking about it, and for all I knew the whole world could have been watching Fred let out his emotions. And I thought later it was almost too bad that they didn't see that, because he's always carried the reputation of a guy who can take it or leave it, and I know there's a flame burning inside his heart. He wants to be a great player much more than he ever lets on, and it's too bad. It would have been a wonderful opportunity for people to see how much it means to him. How much he wants it."

Nantz still remembers it as the most emotional moment he's ever had in his professional career.

Sometimes, as Judy Garland sang, the dreams that you dare to dream really do come true.

Couples's was a size 42, in green.[12]

Couples came into the post-round press conference carrying his jacket, not wearing it. This, the reporters noted, was different. But it gave him a chance to put it on one more time for the cameras and photographers, a routine that brought a boyish grin to his usually serious face.

Primarily because his main competitor for the green jacket had been his mentor, Raymond Floyd, Couples explained some of what he had learned from his friend.

Later on, he would also credit advice from Tom Watson.

"I was excited for him," Couples said about going up against Floyd. "I wanted to beat him, but I thought it was pretty neat that here is a guy I played with yesterday, and he had a great day, and he is coming on Sunday. As much as he has helped me, I wanted to end up beating him if I can. He is a great person and he has been there. He is 49 years old—almost 50—and he knows how hard I am trying, and he has helped me a lot.

"He told me when you get a lead, get more of a lead. He is a real good front-runner, and there are guys that aren't. I think that I am getting better, and I don't think just because someone tells you to do it, that you are going to get a lead and win. You need to understand how good a putter he is when he hits the ball, we all know how good he putts, and that is why he is always there when he is in the lead. Raymond will be the first to tell you, you don't need to knock it in the hole on a par 5 for an eagle. You can knock it on and two-putt and pick up ground, and I learned that from him."

Later that evening, Fred and his friends celebrated his very personal victory after he returned from the members-only dinner.

"Paul Marchand had taped the final round," Jim Nantz explained. "It was cued up, and we watched it, and took turns wearing the green jacket. I really think Deborah must have had the coat on second, or else I did. We all did. Even my dad. We sat in the den and watched the opening and shuttled through, and it was a late night, a great night that you didn't want to end. It was surreal. Almost like a college experience again among friends and family."

Joe LaCava was also there, as was Phil Mickelson's caddie, Jim McKay.

Paul Marchand recalled the impact it had on him. "I told Jim Nantz next to getting married and having a child, the most significant thing for me was Fred winning Augusta. It was unbelievable to be there and witness it."

"Fred had made a powerful statement to the world, and we all shared it," Nantz said.

The Masters 1992
Fred Couples—detail of the final round

Hole 1: Tea Olive   400 yds.   par 4
Driver, 9-iron, two putts from 20 feet.

Hole 2: Pink Dogwood   555 yds.   par 5
Driver to azaleas. Unplayable. 6-iron, 9-iron to
30 feet, two putts for bogey.

Hole 3: Flowering Peach   360 yds.   par 4
9-iron second shot to a foot for birdie.

Hole 4: Flowering Crabapple   205 yds.   par 3
4-iron to 15 feet, two putts for par.

Hole 5: Magnolia   435 yds.   par 4
Driver, 6-iron to left bunker. Sand wedge, two
putts from 20 feet for bogey.

Hole 6: Juniper   180 yds.   par 3
7-iron to 30 feet, two putts for par.

Hole 7: Pampas   360 yds.   par 4
3-wood to trees. 5-iron to greenside bunker.
Sand wedge to 3 feet, one putt to save par.

Hole 8: Yellow Jasmine   535 yds.   par 5
Driver, 2-iron, two putts from 18 feet for birdie.

Hole 9: Carolina Cherry   435 yds.   par 4
Driver, 7-iron, one putt from 20 feet for birdie.

The Masters 1992 *(continued)*
Fred Couples—detail of the final round

Front nine: 35, one under par

Hole 10: Camellia   485 yds.   par 4
3-wood, 7-iron to greenside bunker. Wedge to
10 feet, one putt for sand save and par.

Hole 11: White Dogwood   455 yds.   par 4
Driver, 8-iron to 20 feet and two putts for par.

Hole 12: Golden Bell   155 yds.   par 3
8-iron to front bank. Chip to two feet and one
putt for par.

Hole 13: Azalea   465 yds.   par 5
3-wood to trees. 7-iron lay-up, wedge to 20 feet
and two putts for par.

Hole 14: Chinese Fir   405 yds.   par 4
Driver, 9-iron to eight feet. One putt for
birdie.

Hole 15: Fire Thorn   500 yds.   par 5
Driver behind a tree. Rolling hook 7-iron
around trouble, wedge, and two putts from 15
feet.

Hole 16: Red Bud   170 yds.   par 3
7-iron and two putts from 20 feet for par.

Hole 17: Nandina   400 yds.   par 4
Driver, wedge, two putts from 60 feet for par.

Hole 18: Holly   405 yds.   par 4
Driver to fairway bunker. 7-iron to 30 feet and
two putts for championship.

Back nine: 35
The week: 69-67-69-70, 275

For much of the previous year, Couples had publicly mentioned help he had received from Tom Watson during a visit to Kansas City. Between then and the Masters, Couples won six times, was second twice, and was third three times. In 25 tournaments around the world, he was in the top six 20 times. He was hands down the hero of the Ryder Cup in 1991. Whatever Tom Watson told him, whatever words of advice and encouragement he received from veteran Raymond Floyd, Couples was able to finally turn his enormous potential into reality. The reality of his dreams.

15

Life at the Top

> *"It was the best of times, it was the worst of times."*
> —Charles Dickens, A *Tale of Two Cities*

By the time Couples won at Bay Hill, there wasn't a person on the planet—except perhaps his fellow golfers—who didn't want to be near Fred Couples. Who didn't want his autograph. Who didn't want to shake his hand, buy him dinner, or offer him a deal. He was the number one attraction, number one in the world. When he won the Masters, he was better than that, whatever better than number one in the world was.

And yet, when Deborah arrived in Augusta, she said she wasn't supposed to be there. She was going to skip Augusta? The tournament that meant more to her husband than any other had since she had known him? When he was playing better than he ever had in his life?

By the spring of 1992, the real question was, how could Couples play the kind of golf he was playing in this kind of environment? No one, least of all Couples himself, has ever come up with an explanation. He just did it. That alone should answer any questions on mental toughness.

After the Masters, the dynamics of the Couples household were subjected to the external pressures of the spotlight. The hot glow of success brought demands for interviews, and requests for appearances. Couples was going to need more than the asbestos shorts Nick Faldo had mentioned. He was going to need an asbestos mind and soul.

Would he burn up, burn out? With the newfound fame, Couples's life could take any number of twists and turns.

Deborah had sounded a warning of her own before the Masters: "If all the attention gets out of hand, Fred could back off from being as good as he can be. To Fred nothing is worth the sacrifice of losing your peace of mind. Maybe that's why he didn't accept the responsibility for his talent sooner. He really wasn't ready."[1]

It was a curious way of putting it. Everyone who knew Couples felt it was the result of a lack of confidence, that he didn't know how good he could be.

Meantime, articles spewed forth like an erupting geyser.

Before April was over, Jaime Diaz wrote two Couples features for the *New York Times*. The first summarized his successes to date and included quotes from fellow pros like Corey Pavin, who said, "Fred is just starting to get great now." Mark McCumber added that Couples was "labeled as not being determined, but he's the most mislabeled person in sports. He couldn't have done what he's done if he wasn't determined."[2]

Paul Marchand remembered how the attention affected Couples. "After the Masters, one of the damnedest things happened. Fred played Greensboro, and he had a detail of state troopers with him. He had gone from being kind of a cult figure where people who knew him loved him, and now he was in the mainstream as a cult figure. It was apparently pretty overwhelming."

The next week at Houston, Couples stayed with Marchand, which he would not ordinarily do because it's too far from the golf course.

"He would just come home at night and just lie on the rug and look at TV," Marchand recalled. "I literally felt like maybe the guy needed to see a doctor. He was so tapped out. He'd been on this stretch since about 1991, capped off by this Masters win. The world was looking at him. It makes you really appreciate what some of these guys go through. It takes your energy. You need to know how to handle it in order to keep playing well.

"Fred's such a nice person, most of the time he's going to try to do what other people ask him to do," Marchand continued. "I really was concerned that, like anybody who gets to that top level, you've got a whole plateful of things that have nothing to do with golf."

Fred Couples from June 1991 to April 1992

U.S. Open	T3
Federal Express St. Jude	Won
Centel Western Open	3
British Open	3
Dutch Open	T6
Scandinavian Masters	T6
PGA Championship	T3
B.C. Open	Won
Toyota World Match Play	T5
Tour Championship	T16

Fred Couples from June 1991 to April 1992 *(continued)*

Visa Taiheyo Club Masters	T5
Sun City	T5
Johnnie Walker	Won
T of C	T3
Bob Hope Chrysler Classic	T6
Northern Telcom	T16
San Diego	T25
L.A. Open	Won
Doral Ryder Open	T2
Honda Classic	2
Nestlé Invitational	Won
The Masters	Won

Offers that come to a player who has won the Masters are bountiful. This was particularly so that year, when Couples was the first American player since 1987 to win the coveted green jacket. But nobody in the Couples camp had experience dealing with situations like this. As good an agent as Lynn Roach is, Couples was still a newcomer to the majors mill.

But Couples's stay at Paul Marchand's also pointed up some other difficulties. "That's also when it started being apparent that he and Deborah were having a problem," Marchand explained.

So, after the Masters, Couples's game was ready for superstardom, but his personal life wasn't. In addition, the more private the person is, the more difficult the limelight.

Wayne Grady, who was vaulted into autograph status when he won the PGA Championship in 1990, said he was so taken aback by the situation that he finally consulted Jack Nicklaus who told him that it was just something he had to do because he was a PGA champion. When Nicklaus speaks, players listen.

Arnold Palmer, it seems, has always thoroughly enjoyed being Arnold Palmer. And that's another reason they call him the King. Never has one person so gladly signed so many autographs and done so many interviews and given so many speeches as Palmer. But Palmer is an extrovert.

Fred Couples's personality is the opposite. He was the one who was so shy he didn't even date.

At the Byron Nelson tournament in May, Couples admitted he was struggling with the magnified attention, that the early season had worn him out mentally more than physically. He mentioned his poor finishes—

for him—in Greensboro and at Houston. He had played 11 events in 13 weeks.

"I need some rest," he said. "But after three weeks off, I should be ready for the U.S. Open."[3]

Rick Reilly wrote about Couples for the third time in as many months, saying, "Couples is like chocolate: Nearly everybody likes him and most people like him a lot."[4]

Couples missed the cut at the Byron Nelson.

He returned to defend in Memphis, but did not play well enough to make it to the weekend. Then he headed for the U.S. Open at Pebble Beach.

U.S. Open week, *People* magazine published a two-page photo spread featuring Fred and Deborah. This sent mixed signals. Here was a guy protesting about having a tough time adjusting to the attention, yet he was doing photo shoots for *People* magazine. It was confusing to most everyone because Couples hid the fact that he was struggling to keep his marriage intact.

As the reigning Masters champion, Couples was the only person that year who had a chance at the grand slam, so he became a pretournament favorite at the U.S. Open at Pebble Beach.

He was a bit uneasy with the new position. It was noon. He faced the press and answered questions about whether he lost momentum by taking time off:

"I was on a pretty good pace for a long, long time. From L.A. to the Masters, I was in the last group on Saturday and Sunday. The wear and tear was hard on me. I've taken too much time off, but I feel it's good to do that. There's no way I could keep playing the way I was every week."

Dave Anderson of the *New York Times* took exception to this. He asked if Couples hoped not to win at Pebble Beach so as not to have people after him, and Couples's response was "No. I'd love to win every tournament, but I don't see how anybody can play his best all the time."[5]

Anderson followed up by writing for the next day's column that "the trick for the best golfers has been to try your best to play your best when it matters the most, at the four major tournaments. . . . Couples doesn't seem to have tried his best to play his best."

Well, actually, the tournament hadn't started. But Anderson was picking up on the almost tangible negative vibrations Couples had been giving off. Couples had never been one who could disguise his feelings. Anderson was correct. Something was wrong, but it wasn't just Couples's golf game.

It's the job of reporters and writers to listen and watch and pay attention to change, to notice the small things that are lost on other people.

Something had convinced Couples that all this attention was a bad thing. He needed help to make it a good experience. He should have been one of the happiest guys in the world, but it was absolutely clear to people in the pressroom that he wasn't.

Paul Marchand and his wife had just had a baby, so Couples didn't have the benefit of an on-site instructor that week. He'd opted to play some friendly matches with Paul Azinger against Ken Green and Mark Calcavecchia. He cited the fact that scores would be close to par, and said he liked that.

He was asked about being a superstar:

"I don't go to a tournament to talk about myself. I don't think I'm a superstar. Michael Jordan is a superstar because he can dominate every night he plays. Eight months, yeah, I've done really well. A superstar is a Jack Nicklaus or Arnold Palmer who did it for 35 years. I did it for eight months."

As much as Fred shied away from the attention, Deborah seemed to enjoy it. She attended the press conference, nattily attired, and afterward, while Fred disappeared with Chris Berman, who was making an infrequent appearance in the golf pressroom, Deborah conducted her own interview with a circle of reporters. She announced that she was working on a deal to design clothing for a company in Japan.

At week's end, Couples finished in a tie for 17th in a cold and blustery contest that finally provided Tom Kite with a much-needed U.S. Open title and relief from the never-won-a-major label.

After the Open, many of Couples's new endorsement deals made the news. The June 29 issue of *Advertising Age* announced a three-year deal with Cadillac for personal appearances and advertising. The other two spokesmen for Cadillac at the time were Arnold Palmer and Lee Trevino.

The July 6, *Forbes* "Informer" reported that with the amount of Charter Golf (Ashworth) stock Couples owned, he was the second-biggest shareholder, and with the stock price of $6.50/per share, his investment was worth $3.4 million.

Couples soon developed a promotional relationship with Rolex, appearing in the company's advertising. He already had a golf-ball deal with Maxfli. Couples was signed, sealed, and delivered. He was set for life, really. Lynn Roach had been lining up people right and left.

Then, after Pebble Beach, Couples seemed be on the road to contending again. He finished ninth at Westchester, and third at the Western Open before departing for Scotland and the British Open.

And that's when all hell broke loose. Couples missed the cut and wanted to leave immediately. Deborah, by all accounts, wanted to stay. She created a stir in a public establishment by dancing on a table and starting to unbutton clothing. Billy Ray Brown, a PGA Tour player who also went to the University of Houston, lifted her off the table and got her out of there before she made more of a scene.

Paul Marchand saw Couples Stateside almost immediately afterward, and it was apparent to him that Fred and Deborah were splitting.

"I found out later they definitely had an incident or two over there. I remember looking at the plane ticket in the rental car that had the airfare for the British Open, and I said, 'Man, that is some airfare.' And he said, 'Yeah, you've got to finish fourth almost to make your expenses.'"

They didn't talk about it any more.

With no announcement as to what would happen in his marriage, Couples teed it up again at the PGA Championship at Bellerive, outside St. Louis. There were rumors from the reporters who had attended the British Open, naturally. But Couples seemed—outwardly—OK.

One very negative article was written about Couples not signing an autograph for someone in St. Louis. He later referred to the reporter using an unmentionable expletive, and that was printed, making matters worse. But two days later he was back, signing again.

"There were a few people who thought I did that [signed more autographs] because there was a bad article," he recalled later. "Funny enough, the guy who wrote the article watched me play, and after that round I stood and signed autographs for an hour, too. So I don't have a problem doing it.

"I'm very shy. I don't like to have people in my face. When I get used to that, I'll enjoy it, but I don't think anyone would love to go to work and, before they get to the office, fight with three or four or five hundred people every single day. At least I don't.

"But I enjoy kids, and I'll look after them as much as I can," he added. "And if I offend people, I don't mean to, but when you meet so many people, you're bound to have a few walk away disappointed."

To have spent hours signing autographs for fans, then be ripped to shreds by a reporter was difficult for him to bear. He never once used the difficulties in his personal life as an excuse.

Like others who had struggled after winning a major, Couples also sought advice from experts like Arnold Palmer, Ray Floyd, and Tom Watson about finding your way through the popularity that comes with success.

The difficulties in his personal life at that time magnified his sensitivity to the media regarding some of the negative things that had been written about him. "I don't want to sit there and talk to them for a half hour and wake up the next day and not know what they are going to write. So you have to find the right people," he explained.

"I feel like I'm doing what's best for me. And I'm going to learn, that's for sure," he concluded.

At the PGA, he finished in a tie for 21st. Nick Price won the Wanamaker Trophy with Squeeky Medlin on the bag, and Squeek became the first caddie to win the same major back-to-back with two different players.

Though nothing was said to anyone, Couples moved to Rancho Mirage. With the decision made to separate, there was but one thing to do. Play golf. And in that arena Couples seemed to be back on track.

He finished third at the World Series of Golf in Akron, with his highest scores two 70s. At the Canadian Open, he was 9th. He defended at the B.C. Open and tied for 13th and concluded the regular season at the Tour Championship tied for 5th with his friend Raymond Floyd.

At season's end, it was clear that Fred Couples would win the PGA of America Player of the Year Award, the Vardon Trophy for the second time, and the money title. But it now looked like he was facing divorce proceedings.

Stories about Deborah surfaced.

One woman recalled a time when Deborah was playing in the wives tournament at the TPC, took a club and did a whirlybird with it, and heaved it down the fairway because she didn't like the shot.

Another woman remembered a charity luncheon where, after a glass or two of wine, Deborah remarked, "Who died and made you God?" The woman telling the story did not believe that what had been said necessitated that kind of a reply.

But Couples has never said anything critical about Deborah publicly. Most people who witnessed any evidence of marital strife are mum about it, preferring to change the topic. Couples couldn't run to his family because they'd been against the marriage. Friends like John McClure said years later that remembering those times was painful for him, and it wasn't even his own problem.

Make no mistake. Fred did love Deborah. Anyone who thinks otherwise just doesn't know Fred Couples. But when it was over, it was over. He closed the door on it and went on with his life. Years later, Couples admitted that many people questioned him about Deborah, saying he should leave her. But until that summer, he remained.

Deborah's gregariousness might have worked in Fred's favor and taken some of the pressure off him—if she had been there to help when the demands seemed unrelenting. But, it didn't work that way. She was smart enough to find him, and for reasons that will continue to astound everyone, silly enough to let him go.

While the year brought difficulty, it ended with a cascade of career benefits. Couples did so well that a week before Thanksgiving, Steve Hershey of USA *Today* gave him a new nickname: Mr. November. It was apt. Couples was a money machine for four and a half weeks.

At La Moraleja II Golf Club in Madrid, Spain, in the World Cup, he and Davis Love III paired to bring home the trophy, the first U.S. victory since 1988. As a winner of the Masters, he was invited to play in the Grand Slam, and although he did not perform as well as he would have liked, he still made $200,000.

In a quick swing to Kapalua, he cooled, netting just under $30,000. He and Ray Floyd paired up once again in the Shark Shootout, where they each earned a little over $60,000.

He was asked if he was tired with all the end-of-season play and replied, "When I stop, I'm going to get tired. Right now I haven't slowed down. . . . But I've waited a long time to where I can get to have some fun and enjoy the so-called 'unpressure' of all this stuff."

His new-found fame even brought an invitation to the Skins Game, the cherry on top of the Silly Season events. And in a weekend that produced a 5.3 earthquake and appearances by Deborah Couples, Violet and Tom Couples, and Tawyna Dodd in the gallery, Fred proceeded to take home $210,000.

By the time November was over, he'd pocketed $746,858.50 for the month, including his fifth-place finish in the Tour Championship. Mr. November indeed.

Couples's 11th month in 1992 would have put him in 12th place on the 1992 PGA Tour money list. For the year. Even without the Tour Championship, he would have finished 18th, a few dollars ahead of Greg Norman's take for the entire season.

But deep inside, his heart had to be heavy. His relationship with his first love was now over, as far as he was concerned. Life would never be exactly the same.

16

Breaking Up Is Hard to Do

> *"What I want is the bank account*
> *of Fred Couples's soon-to-be-ex-wife."*
> —Rocky Thompson, Tour Awards Dinner,
> La Costa, January 1993

Fred Couples is not the only professional golfer or professional athlete or person to be divorced. His was just more public than most. It was like a Hollywood breakup, complete with tabloid reporting.

Like everything else Couples did after the 1989 Ryder Cup, he was destined to live under the probing eye of the media. Whether it was, as Ron Drapeau suggested, his indescribable personal charisma, the lifestyle that Deborah was living, the fact that he'd won the Masters, or some combination, Couples could not escape the spotlight. People just wanted to know. And for a while, Deborah wanted to tell them.

Beginning in the summer of 1992, Couples moved away from the Polo Club and lived quietly at Mission Hills Country Club, until things were more settled. He and John McClure played golf when McClure was in the desert on business, about once a month. Throughout these tumultuous times, McClure was a steadfast friend and trusted confidant.

It was said that, at first, Deborah didn't believe Fred was serious about the split. But it didn't take her long to comprehend the situation, and by the end of 1992, she had filed for divorce.[1]

As the legal drama unfolded, Couples began seeing Tawnya Dodd, who was living near Corona, California. She accompanied him to the Tournament of Champions in January of 1993. During the players banquet, Rocky Thompson, senior Tour player, was full of his usual routines, one of which was his own wish list for the upcoming year. "I want Fred Couples's face," Thompson began. "And I want Fred Couples's body. And

Fred Couples's swing. His hair? I want anybody's hair. And I want the bank account of Fred Couples's soon-to-be-ex wife."[2]

Couples blushed deeply. Thompson had said what half the world was thinking.

The fact that Couples was PGA Tour Player of the Year for the second consecutive time seemed to be lost in South Florida, where the Palm Beach newspapers covered virtually every angle they could uncover about the pending divorce proceedings.

Golf writer Larry Dorman suggested to Couples that he find "a different lawyer, somebody who knew Palm Beach. Somebody a little meaner than the lawyer he originally hired."

Couples attempted to remove himself from the swirling circles of gossip. The best thing for him was that he was living out west and didn't have to see the articles. The second-best thing was that in this time of personal crisis, his friends and family rallied to support him.

Cindy, his sister, announced that she was glad Deborah and Fred were getting divorced. "I never liked Deborah from the first time I talked to her on the phone," she said years later.

She said in a magazine article that her mother and her father had seen more of Fred in the months since the separation than they had in the 12 years that Fred and Deborah were married.[3]

But some people close to Fred felt that Deborah may have jump-started the laid-back Couples early in his career. "She was a very aggressive lady, and she pushed him, and she got him out the door," Uncle Pete noted.

John Horne added, "I don't care what's said about Deborah. If it was not for Deborah, he may not have had the drive to do what he did. He did not always know what to do. He needed somebody to get his entry fee to Tour School. To give him direction."

In the midst of this mayhem, the golf season began.

Things started swimmingly in 1993. Literally. The first round at La Costa was washed out. The 10th fairway was a lake all the way across, complete with ducks paddling in it, until the city officials in Carlsbad pulled a plug out in the lagoon across the street from the resort and allowed the water to drain away. No one knew where, but it vacated the premises. Pumps ran all night.

By Friday morning, the 10th fairway was mostly green instead of murky brown. Because there were so few players, the entire field played 36 holes. By Saturday, conditions had improved to a water torture: off-and-on showers all day long. The pumps droned on, their low rumble echoing through the valley between rocky cliffs.

When everyone had finally wrung themselves out, Davis Love III was crowned the Mud King; he brought home the trophy with a 67-67-69-69.

Couples finished 10th and went undercover for four weeks. In February, he was at the Johnnie Walker Classic in Singapore, where he shot 73-65-70-69 for a 277, which was eight back of the winner, Nick Faldo.[4] Then, at the Bob Hope, Couples claimed he was rusty. But he shot 68 at Bermuda Dunes to get things started. He said his goal for the year was to get to the top of the money list by season's end.[5]

Rust or no, he played well enough to be one shot off the lead at the end of round two. When he was called into the interview room, reporters were a little hesitant with their questions, but Jaime Diaz finally asked him about his personal situation.

"It's not sad, but it's too bad we couldn't work it out," Couples told him. "It didn't affect my play, or maybe it did, and I'm too naive to figure it out. It's been tougher than I thought it would be. . . . I've got to get the other stuff out of my mind and start playing golf."[6]

Couples contended all the way through, until Sunday. Then Tom Kite, who thought he was still a kid, decided to demolish the record books and shot a 62 on the Arnold Palmer Course at PGA West. He set a new tournament record of 35 under par. It was his second 62 in the desert in four months. It was an astonishing round of golf, and Couples, with a round of 72, finished 13 strokes behind.

Perhaps Couples's finish was a result of the fact that he had other things on his mind.

"I really need to start practicing," he said to Steve Hershey. "Each week I say this is the week, but . . . well, I want to practice, but little things keep getting in the way."[7]

Right. Little things like his divorce.

Eventually it came out that Deborah had asked for just over $160,000 a month in temporary support. People were dumbstruck. No one could figure out how one woman needed that much money to "get by" each month. Even with polo ponies. It was beyond comprehension.

Polo expenses, according to several sources, became a sore spot in Fred and Deborah's marriage as early as 1990. Even Jay Haas told the story of teasing Couples about Deborah's polo in 1988. But as Couples often said at the time, he was doing what he wanted to do and saw no reason why Deborah should not be able to do what she wanted to do, too. That was until he found out what it was really costing him—reportedly $300,000 in 1992 alone.

While Couples was a multimillionaire at this point, he was not at the stage of inherited wealth like the Busch brothers of Anheuser-Busch, who stabled their 60 to 80 polo ponies in South Florida for the winter. But he loved Deborah very much, so he had indulged her.

The third week of February, Couples went to face divorce proceedings. The following week, he was slated to defend at Riviera. Golf for him became a welcome relief from the legal hassles.

Steve Hershey, ever watchful for changes in Couples's composure, reported Couples's admission that he had let his game slide. "I let that happen," he said without excuses. "I had played so well for so long, then finally won the Masters. I started taking my game for granted and not practicing as much."[8]

But in an article for *Golf Magazine*, he told Dave Kindred that another reason was that his marriage was on the rocks and that it got worse as spring turned to summer. "People would say, 'How's Deborah doing? Is she going to come out [to the tournament]?' And I'd say, 'Oh, she's doing great. She'll probably come out next week.' What was I going to say, 'No, things are horrible, we're separated'?"[9] Couples kept the whole thing to himself for as long as he could.

Thursday at Riviera, under sunny skies, Couples shot par. Jim McGovern, Russell Beirsdorf, and Jay Don Blake were four under.

Friday's hideous weather canceled the second round, and it was decided that the event would be a 54-hole tournament.

After the second round on Saturday, Couples led, tied with Marco Dawson, Donnie Hammond, and Payne Stewart. Lurking, as Gary McCord is so fond of saying, just one back, was Tom Kite.

On Sunday, Kite shot a 67 to Couples 71 and walked off with the title. Couples finished third, but it was not what he wanted.

Couples commented after the tournament, "You win a bunch of tournaments in streaks, except for Tom Kite, where he wins early in the year, the middle of the year, or later in the year because he's so good."

But for Tom Kite, it was a sweet reward.

The next week at the Doral, Couples roomed with Jim Nantz. Nantz was still the king of trivia, and the two of them spent hours watching and talking sports. Paul Marchand came in for the weekend, and they requested a rollaway bed. It was almost like college, only this time they all had suitcases ready to go, and the microphones were live on national television.

Couples also experienced his first reported back twinge. However, he finished out the tournament in a tie for sixth, with three rounds in the 60s, his final round a 67. In retrospect, one has to wonder if that was a sign of the problems that would surface one year later, to the week.

It was on to the Honda Classic.

On Thursday fans wore tank tops, shorts, sunscreen. They were ready for some hot golf and got their wish. Couples opened up with an eight-under-par-64 to take the first-round lead by the throat.

In the second round, rust returned, and Couples finished with a worse-than-average 73. He was one behind Larry Mize. It was reported that Deborah had been somewhere on the course, but that she was not in Couples's gallery.[10]

Then nature took over. A swift-moving, near-hurricane-force storm with heavy lightning and torrential rain hit the course, knocking down bleachers, seating, tents, banners, and anything else it could demolish. Skyboxes were actually in the sky for a time. The third round was canceled as volunteers and staff struggled to put all the temporary obstructions back so that golfers would be able to get free drops from them.

On Sunday, Couples played exceptionally well for 10 holes and was ahead of the field by four strokes. Suddenly, at the 11th, he became the Tin Man in the Wizard of Oz. Everything that had been so smooth locked up. A noxious rust attack.

At 11, he missed the green right on the par 3, made an inadequate pitch to 10-feet, and missed the putt. Bogey. He redeemed himself with a birdie at the par-5 12th. At the 13th, he left his 9-iron short and took three to get into the hole, missing a three-footer. Eyebrows shot up in the press room. Missed three-footer?

On the 14th, he was in a divot and said it felt as if the turf opened up the clubface. He missed the green with a 9-iron and made another bogey. Two in a row. The press contingent moaned, fearful they would have to rewrite the stories they'd already started. However, he was still two ahead of Mize. He parred the 15th.

Then he did something really ridiculous. It was the kind of thing that makes Couples such fun to watch—his game can be so unpredictable.

Couples had lost this tournament the previous year, putting a ball in the water short and right of the 16th green. This time, his drive landed in the light rough on the left side of the 460-yard par 4. Then he selected a 4-iron from 190, which was plenty to get him home.

Who is to argue with Couples's technique for getting out of trouble or even marginal difficulty? Yet, it was less than perfectly struck. It flailed in the wind like a wounded duck and flopped into the water. His follow-up landed eight feet, but his psyche must have been damaged, because he missed the putt. Double.

Later, he denied that it was pressure. "I think it was the lack of pressure, or lack of feeling like I knew what I was doing. I was playing like a choking dog coming in."

Where was a golf medic when he needed one?

He said he was playing more like his father than like himself or like a supposedly good golfer. Gary Van Sickle in *Golf World* took issue with that, saying that Couples's father would probably play much better.

It got worse. Couples pushed his 3-iron into the bunker right of the 17th green, a 215-yard par 3. He was lucky the bunker was there, because otherwise his ball would have ricocheted from the bank into the water right of the green.

Miraculously, he holed the bunker shot to tie for the lead. "It was skill to get it out, but lucky that it went in," he said about the 60-degree wedge shot from 40 feet.

On 18 he drove into a fairway bunker. He pulled the second shot into a second bunker. Amateurs could identify with his play. The third shot was from an uphill lie, 158 yards away, water in front of the green on the right. He chose a 6-iron, certainly more club than the distance alone called for, but there was wind. It landed 30 feet from the pin, but he called it the best shot of the day, mainly because he had reached the green and still had a chance to win. As his long approach putt rolled toward the hole, it looked so good he started running, but it slipped by. He two-putted for a par and tied with Robert Gamez, who wasn't even on the leaderboard through nine holes.

The playoff started at the 10th and went back to 18 again, where Gamez's second shot came to rest in a divot and his third plunged into the water, handing Couples the trophy.

In the emotional firestorm of Couples's life, winning again was a monumental achievement. "Going out there, after being five under, I was thinking about golf, and I really felt like I let my mind wander when I was standing over the ball," he said later. "I was not thinking of anything else, but it's hard to win because, really, what I'm trying to do with my golf game. . . ." He became circular, as he is wont to do when he realizes he doesn't want to reveal what's on his mind. "I just feel like people are pulling so hard for me to win, and it became a struggle of not really thinking what I was doing."

As Couples came up the last hole, the fans cheered raucously, just as they had done all over the country and, literally, all over the world for several seasons. The fans to the far left of the 18th green, where the bulkhead extended to another grassy area, had attached paper letters on the bottom of chair seats, and as he came into view, they lifted the chairs, spelling out "Couples."

"You know, things like that, it's fun to look at. A lot of people pull for me on Saturday and Sunday. A lot of people bring posters out or pictures or whatever. And it's fun when you see that, it gives you a big boost when you need a two-putt to win."

Gary Van Sickle had his own opinion of the increasing numbers of Fred Fans:

"Actually, the way he won simply reinforced the three reasons Couples is so popular with his public:

"One, he's longer than long, and everybody wants to be a gorilla.

"Two, he seems cooler than iced tea, and everybody wants to be that cool. Even Bond, James Bond.

"Three, he's human. He screws up, even when he wins. Everybody wishes they would get away with that."[11]

Van Sickle even got a quote from Tom Watson to substantiate his theory: "Nick Faldo plays mistake-free golf. Freddie is so good, he can make a mistake or two and still win," Watson told him.[12]

The next day Deborah was on the tabloid TV show *Hard Copy*.

And the *New York Times* had an article on the divorce, which they called the Ex-Factor. Couples had talked to Jaime Diaz about the situation and said, "When my parents say, 'Son, are you all right?' I say, 'Yeah, yeah, yeah,' but I could tell them that every single day, and they still kind of don't believe it. I had the chance to prove it by playing good golf. And that's the best way I know how."[13]

The *Times* had the facts right, except for Deborah's age. She had asked for $168,000 a month. Her attorney estimated his bill would be around $750,000. A judge awarded her a $52,000-a-month allowance until the case was settled. Couples claimed Deborah spent nearly $300,000 on polo in 1992 and that her preoccupation with the sport contributed to the split.[14]

USA Today followed up, asking Couples about numbers that had been quoted in the West Palm Beach paper that said he had legal fees in excess of $300,000.

"That's cheap" was his answer. "I just know in July [when the divorce is final] I'll be one happy dude."[15]

However, Couples admitted that the whole situation had been painful, like a death in the family. Unfortunately, sooner than he would like, he would have a means to verify that statement.

Steve Hershey mentioned that the split was rivaling the Roxanne Pulitzer saga in terms of coverage in West Palm Beach. The sooner Couples got out of south Florida, the better it would be for him. He missed the cut at Bay Hill, finished 39th at the Players Championship, took a week off to practice, and then headed for Augusta to defend his title.

Naturally, there was a great deal of pre-Masters hoopla about Couples. But when all was said and done, it was Bernhard Langer who went home with the green jacket, his second.

Couples's entourage included Tawnya Dodd, John and Dallene Bracken, and Tammy and Lynn Roach. Several of Tawnya's relatives were also there. John McClure made it for the weekend, and he might have been the only person at the tournament without a credential. How Couples got him onto the course is still a mystery; and once there, with the Sunday round completed, Couples couldn't figure out how to get McClure back through the clubhouse without a badge.

Someone reminded Couples he was still defending champion and that probably no one would argue with him if he just put an arm on McClure's shoulder, looked the security guard straight in the eye and said "He's with me." That the defending champion at the Masters did not want to disrupt the order of things even for his good friend exemplifies the way Couples sees himself. But this one time Couples used the authority temporarily granted to him.

Couples had good finishes the rest of the spring. He was 5th at the Byron Nelson, 4th at the Memorial, 16th at Westchester. And he was 16th at Baltusrol, where Lee Janzen won his first U.S. Open.

If Couples had not been number one in the world the previous season, no one would have noticed the seeming slide in his play during the summer of 1993. He was 25th at the Western Open, and 9th at the British Open, which was won by Greg Norman, who had four rounds in the 60s and a patented low Sunday score on Sunday of 64. At the Buick Open he was 13th.

At the PGA Championship, which was held at Inverness in Toledo, Couples finished 31st while Paul Azinger won, getting the major monkey off his back. Little did anyone realize that Azinger, too, had other things on his mind. His shoulder had been bothering him, and his battle with cancer was about to begin.

Obviously, off-course issues were still alive for Couples, because at the PGA Lynn Roach was asking people if they would appear on Couples's behalf in depositions. The divorce that was supposed to be final in July wasn't over yet. From the Honda Classic on, the Fred Couples everyone thought they knew had seemingly taken a hall pass—straight to legal proceedings.

He was second at the Canadian Open, although he never led, finishing with a final round of 69. As it happened, prior to the event, he'd just had a session with Paul Marchand.

Couples must have known—as Marchand puts it, "he has a special built-in gyroscope"—that he needed a look-see. He wanted to get back on track because the Ryder Cup was coming up.

Tom Watson had actively lobbied for the hot-seat captain's position in 1993, intent on erasing the bad memories U.S. players had at the Belfry. With five British Open titles, Watson was as much at home in the British Isles as he was in the States. He was the perfect captain for the situation.

Team members included five repeaters from Kiawah Island in 1991: Chip Beck, who finished second at the Masters in 1993; Payne Stewart, second in the 1993 U.S. Open to Lee Janzen; Paul Azinger, 1993 PGA champion; Corey Pavin; and Fred Couples. Azinger and Couples were the top two in Ryder Cup points.

Rookies were Davis Love III, John Cook, Jim Gallagher, Jr., and Lee Janzen, U.S. Open champion in 1993.

Tom Kite, 1992 U.S. Open champion and 1993 Bob Hope and L.A. Open victor, had not been on the 1991 squad, but he had been on six others. Watson was not worried about Kite.

Captain's picks were Raymond Floyd and Lanny Wadkins. Floyd at age 51 became—again—the oldest member of a U.S. Ryder Cup team. Wadkins had already won 18 Ryder Cup matches, and Watson wanted winners.

"Raymond was selected because he and Fred obviously had something going on the golf course," Watson remarked later. But as Couples had said, Floyd played younger than his chronological age. The selection turned out to be the right move, but not because of Couples.

The Europeans, again headed by captain Bernard Gallacher, had their own ideas about retrieving the Cup. Their big guns were in force: Nick Faldo, who was number one in the world at that time, though majorless in 1993; Bernhard Langer, 1993 Masters champion; Seve Ballesteros, this time a captain's pick; and Ian Woosnam, Colin Montgomerie, and Jose Maria Olazabal. The rest were Sam Torrance, Mark James, Costantino Rocca, Joakim Haeggman, Barry Lane, and little-known, Peter Baker.

Ballesteros, in full braggadocio, remarked that the only reason the Concorde was landing in Europe was to bring the Ryder Cup back to them.[16]

On the first day, Pavin/Watkins and Kite/Love were successful in the morning matches, but Stewart/Azinger fell to Woosnam/Langer. When Floyd and Couples went down 4 and 3 to Faldo and Montgomerie, the score was even at 2 each.

In the afternoon fourball, Europe advanced, winning two and losing one point. Watson rested Floyd, and paired Couples with Paul Azinger, throwing them to the beasts: Faldo and Montgomerie. This match wasn't just tough. It was impossible. They didn't even finish on Friday. Play was suspended for darkness, and they all returned to the course early Saturday morning to play the last hole. It looked as if Couples and Azinger would win, but Faldo forced a halve by draining a 12-footer for birdie.

After the first "day" was completed the score was close, as expected: Europe 4½ and United States 3½.

Couples and Azinger had done well enough for an encore and again drew Langer and Woosnam on day two. There was no joy as Couples and Azinger went down 2 and 1 in the morning foursomes that saw Europe take three out of four matches to increase their lead to 7½–4½.

The afternoon fourball awaited, and making matters worse was the recent U.S. record that had carried over into this Ryder Cup.

Fourball Matches Won	1991	1989	1987	1985
United States	2	2	2	3
Europe	6	6	6	5

If the United States repeated its previous performances, the Europeans would have a commanding margin heading into Sunday's singles matches.

Watson went to an untried combination, John Cook and Chip Beck, who delivered an extraordinary performance, delivering a much-needed point for the U.S. team by beating Faldo and Montgomerie 1-up. Watson was thrilled with their performance and later commented that the Beck and Cook pairing "was the heart of the victory."

Pavin and Gallagher must have had razor blades for lunch, because they followed by making absolute mincemeat of James and Rocca, winning 5 and 4.

With the United States winning the first two matches, Azinger and Couples drew Ian Woosnam and Peter Baker. Three of them had won majors. Eight times out of ten, at least, anybody would pick the U.S. team, simply because of the records. But on that afternoon, Peter Baker played golf as if he had been cloned from Corey Pavin's mustache.

Baker, an untouted player, made six birdies in the first 14 holes. He and Faldo blew away Couples and Azinger, 6 and 5. They would have blown away Ben Hogan and Byron Nelson the way Baker was playing.

The final pairing on Saturday pitted Floyd and Stewart against Olazabal and the Swede, Joakim Haeggman. Watson may have dispensed

Advil and Sportscreme to get Floyd through the 36, but the bionic veteran rose to the occasion.

Stewart and Floyd held on to win, 2 and 1.

Watson had coaxed the U.S. team out of a deficit and back into position. Not only that, they had won 3 points in the betterball on Saturday and 4½ overall. It was a better fourball total than any U.S. team had earned since 1981.

The U.S. team was back in it, 7½ to Europe's 8½.

Then Sam Torrance was forced to withdraw because of an infected toe. In a gesture of sportsmanship, Larry Wadkins offered to sit down on the U.S. side. Each team was awarded half a point. Sunday began United States 8, Europe 9.

Naturally, it didn't play out as anticipated. New heroes were born. Reputations were made. Such is the stuff of the Ryder Cup.

On Sunday, half the matches went all the way. Only one was a blowout. Tom Kite, playing the next-to-last match, trounced Bernhard Langer, 5 and 3.

Jim Gallagher, Jr., had the awesome task of playing Seve Ballesteros, and he succeeded, 3 and 2. Payne Stewart, whose confidence had returned in full force, handled Mark James by the same score.

Everything else was much closer.

Chip Beck, in the first match to come to the 18th, edged Barry Lane, 1 up. Beck had been three down and mounted a back-nine comeback charge.

Lee Janzen drew Colin Montgomerie and was treated to a 1-down loss, but Montgomerie was second-high point man for Europe in 1993.

Pavin witnessed another putting exhibition by Peter Baker, who won their contest 2-up.

Couples drew Woosnam and took him to 18 before halving the match.

Paul Marchand recalled it as one of the best-ever matches between Woosnam and Couples. "It was back and forth all day. At the last, Fred putted up for a gimme on the 18th. Woosie had 10 feet for birdie and hit his putt past the hole four or five feet, and the look on Woosnam's face was like, *What did I just do?*"

Woosnam's last putt did everything to stay out of the hole before dropping in. Woosnam put his hands over his face and Fred had his hands on his head as they approached each other for a handshake like two weary prizefighters.

The final score: United States 15, Europe 13. The Ryder Cup was going back to the United States on the Concorde. Seve Ballesteros and the rest would have to wait two more years.

As Johnny Miller had said in 1991, winning silences the critics. Fred Couples had not played to the same level in 1993 as he had in 1991, but he did not repeat his 1989 performance. He was 0–2–3, earning 1½ points.

A couple of weeks afterward, on October 8, Couples's divorce proceedings concluded. There was a lump-sum settlement of about $3 million, plus the house and whatever had been paid in interim monthly support. Couples himself does not know the total to the penny and would rather not recalculate it. Sometimes it's better to look forward. And for Fred Couples, this was one of those times.

Part of the divorce agreement precluded Deborah from writing any books, making any public appearances, or otherwise profiting from the marriage.

With legal loose ends tied up, it was time for Mr. November to strike again.

Couples began his postseason assault at Kapalua. The first two rounds he remained in the shadows, letting the leaders think they were safe.

After the third day, Couples was ahead by two strokes over Mike Hulbert.

Couples made only one bogey in the final round, his first in 47 holes, at the sixth. For the entire week, he had only three, two on the first day.

Finally, Love III began to make a move, and Couples put his game into overdrive, birdieing three of the last six holes—the 13th, 15th, and 16th—to take a choke hold on first place and close out the contest by four shots.

"Fred played 72 holes without a three putt which was remarkable on those greens," said Mark Rolfing.

Couples and Love packed their Hawaiian shirts, donned World Cup outfits, and flew to Lake Nona, in Orlando, Florida.

They both expected some additional pressure since they were defending against some great teams. Couples expressed some concern about his game, which he viewed as less finely tuned than it had been the previous year.

Yet in the first round, Couples and Love opened up a three-stroke lead on all countries. The South African team of Ernie Els and Retief Goosen gave chase. Couples had a 66, one of his favorite numbers, and Love posted a 71, high for him.

During that round, Davis Love saw an amazing display of luck and skill on the 532-yard, par-5 ninth hole. "Fred holed a 2-iron, off a downhill lie, out of the first cut of rough for a double eagle. That's probably the best shot I ever saw him hit, and that wasn't a normal trouble shot," Love recalled.

After two rounds, the thunder of approaching spikes could be heard. The Zimbabwe team of Nick Price and Mark McNulty was gaining. They were only one back of Couples, who had fired a 71, and Love, who had improved to a 69.

The third day, the U.S. team advanced to a three-stroke margin, again over the Zimbabwe twosome.

The last day, Couples and Love left nothing to chance. They teamed for a five-shot spread over the field, with Price and McNulty the closest competitors.

Couples chipped in at the first hole and made a 40-footer on the seventh for another birdie to get the team going.

Then he almost hit Nick Price on the 14th, a 309-yard drivable par 4. The green wasn't visible from the tee. As Price took his putter back to attempt a three-footer on the green, a golf ball rolled almost between his legs and stopped within a foot of his ball. Price jumped, startled by the shot.

"It took us a long time to play the 13th hole," Couples said afterward, apologetically, "so when we got to the 14th tee, we assumed they were already off the green."

"I was watching my tee shot when I saw them coming off the green," Love added. "Obviously, we never would have hit if we knew they were still on the green."

Price made his par. Couples made his four-footer for eagle. Davis Love came up with a great line: "When we're driving a par 4, get off the green."

Couples and Love won the World Cup. Bernhard Langer won the International Trophy for individual low score.

Couples said afterward, "It means a lot to win for your country. It's fun when you can share a win with a teammate."[17] He said, when it was over, that he had thought they'd be the team to beat if they stayed on top of their games.

Couples skipped the Shark Shootout in favor of the Dunlop Phoenix in Japan, where he could collect appearance money. He was fifth.

Then it was on to Skins, again at Big Horn, but this time with Arnold Palmer substituting for John Daly, who had been suspended by Commissioner Beman for picking up his ball and disqualifying himself during play at Kapalua.

Payne Stewart was defending champ. Paul Azinger, fresh off his victory in the 1993 PGA Championship, yet worried about upcoming medical tests, was the fourth.

Once again, birdies ruled the first day. The prize money was the same as the previous year: $20,000 for the first through sixth holes, $30,000 for the seventh through eleventh, and $40,000 for the last six.

Arnie started out hot, birdieing the first hole to the delight of all who had turned out to see the King. But Couples birdied also, and the money stayed with the banker.

At the sixth, Couples collected $60,000 for two holes. He was relieved to have some loose change to add to the growing November pot.

Players tied with pars on seven and eight, letting the money ride. Then, at nine, Couples got greedy and took it all, $90,000.

Sunday morning when play began it was cool, but Couples had loosened up enough on the practice range to make a seven-footer on the 10th for birdie to boost his total to $180,000.

The 13th was lucky for Payne Stewart, who scooped up $100,000. Stewart won again at the 16th, this time pocketing $120,000.

With two holes to play, Palmer was skinless. At the 17th, the treacherous par 3, Stewart and Couples halved with pars. Carryover.

They all came to the 18th and watched with anticipation as Palmer made his birdie putt. It didn't drop, but Couples's did, and he added another $80,000 to his bankroll.

In the end, all the money was split between Couples and Stewart, but Stewart had the most and became the only player to win three Skins contests in a row. His Thanksgiving weekend total was $280,000. Couples's take-home was $260,000.

When Couples took away Palmer's last shot, he said, "I haven't felt that bad all year." Palmer, of course, did not need the money.

Cindy, Fred's sister, was in the gallery with their mother, Violet, and has a vivid memory of one of the fans.

"I remembered seeing this lady in a wheelchair who told us that Fred was absolutely her favorite golfer, and that she was at the event because her son had asked her what she wanted for her birthday and she said this was it: to see Fred at the Skins Game," Cindy explained. "So it was arranged and they put her at a hole in the wheelchair, and then they'd move her three or four holes up.

"We saw her on the 18th green, and she said that she had really enjoyed it. So I got an autograph and sent it to her just because I wanted to. And I got a letter back from her saying how much it meant to her, because she had breast cancer, and when she was recovering what got her through it was watching Fred play golf on TV. That's why it had meant so much to her just to see him in person. I had to fight from crying when I read the letter."

Couples's November Totals

Kapalua	$180,000
World Cup	$130,000
International Trophy	$ 50,000
The Skins Game	$260,000
Total:	$620,000

Plus what he made in Japan. Mr. November strikes again.

By the end of 1993 Couples had a new house in Plano, Texas, which he was sharing with Tawnya Dodd. The location was good because Texas has no state income tax. As the writers joked, he had to move somewhere because he lost Florida in the divorce. Fred and Tawnya started looking for furniture, and for a time they suffered the problem of lots of rooms with nowhere to sit or sleep. They even moved in before all the utilities were hooked up and for a few days were heatless.

For Fred Couples 1993 had been expensive and painful. But he would have given even more to anyone who could have prevented what would happen in 1994.

17

Words Aren't Enough

*"I don't even want to think about how much it
hurt Fred."*

— Jim Nantz

Nineteen ninety-three was a year Fred Couples wanted to kiss good-bye as soon as possible. The divorce and resultant publicity had stretched him.

He occasionally snapped at caddie Joe LaCava, according to reports in the *New York Times*.[1] LaCava, however, knew better than anybody what was going on, and so, like most of Couples's true friends, he just hung in there knowing the real Fred Couples was just around the corner. Someplace.

"I wanted to be the biggest jerk I could be," Couples said sometime later. "For some reason, I thought it would make me feel better."[2]

But it didn't, down deep.

The real Fred Couples has as much natural animosity as a teddy bear. Yet, he was often one big, brooding, Italian storm cloud. Who could blame him? It sure looked like nice guys were finishing last.

His first tournament of the year, La Costa, was for winners.

"I played well at times last year [1993], but having to deal with the divorce was something that was always on my mind. When I did play, I tried to keep my mind on what I was doing, but there was no way, in my mind, that I was going to beat Greg Norman, Paul Azinger, or Nick Price on Sunday. I feel like I need to get back to the point where I've got the confidence in my game that I know I can beat those guys," he explained.[3]

Despite having the flu that week, he was tied for the lead after the first and third rounds. On Sunday, Couples was tied with Phil Mickelson at the end of regulation.

During the playoff, in what can only be described as a hangover from 1993, he hit a shot he didn't like from the fairway bunker on the 10th—the second hole of sudden death—and uttered an unmentionable expletive, which was caught by on-course microphones. If he'd been a wordsmith, he might have explained that he and his caddie were talking about an upcoming tournament stop: Phuket, Thailand. But the accent was on the wrong syllable, and he was fined by the Tour.

After the cursing, Mickelson won.

Couples zipped up his suitcase for some guaranteed money in Dubai and Thailand. In Dubai, he missed the cut but stayed extra days as a guest TV commentator. In Phuket, Thailand, he finished second to Greg Norman, who birdied the 16th and 18th in the final round.

So Couples had two seconds and some cash. After an 18½-hour flight back to L.A. he was ready for his pre-Augusta run. Riviera was the perfect place to start.

Larry Dorman wrote that he looked cool. "And in L.A., that's half the battle."[4]

The first round Couples posted a 67, but he was three back of his friend, former champion Tom Purtzer, who shot 64 to take the lead.

The second day, the weather turned cool and windy. Purtzer had the turnaround typical for anyone shooting low. He shot high, but so did the field. All except Corey Pavin. Pavin posted a 64, despite wind gusts to 25 miles per hour and temperatures in the 50s. He was 10 strokes better than the average of the field, which was 74.55. Only five players broke par, and Couples was one of them, with a 67.

However, on Saturday, Pavin did what Purtzer had done, and after shooting low, skied to a 72 in the third round. Couples chugged along, posting a 68 to take the lead.

Sunday it was head-to-head, Pavin and Couples, and while Couples played respectably, par was not good enough to best Pavin. Couples had a bad putting round. Pavin didn't. That, basically, was the difference. Nobody else even threatened all day.

Golf is funny. Sometimes everything a player looks at drops. Some days everything lips out or breaks off at the hole. Whether it's jet lag or the alignment of the stars or what people have for breakfast, if anybody could figure it out, there'd be no need for sports psychologists. Couples left an approach putt short on the second, and then, mysteriously, the club seemed to explode in his hands as he hit it six feet by on the come-back. He missed two more birdie attempts, and then pulled even again at the 12th. Inexplicably, he missed a two-footer at the 14th for par.

Pavin hung on to his lead, and at the 16th sank a 25-footer for birdie on a green where 25 feet is about as far away as anybody can get. That was the clincher, and Pavin won by two.

Psychologists might argue that somewhere inside Couples's brain he wasn't ready for the media spotlight again. Champions don't miss two-foot putts.

This season the Bob Hope tournament was played after L.A., but Couples was world-weary and dropped off the charts for two weeks.

His game came around again at Doral. Paul Marchand was there, helping to tweak Couples's game, working on putting techniques and helping Couples get his swing into the right groove.

After three rounds, Couples was near the lead, which was held by Billy Andrade at −12. He was on the range warming up prior to his round when something went terribly wrong at the top of a backswing. He looked at both Marchand and LaCava and said that if he moved a muscle he was going to scream.

"Somehow, they got him into a golf cart," Marchand recalled. He was taken to the Centinela trailer, but he could not continue.

He was diagnosed with three different problems. First, he had a herniated disk. Second, he had the normal amount of "degeneration" for a professional golfer. And on the range at Doral he had pulled muscles and other connecting tissues around his sacroiliac joint.[5] Anyone who has experienced that sensation can understand that Couples's first move was to spend two days in bed.

Was it a combination of age and physical use? Was it the mental stress of the post-Masters victory plus the divorce? Was it a combination of those things? He would never know. He just knew he needed to find a way to get better.

"I started to play a little bit [two weeks before the Masters] and couldn't get out of bed one day, and then I got a little scared," Couples admitted. Unfortunately, he would miss the Masters.

Yet Couples would have been happy to keep his back problem if that was the only bad medical news he received. Shortly after his back problems were diagnosed, his mother was diagnosed with an inoperable cancer.

"I don't even want to think about how much it hurt Fred," Jim Nantz was quoted as saying. "She was a very special woman, and there was a real bond there."[6]

To this day, Paul Marchand can't talk about Violet Couples without tears coming to his eyes.

"It was a weird year," Couples said many months later, referring only to his playing schedule, "because I came back the week before the U.S. Open, and it's not exactly when you want to come play, but I'd missed enough tournaments, and, of course, the Masters, so I really wanted to get out and play."

He didn't return without a medical clearance.

"Even my first week back, I was with my doctors," he explained. "They came and watched me hit balls. They're not golf teachers, they're doctors. So they don't know if I'm hitting it good or bad or what, but they wanted to know if I flinched or if it hurt."

According to on-site reports, it didn't take Couples long to hit the ball 300 yards straight down the fairway.[7]

He had been out 97 days, according to the *New York Times.*

At the U.S. Open, the press showed him courtesy by not asking him about his mother who had passed away on Mother's Day. Nor did anyone dwell on his absence from tournament golf. He had been in Seattle for close to a month, and golf was the furthest thing from his mind.

Couples did not like his chances for doing well at Oakmont, but he wanted to play.

"I need to look at it really as I want to play well, but I also want to be careful in what I am doing and not trying to go out with a 5-iron in eight inches of rough because of the situation. Last week I hit the ball very well from tee to green. I chipped and putted good at times and very bad at times. That is kind of the big problem. Here, you know, you can't get away with four, five bad holes. If I miss three or four fairways in a row on nine holes, turning three or four over, that is too much to come back from.

"I just need to keep involved in practicing. The problem is—that is what bothers my back. I could probably play every day, but hitting balls for a couple of hours is not what I want to do yet. That is also my concern. This is the U.S. Open, and I want to play my best, and I really can't go out to the range now and just cream balls all afternoon."

In the end, this was the Open that had people passing out from heat-stroke in 100-plus-degree days, temperatures even worse than those the previous year at Baltusrol.

Sunday, a moan went up in the pressroom when it became apparent that the day would finish in a three-way tie between Ernie Els, Colin Montgomerie, and Loren Roberts. Loren Roberts took Ernie Els 20 holes before succumbing.

The sentimental highlight of the week was the thundering round of applause that greeted Arnold Palmer as he came up the 18th fairway, playing in his last U.S. Open just a few miles away from his hometown of Latrobe. He wiped tears from his face on the walk-up, and again, in the press room. Burying his eyes in a towel momentarily, Palmer composed himself enough to make his remarks to the media, take questions, and say his thanks. As he got up to leave, the entire roomful of reporters, defying an unwritten rule that forbids applause by the press since it indicates favoritism, stood and cheered the King.

Couples finished tied for 16th. Now he faced the problem of trying to play the minimum of 15 tournaments required by PGA Tour rules.

"I will probably play some tournaments I haven't played in a while," he said. "I don't know what ones just yet. But if I can get through three weeks at a time and take a break, I will be okay. My biggest concern is really traveling . . . picking up luggage if I don't have to."

He played the following week in Hartford, finishing tied for 15th, and the Western Open, where he tied for 26th. Out of concern for his back, he skipped the British Open. Nick Price won the year's third major, in what would become a second monster year for Price.

For his next set of three tournaments, Couples chose the Buick Open, the PGA Championship, and the International.

The first day in Flint was completely rained out, and round one was played on Friday. Corey Pavin was near the top, one stroke back of Fred Funk, who led with a 65. Couples posted a 72.

But the story that day was the return of Paul Azinger. He had his hair back after undergoing chemotherapy. He was healthy, and he was happy to be back.

The second round was played on Saturday, and the cut came at even par. Pavin led by a stroke, and Couples, boosted by a second-round 65, was just one back.

Tournament officials decided to go for a 72-hole tournament, with the field playing 36 holes on Sunday.

It was a double whammy for Couples. He was faced with battling Corey Pavin, who had beaten him at Riviera earlier in the year, and he had a back that barely went 18 holes plus a warm-up. Could he finish, never mind beat Pavin?

But, as Couples himself had said to Steve Hershey the year before, sometimes he was lucky. When something bad happened, he would turn around and something good would happen. It did in Flint.

On Sunday Couples shot 65-68 to Pavin's 70-71, and no one else even came close enough to scare him.

He even considered it a bonus to go 36 holes that day, because he was playing so well in the morning. "It gave me a little boost for the afternoon, and after four or five holes, I knew I was going to be done [physically] at the end," Couples said.

"I ended up birdieing the ninth hole to fall back. Then, the back nine, the biggest shot I hit, besides 18, was on 13. I hit a 2-iron from 228, all over the pin, to 10 or 12 feet and made it for eagle, which was my third eagle in a row on that hole."

As Couples finished his second shot on 18, the gallery reacted with wild applause, but he checked the scoreboard. "I thought it was over when I hit that shot, whether it was two feet or five feet or whatever. As soon as I got to the green I looked back, and Corey birdied 17, which kind of puts a lump in your throat, and then when I got up there, it was very close. I'd missed those before, but with a one-shot lead, playing that hole, the odds of birdie are very slim, so it was a little easier to putt."

He said his back was fine. "There was no problem, but I am very, very tired. . . . I guess adrenaline or being pumped up by leading certainly helped. If I'd fallen behind, I might have lost a little energy," he admitted.

The next week at the PGA in Tulsa, which was at Southern Hills, he may have thought about the 29 that he'd posted years earlier on the back nine. He might have remembered John Bracken being on the bag. But when Sunday came, he had finished 39th. In an effort to play in 15 events, he went to the International, and, after that, the World Series of Golf, where he finished eighth.

Despite his 97-day layoff, he was rising in points for a new event that debuted in September called the President's Cup.

This event came about because foreign players who participated on the Tour, but who were not eligible for the Ryder Cup—Greg Norman in particular[8]—wanted a new contest. Many of the international players had become big draws on the PGA Tour, and Deane Beman, the outgoing commissioner, could see the long-term value in putting just such an event on the Tour. Pressures from other organizations trying to create similar events caused the Tour to unveil the event in 1994. However, there wasn't a big enough talent pool in any one country to compete with a U. S. team, so the United States played a team consisting of players from all foreign countries except Europe.

Unfortunately, Greg Norman, the player who had been most vocal in favor of the event, withdrew due to severe gastrointestinal problems.[9] And Ernie Els, U.S. Open champion, had prior commitments.

"All of us were champing at the bit to get a shot at Greg," U.S. playing captain Hale Irwin commented.[10] Norman, at that time, was number one in the world.

David Graham was the first International team captain, and his charges were Robert Allenby, Fulton Allem, Steve Elkington, David Frost,

Bradley Hughes—the substitute for Greg Norman—Mark McNulty, Frank Nobilo, Nick Price, Craig Parry, Peter Senior, Vijay Singh, and Tusukasa Wantanabe. Even the Ozakis weren't available in 1994. And everyone in golf knows that to have Asia represented, there has to be an Ozaki.

The U.S. team consisted of Fred Couples, Jim Gallagher, Jr., John Huston, Hale Irwin, Jay Haas, Scott Hoch, Tom Lehman, Davis Love III, Jeff Maggert, Phil Mickelson, Corey Pavin, and Loren Roberts.

The event was two sets of five matches for two days, for a total of 20 points, plus singles on the last day for an additional 12 points—32 points in all.

Couples and Davis Love III, the World Cup duo, won two matches. Because of his back problems, Couples played only one match per day.

On Sunday, Couples faced Nick Price, and the match went to the wire. Couples finally outlasted him, 1-up on the 18th hole. But at that point it was only pride at stake, as the United States had the contest in hand, eventually winning, 20 to 12.

Couples wound up his year with a 15th-place finish at the Texas Open, which was won by Bob Estes, then finished last at the Tour Championship in San Francisco.

Though 1994 was a difficult year for Couples off the golf course, by the end of the season he was ready for some much-needed fun. Once again, Mr. November was ready.

Couples began at Kapalua, where he played a practical joke on Mark Rolfing, nearly giving him a coronary in the process.

"He was scheduled to come in on Monday," Rolfing remembered. "Lynn Roach was there, playing in the pro-am, and said he didn't know if Fred would be able to make it because of his back."

Rolfing asked if Fred had a reservation for the next day, and he did. But Tuesday came and Couples's back was still a problem, but he was going to try again Wednesday.

"We had a production meeting for ABC at the Ritz Carlton on Wednesday," Rolfing said. "Fred was supposed to have arrived at 5:30, and I was coming in to the hotel at about six. Lynn saw me come in, and he walked over and said he had some really bad news. He said he was certain Fred had gotten on the plane, that he'd even gone all the way to the airport to pick him up, but when he got there, no Fred.

"My heart sank. I didn't know what to say," Rolfing said. "All along Fred was standing around the corner listening to all this, and he jumped out and almost caused me to have a heart attack."

In the tournament, Couples lurked but did not lead. Then, in the final round, he came to the 11th hole, a 168-yard par 3, tied with Bob Gilder and Tom Lehman. Couples selected an 8-iron. He swung, he stared, he posed. And, as the golf gods watched, he made what he called the first ace of his career. Only Uncle Paul knew differently.

"I think I had one when I was kid, practicing and hitting four or five balls each hole," he said afterward, "but this one was very exciting."[11]

There was a report that Joe LaCava got the car, but he didn't.

"The deal we made was actually that I got the car if he was closest to the pin on 18," explained Joe LaCava, "but I kind of knew he wasn't going for it because, normally, if he was leading the tournament he would be shooting away from the pin because all the trouble there is left.

"So when he hit the hole-in-one on 11, we both looked to the right and there was this big old Continental and I kind of looked at him and said a car's a car, teasing him about it. And he said that's not the deal we made! That's not the deal we made! And he was kidding, too. He kept the car, and that was fine. He made the hole-in-one, and that helped him win the tournament."

Again, it was good luck at the right time.

"Winning here gives me confidence for the next couple of months," Couples said. Uh-oh.

Next, the Couples and Love machine headed for Puerto Rico and the World Cup.

Theoretically, any one of the 32 international teams can win the World Cup. However, that theory evaporated when Couples and Love got off the plane. The field did see a slight possibility of an advantage when it was reported that both men were exhausted from the flight and the four days of wind at Kapalua.

Couples and Love seemed oblivious to the jet lag, with Couples firing a 65 and Love a 67 on the first day of competition. But the rain was so torrential that play was called off, and those in the last groups returned to the course Friday to finish up.

Couples and Love, however, were −12 for the first round, three shots ahead of Mark McNulty and Tony Johnstone of Zimbabwe. To celebrate, they were guests of honor at a cookout hosted by caddies Joe LaCava, "Six-Pack" Jack Keating, "Electric" Ed Bigoss, and Jeff "The Shadow" Jones. It was a sumptuous menu of chicken, rice, red beans, and pasta, followed by an extremely serious discussion of the important issues of the day, including sports and classic cars.[12]

On Friday, warm tropical weather returned. Couples added some heat of his own with seven birdies and an eagle for a 63, while Davis Love carded a 66. They were now −27 under, 13 shots ahead of their nearest threat, the Malaysian team.

When Saturday ended, their score was ridiculous: −34 on the basis of Couples's 68 and Love's 69. McNulty and Johnstone were like lion cubs scratching at the king of the pride, 11 back.

What was the secret?

Love believed, "If I can keep Fred interested in something other than golf, we'll be fine. I'm not going to try to tell Fred Couples how to play golf, and he doesn't want me to. We don't push each other or get in each other's way."

The company, the cuisine, and the conversation were good enough for Couples and Love to finish an astonishing −40—count 'em, 40 shots under par. The next-closest team was McNulty and Johnstone, 14 shots back at −23.

During that round Couples hit one of the worst shots Davis Love has even seen him hit. "He topped it. Rolled it off the end of the tee on the 18th. But he came back and made par. He's definitely got all the shots, but he's not real sure when they're comin'," Love said with a smile. "He also hit a million good ones too."

The −40 set a new record low score at the World Cup. Couples's individual score of 265 won the International Trophy with a record −23 for the 72 holes of play. When asked about defending the title in 1995 in China, Love answered, "They might be sick of us, but Chinese is my favorite food."[13]

November was only half over, and the Shark Shootout was slated for the third week. So it was back on an airplane, another 3,000 to 4,000 miles, and bingo, Thousand Oaks, California.

This time Couples's partner was Brad Faxon by an arrangement between their caddies. After the first round, which was alternate shot, Lanny Wadkins and Andrew Magee fired a six-under-par 66 to lead Couples and Faxon and Chip Beck and Jeff Maggert by two strokes. It looked as if the caddies had scored a 'place,' at least.

The second round, Ben Crenshaw teamed up with Mark Calcavecchia to go 10 under par in better ball and capture the lead. Couples and Faxon and Wadkins and Magee were just one back, ready to pounce.

On Sunday, all waved white flags at Couples and Faxon, who posted a 58 on the last day. Why were they a good team? Faxon replied quite seriously, "Fred Couples and anybody is a good team." Quite a statement.

Couples had his own view of this time of the year, which he called the off-season. "That's where I thrive. I get to play with some of my buddies. I like sitting around at night talking to Davis and Brad Faxon at the Shark Shootout and, of course, Kapalua. A lot of families go over there, so it's a nice time, and I learn a lot about my game from relaxing. It's one of those things—you either play good or you don't, and out here [on the Tour] when I don't play well, it really bothers me, and that's not good for me."

But wait. There was still a week left in the month, and it was more or less a cab ride from L.A. to Palm Desert for the Skins Game. No jet lag. He'd be rested.

Tom Watson, winless on the PGA Tour since 1987, was invited to the contest, which was historic in a way since Watson was a member of the original Skins foursome when it started in 1983. Couples, Paul Azinger, Payne Stewart, and Watson readied for battle.

After nine holes, Azinger and Stewart had pocketed $80,000 each and Watson had $50,000. Couples had a goose egg.

On Sunday, Couples was eager, but neither he nor his competitors were able to make a move. Pars tied through the 13th. The birdie barrages of years past had disappeared.

Finally, at the 14th hole, Couples made a six-foot birdie putt to win five skins and $170,000.

The deadlock returned.

Ties prevailed through the 18th, and the four went to a playoff. It was settled quickly, but with drama.

Watson had a 20-footer, gave it a good roll, and miraculously it fell right into the cup. Then Couples faced a makable birdie putt of 10 feet to tie and force continuation of play. When he stroked it, it looked good, but it grazed the hole on the right side of the cup, handing $160,000 and the Skins title to Tom Watson.

Couples was a Skins bridesmaid for the third season in a row. But at least Watson now had received payment for the 3-wood and the advice.

Couples's End-of-Season Earnings

Kapalua	$180,000	Hole-in-one; car
World Cup	150,000	
International Trophy	100,000	
Shark Shootout	150,000	
Skins Game	170,000	
Total:	$850,000	

As the year wound down, Couples took time out for friends. He had introduced John McClure to friends in one of Ross Perot, Jr.'s, businesses in Dallas. McClure did some consulting during the summer and fall, was offered a permanent position, and decided to take it.

Couples immediately suggested that McClure stay in his guest house, which was good for both of them. McClure was a native Texan, so he was at home in Dallas. He was almost as shy as Couples. They played golf together and trusted each other's opinions on all kinds of matters. They both hated spending money foolishly or losing it. They both looked good in Ashworth. McClure was such a good friend that he sometimes watched over Tawnya's son when Fred and Tawnya were traveling.

Just before Christmas, Mark Rolfing and Couples hooked up again at the Johnnie Walker World Championship. Rolfing remembered not the golf but a story about pancakes.

"Fred is the kind of guy who really cares about everybody, and that's a rarity in a superstar," Rolfing began. "To give you an example, Fred and I were rooming together at the Johnnie Walker in Jamaica along with Brad Faxon in a villa. It was a real nice set-up, and we had a couple of Jamaican ladies who cooked us all our meals.

"I got up one morning and went downstairs, and Fred was sitting by himself at the breakfast table and in his shorts and T-shirt. His hair was a little messed up and he had his chin in his hand. I asked him how he was doing, and he said, 'Rolf, we've got problems.' He looked very serious. I asked him what kind of problems. He said there were raisins in the pancakes, which I couldn't see as a problem. Then he said, 'I hate raisins.'

"When I suggested that he ask the lady to make some pancakes without raisins, he said no, he didn't want to do that. He didn't have to say it, but I knew he didn't want to make her feel bad. I always remember it as a perfect example of him being concerned about somebody else's feelings."

Couples diplomacy at its finest.

By the end of 1994, Couples had amassed 11 U.S. titles and a major championship. His 10-year extension from the 1983 TPC had run out, but he had another from the Masters.

He finished the season 23rd on the money list with $625,654 in regular-season earnings. His scoring average was 69.28, second on the Tour—astonishing, considering the circumstances. He'd made every tournament count even though he'd shouldered the burdens of his mother's passing and his own physical ailments.

The question that fans and followers asked themselves was without having to face difficult personal issues for the third year in a row plus health problems, just how good could he have been?

18

Charity Begins at Home

*"One of our original goals was to endow a golf
scholarship at the University of Houston."*

—Jim Nantz

It's nice to see people give something back. Golfers—pros and amateurs—
give a lot that goes unnoticed, unheralded, and unpublicized.

The NFL likes to brag about their charities, but over the years the PGA
Tour has raised over $338 million in total contributions. It is raised
through a combination of corporate contributions, hardworking tournament directors who raise funds through pro-am sales, ticket sales, corporate hospitality, and efforts of volunteers. The players provided an amount
equal to about 25 percent of their purses to charity. This is due in large
part to Deane Beman's reorganization of the PGA Tour as a nonprofit
charitable organization in the mid-1970s.

Beyond that effort, many players have their own charity events. The
more successful a pro becomes, the more inclined he is to pay back to the
community where he lives and to society as a whole. Most pros realize that
if it weren't for the people who come out to see them, there wouldn't be
any big paychecks in golf, and they realize there are many people they can
help by lending their support to various causes.

In 1989 Couples began going to the Claude Harmon Pro-Member at
River Oaks. "It is named for Dad," Dick Harmon explained. "Fred plays
every year. He is quite gracious about doing that because we don't pay
players to play in it. Fred has not ever missed one." The Pro-Member benefits the Claude Harmon Foundation, which gives scholarships each year
to the University of Houston and Rice University golf teams. It is held
before or after the Houston Open when many players are in town.

"Going to events like the one Dick Harmon has made me realize how important it was to get involved in something on my own and with my friends," Couples said about his awareness that he wanted to be more than a recipient of prize money.

Some years, when Couples has not entered the Houston Open, he has come to Houston just to play in Harmon's event. He has been castigated by the press for skipping the Tour event and showing up instead for Harmon's pro-am. The press has presumed it was a paid appearance. He didn't reply to the critics. He didn't tell them he had come for a friend. He knew that Dick Harmon had made a difference in his career. Showing up was one way to repay Harmon.

In 1993 Couples became interested in an idea that Jim Nantz and Charlie Epps had discussed 15 years earlier to raise money for charity and for scholarships at the University of Houston. It became the Three Amigos, a charity tournament started in 1994. Charlie Epps recalled its origins:

"When I was golf pro at Houston Country Club in 1978, Paul Marchand came out and asked for a lesson. We developed a relationship then. I met Jim Nantz, and we all became friends. I would have them over for dinner. We'd talk about the future."

Epps told them that when they became rich and famous, they couldn't forget him and that they were going to get back together.

"After school, Jim was going to Utah," Epps continued. "We had always talked about starting a golf tournament. I told them all it was important to come back to their community, to give back. For about 10 years, everybody was out doing their deal. We didn't see each other that often, but kept the idea alive. Then Jim called me and said, 'Let's do it. I'm ready, and I think I can get Fred.' And I said, 'Let's include Blaine.'"

Epps noted that for Blaine McCallister, raising money to support research for his wife, Claudia, is really important. "Claudia is one of the main reasons I do this event," Epps added. "She wanted to do something for her rare disease, PXE. It's a motivating factor.

"The title came because they were suite mates," Epps said. "We kept coming back to the Three Amigos."

"It's now the second largest fund-raiser in the city of Houston," Nantz added proudly, "second only to the Houston Open. We gave over $200,000 to charities in 1997."

Nantz also noted that in the past the Three Amigos event was featured on ESPN with Blaine, Fred, and Jim acting as hosts of the weekly program *Inside the PGA Tour*.

"The first year was six months after Fred's mother had passed away," Epps said. "The evening of the dinner, the three guys got up in front of everybody and were honest and talked. Fred talked about his mother. Blaine talked about his wife. Everybody got caught up in the emotion of it. It allowed people to see what these guys were about."

Dick Harmon has gone to the dinner each year. "Fred does a good job," he noted. "He's a much better speaker than he gives himself credit for. When he had to explain the charities, where the money was going, he absolutely broke down when he talked about his mother. Jim Nantz was behind him, and the two of them just hugged. It showed you that Fred has a big heart."

Epps noted that although there are many one-day golf events, he believes that theirs is one of the most successful. "Each one of the players has strengths. Fred is a big draw. His charisma is second to none in this day and age."

The event is a success, according to Epps, because of Jim's and Fred's and Blaine's connections.

Some of the charities that have benefited in the past include Alzheimer's Disease and Related Disorders Association, Inc.—the Greater Houston Chapter, PXE (the eye disease that afflicts Blaine's wife, Claudia); University of Houston Scholarship Fund; Houston Children's Cancer Research Fund; and the Millie Medlin Violet Sobich Couples Fund.

"One of our original goals was to endow a golf scholarship at the University of Houston," Nantz explained, "because that's where we all got our start. We just sent a check to the university for $150,000 for the first-ever golf scholarship in perpetuity. This year, we will endow the first-ever permanent basketball scholarship in university history. We wanted to do that because both golf and basketball have such rich traditions at Houston."

Epps said he was impressed because Couples, Nantz, and McCallister have shown how much they appreciate the University of Houston and understand the importance of making a contribution to communities where they have lived and worked.

The same year that Couples became involved in the Three Amigos, he and longtime friend John Bracken, along with Couples's agent, Lynn Roach, began working on a two-day charity event in the Seattle area. It has gone by two different names to date, and it took a temporary hiatus during 1998 because the PGA Championship was at Sahalee, just outside Seattle, and Couples and Bracken did not want to appear to be in competition with the PGA.

There are several reasons Couples wanted to start the event. One was to raise money for local charities. The other was to give youngsters in the area a chance to see PGA Tour players in action.

Unlike other major metropolitan areas, Seattle had not had a regular Tour event or even a special golf event in decades. The PGA Championship had last been held in the Northwest before Couples was born.

The way the idea for the tournament evolved was almost accidental, according to Bracken:

"I was in the rental house with Fred at Augusta when he won. That was the first time I had ever met Lynn [Roach], although I had talked to him on the phone a couple of times. Lynn came over one night, and we were sitting with Fred watching TV and Lynn was giving us a bad time about Seattle being a triple-A town. Lynn said, 'If you're such a great sports town, why don't you have a golf tournament?'

"Fred went to bed, and I said to Lynn that if somebody were to put their name on it—i.e., Fred—we probably could. That idea kind of died that night, and the very next year, 1993, during the same tournament, Lynn started in on me again, now representing the past champion of the Masters. And I said, 'Hey, this thing could be a home run if Fred would be the host and invite some guys. You're his agent. I'm his friend. It's hard for me to try, you know, to say "Fred, you should do this." So, if you want to bring it up to him, and he thinks its a good idea, we'll go with it.'"

Roach went to Seattle, and Bracken, through his contacts, set up meetings with some businesses and convinced them that the tournament would be a success. Couples wanted Bracken to run it.

"I was a golf rep for Wilson Sporting Goods," Bracken explained, "so I had to think in a hurry. I knew I couldn't do both well, so I had a short conversation with Fred, making sure that it was what he wanted to do—and if he didn't it was no big deal—but if he wanted to make it happen that I would be there and do the best I could, and I wanted to know if he was there for the long haul and he wanted to do it. And he did."

The Ernst Championship, hosted by Fred Couples, started in 1994. Ernst was a regional hardware chain. Between the third and fourth year, Ernst was eventually pushed out of business by larger national chains. Although the tournament lost its sponsor, the tournament's founders kept it going and renamed it the Fred Couples Invitational.

"We put together a combination of other local and regional companies," Bracken explained. "Because it took on Fred's name, it made the marketing and everything easier because it said "golf" right away."

Bracken admitted that Couples was a little bit gun-shy about using his name on it but that he wanted the tournament to continue, and so they all decided it was the thing to do.

The charities that benefit have rotated a bit since the inaugural year of the event but include cancer research and children. "The Fred Hutchinson Cancer Research Center in Seattle is world renowned," Bracken explained. "Fred's family has some cancer history. Fred also wanted to encourage kids to start playing golf, and so we split up between Washington Junior Golf and Inner City Golf."

Bracken thinks Couples waited until he was truly established to start the event. "Fred didn't really think he was a big enough deal to have a tournament until after he won the Masters. He could have done a tournament 10 or 12 years earlier, but if he did something, he wanted it to be big, and we wanted to raise enough money to make a difference. He wanted to have a respected enough name that he could bring the best players on the Tour for the kids and adults to go out and watch, and I think he's done a great job with that."

In the fourth year of the tournament, 1997, Arnold Palmer agreed to play. Palmer likely would have played before, but nobody in the Couples camp could get up enough nerve to ask him.

"With Arnold, Lynn said, 'Fred, *you* really need to invite Arnold,'" Bracken explained. "Arnold had just invited Fred to play in his deal in Latrobe, and Arnold had said, 'Any time I can do anything for you, let me know.'

"Fred made the mistake of telling us that; so we said 'Come, on Fred. Call his bluff. Ask him to play in your deal.' Then he'd see Arnold and it would be, 'Oh well, the situation wasn't right. I couldn't do it.'

"So then he went to Bay Hill. He was on the range and he walked up to Arnold and was going to have the discussion with him, and he got sweaty palms. He said hi to him and talked to him and the words just couldn't come out. Fred told me a couple times that Arnold Palmer is the only guy who really makes him in awe. Nicklaus and Trevino he's gotten to know well enough, but something about Arnold Palmer, the ambiance of Arnold Palmer, makes him really nervous, and he can't talk. So I guess that's a credit to Arnold and the way people look up to him."

But it didn't solve the problem of how to invite the King to Couples's tournament in Seattle. What they decided to do was write a letter.

"Fred actually wrote to Doc Giffin, and Doc called us up right away and said, 'Sure, Arnold would love to play,'" Bracken recalled. They couldn't believe it was that easy.

Couples's contribution to Seattle doesn't begin and end with playing golf, according to Joe LaCava. "I found this out by accident, because he didn't want anyone to know. I was just around a conversation during the tournament—I know Fred would not want to make a big deal of it—but he gave whatever he won back to the Cancer Society in the area, $70,000 to $80,000. So he played basically for nothing."

In its first three years, Couples's Seattle event raised over $330,000 for local charities, which included the Fred Hutchinson Cancer Research Center, the Seattle Athletic Facilities and Education, the Washington Junior Golf Association, and Inner City Junior Golf.

While these are special events that benefit many, there are other things that Fred Couples—and he's not alone in doing this, as he would be the first to point out—has done to help other people individually.

One was several years earlier, in 1991, for Micah Mefford. Micah, who at the time was living in Virginia, Illinois, was born with congenital heart problems.[1]

"When he was five weeks old, he had open-heart surgery," his father Marquis Mefford, explained. "He had more surgery when he was four years old and wore a pacemaker."

But Micah's health would never approach that of an average child, and he and his parents knew the time he had left was short.

But Fred Couples and fellow Tour player, Billy Britton made one of his wishes come true.

"Micah informed me one day that his favorite golfer was Freddie Couples. It was just before Fred really took off [1991]. He kept telling me about Freddie," Micah's father explained.

"I started watching," Mefford went on. "I happened to have a friend, Matt Mays, and his college roommate was Billy Britton, who plays on the Tour. Listening to all this, Matt decided to do something."

The "something" took about two months to work out. It was in the spring of 1991. "Matt got hold of Billy and explained the situation, and Billy suggested a letter to Fred. I think it was just that Micah would like to see and meet Fred. He wrote the letter," Mefford explained. "Fred agreed. They would do something during the Western Open."

What Britton and Couples had in mind was more than a handshake. They were going to give Micah Mefford an experience that even most CEOs don't have. They were going to play a round of golf with the 11-year-old. The only stipulation Couples had was that it needed to be a private golf course without a lot of people watching, without the press.

At the Western Open, Couples had a morning pro-am tee time, and Britton changed his tee time with Scott Hoch so they would both have the afternoon free. La Grange Country Club agreed to take them and arranged to have no one else on the course at the time.

"I didn't know what was planned," Mefford said. "Our plans were just to go to the Western Open. Then Matt called me at 11 P.M. on a Tuesday evening and asked me to go to his house. He told me he'd been working on a little deal for Micah to play golf with Billy Britton and Freddie Couples."

But they told Micah that they were going to La Grange Country Club to get tickets for the tournament. The head pro put on an exhibition to stall for time while they waited for Couples and Britton to arrive.

"Micah got a little bored wanting to go to the Western Open," Mefford continued, "but then the tee announcer said, 'Now, on number one tee, Micah Mefford and playing partners touring pros Billy Britton and 1991 Memphis St. Jude winner Fred Couples.'

"Micah walked up to the tee, and Fred said, 'I hoped you're on your A game today.' And Micah answered, 'I hope you're on yours.'

They had played just five holes when a storm came up. They all took shelter in the clubhouse, where a special room had been set up so they could visit.

"We were in awe of Billy and Fred," Mefford said. "We were there for an hour before the storm passed through. Micah asked, 'Do you think we can play?' I told him that I was sure Billy and Fred had other obligations.

"But it was Fred who looked at Micah and said, 'What's it look like? We've got holes to finish.' They got back on the cart. We all went out to a par-5, dogleg right and pulled to the center of the fairway, and Fred took out two Maxflis and dropped them there and said, 'Two pretty nice drives, huh, Micah?'"

When they had finished nine holes, Couples asked if they had cameras and everybody started taking pictures. Couples and Britton left. The next day, the Meffords went to the tournament.

"I told Micah that Fred was at work, so we didn't want to bother him," Mefford recalled. "Fred had finished the front nine. Micah had a chair we brought for him because he got tired easily. He was sitting right near the 10th tee, wearing a Cardinals baseball hat.

"At the tee box Fred said, 'Hey, Micah, go along the fence. I have someone I want you to meet.'"

Then "Fred came up and shook hands again and said, 'Here's a good Cardinal fan,' and introduced us to Jay Haas," Mefford remembered.

Couples was playing Tommy Armour clubs at the time, and unbeknownst to the Meffords, he contacted the Armour Tour rep in the Chicago area. Two weeks later, a full set of Tommy Armour 845s junior size were delivered to Micah Mefford. Micah sent a picture to Fred of himself with his arms around the golf clubs.

Micah Mefford died March 13, 1992, just seven months later.

But the story wasn't quite over. During the Masters in 1992 a very peculiar thing happened.

"When the ball stopped from going in the water on the par-3 12th hole," Marquis Mefford explained, "the announcer said that it always goes into the water. But it sat there about eight inches from the water. Right when the ball stopped, my phone rang and a voice said, 'Micah stopped that ball.'"

Then the line went dead.

Mefford questioned all his friends and relatives, and none of them had made the call to his home.

Mefford didn't see Couples again for four years, until the 1995 Western Open. Couples came off the course, and went to the autograph tent, but Mefford stood back and waited. He saw Couples go to the clubhouse and guessed the golfer would go out the back door, which he did.

Mefford explained: "As he was walking by, I walked up left and back of him and said, 'Excuse me, Fred, I didn't know if you remember me.' And he took a second look and said, 'Of course I remember you. I still have the picture that Micah sent me, and I look at it often for inspiration.'

"All of a sudden you could hear a commotion in the background," Mefford said. "And I told him it looked like he'd been discovered. We shook hands, and I wished him the best."

19

Déjà Vu

*"I'm looking forward to a big year.
I don't think that's going to backfire."*

—Fred Couples[1]

At La Costa for the Tournament of Champions, Couples explained his situation.

"I didn't get to practice last year. After practice, the next day I would be miserable. I would be tight. My back would hurt." He planned to enjoy this first week, go overseas for some guaranteed money, and then start working toward Augusta. He had already scheduled time with Paul Marchand.

"When he comes out or when I see him, I play extremely well after that. It's the old crutch of having a guy that you believe in telling you that you're swinging good, that you look good. One mishit, I think I'm back to playing terrible," Couples explained about their relationship. "He really takes care of me mentally, and that's where I struggle sometimes. I know, physically, I can play day in and day out. Paul gets me back on my game.

"There's a couple ways you can play. One is you go out there and people say it looks easy. And sometimes it really is. And sometimes you're playing where you've got to battle and battle and battle, and I don't do that very well. I seem to get on a ride, and I play well for a couple of months."

Like January of 1995, for instance.

At La Costa he wasn't brilliant, but considering that he'd just come off a year when he was out for nearly three months, he was pleased. He finished fifth.

Joe LaCava remembered the beginning of that season like no other. "He went to Dubai early because he'd missed the cut the year before and felt like he owed them a better performance," LaCava recalled. "He certainly tried [in 1994], but he just didn't make the cut, didn't play well. And he was making appearance money. So, in 1995, he got over there early and practiced Sunday, Monday, Tuesday, Wednesday. And I was kind of surprised by that."

However, in his two-week adventure, Couples became another historic footnote. He became the first American golfer to win back-to-back overseas events on the PGA European Tour since Charles Coody in 1973.[2]

It was also the first time Couples had won two in a row, although he'd been close on occasion. Unfortunately, it was abroad and the U.S. audience didn't get to see him beat Colin Montgomerie by three and Nick Price by four, Greg Norman by five and Ernie Els by six in Dubai, or Price by two and Norman by four at the Johnnie Walker Classic, this time played in Manila, Philippines.

The galleries in Dubai were small, but Couples's arrival in Manila was said to have caused "the same sort of frenzy as the Pope on his recent visit."[3] Well, they are both Catholic.

Peter Jacobsen won at the AT&T and the following week in San Diego, proving that Couples wasn't the only player who could win back-to-back events. Jacobsen said it was fine with him that Couples was overseas, because, "it gave me a better chance to win — just kidding."[4] The two were good friends, and Couples later said he was glad Jacobsen was having his best year ever.

Couples collected $697,750 in purses and appearance fees for his two-week flyby of foreign places.[5] That's a season for some players. Now he was ready to throttle up in the United States.

At Riviera, the throngs were out in force. Riviera had become a new curiosity because O. J. Simpson had played a round there the night before his ex-wife was murdered. Paul Revere Middle School, location of Sydney Simpson's dance recital, was the location of one of the tournament parking lots.

On the golf course, Corey Pavin became the first back-to-back winner in L.A. since Arnold Palmer in 1966–67, and Paul Harney in 1964–65, and Ben Hogan in 1947–48.

Couples finished in a disappointing tie for 19th, packed up, and headed for Doral.

Joe LaCava was ready for a big year. "Fred was ready to practice. He was determined that year. I remember him being so high and I was thinking, 'God, no one can beat this guy the rest of the year. He's going to win everything.'"

Then it happened again. The back. This time Couples didn't complete a round.

LaCava shook his head as he recalled the incident. "That's going from being as confident and high as you can to being pretty low—thinking this guy may not play again, let alone beat everybody."

LaCava wasn't kidding. This time it was more serious than pulled muscles. Couples rested and got more medical advice. The diagnosis was that the space in his spinal column holding the nerves was too small. That caused pressure on nerves, which caused him pain. He had won two tournaments in a row, and now he didn't know how he would be able to play again.

He was very worried. But he didn't tell many people that.

After two weeks off, he tried playing with the pain, finishing 37th at Bay Hill and 29th at the Players Championship. Those who knew him could tell that there was a problem. It was what he didn't say, the way he didn't act, and the fact that his golf wasn't as good as it should have been.

He even played in New Orleans, a spot he rarely visited after the early years, and then was 10th at the Masters. Ben Crenshaw won at Augusta in an emotional victory, virtually collapsing in tears at the 18th from a combination of sheer joy at winning the title again and sorrow over the death of his lifelong teacher, Harvey Penick, the previous week.

Couples missed the cut at the MCI Heritage Classic, then dropped out of sight until the Kemper Open in June, where he struggled to find his game but couldn't. The next week at the U.S. Open, in the rolling sand dunes of Long Island's Shinnecock Hills, he failed to make the cut again.

On Sunday, Corey Pavin, who was overdue for a major, hit a brilliant 4-wood to less than five feet on the 18th hole to cap a spectacular week of golf and get the major monkey off his back for good.

For most of the summer, the only regular appearances Couples made were in Ashworth ads.

However, he did accept one invitation extended by Paul Marchand, to play golf in Maine at former President and Mrs. Bush's property, called Walker's Point.

Marchand had been invited to go to the Bush family property in Kennebunkport in 1994, and in 1995 "the President asked me if I would like to invite two others to join me, so I invited Fred and Jim Nantz." Jim and Lorrie Nantz, Fred Couples and Tawnya Dodd, and Paul and Judi Marchand went to Maine. The property had been in the Walker family several generations. As many serious golfers know, the former president's grandfather on his mother's side donated the Walker Cup trophy.

In the morning they would get up early, choose up sides, and play golf at Cape Arundel, a par 69 on an inlet of the bay coming through Kennebunkport.

"We played golf every day in under three hours. President plays fast," Marchand noted. "Fred loved that. It was a fun course.

"We played there four days, mixed up who was with who. On the third day I shot 65, and nobody knew I was there because Fred shot a 62 and set the course record.

"The fourth day, President Bush took Jim, and I think Fred was seven under after 11, then one over coming in. President Bush made a 10-footer the last hole to win the match. Fred was happier about that than his 62.

"I got a note, a copy of the letter that the President sent to Fred about a month later, and it said, 'Congratulations. You made the Cape Arundel newsletter. Front page.' Nowhere did I read about my 65!"

Back on the regular Tour, Couples was virtually invisible until his defense of the Buick tournament in Flint, the week before the PGA at Riviera. There he was sixth. He had played mostly to show Lanny Wadkins that he wanted to participate in the Ryder Cup. Because of the time he'd lost since 1994, his only shot was as a captain's pick.

At the PGA Championship, Couples and Corey Pavin were favored, since the two of them had won on Riviera four times since 1990.

However, Ernie Els played three magnificent days of golf, and when Saturday's round was concluded, everyone just about gave him the trophy. He'd already won a U.S. Open on a more difficult course. But on Sunday, Els took a wrong turn somewhere out there in the kikuyu, eucalyptus, and iceplant, and Steve Elkington, who had been six strokes back at the start of the day, won the PGA Championship in a playoff with Colin Montgomerie.

Couples was disappointed with his 31st-place finish, but he received great news the following day when Lanny Wadkins announced his captain's picks for the upcoming Ryder Cup at Oak Hill: Couples and Curtis Strange.

Wadkins said he'd played 36 holes with Couples at home in Dallas and was confident that Couples would be able to go the distance. But there was a little more to it than that, as John McClure recalled:

"Lanny was trying to get Fred to join Preston Trail in Dallas," McClure explained. "Fred hadn't played much because of the back problems, but he wanted to make the Ryder Cup team.

"Lanny said we ought to have a game, and said he'd take Gordy [Gordon Johnson, the head pro]. Fred said, 'My guy's an amateur [McClure], and he needs a half a shot.' We played 36 holes one day and 18 the next day. We started on the back nine in the morning and decided to play for five bucks, 1 down automatics. We played the front nine, and Lanny shot 31 on his own ball and we lost, 2–1 and 0. Then Fred shot 29 or 30 and ended up with a 64 with a double."

After lunch, they teed it up again.

"We got to about the seventh or eighth hole, and Mickey Mantle, who was one of Fred's dad's heroes, was just out of the hospital. He came out to watch us play for a few holes, because he liked Fred. His son took a picture of us—Lanny, Gordy, Fred, David Frost, who was out practicing, Mickey Mantle, and me.

"We had so much fun, we played the next day. I think Lanny picked Fred for the Ryder Cup team based on what Fred did those two days. He hit one bad drive, made double—hit a tree, went in water, and dropped—but other than that never missed a shot."

The only question anyone had about Wadkin's pick of Couples was whether his back would be willing.

The Curtis Strange selection caused heated debate in the press corps before and after, but Strange had won the U.S. Open at Oak Hill.

Couples's journey to Oak Hill started at the World Series of Golf, where he played the individual winner of the World Cup in 1994. He finished tied for sixth and went to the Canadian Open and tied for 34th. At the B.C. Open, which he had won in 1991, he tied for 20th.

Then Couples headed for Rochester. It was cold, rainy, dismal. And even when the sun came out, it was chilly—more like European weather.

Yet for Couples, the week started with a happy occasion. He became engaged to Tawnya Dodd. It happened on the way to the players' banquet. Tony Porcello, a Seattle friend in the jewelry business who delivered the ring to Couples, said it was not a decision made in haste.

The pre-event hype had the U.S. team as a stone-cold lock. The Europeans were supposedly getting old, on the one hand, and had too many rookies, on the other. The heart and soul of the team, Seve Ballesteros, had lost his game completely. Ballesteros even joked during a press conference that he'd cleaned out the bush on the course for the members and that he'd been places most of them had never even seen. But as Peter Jacobsen wisely noted about Ballesteros, "I think you could put Seve with the paper boy, and Seve would probably bring him through."[6]

Lanny Wadkins had 12 guys he liked, respected, and was determined to whip into shape to keep the Ryder Cup. The veterans were having good years, with Crenshaw winning the Masters, Love winning New Orleans, Pavin winning at L.A. and the U.S. Open. Jay Haas was a Ryder Cup veteran from 1983. Even Couples, with his bad back, had won twice, albeit abroad.

New "kids" were far from being fresh-faced boy wonders, except, of course, for Mickelson, Hollywood grin and all. Brad Faxon had played the Tour since 1983; Jeff Maggert, since 1986. Loren Roberts had turned pro in 1975. Tom Lehman won at Colonial in 1995. Some of these guys weren't just experienced in the trenches—they had seen the bottom of the trenches. They were street fighters in golf clothing.

The Europeans had Ballesteros, Woosnam, Langer, and Faldo. Olazabal was out with injury problems. Montgomerie had become world class. The rest of their cast was familiar: Mark James, Sam Torrance, Howard Clark, Costantino Rocca. David Gilford wanted to avenge his 1991 performance at Kiawah.

Their team had two "kids" in Per-Ulrik Johansson and Philip Walton.

Friday and Saturday came and went, and it looked as if Wadkins was the only American captain ever to figure out how to beat the Europeans soundly in better ball. The United States actually won six of the eight fourball matches, a total equal to the number of fourball matches won in 1987, 1989, and 1991 combined.

Couples and various partners won two matches and lost one. Jay Haas and Couples played on Friday morning in alternate shot and had problems. At one point, Couples played up the 10th hole while they were on the 13th. But that kind of thing happened with Couples, as they all knew. They made par on the hole and won it. However, they lost the match 3 and 2 to Rocca and Torrance, who were described as patient plodders.

On Friday afternoon, Couples and Love showed why they had won the World Cup three years running when they teed it up for better ball and won 3 and 2, defeating Faldo and Montgomerie. Prince Andrew followed the action.[7]

On Saturday morning Couples sat out, which was probably wise, considering his erratic play in the Friday alternate shot and the state of his back. But he paired with Brad Faxon in the afternoon against Montgomerie and Torrance. It was one of those matches where birdies tied holes. The Europeans finally made an error at the sixth, and Couples's par won for a 1-up lead that they added to as the match continued. By the 12th, they were 3-up and cruising. When Monty and Torrance birdied the 13th, it looked as though the momentum was changing.

Couples was in the rough around the green in three. Then he hit one of his miracle flop shots and, as Joe LaCava remembered, "when he chipped in at the 13th to tie the hole, the crowd went nuts. It was probably the loudest thing I've ever heard." This is the Joe LaCava who'd been through two victories in L.A., a Masters win, and three previous Ryder Cups. Even the stately oaks around the green must have been moved.[8]

Couples and Love went on to beat Montgomerie and Torrance, 4 and 2.

At the end of play on Saturday, the United States actually had a solid advantage of 9 to 7.

In the history of Ryder Cup, 69 years, the United States had lost the singles portion only two times: 1940 and 1985. With only 14 points needed to keep the Ryder Cup, the U.S. team didn't even have to win a majority of the matches. That was probably the problem. Everybody thought it was ok not to win.

Hole-outs and even a hole-in-one played parts in Sunday's outdoor adventure story. The only things missing were ropes, trail mix, and hiking boots—and, at the finish, rescue helicopters, although the Concorde did buzz the course.

In emotional events like the Ryder Cup, intangibles count. For Europe, it may have been the outfits. Saturday evening, Seve Ballesteros had told his teammates they had to wear blue instead of green because blue was his lucky color.[9] Who was to argue? If Seve said blue was lucky, then blue it was.

The wives of the European team even wore blue, complete with the little gold stars.

The score stood at United States 11, Europe 9 on Sunday when Couples and Woosnam began their match with obligatory first-tee photographs. Couples bent down, to even up his nearly six-foot frame with Woosnam's five-foot-four-inch height. The gallery gathered around the tee chuckled. It started in friendly fashion.

Woosnam lost his humor in the right rough off the tee. He had to take a drop from the television cables, and could get only to the rough near the green. It was bogey. Couples had the early advantage.

At the third, Couples missed a short putt for par and the match slipped to even. Then, at the fourth and fifth, it was a replay, with two missed putts, and Couples was 2-down.

Woosnam gave one back with a bogey at the seventh. At the eighth, they both birdied, Couples with an approach to about four feet. At nine Woosnam made a 15-footer for birdie and took his 2-up advantage back, but it lasted only one hole.

No matter where they played from, between the 11th and the 16th, the score stayed the same, 1-up in Woosnam's favor. The closest Couples could come to a strike was a lipped-out birdie attempt at the 12th from inside six feet.

At 17, both hit the fairway. Couples backed off his second shot. Cheers had erupted from a nearby green. It was worth the wait: his second shot landed about 15 feet from the pin. When he made the putt and Woosnam couldn't match it, the score went back to even with one hole to play. They had been slugging and slogging their way through as many roughs as fairways, and after 17 holes they were even.

The 18th was a deciding hole for more than one match, but theirs was the first to reach it. Couples found the left rough off the tee, Woosie went to the right side. Either of them would have paid a few thousand dollars to have been in the fairway at that point. Woosnam hit first. He landed inside 15 feet, some said closer to 12. It was makable.

Couples came out of the rough—squarely into the front bunker. It looked as if he would surely lose the hole and the match. But with Couples it always looks that way, and like Houdini, he escapes. This time the sand wedge landed four feet from the pin. Unfortunately, with the number of short putts he'd missed that day and with the pressure of the Ryder Cup, it wasn't a lock. Woosnam had first shot at it: a putt to win the match and the point. But it slipped by the hole. Couples made his. They tied. Shook hands.

Woosnam, hugging his wife, began to cry, knowing he'd been ahead for 13 straight holes with only a halve to show for it. He knew how far behind the Europeans had been at the start. He knew they were wearing Seve's lucky color. And he had never won a singles match in his Ryder Cup career. However, he'd played Couples twice, and that was part of the reason.

Couples said that he was "thrilled to halve with Woosie."[10]

United States 11½, Europe 9½.

The match between Ben Crenshaw and Colin Montgomerie favored Crenshaw on the greens and Montgomerie from tee to green. With 10 scoring changes during the day, it was enough to give the gallery and the players a case of the shakes.

At the 13th, they were tied again. Then lightning struck. Montgomerie went 3-3-3-3, defeating Crenshaw at the 17th, 3 and 1.

Montgomerie was just the second player to birdie the 17th. Couples had also done it. No one else would.

United States 11½, Europe 10½.

Lanny Wadkins chewed on his walkie-talkie antenna.

The precarious lead did not last long. When Faxon was defeated on the final hole by Gilford, the score was evened once more. But Corey Pavin outgutted Bernhard Langer to give the U.S. a one-point margin, 12½ to 11½, that registered briefly until Loren Roberts fell to Sam Torrance to tie it once again.

In the last match, Mickelson was comfortably ahead, and the U.S. was fairly sure of his success.

The focus shifted to the Faldo-Strange duel, which went the full 18 holes, Strange pushing him all the way, until Faldo escaped with the full point. Ballesteros and Faldo hugged each other in the emotionally charged moment, both of them crying. It was then 12½ to 13½ in Europe's favor.

Jay Haas had fallen behind Philip Walton but dug deep to stay in the match, holing out from a bunker on 16, winning the 17th with par, and pushing the match to the last green. On the final hole, Walton admitted afterward, "While I was playing, my legs were shaking." Yet this little-known player from the other side of the Atlantic won the deciding point.

As Ian Woosnam popped the cork on a magnum of champagne, the European fans, draped with flags from various countries, began singing, "Philip Walton, we love you."

It was only the second time in the history of the competition that the U.S. team had lost the matches at home.

Couples had finished 2-1-1 for his second-best Ryder Cup effort. As captain's pick, he had performed fifth best on the team. He'd gone 0-3-2 in 1993; 3-1-½ in 1991; 0-2-0 in 1989.

With many weeks off during 1995, Couples did not qualify for the elite Tour Championship for the first time since it began in 1987, but as usual he played in November, though he started out more slowly than in previous seasons.

He finished ninth at Kapalua. Was he beginning to slip? Perhaps he viewed it as a way station en route to China for the World Cup, where he and Davis Love III would defend for the third time with a chance to break the mark set by Jack Nicklaus and Arnold Palmer.

"There were probably three or four or five thousand people watching us on all the holes," Couples said, about the experience of playing in China. "The first day we played with the Chinese players, and they were nervous. There were a lot of cameras and portable phones. But we realized what was going on, and by the end of the week it was fun."

One player quipped that he didn't know if he was playing golf or participating in a telephone commercial.

However, Couples and Love came through the first round with a 68 and a 65. They were −11, but Jesper Parnevik and Jarmo Sandelin were only three back.

In the second round, Couples and Love went 69 and 67 and held a one-stroke advantage over the Swedes.

By the end of day three, Couples and Love distanced themselves from the field with 70 and 68, respectively. The Japanese team of Hisayuki Sasaki and Hiroshi Goda had pulled into second. At this point, Couples and Love were at −25, a full 10 ahead of the nearest contenders.

In the final round, Couples posted a 69 and Love came in with a 67 to win the World Cup for the fourth time in a row. They knew they were making history in several ways.

They tied their own record margin of winning by 14 shots over the next-closest team, but they finished only −33, seven strokes higher than their completely devastating total of −40 the year before.

As a team they were 121 under par for the event, 73 under par in the last two years, and had three of the four best winning scores ever posted in the event. Additionally, the record of a 14-shot victory margin, which Couples and Love had achieved twice, was one they shared with the team of Hogan and Snead, who were victorious for the United States in 1956.[11]

And, of course, they put China on the golf map in a big way.

After a long flight to the states, Couples unpacked his bags for the Shark Shootout at Sherwood Country Club, where he and Brad Faxon defended their title. They never contended or led the event, but they finished with a final-day 57, in a tie for third with the team of Tom Lehman and David Duval. The cash register still rang up $51,000, which was not a bad tune-up for Couples's annual pilgrimage to the Skins Game the following week.

At Bighorn, the last time the event would be contested on the rocky slopes of the Santa Rosa Mountains, galleries welcomed returning Skins champion Tom Watson, U.S. Open champion Corey Pavin, Peter Jacobsen, and Fred Couples.

Surprisingly, after three spectacular years at the Skins Game, Couples was completely shut out on the first day. The glory was Corey Pavin's.

On Sunday, $30,000 was still riding, a carryover from the previous day.

Three players—Couples, Watson, and Jacobsen—parred the 10th. The 11th was now worth $90,000. As though he had not missed a beat, Corey Pavin birdied it and scooped up the prize. Of the 11 holes, Pavin had won 10. He was a thief disguised as a golfer.

No one could win another hole outright. The 12th, 14th, and 16th were tied with pars or birdies. And they came to the 18th with $270,000 on the line.

They tied again, forcing a playoff. They replayed the 18th, and Watson and Jacobsen were eliminated when Couples and Pavin both made birdies.

Then Couples and Pavin both parred the 17th. Then the 18th. Then the 17th. And finally, on the fifth playoff hole, Couples made a 10-footer and collected $270,000. Seven holes' worth of cash all at once. It was a record for money won on a single hole, surpassing the $260,000 that

Payne Stewart won in 1991. Zero to 270 in seconds. Better than any race car around.

It was also good enough to declare Couples Skins champ, guaranteeing a return trip to the desert in 1996.

Mr. November IV

Kapalua	$ 21,333.34
World Cup	$200,000.00
Shark Shootout	$ 51,000.00
Skins Game	$270,000.00
Total:	$542,333.34

It was well below his earlier *ca-chings* on the cash machine, but Couples had finished 63rd on the money list, and this topped his season-long earnings by a little over $240,000. His November earnings would have put him in 33rd place on the Tour money list for all of 1995.

But he wasn't quite done for the year.

He had received an invitation to the Johnnie Walker World Championship in Jamaica. There were only 19 players in the elite, invitational field.

Wayne Riley, the Scottish Open champion, held the first-round lead with a 66 that included a chip-in birdie on the first hole.

Couples had more than his share of ups and downs, with two birdies and a bogey on the front side, a double at the par-4 12th, a garden-variety bogey at the 13th, an eagle at the par-5 14th, and a birdie at the 18th.

The second day, he shifted into high gear. He was up and down on the front with two birdies and two bogeys for even par. The back was more interesting, however. He chipped in at the 10th from 25 feet to get things going his way. He cruised to the 13th, where he bogeyed; birdied the 14th, a par 5, from five feet; and finished birdie-birdie-birdie.

At 16, he made it from three feet, which is where his sand wedge landed. He hit the par-5 17th green in two and two-putted. And at the 18th, he again wedged it close, to two feet, a virtual kick-in birdie.

He said his back had tightened up and that caused him to hit the ball better. "I can't explain it"[12] was all he could add. It was a 67, good enough to tie for the second-round lead with Riley and Singh.

On Saturday, Couples posted a 71, but it was a round that hung on a lucky break. The golf gods obviously liked Jamaica, too. Couples came to the par-3 15th with a three-shot edge. On the tee, he hit 5-iron and just didn't make a quality pass at the ball. Miraculously it crossed the river and landed near a cart path, which interfered with his stance. The good news was that he got a drop. The bad news was that after the drop he would be making a baseball swing. Of course, he had a hereditary advantage there. He escaped with a five and considered himself lucky that the ball didn't go into the hazard. Then he got a stroke back with a birdie at the 17th and finished one shot ahead of Vijay Singh.

Couples's play on the front nine of the final round was abysmal. He birdied the first, then bogeyed the second and the fourth. The extra stroke at number two was from a bunker, and at four from a creek. That's right. A creek. He couldn't find the green in regulation on the fifth and then took two putts to get in, and at the seventh he had an attack of three-puttitis.

At the end of nine, Loren Roberts emerged as the leader. Vijay Singh was one back, and Couples was three back.

Couples seemed to be on snooze control instead of cruise control until the 16th, when suddenly the alarm clock in his head went off and he commented to Joe LaCava, "If I finish three-three, we've got a chance to get into a playoff."[13]

LaCava didn't wince, grimace, laugh, or even change expression. He handed Couples his driver. Couples would have to go eagle-birdie to get into a playoff.

As Couples explained later, "Walking down the 17th, I noticed that there was no reaction from the gallery."[14] That meant Roberts, playing in the group ahead, hadn't birdied the hole. Couples hit an 8-iron to 25 feet and made the downhill eagle putt on the par 5. At the 18th, he hit his wedge to 20 feet, which was far off the mark, but he made the birdie putt, forcing a playoff with Roberts and Singh.

On the first playoff hole they all parred, although Roberts was the only golfer in the fairway off the tee.

They replayed it. Groundhog's Day golf. This time everyone made the short grass. Roberts's second shot landed 18 feet from the pin. Singh was next, lobbing a brilliant shot to five feet, and he looked like the sure champion, because Couples came up 15 feet from the hole.

Roberts lagged up and made par.

Couples was next, and he calmly rolled his right in the heart.

Singh must have been rattled by Couples's stunning comeback, because his putt slid past. Suddenly the championship belonged to Fred Couples.

In the five years of the Johnnie Walker World Championship, Couples had won $1,517,500. "The first million I made here is gone," he said after collecting the trophy and the check. "Maybe I can hang on to this

$550,000." He'd won the first year of the event in 1991 and the last year of the event in 1995.[15]

Couples finished 1995 with his third victory on the European Tour. In between, he'd had injury problems that caused him to reevaluate whether and how he could still contend, never mind win. But he'd figured out a way to be at least sporadically brilliant. With four victories in 12 months (counting the World Cup), it was his winningest season ever, even though all of the victories came outside the United States.

On the U.S. Tour, he finished lower than he had since 1986, owing to the back problems that started at Doral. His other stats slid. He was 15th in scoring because of poor—by his standards—rounds during his effort to play the required 15 events. However, on the world money list, he was 15th, with $1.4 million,[16] not counting appearance money for Dubai and Manila.

He and his banker were probably still on speaking terms.

The victory at the end of the year became a springboard for 1996.

20

America's Player

"His final three. The only thing that could overshadow the Final Four."
—Headline of a Lynx ad

For the first time in the 1990s, Fred Couples was not at the Tournament of Champions.

His 1996 season started at the Bob Hope tournament. Couples-watchers noticed he was still struggling with his back condition. He managed seventh place, but had been just one shot off the lead after four rounds.

His next move was the Johnnie Walker Classic in Singapore, where he was defending champion. He finished sixth and came back to the States, then took a week off.

In San Diego at Torrey Pines, though he was not on top of the leader board, he was considered a serious contender because he began 68-65. After the round, he said he "couldn't do anything" because of his back. By Sunday night he was tied for 12th.

In L.A., his favorite place, he tied for second with Mark Brooks, Scott Simpson, and Mark Wiebe, but he never led, carding 68-70-70-71, one short of a playoff with eventual winner Craig Stadler. Things got worse. He played poorly at Doral, finishing 58th, and did not enter the Honda Classic.

Couples's next event was in Dubai, where he was also defending champion. Unfortunately the Dubai event had changed weeks, putting it up against one of his favorites: Arnold Palmer's event at Bay Hill.

The schedule conflict created headlines, fueling the debate about whether the Silly Season was hurting the West Coast events. But that wasn't 100 percent accurate. Norman was gone to Australia to support events there. South African players—Ernie Els and Nick Price—went home for a long holiday. They all returned to the United States in March.

For Couples personally, the Dubai situation was more than a schedule conflict. It was a personal conflict, because he felt he needed to be two places at once and couldn't be.

"If I hadn't won at Dubai, I would have gone to Bay Hill," he said the Wednesday before the Players Championship.

He was asked about appearance money for foreign events and about the Silly Season. Couples was a good person to ask because he had learned to balance them all. As a rule, he did not skip the West Coast swing. Several tournaments there had been favorites of his for years, and he used to say he liked to play them and make money and then take time off later in the year.

"Great question," he responded. "I can only respond from my point of view. I've done it.

"I played the British Open in 1984 and loved it. That's the British Open. You don't get paid to go there. The next year, not playing well, I didn't go.

"That would never happen if someone were to invite me to a tournament and pay my way and give me money. If I was playing poorly, I would go. That was the way I used to look at it.

"Personally, I enjoy going to play against Colin Montgomerie, Ian Woosnam, Michael Campbell, all those guys. It gets me away and makes it more fun for me.

"I don't play the Phoenix Open anymore because I go to the Johnnie Walker. But I definitely would have played Bay Hill except it was the same week as Dubai. I wouldn't go to Dubai for a handshake, but two years from now I might not be that good a player, and they might not ever ask me to go back again. So I'm taking advantage of it for me.

"I see all these players who go travel and make money, it's their call. I look at it as being fun to have an opportunity to play golf and get paid, too. And it's exciting to go to China or Hong Kong to play golf."

Because Couples often played at least half of the West Coast events, no one could accuse him of playing the Silly Season and skipping early-season tournaments. But at that point, he was struggling with a bigger problem: his back. He was still trying to figure out how he could play a round of golf and practice and get up the next day and be capable of playing.

"Last week I tried to push a little bit, and the next day . . . I'm not going to say I couldn't get out of bed, but I couldn't play the next day. And when you do that, and you're at a tournament, you have no chance. To go out and beat these guys, you need to practice. There's no way you can just show up and win."

He admitted that he was, in his own mind, pressured by time.

"I'm in a hurry. Two years ago, it [the back] was not too bad. And it got worse the second time. This is possibly career threatening. But there are not many sports where you can have 15 years of work, and the first and last years are not your best. I need to figure something out for me."

Couples explained that he was getting assistance from therapists. "A lot of days are great days. But I can't follow up a 67 or 68. Is it a big deal? Not really. I've learned to accept it as long as I'm not shooting 77 and 78, and I don't have a problem and feel good most every day."

He did not want to use his back as an excuse for bad play. He reminisced about winning his first tournament in 1983 at Kemper.

"It was one of my first chances to win, and I realized I learned a lot. Someone was going to win, and I was playing them. It was just one of those fluke things. To shoot 77 and win."

But he added, "If you never get your first win, you never know how important it is. It took me a little while to win the TPC here. I struggled a little bit. It's the thrill of a lifetime. It's what you strive for, no matter whether you're someone no one's heard of or one of the greatest players. You still need to get a first win somehow."

Sometimes it's intangibles that get the week off to a good start. Maybe remembering better times put good things into Couples' game, because when he teed it up on Thursday morning he came out strong with a 66. Justin Leonard and Kenny Perry were leading with 65s.

Paul Marchand came in for the day, as Couples explained in a postround press conference. "I asked him to come down Thursday morning just in case he saw something that he could tell me then versus seeing it at Augusta. I have not seen him in a while."

As Paul Marchand had explained, at this point he was more or less a reminder for Couples. When they got together, it was like a refresher course in all the things Couples already knew he should do.

This was also the month of Tommy Tolles's coming-out party. Tolles had held the third-round lead in New Orleans, the week before the Players Championship. Prior to that, Tolles was a hardly known, second-year Tour player who had honed his skills on the Nike Tour.

After a first-round 66, Tolles added a 64 and climbed to the top of the pack.

Couples was sort of hanging around. The second day he posted a 72. He was five back.

On Saturday Couples made a semi-move with a 68 and improved his position to −10, four behind Tolles, two behind David Duval, and tied with Colin Montgomerie.

He was asked about the other contenders, especially the first-timers like Tommy Tolles.

"I think, whether he has never won before, you know, he is the guy to catch. If the weather is good, he could be 15 or 16 under before he is done today. If he doesn't, and he comes out tomorrow, and plays good at all, realistically, I have no chance. So I think it is great. I'd like to see everyone have a shot at winning."

When questioned about the pressure of the money, $630,000 for first place plus the 10-year exemption, he admitted it probably would affect the younger guys, but said it wouldn't bother him in the least.

"I couldn't care less about $630,000, but that is not going to make it any easier for me tomorrow. The fact is that I can go out there and play a great round and so can Tommy Tolles or Michael Bradley. They are just as capable as I am. It is not like they are going to fall apart tomorrow. So the exemptions, all that, it could be a part of struggling, but I think this course will make you struggle more than anything."

Someone in the media quipped that $630,000 was like a bad November for him, and everyone laughed. So did he.

"Well, you know, yeah, that is not nearly enough," he joked. "Oddly enough, I don't know, that is a lot of money to play for. I think it is great. This is our biggest tournament. I see no reason why if it can be bumped up, we shouldn't play for it."

He left the media center claiming to be headed for his back therapist and a night of heavy basketball viewing. The NCAA basketball March Madness was in full swing, and he didn't intend to miss a shot.

On Sunday he proved he could go from number one to done to back again. He did it with flair, with drama, with style, and with power. It was wonderful to behold, unless one happened to be Tommy Tolles or Colin Montgomerie or David Duval, the contenders who were pretenders to the Couples throne.

It wasn't any place close to an average finish, either. It was a stunner, a come-from-behind victory with all the joyous enthusiasm of a Nicklaus at Augusta in 1986.

"I hit two great shots on the first hole and missed a fairly makable birdie putt. Second hole I drove it in the right trees, up by a root. I was trying to go over the palmetto bush and under some other trees and maneuver it up the fairway. I thinned it right into the palmetto bush. It trickled into the rough. From there I had 220. I cut a 3-iron in front of the green and in the left rough, not too bad, and chipped it to about six feet, and a huge putt. [He made it for par.] To make bogey there is . . . that would not have been good."

"On the third hole [par 3], I hit a 7-iron, 20 feet, made it.

"Fifth hole, hit 6-iron, three feet, made it.

"Sixth, hit a wedge, 25 feet.

"Eighth, I hit a 4-iron to two, two and a half feet, made it.

At the 11th he missed a short putt, and it actually may have been what helped him win.

"It was embarrassing," he said sheepishly. "At that time it was too good of a round. I mean, a three-footer or four-footer, but this was like straight in from two feet. And I am not saying I have never missed any, but you really want to tap it in and crawl into the cup and not let anyone see it. It is just a bad feeling."

At the 16th tee, Couples was a shot behind. He hit a standard-issue thundering drive. Then, on his second shot, the shot that really won the tournament, he was trying to hit a "big old fade. I started it at the middle of the green and it kind of cut over there to the right edge of the water."

Those out on the course held their breath as it headed for the green, looking like it was going to find the lake to the right of the dastardly but familiar par 5. At the last minute, it took a miracle hop. Another Fred Couples lucky break. Then, when he made eagle from 25 feet, it was as though destiny was on his side once again.

Gary Van Sickle described the reaction after Couples dropped the putt: "It was loud, of course, and more than a roar, really. You actually felt it."[1]

And if there were ripples in the water, if the coverings on the skyboxes reverberated, or if the alligators in the water around the island green actually shimmied from the decibel level, it would not have been a surprise.

Colin Montgomerie said that no one had to tell him who had hit the shot or what it was for, although he also admitted thinking it might have been a hole-in-one on the 17th. Not an eagle at 16.

Tommy Tolles said that he had been to a lot of golf courses and a lot of tournaments and that it wasn't often a crowd made such noise.

Then Tolles and Montgomerie saw the one at 17. It happened just after Colin Montgomerie put his second shot into the water at 16.

Couples continued. "On 17 [the par-3 island green] I was aiming pretty much where it went. There is a small little ridge and I flew it a little too far, and it was an uncomfortable shot at first. It was a weird yardage. They put the tee way to the left, which they had never done." It was 137 yards, and he used a 9-iron but said he was jumpy when he hit it. Understandably.

"It flew in the back part of the green and stopped up at the tier. I just felt good over the shot and I hit it where I was looking, which was safe," he added.

The thing was, he made the putt. Again, a 25-to-30 footer. This time for birdie. The repeat roar was like an aftershock. Was it live or was it Memorex?

Montgomerie, meanwhile, received a penalty shot at the 16th and virtually ended his chances for the title.

Couples had gone eagle-birdie on two of the toughest holes the Tour played all year. Yet even the 18th, the testing finisher, wasn't routine.

"I thought I was a couple of shots ahead on the tee," Couples explained. "It is still an uncomfortable tee shot for me, because I don't really draw the ball, and I just hit it straight, pushed it out to the right. But, you know, not the end of the world. When I got there, I just took another club. I hit a 2-iron from I think 212 to the hole, and I just played a big banana shot and actually hit it right where I was trying to hit it, which was on the right side of the green. It hit and stayed in that little swale, and I lagged it up there very close and made par.

"One shot that I have no problem hitting is a fade or a slice, and I really think if I went out there and hit ten more, four, five would be on the green and four, five would be further right. It just was not that difficult of a shot. You know, I've played enough of them."

Tolles played the last three holes one over. Montgomerie played annoyed.

At the end of the day, Couples claimed he was just trying to get to 17 under. He finished one better, at 270, not a record by any means, but a very wonderful victory at a time when he needed it for himself.

He admitted to the press that he had been concerned his physical condition might hold him back. He explained that Tom Boers, his therapist, had come in Tuesday and had been a great deal of help. This finish and the fact that he held up physically gave him hope.

"I would love to play like this. I think if I continue to play like this, I will work my way back into winning tournaments," he said, meaning more than one a year. "I would say this tournament ranks right there as the best tournament I have had. It was perfect timing. The Masters is the biggest one I have ever had. I think at the Masters [in 1992], I was one of the top players at the time, and I don't think I am too far now, but to win here really shows me that I can still win."

He did, of course, receive another 10-year exemption, to which he replied, "I wasn't really planning on playing till I was 46, but at least now I will be exempt."

That Sunday he thumped the field with an amazing display of power and courage and talent, proof of the comeback that had started at the Johnnie Walker. It was an exclamation mark in an ongoing career of thrilling moments. But because of what Couples had gone through in the four previous years, it was a fabulous victory at a time when he needed it. He was back, so much so that the next series of Ashworth ads showed a follow-through revealing precious little about the clothing and showing mostly Fred's back.

During the week he had removed the Lynx Black Cat long irons and gone back to the old Lynx 2-, 3- and 4-irons. He put in a new sand wedge because the grooves on the old one had worn out.

The next week in Atlanta he finished fifth, working his way toward Augusta.

But at the Masters, he was disappointed, starting with a 78 that did not compare well measured against Greg Norman's 63. He finished tied for 15th place, 288, even par. Greg Norman was expected to win on Sunday. Nick Faldo, his nearest threat had started six strokes back, and Norman looked unbeatable until he handed his title to Faldo on the back nine.

Couples played at the Colonial, and he got to Fort Worth in the early rounds courtesy of a helicopter, a loaner from Frank Zaccanelli, then GM of the Dallas Mavericks. He took heat in the media room for his choice of transportation but pointed out that the helicopter was easier on his back than the 90-minute drive from Plano. He finished fourth there and was beginning to look like a contender again.

Then, the Monday after the Colonial tournament, Couples pulled a muscle in his back and was sidelined. It happened while he was chipping, not during a full swing.

Couples pulled out of the tournament at Westchester, hoping it would improve his chances to play the following week at the U.S. Open. But when the time came, he also withdrew from that event.[2] It was frustration and difficulty he didn't need.

Oakland Hills, which Hogan had called the hardest golf course in the world, proved to be just about that difficult for everyone but Steve Jones, who outlasted everyone on the severely raised, lightning-fast greens.

Couples's back muscle finally recovered, and he teed it up at the Canadian Skins Game and then went on to the Western Open. At Cog Hill, he played a little closer to par than he would have liked, 72-69-72-70, and finished in a tie for 26th. But he was able to play again, and that meant he could go to the British Open, one of his favorite golf tournaments.

The British Open in 1996 boasted an international leader board for the first two rounds. On day one, Hidemichi Tanaka from the Asian/Japanese Tour and Americans Mark McCumber, Mark O'Meara, Brad Faxon, Mark Brooks, Loren Roberts, Tom Lehman, and Fred Couples were all within two strokes of the lead, which was held by Englishman Paul Broadhurst. Americans were not favored because no American pro had ever won at Royal Lytham and St. Annes. The only U.S. player to have success there was Bobby Jones, as an amateur in 1926.

In round two, Nicklaus shot a 66 to take attention away from the rest of the field, including leader Tom Lehman. Faldo posted a 68 and was within two strokes. Couples was one more back, but there were 10 players between his score and Lehman's.

The third day locked up the championship for Lehman. He posted a 64, with a bogey at the last hole, to separate himself from the field and give himself a little breathing room on Sunday. He'd learned that lesson at the U.S. Open. His lead was the largest since Tony Lema's, who was seven ahead of Jack Nicklaus in 1964. Faldo, the nearest competitor, was six strokes back. Again.

On Sunday's first nine holes, it looked as though Couples's physical problems had been cured overnight by a TV faith healer. He shot a 30, five under par (35), but on the incoming nine he skied to a 41, six over par, as though the other half of a split personality materialized at the tenth hole. Perhaps he believed he would have to post a second 30 to win. He had been a virtually unreachable eight shots behind Lehman at the start, then made up five of them on the front.

As it turned out, Lehman posted a 73, two over par, and if Couples could have managed to shoot one under on the back, he would have tied Lehman and gone to a playoff.

A few weeks later, at the PGA Championship in Louisville, Kentucky, Couples and representatives of a group of investors including Ed White, Paul Little, and Joe Leach, announced the completion of a buyout of Lynx from Zurn at a Wednesday morning press conference. They said it had been done in record time. The investors included Bob Bennett, Fred Couples, Rick Dees, Clint Eastwood, John Elway, Brett Hull, Bob Husband, Jim Lampley, Jim Nantz, Jack Nicholson, Allen Paulsen, Lynn Roach, Patrick Roy, Pete Sampras, Jeff Silverstein, Roger Staubach, Jerry West, James Worthy, and others who were either not involved directly in the deal or who were not as famous.

The total price for the buyout was between $25 and $30 million, and according to White, they had more investors than they could use. A press release from Lynx dated August 7, 1996, indicated that $37 million was "offered and funded" by GTL Securities, a Canadian merchant banker and that "a 100% subscription rate was accomplished within 90 days." For 1996, Lynx sales were reported at about $45 million, up 50 percent from the previous fiscal year. The investors planned to take the company public with an offering on the Toronto Stock Exchange.

Couples, likely distracted with the off-course, club-company activities, opened with a 74, then added another 74 in the third round to finish 41st. This was not the way Fred Couples wanted to play in major championships, particularly not after his 1996 triumph at the Players Championship.

The PGA was won with a gritty final-round performance by Fort Worth native Mark Brooks, who simply refused to succumb to the pressure of the situation and the narrow fairways. He shot two under on the final day and ended the round in a sudden-death playoff with Kentucky native, Kenny Perry.

Less than a month after the PGA a new force in the game put a choke hold on every other story. Fast on the heels of his third U.S. Amateur victory, Tiger Woods announced that he was turning pro. Immediately various tournaments sent invitations, and before anybody could say Nike, he had a full slate of PGA Tour tournament invitations on his schedule for the fall of 1996.

For Couples, the next tournament was a special event, the President's Cup, this time captained by Arnold Palmer. He did not intend to play poorly.

Prior to the matches, a huge controversy developed when several players on the international team, reportedly headed by Greg Norman, asked that David Graham be replaced. Whoever headed the uprising, and whatever the reasons, Peter Thomson, winner of five British Opens, became the captain of the International team.

This year, all their name players attended: Norman, Price, Els, Elkington, Singh, Nobilo, Frost, Ozaki, Parry, Senior, Allenby, McNulty. And the U.S. team was strong with Lehman, Pavin, Brooks, O'Meara, Love, Leonard, Mickelson, Duval, Hoch, Perry, Stricker, and Couples.

Former president George Bush was the Honorary Chairman.

Unfortunately for the event, that same week Tiger Woods teed it up at the Quad City Classic, and on Saturday, when Tiger took the lead, many of the writers who had been covering the President's Cup spent Saturday afternoon trying to figure out how to get to Moline, Illinois.

Couples said what he liked about the President's Cup was "to have people that you have looked up to your whole life, like Arnold Palmer, to be around for a week. I think that's great. Having him around, having him tell stories, and having him get charged up and trying to get you charged up."

Before the competition started, the American players celebrated Palmer's birthday, complete with a cake. They hoped to bring him a victory, a present they knew would mean more to him than anything else they could do.

Palmer put the winning World Cup team of Couples and Davis Love III together, figuring they ought to be a lock for most of their matches. The first day, it looked like a sweep for the U.S. team as Couples and Love took out Greg Norman and Robert Allenby in fourball (2 and 1) and again in foursomes (1-up).

At the end of the day, it was United States 7½, the International team 2½. It looked like a walkover. A snooze. A mail-in victory.

The quip of the day was when Palmer was asked what the president had to say. "Which president?" Palmer asked. He goes way back with presidents. Back to Ike.

Once that was clarified, Palmer said, "When a president of the United States sees fit to come out and condone an event like this, I think that's a great thing for the event."

Couples and Love, a combination that was now beginning to sound like a daytime soap opera or a rock group, met with reporters. It was the first time they'd played back-to-back matches, Love explained. "For an all day thing," Love added, "I think it was a really good day. We both can get a little disgusted with ourselves, and I didn't think we really did today."

They'd played two matches and endured a rain delay. It had taken a while.

Couples commented on the closeness of the play: "We knew, basically after Greg hit his putt, we could win the match by Davis making it or by his missing it. It's still the last match, and you miss it, you lose another full point, you find yourself further behind. It's not like Davis and I are the best team for our team, but they had said that they felt they were invincible, and Davis and I asked to play them," he explained.

Not exactly a schoolyard "Oh yeah?" But not far from it.

Davis cited the World Cup as helpful because "we learned each other's games in 16 six-hour rounds at the World Cup. We learned patience with each other and with our games. You laugh, but it's the truth, that tournament has done a lot for our confidence.

"We've played so many rounds together, I've seen every miss and every good shot he can hit and vice versa," Love continued. "He puts me up there in the trees at 16 or 15, it's just payback for me hooking him down there in the trees on 12. It doesn't bother me. It bothers him a lot more than it bothers me. And we have fun. I know he's going to come on strong at the end no matter what. I'm walking 200 yards ahead just with my putter, waiting to putt my birdie putt. It's a lot of confidence in each other."

Couples cited some loose shots he'd hit and mentioned that playing with Love had helped him pick up his game a notch.

But Peter Thomson didn't win five British Opens without learning a thing or two about golf. His side came out the second day like birds of prey with talons outstretched, ready to ensnare unsuspecting victims.

The score tightened up a little after the morning, with the International players winning three points. It was 9½ United States to 5½ International team.

In the afternoon, the bloodshed began. The U.S. team won only a single point—in the very last match on the very last hole.

O'Meara and Hoch in alternate shot against Singh and Elkington played their first two shots in a ravine to the left of the 18th fairway. O'Meara hit a low smother hook off the tee, and Hoch could only advance it further in the trouble. Then O'Meara redeemed himself with his wedge, hitting a miracle shot that landed a couple of feet from the hole. Hoch made the putt, and the United States captured the point, and at the end of the day it was United States 10½ to International team 9½.

On Sunday, in singles play, the U.S. team needed to win six of the 12 points to win the matches. Many of the players spoke about their desire to win for captain Arnold Palmer. Some just had better luck on the course than others, and it came down to two matches.

In what had been an up-and-down, David and Goliath–type battle, Corey Pavin went down to Greg Norman 3 and 1. The score was then tied, 15½ to 15½.

Only Couples and Vijay Singh were left on the course. Couples remembered, "When we teed off, I said to Vijay, 'I hope it doesn't come down to us.'"

But it did.

It had been close, and coming down the 17th hole, Couples was 1-up.

"The second shot was basically trying not to miss it to the left and do anything crazy. I blocked it out there, then he hit a good shot. When I got up to the green, the putt really wasn't that hard from the standpoint of rolling up there and trying to two-putt."

But at that point the captains, all the team members, and their wives and fiancées or girlfriends, plus galleries were on hand watching the two remaining players.

"It's nerve-wracking—that's obvious. . . . I knew it was going in three or four feet from the hole, and I turned around and the first guy I laid eyes on was Mark O'Meara, so I ran at him and had a good time. It was a great feeling, great for me."

The 25-foot putt went in, and Couples went into his imitation of Air Jordan and celebrated with O'Meara.

"We won six matches today, which was not easy," Couples added. "To win and have the putt made it even more special. But we came to win, and we did, and we beat a great 12 guys. We were fortunate."

O'Meara added, "I've been with Freddie in a lot of Ryder Cup events, and I know Davis and he paired together tremendously in a lot of events. I've seen Freddie on the 18th hole, too, been the other way. So I couldn't think of a better person and a more solid player to pull it off, and that's why I was so jacked for him when he made the putt, because he and I spent some time together after it wasn't such a great day at the Belfry. Golf has a funny way of redeeming itself."

For Couples, he had had the chance to be a hero once to himself in March, and a second time for his team in September. He finished out the year with a rare appearance at what used to be called the Southern Open but was now the Buick Challenge, and he was sixth. He also went to Las Vegas, where he finished eighth in the shadow of the New Kid, Tiger Woods, who found the winner's circle for the first time as a professional.

All the golf headlines for the rest of the year began with Tiger Woods's name somewhere close to the first paragraph, or the stories didn't get read. It took some of the pressure away from Couples, and in a way that was fine with him.

He had reclaimed his stature, professionally, with a sixth-place position on the Tour money list and a victory at the Players Championship. He'd won $1,248,694 in the United States. Though he had problems with his back, he had figured out how to play. Playing golf was important to him. It was what he did best.

He was second in scoring with a 69.57 average. His final-round scoring average, a relatively new stat, was the third best on the Tour at 69.75. Thinking back to what Steve Hershey had written about being able to bring it home on Sunday, it was clear that Couples had almost mastered that in 1996. Certainly the 64 at the Players Championship was a convincer.

Though he and Davis Love III did not defend again at the World Cup in 1996, Couples picked up the Sarazen World Open. Gene Sarazen had agreed to be honored at Three Amigos in Houston, so Couples, naturally, wanted to play in an event that Gene Sarazen was hosting. But he also added, "At Augusta this year, Gene Sarazen came up and said, 'I've got an invitation for you to play in my tournament. . . . Would you like to play?'" However, he never contended and finished tied for 26th.

From there, it was on to Kapalua where he led the first round firing an eight-under-par 63 at the Bay Course in wet and windy conditions.

The weather continued to be unusually nasty, as though gremlins had decided to take a Hawaiian vacation. But Paul Stankowski was unflappable, and pulled a stroke ahead of the field on Saturday. Couples was two back, in third behind the tenacious twosome of Gilder and Jones.

The rain stayed for the final round, and the trade winds continued to blow. Stankowski disregarded them, however, and shot a steady 68. Couples finally pulled himself up by his bootstraps and shot a 67 to finish one shot out of first. He collected $130,000 for second place. Gilder and Jones were finally separated by—guess who—Davis Love III.

For the first time in five years, Couples was not in the field at the Shark Shootout. He spent the two weeks sharpening his clubs for the Skins Game.

Making matters more interesting was the rest of the field. Tiger Woods, at 20 years of age, made his first appearance. John Daly, after battling demons, was invited to return. It was hyped as the contest between the two longest hitters the Tour had ever seen.

Couples, the defending champion, was almost relegated to second fiddle. And in a sentimental move, Tom Watson, who had won the Memorial, breaking his streak of nine winless years, was also invited to play. Watson had more majors and titles than the other three combined.

The tournament also changed venues, returning to the flatter terrain of the desert floor at Rancho La Quinta.

Watson started off strong, with a 12-foot birdie putt on the first hole for $20,000.

At the second, Daly and Woods tied with pars. The $20,000 carried over to three, where Couples made his presence known with a second shot to a foot and a virtual kick-in birdie putt to rake in a quick $40,000.

At the fifth, Woods broke through, winning $40,000.

Not to be outdone by the kids, Watson scooped up $80,000 for three holes with a birdie on the eighth; $30,000 carried over to the tenth hole on Sunday.

Sunday was so chilly there was a 30-minute frost delay, and when play started, Couples couldn't seem to find the magic. He was among the spectators.

From the 10th through the 14th there were ties with pars or birdies. The money was adding up, but nobody could break out; $240,000 waited for the best man to take it away.

Then, at the 15th, a 338-yard drivable par 4, the big hitters let loose. Woods and Daly both went for the green. Couples and Watson hit irons. But before Daly and Woods reached their balls, Couples had put a sand wedge inside eight feet. He was salivating. When his putt curled in on the low side of the hole and nobody else birdied, *ca-ching*: $280,000 in the bank.

Again they found the tie zone, with players making pars on the 16th, birdies on the 17th, and pars on the 18th, forcing a playoff.

On the first extra hole, the 18th, Watson, Woods, and Couples parred. Daly was eliminated. Playing the 10th for the second time that day, Tom Watson birdied the par 4 with a five-foot putt and pocketed an additional $120,000. Putting demons begone. However, Watson's total was not enough to unseat Couples, who now repeated for the first time as champion at the Skins Game.

The contest between Woods and Daly had driven up television ratings on Saturday to 6.2 nationally, but it still didn't break the 1986 Saturday mark of 7.0. Both days were higher than the ratings of any Tour events that year.

Mr. November V

Sarazen World Open	$ 12,206.25
Kapalua	$130,000.00
Skins	$280,000.00
Total:	$422,206.25

It was Couples's worst November since 1991, and he had still totaled nearly half a million dollars. He set records at the Skins Game, becoming the number-one money winner in the 14-year history of the event, with $1,190,000 in his five appearances. He became the only player to win a million dollars in the event. And he still held the record for the most money won at once, with $270,000 on a 12-foot putt on the fifth playoff hole in 1995, the only hole he won in the two-day event that year.

Mr. November, Totals 1992–1996

1992	$ 676,858.50
1993	$ 620,000.00
1994	$ 850,000.00
1995	$ 542,333.34
1996	$ 422,206.25
Total:	$3,111,398.09

And a car. But who's counting?

21

Year of the Tiger

*"Last year I basically just kind of played golf,
and whatever happens happens."*
—**Fred Couples on his 1997 season**

Nobody ever starts New Year's Day thinking the worst. It's just that sometimes the worst is waiting. By the end of 1997, Fred Couples had to be feeling like a human bull's-eye.

Things went well at first. Couples tied for fourth at the Tournament of Champions. His next outing was the following week at the Bob Hope tournament, where he finished in a tie for ninth, shooting a 64 in the third round and a 65 in the final one. However, he couldn't upstage John Cook, who won for the second time in the desert, finishing 62-63 for his second Bob Hope title in the nineties.

The third week found Couples in Australia playing in the movable Johnnie Walker Classic. Ernie Els won and Couples was fourth.

Though he'd been leader-board material all three weeks, he took to the couch.

His next appearance in the States came in Los Angeles as he began his real season, the annual push to Augusta. There he finished ninth and headed east, stopping off in North Florida for a press conference to promote the upcoming Players Championship. He was all smiles and handshakes, as though things were going very well. A private plane waited to take him from the St. Augustine airport to a pro-am function for the Doral tournament.

But within a few days, life took another strange turn.

At Doral he was slated to pose for photos for a story in *Golf World* called "Made in the Shade." Looking at the result, anybody who knows him well had to know there was something upsetting going on that week.

The reporter hardly quoted Couples at all—hard to imagine after a 30-minute interview.

Couples missed the cut and hid out for the weekend, talking things over with Jim Nantz. He was supposed to play Bay Hill, but he pulled out just before the tournament started. And when he returned to Ponte Vedra at the end of the month to defend his title, it was clear from the moment he entered the pressroom for his defending champion's press conference that something was troubling him. He had the storm cloud look, like he'd just shot an 83. He was slumped down in his chair. His body language fairly screamed unpleasantness. The first thought that crossed everybody's mind was his back.

After two or three questions, he finally confessed to a roomful of fairly astonished reporters that he and his girlfriend were breaking up, and there were other problems associated with that.

It came out in a peculiar way. Couples was asked standard questions and said, "I am a little bit edgy, whether it is being the defending champ or, you know, just being here and not quite prepared."

Someone asked him why not.

"You know, that is a good question," he answered. "I haven't been playing the last couple of weeks for a reason, which is really not that big of a deal. It just happens to end up being a big deal, and I am sure it will come out and people will know. But no one has died. Just, life seems to go on, but it can be difficult for me for some reason. I don't know why."

Well now, he'd done it. He'd confessed to a problem and then said he didn't want to discuss it. You'd have thought somebody yelled fire. Eyebrows were shooting up like fire extinguishers, and everybody was whispering to the person sitting next to them, trying to guess what was up now.

"So something happened?" a brave soul said, prodding him a little.

"Something happened, yeah," he said.

The room was so quiet people could almost hear each other breathing. Again he declined to elaborate. He was asked if whatever it was made it harder to focus on his game, and suddenly he decided to come clean.

"I guess the best way to say it is, I broke up with my girlfriend," he finally admitted.

"No alimony?" asked one writer who had been around for the divorce.

"Well, you know, I can't comment on that just yet," Couples answered. That reply broke up the room. They all knew what he'd gone through with Deborah.

"That is the problem." He paused.

Another laugh. His timing was nearly as good as Bob Hope's. If it had been a purposeful stand-up routine, it would have been a success. They got the drift and moved on.

Later Couples turned comedian again. One questioner asked about 16, 17, and 18.

He quipped, "Are those divorces?" And the media people broke up once more. With the one-liners he was laying on them, he could have been invited to Vegas as an act.

The week was endured by Couples, but it was embraced by Steve Elkington, who, as he put it, "blew away the best field we've ever had." And he was right. The top 50 players in the world were there.

What Couples didn't say in the media room was that he had also met someone new. There were no names mentioned, but it would later be learned that the new love interest was Thais Bren, a stunning 30-something mother of two who was getting divorced.

Couples had met her and her husband the previous year through mutual friends in the Los Angeles area, but it was one of those hello-nice-to-meet-you things. She was married and he was engaged.

A year later, things were different for both of them. Then, two weeks after they started seeing each other, she found out she had breast cancer. When she told him that it was a problem he didn't need, he disagreed.

Couples made his way to the Masters, now with an additional mental burden. While he was on the fairways, the new woman in his life underwent medical treatments. He had told her that they would go back to Augusta together the next year, when she recovered.

As everyone in golf knows, 1997 was the year that Tiger Woods cut a swath so wide through Augusta, Georgia, that it caused writers to resurrect the statement Bobby Jones used to describe Jack Nicklaus: "He plays a game with which I am not familiar."

The records that Woods set at Augusta started with the record score of −18 and went from there: Most shots under par, back nine, −16. Low middle 36. Low first 54, tied with Raymond Floyd. Low last 54 holes. Largest 54-hole lead. Youngest champion. Youngest 54-hole leader. Largest margin of victory. Most threes in one tournament.[1]

That was just his performance on the course, never mind his assault on cultural barriers. Woods said afterward that during the week he thought of the people who had come before him, of Ted Rhodes, Charlie Sifford, and Lee Elder.

The Masters ratings were the highest in the history of the telecast. Woods's assault on the azalea bedecked hills of Augusta, Georgia, will forever be a part of golf and Masters history.

Couples's play was decent, considering the circumstances. He opened with par golf, five back of John Huston, the first-round leader. At the end of the second day, he was five behind.

Jim Nantz, known for his superb memory and ability to identify the moment to remember, mentioned for the record that at 5:30 on Friday, April 11, Woods had taken the lead.

"Taken" was gentle for what Tiger did. He handcuffed the lead and tied it to a chair, brought out the duct tape, and refused to let it go until he got the green jacket he wanted. Might be the only time a major championship has been held hostage for a piece of clothing. But some things mean more than money. And in the case of Tiger Woods, waving a green jacket in front of him was tantamount to waving a red cape in front of a raging bull.

On Saturday, Woods shot a 65 to pull nine shots ahead of his nearest competitor, who turned out to be Costantino Rocca. On Sunday, Woods took a victory lap.

Couples finished seventh. He left Augusta and soon received more bad news. His father had been diagnosed with leukemia. They would start treatments later in April.

If it seemed as if Couples began going through the motions, that's because it was all he could do. It was a miracle he could play at all. He shot a 78 in the last round at the tournament in Houston, then went to Seattle.

He began dividing his time between visits to see his father and trips to L.A. to spend time with Thais. His play was limited. He made a half-hearted effort at the next major at Congressional, where he opened with a 75 and finished in a tie for 52nd. Friends Tony and Ann Porcello and John McClure made it to Bethesda to watch and be there if he needed them.

But that week Ernie Els won his second U.S. Open when Tom Lehman missed his shot to the green on 17, a 7-iron from 190 that he caught a little heavy.

Couples played in only one other tournament between the U.S. Open and the British Open, and that was in Chicago at the Motorola Western Open, where he finished tied for 62nd. This was a guy who would ordinarily be in the top 10 when he had the flu, when his back was bothering him, when he was having a migraine. His heart wasn't in it. His mind wasn't on it.

At the British Open, one of his favorite events, he was, miraculously, in contention all the way until Sunday. After a first-round 69, he was just two back of Jim Furyk and Darren Clarke. After the second, he was four off the pace with a 68. Darren Clarke led.

At the end of round three, Jesper Parnevik was two ahead of Clarke. Neither of them had won a major, and most wondered if their nerves would hold up. Couples and Justin Leonard were tied, five back.

Couples was clearly the veteran of the field, and during the third round had eagled the par-4 11th (Railway) with a 6-iron,[2] but his off-course concerns and his lack of practice were big question marks. He would also have to shoot in the mid-60s and hope that the leaders crumbled.

Leonard turned out to be the unflappable one. Making substantial birdie putts when he needed to, he shot a 65, matching the second-lowest final round in British Open history.[3] Couples, his playing partner, had the best seat in the house but was unable to mount a charge of his own. He finished seventh, posting a final-round 74, nine shots behind Leonard's winning total.

Couples disappeared again until the Buick Open, which he used as a tune-up for the PGA Championship at Winged Foot, where he was just two back of leader Lee Janzen after his second-round 67. He eagled the 11th hole there as well, this time with a 9-iron from 140 yards to the cup on the short but dangerous 256-yard par 4. Parnevik had been playing with Couples when he eagled the 11th at the British Open, and he said, "You do it every time we play."[4] Couples also birdied the 12th and the 14th, but finished up with a bogey. He hoped that a strong weekend showing would secure him a spot on the Ryder Cup team.

Tom Kite had only two picks, and, as Fred noted, "I can't go up to Tom Kite and say, 'Tom, I want to play. Put me on the team.'"

The question about off-course distractions was beginning to get monotonous. "As far as the other things on my mind, once I tee off, I'm a fairly tough individual, not exactly someone that bears down to the necessities, but I do feel like, when I get out there, I can play. My problem is I am just pretty rusty. I haven't played because I've been doing other things away from the course."

His third round, though over par (73), was still good enough for fifth. But Sunday's 75 dropped him to 29th.

In what had been a year of emotional and exciting major championships, one of Couples's close friends, Davis Love III, finally catapulted the major monkey off his shoulders in a terrifically moving finish that served as a tribute to his late father.

On Monday morning following the PGA Championship, Tom Kite announced Lee Janzen and Fred Couples, as his captain's picks for the 1997 Ryder Cup team.

Kite was said to have been impressed with Janzen's finish in the PGA. Couples, even with his limited play, was 17th in the standings. He promised he'd be ready, and it would be difficult to leave a player of Couples's caliber and Ryder Cup experience Stateside if he wanted to compete.

In contrast to the heat that Lanny Wadkins felt in 1995 at Rochester, Tom Kite's team was described in this way in *Golf World*:

"Five years from now, we may look back and decide the 1997 U.S. Ryder Cup team was our best ever. Seven of its 12 members are under the age of 35. Six of the 12 are major champions. And all three rookies finished among the top five qualifiers, including two [Tiger Woods and Justin Leonard] who are widely perceived to be the game's toughest competitors."[5]

They were, in order of points: Tiger Woods, Justin Leonard, Tom Lehman, Davis Love III, Jim Furyk, Phil Mickelson, Jeff Maggert, Mark O'Meara, Scott Hoch, and Brad Faxon, plus the captain's selections of Lee Janzen and Fred Couples. They looked very strong indeed.

In Europe, Seve Ballesteros had finally been rewarded for his valiant efforts. He was chosen to captain their team. His homeland of Spain was to be the site of the matches, and the venue, Valderrama Golf Course in Sotogrande, Spain, was world renowned for its wonderful, sunny fall weather.

Europe rounded up the usual suspects. By now, most of the names on the European team were household words to golf fans everywhere. Nick Faldo. Colin Montgomerie. Bernhard Langer. Ian Woosnam. Jose Maria Olazabal. Costantino Rocca. And their new kids: Darren Clarke. Ignacio Garrido. Per-Ulrik Johansson. Jesper Parnevik. Thomas Bjorn. Lee Westwood. For the first time since anyone could remember, Sam Torrance wasn't on the team, and neither was Mark James.

Couples, true to his promise, made an effort to get in some special practice time.

"We practiced in L.A. three weeks prior to the Ryder Cup," Paul Marchand remembered. "Fred had been at L.A. North, played a bunch of days in a row to get ready. L.A. North is a true championship test. He had already shot something like 68-67-68-65-65 when I got there."

"The question was," Marchand remembered, "how the possibility of playing 36 holes was going to affect his back. He was very disciplined about cardio workouts and stretching, so he would be able to handle the demands. At our practices, he played good rounds trying to keep his swing compact and getting a little distance from the ball."

Then, of all things, Marchand, Couples, and John McClure stayed up all night watching Princess Diana's funeral. Because of the time difference, it started in the early hours of the morning in L.A. All three of them had really admired Princess Diana, though none of them knew her.

At about this time, Couples also made plans to accompany Thais Bren to her chemotherapy treatments near Chicago. They arranged for a place to stay for the length of time she would receive medical attention.

Couples arrived in Spain early, the Saturday before the matches, and played nine holes. He played 18 on Sunday. He wanted to be ready.

The entourage came two days later. Paul Marchand arrived Monday along with Tom Boers, Couples's physical therapist.

"There were no ropes up Monday," Marchand recalled. "The teams were not there yet. It was just like a fun golf trip. Fred wasn't in the team uniform."

Everyone else arrived Monday. Former president George Bush was there, a guest of the owner of the golf course. Prince Andrew attended. U.S. royalty—His Airness, Michael Jordan—was there.

Because of the number of dignitaries, security was high.

"There were plainclothes militia everywhere," Marchand explained, "with vests and big side arms. If any incident was about to take place, they would have had plenty of firepower."

The teams were in a resort close to the course but not connected to it. A temporary dirt road had been built to transport players to and from the course.

"Tom Boers and I were staying at a place with the PGA and got up for the bus at dawn to commute to the course," Marchand said. He had done that every day, and by Wednesday evening he was beat. "I decided I'd sleep in the next morning since we'd been getting up at dark-thirty to go out there. But that night at the players' dinner, unbeknownst to me, President Bush ran into Fred and said he was supposed to play the next morning with Prince Andrew and wanted me to join them and play as his pro. The course was right down that dirt road at the hotel. President Bush said that they had a 9 A.M. tee time, so he asked Fred to tell me to come over to the course when I got out there."

Nobody called Marchand. They just figured he'd be there early.

"I finally got there, and at the seventh green Fred said, 'Oh boy, are you in trouble. You were supposed to tee it up an hour ago with President Bush and Prince Andrew. Now you've no-showed him.' I thought he was just poking fun at me because I got there late. But Davis said it was true. Fred walked up to the next tee shaking his head. Then Davis said, 'That's what CBS producer Lance Barrow calls having your foot in the bucket. Great foot in the bucket, Paul.'"

Marchand felt slightly better after he saw Mrs. Bush at the turn, because she told him not to worry about it.

"At the end of the day, Prince Andrew came out of the locker room. Fred introduced us, and Prince Andrew said, 'Oh, you're the chap that overslept. Nice to meet you.' Fred got the biggest kick out of that. So now I'm the guy who no-showed President Bush and Prince Andrew."

When it came time to open the matches, the King and Queen of Spain arrived in helicopters. There was pageantry, complete with a display of Spanish horsemen and their steeds. Several who attended were impressed that Seve Ballesteros gave his opening remarks first in English and then in Spanish.

This was a week Severiano Ballesteros had anticipated his entire life, ever since the days he learned the game hitting golf balls on a beach.

Though the U.S. team was highly favored by the American press, everybody should have suspected trouble because Seve was playing at home. After two decades of swashbuckling through car parks and shrubbery, he was finally able to deliver one of the prized competitions in all of golf to the shores of his homeland. He fully intended to invoke whatever golf magic he still possessed to keep the Ryder Cup in Europe. He probably would have had help from the King and Queen if he needed it.

So just as the fans in Kansas City are the 12th man for the Chiefs, Ballesteros was the 13th, 14th, 15th, 16th, whatever they needed, for Europe. Seve was used to dragging half a continent on his shoulders. He defied logic. He played on emotion. And as even Fred Couples admitted, that is what separates this contest from others.

"Having a goal of not how you play but how your team plays is exciting," Couples said of his experience on five Ryder Cup teams. "Some people thrive on it. I seem to *play* like it's anything else. What I thrive on is that it's very emotional."

The rain came to Spain. So much rain that a few members of the media had water in their hotel rooms, and not just in the faucets and showers.

The start of the Friday morning matches was delayed by 90 minutes.

At that point, one might have thought that Seve's plans were going to go awry. But he had already countered with a strategic maneuver. He had asked to switch the order of play. No one could think of a good reason not to. A dip into the record book supposedly revealed that the Europeans had never led after Friday-morning foursomes [alternate shot].[6] And Seve knew that the American record in fourball was more bad than good. Yet he did not want his team to start out behind. They switched. But at the end of the morning, there seemed to be no advantage. The teams were tied at 2 points apiece.

Couples paired with Brad Faxon for a 1-up victory over Nick Faldo and Lee Westwood. Couples birdied the impossibly annoying 17th hole and Faxon parred the last.

The afternoon alternate shot was also a close contest, with Europe winning 2½ points and the United States 1½. Couples did not play. Instead, he and Marchand spent time on the range, practicing, trying to reinforce the good things. "It was late in the day, and there were not many other players there. Davis started hitting 1-irons. He hit them for about 45 minutes, and toward the end of it I said to Fred that I thought that was the best I'd ever seen a golf ball hit. Fred had finished practicing, and he was laughing. 'Look at that,' he would say, shaking his head. Davis was semi-laughing because he was hitting it so high and far and on line in the groove," Marchand recalled.

Marchand came out for the Saturday-morning fourball match between Couples/Love and Clarke/Montgomerie. "On the eighth, Fred holed his second shot, and I got on a plane headed for Madrid." The next day he couldn't believe the results.

"The way they played together in practice, they were just drowning everybody," he added. "They are so experienced and their games complement each other, and the way they look at the course is so similar. They've done so much together. The way Davis was hitting them, I was saying they did not even need to show me the matches."

Although Couples and Love were 2-up at the 11th tee, Clarke birdied 11, Montgomerie birdied 12, Clarke birdied 14, and Monty birdied the 16th and 17th taking the match.

"That's the beauty of Ryder Cup," Marchand noted. "There's such drama. The world level of play is so high now that anything can happen."

Not only was the Couples and Love machine stopped 1-up. Woods and O'Meara were defeated by Faldo and Westwood when Westwood scored five birdies and Woods putted from the back of the green, over it, and into the water in front of the 17th.

Lehman and Mickelson salvaged half a point, the only number that went up on the board for the U.S. team Saturday morning. And now Seve's strategy became clear. It was the U.S. fourball nemesis that he was attacking. Europe was ahead 8 to 4.

In the afternoon foursomes, Couples and Love must have left all their good shots on the range, going down 5 and 4 to Olazabal and Rocca.

It was Europe 10½, United States 5½.

Of the 12 singles matches on Sunday, the U.S. team would now have to win nine to take The Ryder Cup. Not only would they have to beat all the rookies, who were not playing like rookies, they would also have to take out at least two of the Monty, Faldo, Langer, Woosnam, Olazabal conglomerate.

The U.S. team was in a hole so deep, they needed miner's lights on their golf caps; so far down, they may have bumped into Jacques Cousteau. How they had gotten there was anybody's guess. They had the winners of three of the year's majors. They had guys who could hit golf balls through apples.

It was so bad, Kite asked President Bush to come and speak to the team on Saturday night. And he did. He told them that he had been through rough times and he knew what it was to face adversity, to go out and play hard and enjoy it.

When Sunday dawned, the battle was joined.

Couples apparently was inspired, because he waxed Woosnam, 8 and 7, with an eagle on the fourth hole and five subsequent birdies in a performance that tied for the largest margin of victory in Ryder Cup singles history. His was the first match out and the first to finish.

The U.S. team launched a mini-comeback, coming up only one point short. They won eight of the 12 singles matches, a huge achievement, considering their position on Sunday morning. The uphill battle was a monumental effort to gut it out when adversity was throwing lefts and rights faster than the partisan crowd could say "Olé!"

Sunday's play included more than 50 birdies and four eagles.

Couples reflected on the event. "I'd never go back—like this year beating Woosnam and somebody saying 'Jeez, you had nine birdies'—or whatever you had. Or another time where I tied Woosnam at Oak Hill. It didn't matter. I don't even remember the match.

"My performance is as big as anyone else's, but if I don't win a match and we win I would never go home and say, 'I played terrible. It was not fun.' I would say, 'Hey, we won.' And if someone said, 'You didn't win a match,' I would say, 'You know, you're right, I didn't. But we won.'

"I think the pressure's on everybody, and that's a given. And that doesn't mean anything more or less to how you play or how everything works out. Because if your team's way up, like it's been in the Presidents Cup, it's all going to come close. The players are all too good. It's too close to ever have a cakewalk.

"In the 1989 Ryder Cup, the first time I ever played one and lost, I didn't have a clue as to what the whole week was. I didn't know how much fun it was until you realize they actually made a putt and we couldn't win anymore. And I took that pretty hard," he admitted.

But there's always 1999.

"I've made teams and I've been chosen. I've made them every which way. For sure, it's an honor to be chosen. It's also a great honor to make the team [on points]. To be one of the two guys chosen says a little about your game and your experience in playing in team events.

"I think you have to pick someone with experience. I don't know who of the captains would think about picking someone that's never done it, because it's the most . . . the fear in your fingers and eyes and toes on the first tee is bizarre. You are sick to your stomach. And it's the same whether you've been there or not, but once you tee off, you get the feel of it.

"But to be chosen is a thrill and an honor. The Ryder Cup is by far the greatest thing to do in golf. The Presidents Cup, someday, will be like that."

After the Ryder Cup, Couples played in two events in October to get in his minimum. He finished 29th in Kingsmill, ninth in Las Vegas.

Although Couples showed up for tournaments, his body was on autopilot. The fall brought a series of medical emergencies, with treatments for Thais Bren and the deteriorating condition of his father.

He pulled out of the World Cup at Kiawah Island, which he had intended to play. Justin Leonard was a last-minute substitution.

Couples planned to enter the Shark Shootout, but his father's health caused him to withdraw from that at the last moment.

When it looked as if things were stable, he returned to the desert for the Skins Game, only to learn on Thanksgiving Day that his father had passed away.

It was a sad ending to a troubled year. His friends could only pray that he would get some good news soon.

22

◆✦◆

Happily Ever After

"This time I thought it would be a big week."
—**Fred Couples on the 1998 Masters**

After his victory at the Bob Hope Chrysler Classic, Couples took a time out. Caught in traffic going back to L.A., he missed a flight to Thailand, and he actually enjoyed being at home to savor the victory.

He kept his feet up until San Diego, but the determination that he had shown in the desert was not there. He missed the cut with 74-74.

The next weekend he went to Hawaii, a tournament he hadn't been to in years, and finished in a tie for 35th. He tacked on a week of vacation afterward, a late celebration for the Bob Hope victory. He confessed that winning the Bob Hope tournament had put him ahead of schedule. He had peaked early.

"I just kind of relaxed, and I don't want to say gloated about it, but winning is a lot of fun. And at this stage of my career, as little as I play, winning means a lot more. But winning the Hope was a big, big deal. I think it made me think I could win a lot more," he said, and one could almost see him thinking two months ahead.

In Los Angeles, his play was worse than in Hawaii. He tied for 65th, but the tournament was played at Valencia, not Riviera because the U.S. Senior Open would be held at Riviera in July and tournament organizers wanted to restrict use of the course.

Couples stayed out of the fray until the third week of March, teeing it up at Bay Hill, Arnold Palmer's tournament. As usual, he had a plan.

"I brought Paul Marchand out to Bay Hill to work on my game, and the main reason for that was I was basically shooting for Augusta," Couples explained.

In the pretournament press conference he said that he needed to improve the way he was playing. "If I play this way, I am going to finish 40th every week. This is—I can't keep playing like this. It's no fun.

"Before, I could really turn it on pretty quickly. When I saw Paul, I hit balls all day long for three days. And if you don't get any better doing that, then you're never going to get better."

For the first time, he admitted he was considering the Senior Tour on a limited basis.

"I would like to play a few more years, then, you know, quit for six or seven years, and then play the Senior Tour a couple years, just to see everybody. I think it's a great sport. But I'm not going to try to play until I'm 46 or 47 and then play the Senior Tour. There's no way. Ray Floyd, Lee Trevino—there are guys who do it—but they're golf crazy!"

Although Thais was not supposed to make the trip to Bay Hill, plans changed. Thursday was pleasant, but the course was wet from a rainstorm that had shellacked the Orlando area the previous evening. Paul Marchand guided Thais through the gallery since it was her first time there. She said she and her son Oliver were learning to play golf, and she hoped that would get Fred out to practice more often.

At the ninth, Couples pushed a drive a little bit too far to the right, landing in the trees. Marchand said enthusiastically to Thais that she would get to see some of Couples's best work. Her reply was "No wonder he likes to spend so much time clearing brush in the yard." At last, a woman with a sense of humor.

Marchand believed the time at Bay Hill was well spent. "I did not give him any great pearls of wisdom, but he was prepared and thought about what he was going to do. As gifted as he is, to have some structure to how he gets ready to play, combined with his ability to react to the situation at the time—to come up with something at the moment—that's when he's at his best.

"This year was extra special, wanting to show Thais what Augusta was like for the first time," Marchand added. "She had missed the year before while battling breast cancer. So it was going to be a special trip to show her what it was like when he was playing well. He did special preparation at Bay Hill."

The work did not immediately translate to the scorecard. His finish was not up to his usual marks: he tied for 29th.

The next week at The Players Championship, Couples worked on his game, visited with agent Lynn Roach, and received treatment for his back.

Then, after a first-round 67, he was in contention. He'd made birdies at the second, third, and fourth holes, but he shanked a 7-iron from the fifth fairway, although he rebounded with a birdie on the sixth. He also birdied the par-5 16th, with a wedge to six feet, and hit what he termed a "great 9-iron to eight feet on the 17th" for a birdie. But Glen Day, playing in the last group, took the lead.

After the first-round success, things got progressively more difficult, and Couples's finish was not what one would expect from someone who owned the course record at the TPC at Sawgrass. He tied for 42nd, finishing with two 78s.

Couples said he planned to go to Houston Friday, Saturday, and Sunday of the following week to prepare for the year's first major. But that's not exactly how it turned out.

"Before I got to Augusta, I flew to see Paul," Couples explained. "I worked for half a day at Houston, headed for the Masters, and for the first time in a while I thought good things were going to happen.

"I just felt like I was borderline possessed a little bit," he said later in the year. "I talked about the tournament with Thais for months and months and basically wore her out about it." Augusta meant a lot to him, a lot more than he usually admitted to anyone.

Augusta was Easter weekend in 1998. Thais explained that they'd had a holiday celebration for the children early because they had all "known a year earlier that this was going to be Fred's week."

It was like an O. Henry story. Fred wanted to do well for Thais, and Thais wanted the week to go well because she knew how much it meant to Fred.

As early as Doral, Jim Nantz had predicted great things for Couples at Augusta. "It's six years to the day since Fred won at Augusta," he said. He believed Couples would win in 1998. Obviously Nantz felt something that everybody else didn't, something that would, he hoped, show up in time for the tournament.

"Fred had the extra motivation of Thais's coming," Marchand noted. "With him it all added up. From the first Monday when we drove up Magnolia Lane together, I had extra-good feelings that it was going to be a good week.

"He practiced diligently. Played the course. Hit a lot of balls. He almost practiced too much. The facility is good, and he was glad to be there. He spent a lot of time chipping, pitching, hitting sand shots."

On Tuesday Jack Nicklaus, who won the Masters six times, was honored with a special plaque. Few people have any kind of permanent memento there at all. The approximately three-foot-by-three-foot metal marker was presented in honor of Nicklaus's 40th consecutive appearance at the tournament, beginning when he was an amateur. Nicklaus, not known for being outwardly emotional, was moved to tears.

However, the club purposely left room at the bottom of the plaque. "Just in case," Jack Stephens of Augusta National added.

Golf World noted it would have been more appropriate to give Nicklaus his own permanent clubhouse closet.[1] A similar honor had been bestowed on Arnold Palmer at his 40th Masters.

Jack Stephens added that "Arnold Palmer would be deserving of any honor you'd want to give him. He has been a very good influence on this tournament and on golf. I'll put it this way: Before Arnold, we couldn't sell all of our tickets. After Arnold, we sold out all of our tickets and they paid us to put the tournament on television. He was the difference."[2]

Couples's attitude was good. His game was coming around. Then, just when things looked promising, there was a problem. It was his shoulder. He had a funny sensation in it on Tuesday at the course and had Tom Boers check him out afterward. Boers advised him to just take it a little easy on Wednesday. So, instead of playing the course and hitting a few balls, Couples went to the practice putting green.

For several years, Couples had said that he had a problem seeing the line when putting. But he was never more specific about what that meant.

Paul Marchand discovered more about it in two putting sessions, one at the Ryder Cup in 1997 and the other that Wednesday in 1998.

"At the Ryder Cup last September, we were practicing one evening and put two clubs down, shafts parallel, to form an alleyway for putts," Marchand explained. "Fred said when he stood up to the putt, it felt like it was going to start to the right. We had Brad Faxon doing the same thing, and he said it looked straight.

"We put a ball down in the middle of the two clubs. And Fred said he was going to hit that shaft on the top. I tried to position his head to left, to see if that would help it, but that's such a hard thing to do."

They let it go. Couples has said that he once consulted with vision specialists but they said his eyes were fine.

Since Couples had all day Wednesday, he practiced spot putting by using coins as marks on the practice green.

Marchand explained: "He would put a mark down for the line where he intended to putt, and when he stood up to the ball, the line looked way, way, way right. Anytime he would take the mark away and stand normally, then take the putter and point to the spot he thought it would go, that spot was always right.

"So, as an experiment, he closed his right eye. If he did that, then he could put a coin down, and when he stood over the ball, it looked like it was on the same line he saw from behind the ball. I confirmed by asking where he was looking and where he was trying to putt it," Marchand added.

Rain came down on Wednesday in the afternoon, and even the Par-3 Tournament, a tradition at the Masters, was cut short.

The wind arrived, blowing in 40-mile-per-hour gusts. It would be Russian roulette club selection.

The start of the tournament was delayed by 90 minutes so that the grounds crews could finish getting water out of the bunkers and improving on the already perfect condition of the course.

Couples and Marchand had a routine of having lunch in the past champions' locker room before play. "There are about six guys waiting on you and it's a beautiful setting, overlooking that circle on Magnolia Lane and practice tee," Marchand explained. "Fred would go through a little mail while he ate. Then we'd go to the tee and warm up.

"The first day Tiger and Fuzzy were up there and we had a good time shooting the breeze. Fuzzy was working the room even though it was just Fred, Tiger and me," Marchand said laughing.

"The 1998 Masters was the best tournament I've ever been to," Marchand added. It was particularly emotional for Marchand because his mother had died the year before on Thursday of Masters week.

"I was so wrapped up in Fred's play that it did not even occur to me until I walked up on nine what had gone on the year before. If you got down on Thursday, there was no coming back. It's not the best round I've seen him play, but it's in the top three because the conditions were brutal, especially on the greens. The course had not played like that all week."

Couples birdied the first three holes on that cold and windy day and made a couple more before the turn.

Marchand revealed that Couples did something that is unbelievable in the first round of that Masters. "In the 1998 Masters, on the first six holes, he putted with his right eye closed," Marchand said. "He got into the lead, and he quit doing it. When you think about it, leading the Masters with one eye closed, through six or seven, and [to go] that far into the round."

Maybe, thinking back, he should have just kept that eye closed. Gotten an eye patch like the old Hathaway shirt man.

At the first, Couples hit 9-iron to 10 feet and made it. At the second it was a 6-iron to the same distance, but two putts for birdie on the par 5. Fourth hole, a par 3, he was 50 feet away, left it five feet short, and missed the par save. On six, the second par 3, he three-putted from 30 feet.

Then things improved. At seven, a par 4, his sand wedge landed about 30 feet and he made it. Nine was a sand wedge to a foot, kick-in birdie.

He bogeyed both the 11th and the 12th. It was déjà vu 1992 when Couples's ball again held on the slope, but it took him three to hole out.

"Twelve, I barely carried over the water, and it stuck on the bank. I took a shoe off, and pitched it up over the bunker about six feet and ended up missing it. Greg's caddie said it was in the trap. I knew it wasn't in the trap, so I didn't want to say anything. What was I going to say, 'Oh yeah, it's on the bank?' *Again*? The bank's not [been] shaved like it has been since I did that. But it hit over the water and just didn't give itself a chance to roll backwards," he added, making excuses for the terrain.

He was asked if any players had commented about his being two-for-two in banks. His reply was funny, if not believable: "Maybe they forgot I stuck it on the bank [in 1992])."

He birdied the 13th with a 3-wood and 4-iron combination to 40 feet, a routine he would like to have had on Sunday. At the 14th, his ball was blown a foot before he could mark it on the green. Sixteen and 17 were sand wedges for birdie. At 18, his second shot sailed into the gallery, but he chipped to six feet and saved par.

"If it had not rained, I don't think anyone would have broken par," Couples said afterward. He said that his estimate of the course difficulty was 9, maybe 8½, on a scale of 10.

"Obviously it was a big day, and I played a great round and I was leading. I felt comfortable with that," Couples added, never mentioning the one-eyed putting.

Couples was inspired by the play of 1966 Masters champion Gay Brewer, aged 66, who shot par, good enough for a position on the leader board.

Joe LaCava said to Couples during play, "You need to play better to beat this guy."[3]

The first round didn't actually end on Thursday because of the weather delay. Ten golfers were still on the course when play was called at 7:40 because of darkness.[4]

The next morning after the others completed their first rounds, Couples officially became first-round leader. But he knew where he stood. No one else was under 70.

"The end of the second day, I think I was still leading, tied with David Duval," Couples noted in his low-key manner.

As usual, it was exciting.

"At the fourth, I hit a 5-iron 10 feet and made it for birdie," he said after his round. "At seven, I misplayed a sand wedge downwind and uphill and came up short, which was a huge blunder. I didn't get it up and down."

Then it went back his way with a sand wedge on eight to about two feet for birdie. This up-and-down round had gone par-par-par-birdie-par-par-bogey-birdie-par on the front. He was tied with Hoch until he went to −4 with his birdie at the eighth.

"At 10 I underclubbed again, came down the bank, made a good chip to about four feet, and missed the putt," Couples explained.

On 11 he three-putted from about 35 to 40 feet and dropped to −2. He said there was really no excuse. "I had a good drive, played a safe shot with a 9-iron. I putted down to three feet and just flinched at it and missed it."

When Couples finished that hole, for the first time during the two rounds he had fallen out of the lead, and at about the same time, Mark O'Meara tapped in at 18 with rounds of 74-70, two over par for the tournament. Up ahead of Couples, Scott Hoch birdied the 12th to go to −3 and was now the tournament leader.

Couples rebounded at the 12th, hitting an 8-iron to 20 feet and sinking the treacherous putt for birdie. Then, at the 13th, "I laid up and hit a sand wedge about 10 feet and made it." With that birdie, he was back to the top of the leader board again at −4.

But with Couples it's never easy. At the 14th he was in the pine straw, then short of the green, chip to a foot to save par and stay tied.

It was a race against darkness. The late start had them pushing the twilight envelope. Couples played 15 as a three-shot hole that day. The third was a 60-degree wedge that spun sideways, two putts, par.

Duval was ahead of him at this point, and Couples needed a birdie injection. At the 16th tee, with the daylight rapidly fading, he chose a 7-iron for the 164-yard shot, and smashed it up to about 12 feet, and made it for birdie to go to −5, tied with Duval.

On the 17th, Couples pushed his drive into the 15th fairway, which runs parallel, but he made par. On the 18th, he hit his 9-iron a little soft, and the ball just got to the fringe.

Both Couples and Duval parred it. They would be paired on Saturday.

After the round, Couples was asked if he'd lost any distance over the years, and his answer was "I'm just as long. I haven't lost any power. I still swing hard. I still kill. And I seem to pick up distance when I'm driving it well. When I'm a little off, I try to steer it a little. And here, you know, it's a big boost to just stand up there and swing hard." The only comment missing was "Wanna see?"

"It was a typical Augusta deal at the house," Couples explained several months later. "But the golf—I was on my game and hitting the ball fairly well and thought I was going to win from day one, because (a) I love the course, (b) I play well there every year, and (c) I was borderline possessed. Thais was very excited about it."

This might be the first time Couples ever said that he thought he would win a tournament. It didn't come out as bragging, just as a matter-of-fact description of his state of mind after that round.

Saturday was another challenge. The cut had come at 150. Greg Norman was headed home, nursing a sore shoulder. Nick Faldo missed his second Masters cut in a row. Crenshaw was gone, and so were Lehman, Watson, and Price.

Gary Player, age 62, made the cut.

Saturday Couples was again the last one to leave the clubhouse for the practice tee. This was the round that will be remembered as the "Oh, baby!" round, because that's what he uttered as he watched his 3-iron sail the 205-yard distance to the 13th green for a gimme eagle. But when he finished, the scorecard said 71, so naturally there was up-and-down excitement along the way.

He parred the first two holes. The second one should have been a birdie. "I had 5-iron to the green. I'm just trying to hit the green, two-putt. I hit it in the right bunker, hit a heck of a sand shot about five feet above the hole, and putted five feet by." Fortunately for him, Duval also putted three feet past the hole.

Couples birdied the third, a short par 4, with a 3-wood, wedge to 10 feet. At the fourth, the first par 3, he hit "a 4-iron into the right bunker, blasted out, and two-putted for bogey," as he explained it.

At the par-5 eighth, he was much too close to the pine straw and flopped his third up onto the green.

On nine, Couples hit to the right fringe with his second, got down in two, and turned at even par for the front nine, still at −5.

He was tied with his good friend Jay Haas. Mickelson was one back at −4. O'Meara and Duval, who had dropped strokes on the front, threatened at −3.

Naturally, with players on different holes, the leader board that Couples loved to watch was changing all the time. While Couples was putting his second shot into the bunker on the downhill 10th, Jay Haas was at the 11th green making par to stay at −5. And two holes farther up, O'Meara was standing over a birdie putt, which he made to go to −4. Azinger was staring at birdie at the 13th to go to −4. There were roars and cheers all over Amen Corner.

Couples parred 10. But Haas hit into the back bunker and bogeyed, giving Couples the lead outright once again. He stood outside the tee box on 11 with the marker between his feet and the ball to play a fade. He killed it.

A roar came up from the valley. Nicklaus birdied the 15th to get to even. The plaque had room.

Couples's drive on 11 landed 302 yards, leaving him with 153 to the pin. He lobbed up an 8-iron. The wind got it and he yelled "Get up!" It was dry, but not where he wanted. Pin high, but way right.

Nicklaus birdied the 16th, and the noise rivaled the breaking of the sound barrier. It was unmistakably Jack at Augusta. His name was put on the leader board just as Couples approached the 12th tee.

Duval hit a shot right over the pin on 12 and over the green. Couples also overshot the pin. As they walked over the Hogan bridge, Mickelson eagled the 13th to tie for the lead at −5.

Couples's putt was in the throat, but short, and he parred. It was Couples and Mickelson at −5; O'Meara, Azinger, and Furyk—already in the clubhouse—at −4; and Duval and Haas at −3.

At 13, Couples hit 3-wood, 3-iron—"Oh, baby!"—from 205 and made eagle to go to −7, leapfrogging over all the others. The cheers that reverberated could easily have caused the pine needles to vibrate and the dogwood blossoms to quiver in the dappled sunlight.

Up ahead at 18 Nicklaus had driven into the trees, but he made par anyway and was now enjoying his well-deserved walk-up applause. He was one under after three rounds. Ageless at Augusta.

After the wonderful shot at 13, Couples could not match it at 14, and hit a pitching wedge 135 yards and was 30 feet from the hole. Duval was close.

For reasons that can be analyzed only by computer, Duval missed his birdie at 14. Couples three-putted and fell back to −6, tied with Mickelson, but it was only temporary as Mickelson finished bogey-bogey to fall to −4.

At 15, Couples found himself in the folding chairs off the tee. He extricated himself and then wedged from 95 yards to three or four feet and made it for −7. He was shaking his head. Chairs. Birdie. Sure. Duval parred from the fairway.

O'Meara finished at −4, parring 18 from the pine straw.

Couples and Duval made their way to the final hole, and there Couples found what O'Meara had found: trees right. But he was not so lucky with his landing spot. He had 172 yards through some saplings. Couples took a 7-iron and slashed it, hoping it would land someplace decent. Right bunker. It took him two to get down, and his lead went from three shots to two.

"Saturday I went out and played, and when I was done, I was still leading," Couples said, quite simply summarizing what had been an adventure for his fans. "I felt like I left a couple strokes, which got some more people into the tournament. When you get 'em down, you want to bury them. And I felt like I let a couple slip away.

"I practiced a little bit after that round with Paul, almost a waste of time because I was hitting the ball so well. And we laughed and talked and he kept me away from everybody. It was just Paul and I and, of course, Joey [LaCava]. So basically it was pretty quick. I putted for a while and called it a day.

"Then I had no problems. Everyone was all excited at the house, telling me this and that. It was not a big issue. Normally I get a little bit edgy," he admitted. They all knew him too well. In addition to Thais, Lynn and Tammy Roach, Jeff and Susan Strauss, John McClure, Tony Porcello, and Tom Boers were staying with him. They had dinner, and everyone was looking forward to a great final day.

Couples had said that Sunday was like the seventh game of the NBA championship. "There will be a lot of people trying to beat me, and I'm all for it." He claimed to be a "calm nervous." Early in his career, he had explained that he was always nervous before teeing off, but it was a "good nervous."

The next day, the entourage was ready to cheer Couples to what they hoped would be his second green jacket. Uncle Paul from Seattle was in the gallery, along with thousands of fans of both players and many who just wanted to see a great last round.

The cool morning temperatures gave way to sunny shirtsleeve weather by lunchtime.

Sunday's final tee time was 3:10. Players left the practice area, one by one, to make a few practice putts before hitting their tee shots on the first hole.

Fewer and fewer remained at the range. Paul Azinger and Phil Mickelson were next to last and walked away with faces showing the strain. They acknowledged friends, but their skins would have popped like a heated sausage if anyone had touched them unexpectedly.

The practice tee at Augusta National is to the right, the north side, of Magnolia Lane as one drives up. The practice chipping-bunker area is to the left or south side. The hitting area itself is not huge. Narrower than many modern ones, but sufficient for the essentials. It will never need to accommodate resort guests or two-a-day shotguns.

Shrubs, perhaps 20 feet high, flank the northern edge of the range, forming a green wall of protection from the enormous parking area on the corner of Washington and Berckmann Roads. Near the northern edge of the range, between 2:30 and 3:00, Fred Couples was still hitting balls. Paul Marchand was standing behind him, arms folded, giving him the last-minute nod of approval as Joe LaCava walked into the roped area.

On the southern end of the range, no more than 20 yards from Magnolia Lane itself, Mark O'Meara and Hank Haney were making similar preparations. Somehow, it seemed that the winner would come from this pairing.

Couples and O'Meara were friends, but for this one afternoon they stood at a distance each one knowing the other would throw his best shots in an effort to win the green jacket. Two guys who had been through the Qualifying School together. Shared a hotel room because expenses were a problem. O'Meara, who literally had no house when he and his wife Alicia started out on the Tour, going from place to place in their car. Couples, who quit school early, much to his father's aggravation, to follow his dream. To have the two of them come together to play for the green jacket on Sunday 18 years later was one of life's great coincidences.

And in the group just ahead were Phil Mickelson, who everyone said surely should have won a professional major, and Paul Azinger, with his best opportunity since coming back from cancer treatments in 1994.

The more anyone knew about these players, the more agonizing it was to watch. All great guys, yet only one could go home victorious.

When the rounds were over and the scorecards were signed, it would be a career benchmark for the winner. For all the others, it was the ultimate in excitement because it was what they wanted to be doing. Contending in a major championship. They were getting their chance. They just had to make the right shots.

"It was nice being able to play with Fred leading," O'Meara said. "I would classify us as friends. Fred's demeanor is likable, and he's easy to play golf with. The sportsmanship he showed toward me was tremendous, and I think that I did that likewise. It kind of helped us both."

Couples said they had often talked about how they had both started the same year and how far they had come.

It was exciting—so exciting that some of those who did not make the cut stayed and watched. Jeff Sluman was there with friends and family from Rochester. He offered words of wisdom: "You're nervous if you're watching because you can't do anything about it."

Paul Marchand left the practice putting green and waited for the tee off as calmly as he could. "I don't understand it. He's not nervous. There's something wrong. Usually he's nervous," he whispered as the players walked to number one.

Couples at −6 and O'Meara at −4 were introduced, and the shots were hit. The last pair of the final round was off the first tee.

At the first, Couples's shot found the left woods, actually beyond trouble. He came out to a yawning bunker in front of the green and attempted to save par, but was unable to. He dropped a shot to −5. O'Meara parred to stay at −4.

About that time a huge roar went up from a distant gallery. People walking with the last group looked at each other. "Nicklaus," they murmured. They were right. He'd gone to −3.

Couples's drive on number two, the par 5, was huge. His second shot was in the bunker in front of the green. O'Meara was on the green in regulation. Couples came out with a birdie to go even for the day at −6, and O'Meara, who was in birdie range with his third shot, converted to move to −5.

These two knew each other's games. As O'Meara said after the tournament, "I grew up playing golf with Fred, amateur golf and college golf. He's hitting a 6-iron in and I'm hitting a 3-iron, so he had an advantage there."

On the third, a 360-yard par 4, O'Meara was on the right side of the fairway and hit his second shot to 30 feet. It had all the makings of a routine par, except that it was Mark O'Meara putting. "I stroked it up a hill left to right and made it, and that took a little pressure off," he said later. Birdie.

Couples had put his tee shot in the bunker and his recovery was not ideal. They left the putting surface tied at −6.

Before they teed off on the fourth hole, there was a thunderous roar. Nicklaus had moved to −4. A murmur rumbled through the gallery as leader board numbers changed.

O'Meara hit first, a 7-iron, which he pulled. It found the left side of the wide putting surface, so far from the pin that he needed to show his passport before hitting it. Three-putt was a distinct possibility.

Couples's shot was better, about 15 feet.

It looked as if O'Meara would try to lag up, but when he followed through and held the putter blade out, watching it track, it rolled right into the bottom of the cup, bringing some much-needed crowd noise to the final twosome.

Couples watched O'Meara make from 30 feet and from 40 to 50 feet. He would have his work cut out for him that day. He pulled the trigger on his 15-footer and made it. They were tied at −7 and headed to the fifth tee.

Both punched good drives. In the gallery to the right of the hole, two O'Meara fans were talking enthusiastically about their favorite. "Wouldn't it be something if Tiger put the green jacket on O'Meara?" one said to the other. "Yeah," came the reply. "They're best friends at home in Orlando."

O'Meara's second came up on the fringe, but both he and Couples made par and disappeared into the vegetation behind the fifth green to the elevated sixth tee.

On the sixth, a 180-yard par 3, Couples flamed a shot to the far right portion of the green. O'Meara landed his on the lower tier. Couples's two-putt was truly fantastic. They both walked away with par.

For a time the golf course was almost eerily quiet. No roars. No huge moans. No big cheers.

Both hit humongous tee shots on seven, and as the gallery applauded, the players chatted while walking down the fairway. They had done this hundreds of times in other places, but the green jacket had never been on the line.

From the fairway, Couples's second shot was so good that for a moment it looked as if it was an eagle. It missed by two feet. He still had to use his putter, but he left the hole with a one-stroke advantage. He was −8. O'Meara was −7.

At the eighth, an uphill 535-yard par 5, Couples was long and in the fairway, but he pulled his second. It looked like a costly error, but he skanked one out from behind the branches and under the limbs to three feet and made birdie. He was now −9, two shots up. O'Meara had to be talking to himself at this point. But for both players, the game face was in position.

From far back in the pack, David Toms had been lighting up the scoreboard and was now in at −5. His only realistic chance would have been if lightning struck all the leaders as they rounded Amen Corner. But at least everyone knew what they had to beat.

At the ninth, O'Meara made an error off the tee.

"The big turn-around was number nine," O'Meara said. "I pull-hooked a tee shot into the trees and it looks like I'm going to make bogey, and you wouldn't think that would have happened then."

Couples also remembered it well: "I birdied seven and eight, and I had driven it a hundred miles down the middle of the fairway on nine, and O'Meara had hooked it in the junk and pitched out, really not much further than my ball. Maybe 50 yards, 40 yards from the green. He hit a hell of a shot, and I made the blunder of coming up short, and my ball spun back not too far from his ball. And he got up and down and I didn't.

"Going down the fairway [on nine], I was thinking this tournament was where I could play the back nine safely and win. I think the ninth hole, you know, that was just a huge blunder. It was a yard or two short. I hit a sand wedge. I tried to get a little cute and just didn't hit it hard enough. That you could go out and do 100 times in a row and hit it on top. I chose one time to miss it a little bit."

But O'Meara was fired up by his ability to scramble. "That gave me a lot of momentum and didn't get me too far behind. I kept in touch."

They turned with O'Meara −7, Couples −8.

Thoughts of Greg Norman's demise in 1996 came to mind. His problems had started when he backed a wedge off the ninth green.

Thais Bren and Tony Porcello had been so focused on the play while walking on nine that they had stepped, side by side, into a low-hanging tree branch and stopped momentarily to compare bumped noggins.

The crowd was dense and noisy between nine green and ten tee. The players were urged to perform with applause.

"I kind of kicked myself walking to the 10th tee," Couples admitted. "And I went out and played 10, 11, and 12 extremely well."

From 10 tee, Couples hit a 3-wood that looked perfect. O'Meara's shot was equally good, but he chunked his second to make his only bogey of the day. It had to be deflating after having come back from what looked like sure disaster at the ninth.

Couples hit what he considered a makable birdie putt on 10, but it didn't go. However, because of O'Meara's miscue, he regained a two-shot advantage.

David Duval, who'd posted three birdies and a bogey on the front, had also birdied the 10th and 11th. He was in full flight and had pushed himself into supersonic gear. He was at −7, and Couples noticed the move.

"At 11, I didn't make a very good second shot," Couples said, "but got it on the right side of the green and two-putted. On 12," he added calmly, "I hit a good iron." Both players got out of there with pars and turned to the final hole of Amen Corner.

They came to the 13th. With its tree-lined majesty. With its beautiful, azalea-crowned green. Its beautiful bubbling stream—Rae's Creek— sparkling below the putting surface, like a moat guarding the king's palace. Thais Bren, Paul Marchand, and John McClure stood at the turn in the dogleg waiting to see the tee shots land so that they would have a view to the green.

There was a smack, but no ball was visible. Just an enormous gasp from the gallery and then many arms pointing toward trees. And a few moments later, one ball, that of Mark O'Meara, trickled down the fairway.

Soon Couples's ball was not the only thing that had disappeared from view. He was also lost in the forest on the left. Marchand and McClure looked a little ill. Thais did not—perhaps—understand exactly what that meant. But others did. There was a long wait, and finally Joe LaCava's white caddie outfit was spotted through the trees. It looked, miraculously, like there was an opening. Everyone said that if anybody could get it out, Couples could.

"At 13," Couples explained, "I just kind of milked a 3-wood. I always struggle with the hole, and this year I'd had no problem with it. I'd gone birdie-birdie-eagle—I've not seen the tape. [Six months had passed, and he still hadn't watched it. No amount of time was going to make that shot better.]

"I stood over it maybe one waggle too long and kind of closed my stance to aim further right with the extra, the second waggle, and to get the ball back to the left, I came over it, rushed the swing—snap-hooked it. It was a big hook, and on any other course you walk over there and you play it. Here, you don't want to go there. On this course, it draws you over there, so I have a tough time with it. So it was a horrible shot, basically. If you're four feet to the left, it's going to go in the creek. And if you go where I went, it rattles around in the trees. And they found it up on this road.

"It was sitting up in a spot, but it was a full sand wedge to get it out to the fairway. So then I hit a hell of a second shot to get it through the trees. I could have easily taken it back and hooked it around and gone for the green. I thought I could have gotten it out of there."

Paul Marchand explained the part about hooking it around. "When he hit in that stuff on 13—you know how he is out of that—I figure if he has any kind of opening, he's going to hit the shot. He actually had a shot to the green from trees. If it had been Thursday, he would have gone for the green. But he thought, 'Why take a chance.' He hit it off the road and put a pretty good dent in his wedge."

From a location that looked like he needed the chain-saw club, Couples hit a wedge to the fairway. It looked as if par was a possibility. Bogey a worst-case scenario.

"And once I got it out," Couples added, "I basically didn't give myself enough time to really think about the third shot. I rushed it. I thought it was a 7-iron. The pin was tucked up front. Joe thought it was a six. We said let's just hit it in the middle of the green and get out of there.

"I got cute with the shot [the 6-iron] and basically rushed it and choked a little bit and came off it and hit it in the water. Walking up, I thought, 'What is going on? All this talk about us not making a big score. Here we go. I'm gonna make seven.' So I do."

"I'm pretty sure he had 168," Marchand said about the yardage. "He and Joe knew the smart play was long, left. He was not flirting with the pin. If he stood on that club, he could airmail the ball into the azaleas. He needed to hit it smooth. Probably played conservatively for a minute." Often the hardest thing to do under pressure is to hit an easy shot.

Couples was down, but he did not give up. Not with five to play and a two-shot lead when he started the hole. O'Meara made par, and though part of him counted his blessings, the golfer inside him said that he drew his 4-iron too much and didn't get his up and down. It was a missed opportunity because he knew just how explosive Couples could be. He had watched him for 18 years.

As Couples said, he hit two bad shots and one annoying one. But the 13th put a scare in him. For the first time he thought—at least momentarily—that he might be in trouble. Particularly when he saw the scoreboard. Duval was at −8 through the 13th. O'Meara was still at −6.

"The next hole I regrouped," Couples said. "I had a very easy birdie putt, and how it didn't go in, I don't know." The approach had been right over the flag, and he left the putt on the lip of the cup.

"Next hole," Couples explained in a tone that said even he couldn't figure out how these things sometimes worked, "I made eagle. I hit the same shot I hit two holes earlier. I hit 6-iron to whatever—three or four feet."

At that time, no one needed an eagle more than Fred Couples. In the gallery Paul Marchand peered through the shoulders of fans, who were at least three deep. Thais Bren found a small perch to stand on, a part of a corner of a scoreboard. John McClure could not bear to look. He stood behind Marchand, his hands on Marchand's shoulders and his head hung down, resting between Marchand's shoulder blades. When the eagle roar sounded, McClure breathed a huge sigh of relief for his friend. Bren gave a little squeal. Paul Marchand blinked once or twice.

O'Meara was amazed. "He probably hit the ball better than I did tee to green, and made one mistake, a poor tee shot on 13. It was a miracle recovery shot from where he was, and then he hit a poor third shot. A double. To his credit, he made an incredible shot on 15 and made eagle."

O'Meara made birdie and was now at −7. Couples was now at −8 again, and Duval had birdied the 15th to go to −9, but bogeyed the 16th to fall back to −8. After a double and an eagle, Couples was still tied for the lead.

If Marchand, McClure, Porcello—whom no one had seen for several holes—and Thais Bren did not have emotional whiplash at this point, they had at least had some serious fluctuations in ups and downs of their blood pressure.

Now it would just depend on who could gut it out on the way home.

O'Meara and Couples both parred 16.

O'Meara later said about the 17th, "I just told Jerry, my caddie, 'If I can birdie the last two holes, then this tournament can be mine.' I hit a super drive on 17, a great 9-iron approach [135 yards] to just behind the hole, and made a very good putt from eight or nine feet."

The last person to birdie the 17th and 18th holes at the Masters to win was Arnold Palmer in 1960. But O'Meara probably didn't know that.

Couples would like a mulligan on the 17th. "At the 17th, when I was surrounding my putt, I was actually watching Duval through the trees, putting at 18. And I didn't hear any roar, so I thought, 'If I make this, I'm going to win.' So I put a little too much pressure on it, besides not reading it correctly. I thought it was going to break a lot more, and I didn't want to miss it to the right, and I pulled it badly, probably an eight-footer, and I pulled it about a foot left of the hole.

"And then O'Meara makes his putt, and at that time I didn't even realize it was to tie. So then we go to the next hole. I never thought about Mark being just one behind on the 17th green. When I made my eagle, I thought that put me with Duval, and Mark birdied the hole. [He was right.]"

Couples, O'Meara, and Duval were now at −8. In anticipation of a playoff, many people ran from the juncture of 17 green and 18 tee down the hill to the right where the 10th green was located.

O'Meara played the shot he needed to play. "On the 18th, that was right to left, I hit a nice drive. I tried to play it just right of the flag, no need to shoot right at the pin, and it came off just perfect. Driver and 148 yards," O'Meara explained. The putt he faced was 18 to 20 feet.

Couples summarized the finale. "The whole day we were having a great time. And then when I made double, I thought, 'Oooh! Now I'm out of this.' Then when I made eagle, I thought. Ok. It's Duval and I. In a certain way, I just didn't put Mark's birdies together, and he poured that putt in at 17, and we go to 18, and he hit two great shots, and I scrambled around. I hit a good bunker shot, and I was sitting there with a five-footer to tie—I thought—and he rolls this putt.

"It's easy to say I thought he would make it. He's such a good putter. On the other hand, I was also sitting there thinking, 'This is great for me because I'm going to have to make a putt here. I've led the whole thing. I'm going to have to make it.' And at the time he makes it, I'm actually

scrubbing my putter grip—I saw that much on tape—because I'm thinking as I'm doing this, 'I'm going to have to make my putt.' And he makes
it and that was that.

"Preparing for the week, getting there, Jim Nantz was awesome. He
gave me all kinds of notes. I had the same badge number I had in 1992
[70]. It was six years to the day from 1992. It was fun. The only thing not
fun was not winning. But I can't say it was not fun. It was disappointing.
Normally I get [madder] and I take it differently, but I played as well as I
could and only played one bad hole in 72. I didn't really hit too may bad
shots. Mark birdied three of the last four holes to win. He's a great guy. I
was happy for him."

O'Meara was gracious in victory. "This time, the breaks went my way.
I made birdies at the last to end up winning. It is a great feeling. I know
Fred was disappointed, but I hope he was happy for me. Knowing he'd
won before, fans really related to him and pulled for him.

"For me, it was neat that I had my family there on 18 when I made that
putt. Fred was probably shocked and disappointed, but he showed he's a
classy guy. He said, 'That's a great win for you, and I'm happy for you.'
Deep down he's a competitor. I know he was disappointed."

After the round was completed, O'Meara mentioned some words of
advice that Hank Haney had given him. "Hank came in and watched me
hit balls on the range. He's been a driving force on my game. He kept
telling me, 'You can do it, you can win this championship.' He was very
positive about me. He felt good that I could get it done."

O'Meara admitted that he thought about what he was wearing that
day—in case. "I have a little bit of olive green on today. I was going to
put on a pair of black pants and I said, 'No no, there's no reason to think
that way.' You have to think you might have the green jacket on come
Sunday afternoon."

Couples was disappointed, but he had learned the hard way that life
goes on after disappointment.

Marchand said about the end of that afternoon at Augusta, "Fred felt
after the week was over that it was a good one, not a negative thing. It was
a real championship moment. He felt like he'd done a lot of good stuff.
He had shown Thais what it's like to be at the very top. It was a great week
and he played great, even in that bad weather. The tournament was his
to win or lose the whole week. Mark hit the shots coming in. What he said
about Mark afterward was that he'd been happy for Mark.

"Afterward, Fred was standing in the circle in front of the clubhouse
by the car and Jack Nicklaus came out and patted him on the back. Tony
Porcello and Thais were in the car. John McClure was at the wheel. Fred
was very happy. Jack asked him about 13. And he was okay with it.

"It was a lifelong dream for Fred to win at Augusta, and then here was a tournament that by all rights could have and should have been his, and it went another way and he was just the same. He felt good. He was humble, but he played like a champion. His game had risen. It had been a while since he contended in a major tournament. He felt like he handled it when it didn't go his way, and when you can do that you feel like you're a winner. That's what he was."

Though there was no champagne and rerun of the final round, Couples had dinner with Lynn and Tammy Roach, Tony Porcello, John McClure, and, of course Thais, who had helped make the week special.

As the spring wore on, it was apparent that the work Couples had done leading up to Augusta had done wonders for his game. In less than two months he was three or four swings away from five victories in the first half of 1998. Of course, it was those few swings. The first, naturally, was the one on the 13th tee at Augusta.

The second close call came three weeks later in Houston. Though he never led the tournament, he contended after getting past a first-round score of par that put him in 47th place. His 66-70-68 final three rounds were good enough for third, and on Sunday he had birdies on the 13th, 15th, 16th, and 17th but came up just short. David Duval exploded the field with a final-round 64 and won.

Two weeks later, at the Byron Nelson in Dallas, Couples shot up to the top of the leader board with a Saturday back-nine score of 29. Twenty-nine. Two-nine. Halfway though the Sunday round he was at −16, and John Cook, playing along two groups ahead, was at −12.

Cook closed with a more than sporty Sunday round of 65, but it was the 17th that was Couples's ruination. The 17th at the TPC at Las Colinas is a par 3 over water. It was 171 yards that day. A 6-iron. Well, perhaps a 5½ iron. The six didn't quite make it. Or more appropriately, the wind didn't let it.

He felt he had the right club, he felt he hit it solidly. But it hit a rock just short of the green instead of landing left of the pin where he was aiming. "I was shocked," Couples said afterward, "I didn't believe it wasn't enough."[5] Even his playing companion, Harrison Frazar, was surprised. But in the water it went. It was a double. It cost him the tournament.

"I'm going to have to buy a new 6-iron," he quipped.[6] It was the same one he'd used to hit to the green on the 13th at Augusta.

At the time Couples was tied with Cook, and he needed to par in for a playoff or make a birdie on one of the last two holes to win outright.

For John Cook, the victory was some much-needed good news. He'd been having medical problems that had just been diagnosed as ulcers.

They always say it's the quiet guys who get eaten up inside, and in his case it was literally true.

Couples knew by now that when he got hot, he stayed hot. He played at Colonial, where Tom Watson won, then entered the Memorial in Dublin, Ohio, where he had some memories of playing well and others of playing very poorly. He had missed his share of cuts there, but he had also contended at the event that was started by Jack Nicklaus in 1976.

When the weather is good, Muirfield Village is a beautiful setting. It has what can now be called—because Nicklaus was still at the beginning of his design career when he cocreated Muirfield Village with Desmond Muirhead—Nicklaus characteristics of wide landing areas and impossibly difficult shots to sometimes virtually unhittable greens. That is, for everyone but a Nicklaus, one of the best long iron players ever to slip into a pair of spikes.

The tournament is also noteworthy because the terrain and careful routing provide excellent spectator locations. Muirfield Village remains one of the best early attempts at providing fans with an opportunity to see the field of play.

In 1998, 18 of the top 20 players in the Sony rankings entered the Memorial. Greg Norman was out with shoulder surgery. But Els was there, as were Love, Duval, Woods, Lehman, Faldo, Mickelson, Leonard, Janzen, and Brooks. Guys with trophies and records. When the scores were tallied after the first day, former Ohio State player Joey Sindelar shared the first-round lead with Davis Love III, Steve Pate, and Trevor Dodds.

Couples had fired a 68 in the first round, and the highlight was bending his wedge on the 13th. He hit it on a tree in a follow-through. "I smoked the tree," he said about the contact, "so I'm sure it's a 9½ now."

Couples's second round of 67 included birdies on the first two holes, both par-4s, downhill. He hit an 8-iron to the first for a 5-footer. On the second his 9-iron was only 10 feet, and he converted.

He had bogeyed the third by hitting a wedge into the back bunker, which happened because the loft on his wedge was still messed up owing to the tree mishap in the first round.

At the fifth hole, a par-5 with a creek running through the middle of the fairway, "I drove it in the rough, I laid up, hit a 9-iron, probably 10 or 12 feet and made it. At the seventh [also a par-5] I hit two woods in the front bunker. The pin was up front. Blasted out, two feet, made it for birdie."

"On the 8th [par 3], I hit 6-iron, probably 15 feet, made it for birdie."

Then he made the turn and put his second shot at the uphill par-4 10th into the bunker and bogeyed. He finally came back with a birdie at the short but treacherous par-4 14th, where he used an iron off the tee, followed by a sand wedge and a 15-footer that he coaxed into the cup.

At the finishing hole, he selected a 2-iron from the tee. He'd been in the left creek before. His second shot was a 7-iron 20 to 25 feet, and though the green has elephants under the surface, he made it.

The Wild Kingdom hole had been 11, the first par 5 on the back, usually a three-shot hole because of the creek that runs in front of the green. "I hit a good drive," he said, "and went for the green and hit it way right in the trees, up behind a tree, and actually had a shot between a gap. I got it down, and it clipped the tree, bounced back, short of the green, probably 20 to 25 yards. Then I hit a great chip out of the rough, probably a 40-yard shot to about five feet, and made it for par, which was a big hole after bogeying 10."

Perhaps his struggle on the 11th hole at Muirfield Village defines Couples as a player as well as his miracle 3-woods off slopes for birdies and eagles or his wild slicing balloon balls from pencils. By now he had learned that if he wanted to win he just couldn't give up. He was in the woods, off a tree limb, out of the rough, and into the hole to save a par. All because he had his eye on the goal. He wanted to win, and he'd already let big ones get away that year.

When he finished, he was in one of his storm cloud moods. His back was stiff, but he added, "If I keep playing like this, I can't complain."

He was asked about his ability to close. He reminded everyone of the 64 final round at the TPC at Sawgrass, but admitted that in the last couple of months he was oh for two. He mentioned at the very last that he'd almost won the Byron Nelson without touching a club nine days prior.

At the end of the third round, Couples was three ahead of his friend Davis Love III. He had a touch of something—the flu perhaps. Headache, a little nausea.

In *Golf World* Thais was quoted as saying it was just because he had seen *Titanic* and got seasick.[7] He said he didn't line up too many putts by bending down because he didn't feel good enough to do that. Yet he shot a 67 with birdies on 6, 9, 13, and 16. He eagled the 15th, a par 5, with driver, 3-iron, and a 10- to 12-foot putt. At the 18th, he hit a 3-wood into the lip of the bunker, blasted up the fairway to get out, had 81 yards, and spun a wedge that hit on the back of the green and rolled toward the hole. When he made the putt for par, the gallery went nuts.

He didn't know what to say about the fans. He loved to have galleries cheering him on, but his head had been killing him and the noise was brutal.

"I wish they would have been quieter because it would have felt better on the pounding. [If I say that] then tomorrow they won't come out and yell. Most of the places I go, when I do well, people root very hard."

On the final day, anticipated charges from Davis Love III, three back, Ernie Els, and Andrew Magee didn't materialize.

On the front nine, Couples parred the first, but bogeyed the second, even though he took an iron off the tee. "I played a safe shot left, and I pulled it, and I probably had 40 feet. I putted it 10 feet by and hit a very good putt. It lipped out."

At the fifth, the 531-yard par 5, he hit "a three-wood off the tee and a three-wood on the back fringe, and I chipped it down to about four feet and made it." He was even for the round.

On seven he hit what he thought were "two great shots to the back edge—just past pin high and chipped it to a foot and made that for birdie."

At eight, the par 3 with a necklace of sand in front, he made par from a bunker.

"And at nine, you know I hit a driver and I knew where the pin was and I felt like, 'It's easy for me to cut it into the wind,' and I smoked one and I had 102 yards [the hole is 410], and I tried to clip a wedge and flew it. It actually never hit the green . . . to get that up and down was really huge."

Meanwhile, his playing partner, Davis Love III, was on his way to making double at that hole.

After the 10th hole, play was halted because of weather. It came at an opportune time. "When I three-putted number 10, I felt like that was really ridiculous," he said. "It was good that we had a delay. I went back and I got it off my mind. When I went back out there, it gave me the whole time to think about what I was going to do on 11. I was going to hit an iron. I laid up perfectly. I hit sand wedge and made birdie. Then I was back to where I felt like it was a good enough lead to hit the ball and get it in."

Get it in, he did. At 15 he poked driver, 2-iron to the middle of the green and was happy with a two-putt from 30 feet for birdie.

At the 17th, "I hit a three wood and a sand wedge a foot and a half," he noted. That was where the second weather delay occurred. "When we were going down 17, there was a big bolt of lightning, and Davis and I started walking quicker. We thought maybe we could get it in. Obviously they had to get us off the course."

He was picked up in a golf cart, and he rescued Thais from the gallery.

Eventually they finished play and Couples captured his 14th U.S tournament victory to add to five international ones.

"My golf is better because everything is better," he said. "I have to be honest. If I play well every single tournament and keep playing, then I'm a happy guy. And when I start playing poorly, then I become miserable. I don't think I'm any different from anyone else there."

Three or four more swings, and it could have been not just a very good year, but an astonishing year. It was just not to be. He was asked about the age factor and the new players, the kinds of questions he seldom heard in the early nineties.

"There are some times when I feel tired and old, and there are other times, like today," he paused because Jack Nicklaus was sitting next to him, laughing, "so you know age is . . . I mean, Tom Watson won last week, and he's 48. I'm 38. So how old are you? Fifty-eight? [Nicklaus said yes.] So maybe he'll win the U.S. Open at 58. But you know, I firmly believe that if you play and play the game and you've been a good player for a long time. . . I think I'll do fine forever. I don't think I'll ever, you know, become a bad player. I really don't. I don't know how that sounds, but I think I'm very capable of playing at 38, 39, 40, as well as I did when I was 32."

With Nicklaus, who had not merely made the cut but contended on Sunday at the 1998 Masters, sitting next to him, who was to argue the point?

Couples played the U.S. Open, but the week afterward, back home in Los Angeles, he did something much more important.

It was June 25. "GiGi [Thais's daughter] came up and said she wanted to go to a nice dinner," Thais recalled. "She said she wanted fish. She wanted to go out. Someplace nice." Thais thought that sounded a little 'fishy' in itself, but nevertheless, Thais, Oliver, GiGi, and Fred went to dinner at the Chart House in Malibu. "They had just finished remodeling it, and it was really nice. We got a quiet table overlooking the ocean."

Then Oliver spotted a speck in the sky and said "It" was coming toward them. What was coming toward them was an airplane with a banner trailing behind that read, "Thais, will you marry me?"

She was ecstatic. The children were happy, and, besides, they had been in on at least part of the plan.

Thais explained, "Fred told the people with the airplane that because of the traffic in L.A. they had better circle around a lot of times, because we might get stuck on the way and we might not get there in time. So the plane kept going around and around, 10 times.

"He actually got down on one knee, and he dropped the ring, and said, 'Well . . . you didn't answer . . . Will you?'"

And of course, the answer was yes.

During the PGA Championship in Seattle, Jim Nantz announced during the CBS late night report that Fred Couples and Thais Bren would be married September 12. Though he didn't announce it, the ceremony was to be at home not far from Riviera Country Club in Brentwood.

It was a small ceremony, about 40 people—friends, family, John McClure and Paul Marchand, Tony and Ann Porcello. All agreed it was absolutely beautiful. Elegant, but informal. Perfect for the new Mr. and Mrs. Couples.

The newlyweds planned a honeymoon in Paris.

Finally. Happily ever after.

Endnotes

CHAPTER 1

1. Headline in the *Desert Sun*, Monday, 1/19/98.
2. The U.S. Open was played for the first time in 1895, but it is a USGA event, not a PGA Tour event, even though at least 50 percent of the field is composed of Tour players.
3. The PGA Tour was not officially formed until 1968, when the touring professionals split from the PGA of America to form their own organization. Joe Dey was the first commissioner.
4. Reuters.
5. *Golf World*, 1/23/98.
6. NBC telecast, Saturday, 1/17/98.
7. *Desert Sun*, 1/19/98.

CHAPTER 2

1. Seattle is 44th in the national list of rainfall totals, with less than New York City, Boston, Houston, Atlanta, Philadelphia, and Miami. The wettest spot in the United States is on the island of Kauai, with 460 inches per year.
2. According to Uncle Paul, "For years on television he would say, 'I've never had a hole-in-one.' But I knew he had one, but he never acknowledged he had that one. Of course, he was such a little kid he never really considered it. At Jefferson Park one year, they got all these kids for a clinic, and he said he never had a hole-in-one, and one guy in the audience said, 'But Fred, you had a hole-in-one, over here.' And Fred says, 'Well you must know Paul Kaimakis.'"
3. About 15 months before his public verbal sparring incident with Weiskopf.

CHAPTER 3

1. Bill Rogers, Keith Fergus, Bruce Lietzke, John Mahaffey, Fuzzy Zoeller, Bobby Wadkins, Ed Fiori, George Cadle, Tom Jenkins, even Jay Sigel, who stayed amateur until he turned 50 and joined the Senior Tour. All were once on his roster. Later on, Billy Ray Brown and Steve Elkington would follow, also in the belief that the road to the Tour went through Houston. Nick Faldo spent a season there, and Sandy Lyle was there for three weeks but missed home and returned to Europe.

CHAPTER 4

1. One of Fred Renker's nine children is now part of Guthy Renker, perhaps best known for

the Tony Roberts infomercials.
2. This was said before the 1998
   Masters.
3. *Washington Post*, 6/6/83.
4. Ibid.

CHAPTER 5
1. Terry Diehl.
2. USA *Today*, 4/2/84.
3. Ibid., 5/31/87.
4. Ibid.
5. Ibid.
6. Until 1998, 10-year exemptions
   went to winners of certain events,
   such as the Masters, the U.S.
   Open, the British Open, the PGA
   Championship, the World Series of
   Golf, and the Players
   Championship. In 1998 the
   number of years was reduced to
   five.

CHAPTER 6
1. Claude Harmon's sons: Butch,
   Billy, Craig, and Dick.
2. At the Masters on Sunday in 1998,
   Hank Haney stood behind Mark
   O'Meara as he warmed up before
   the final round. Haney then
   walked the full 18, watching every
   shot.
3. The Kapalua event had been
   started by Mark Rolfing. Rolfing is
   also a network golf television
   commentator.
4. These days, John Ashworth is a
   consultant to Ashworth Golf. He is
   spending most of his time in
   Scotland restoring a golf course
   that is next door to another classic,
   Muirfield.

CHAPTER 7
1. USA *Today*, 2/28/89.
2. USA *Today*.
3. *Golf Magazine*, 9/90.
4. Ibid.

CHAPTER 8
1. Since par at Riviera is 71, the 62 he
   shot was −9. Couples has several
   63s at par-72 courses, including the
   TPC at Sawgrass. One week later,
   Greg Norman shot a 62, −10 with
   par 72, on Sunday at Doral, which
   got him into a playoff, and he
   won. Later in the year, at Akron,
   World Series of Golf, José-Maria
   Olazabal shot −9, 61 on the par-70
   Firestone South course, in the first
   round, missing a couple of three-
   or four-foot putts in the process.
2. "He broke the 54-hole tournament
   record. His 62 could have been 59.
   He had birdie putts on at least four
   of the eight holes he didn't birdie."
   —Jim Murray, *Los Angeles Times*,
   2/25/90.
3. *Los Angeles Times*, 2/25/90.
4. *Golf World*, 3/2/90.
5. USA *Today*, 2/26/90.

CHAPTER 9
1. USA *Today*, 5/11/90.
2. Ibid.
3. Jeff "Squeeky" Medlin went on to
   great success as Nick Price's
   caddie, but then developed
   leukemia. After several
   unsuccessful attempts at bone
   marrow transplants, Medlin died
   the week after the 1997 U.S. Open.
   Golf misses him still. His
   photograph is on display at the
   World Golf Hall of Fame. During
   the Players Championship week in
   1999 the caddies' association
   inducted him into their Hall of
   Fame.
4. USA *Today*, 8/14/90.
5. Sexual discrimination was still
   allowed, however. Many women
   took up the banner and sued
   private clubs for the right to be
   members at private facilities.

Marcia Chambers wrote extensively about women's issues in golf in her book *The Unplayable Lie*. USA *Today*, (8/9/90) provided additional insight with reports of two women who felt they had experienced discrimination. Marcia Welch was suing the Wildwood Golf Club in Pittsburgh over club practices in equal treatment for men and women members. ACC assistant commissioner Delores Todd reported she had been denied membership at Forest Oaks Country Club in Greensboro, site of the Kmart Greater Greensboro Open, because of her race.

6. Oak Tree Golf Club had dropped out as a site of the 1994 PGA Championship, but has since changed its membership policies and will now host a PGA Club Professional event.
7. USA *Today*, 8/9/90.
8. Ibid., 8/13/90.
9. As of 1998, the exemption for the PGA Championship changed to five years.
10. USA *Today*, 8/13/90.
11. Ibid., 8/13/90.
12. The Shark Shootout is a modified alternate format, whereas the Ryder Cup is a true alternate format.
13. *Los Angeles Times*, 11/18/90.
14. Ibid.
15. Ibid.
16. Ibid.
17. Ibid., 11/19/90.
18. Ibid.

CHAPTER 10

1. USA *Today*, 2/21/91.
2. *Los Angeles Times*, February 1991.
3. The four: Ben Hogan, Jack Nicklaus, Gary Player, Gene Sarazen.
4. In 1996 John Cook broke the PGA Tour 54-hole scoring record at −24 and finished the event just one stroke short of the all-time 72-hole record of −27. John Huston would finally break the 72-hole scoring record with −28 at Hawaii in 1998.
5. *Golf World*, 7/5/91.
6. *The Commercial Appeal*, Memphis.
7. Ibid.

CHAPTER 11

1. *Bury Me in a Pot Bunker*.
2. Wadkins has a history of having an injury year and then a spectacular season. If he'd always been healthy, he might have won 40 events.

CHAPTER 12

1. USA *Today*, 10/31/91.
2. Ibid.
3. Ibid.
4. Ibid., 12/23/91.
5. The club given to him by Steve Dallas.
6. The elastomer ring looks like an oval-shaped piece of black plastic that attached to the back of each iron, but it was much more sophisticated than that.
7. *Golfweek*, 10/24/98.

CHAPTER 13

1. Reilly had a famous line about Couples being a guy from nowhere, a guy with no press clippings.
2. *New York Times*, 3/2/92.
3. USA *Today*, 3/3/92.
4. That was eclipsed when Hale Irwin won at Medinah. The longest stretch between victories belongs to Butch Baird, who went

15 years, 5 months, and 10 days between victories, from 1961 to 1976. In the post–PGA Tour era, the record at this time belonged to Leonard Thompson, who had gone 11 years, 9 months before winning in Flint in 1989. He said at the World Series of Golf that year that he'd received a card for Bob Murphy to thank him from taking his spot on the trivia list. Since Thompson's feat, Howard Twitty and Ed Fiori have eclipsed him.

5. *Sports Illustrated*, 3/16/92.
6. *Golfweek*, 3/28/92.
7. The largest winning margin in U.S. professional events was 16 by J. D. Edgar in the 1919 Canadian Open, Joe Kirkwood, Sr., in the 1924 Corpus Christi Open; and Bobby Locke in the 1948 Chicago Victory National Championship. After that, 14 strokes, Johnny Miller, 1975 Phoenix; Ben Hogan, 1945 Portland; 13 strokes, Byron Nelson, 1945 Seattle Open; Gene Littler, 1955 T of C; 12 strokes, Byron Nelson, 1939, Phoenix; Arnold Palmer, 1962, Phoenix; Jose Maria Olazabal, 1990 World Series, Tiger Woods, 1997 Masters.
8. *USA Today*, 3/23/92.
9. *New York Times*, 3/23/92.

CHAPTER 14
1. *Golf Magazine*, April 1993.
2. The next year, Couples attended and made his own speech.
3. *Golf World*, 4/17/92.
4. Ibid.
5. Ibid.
6. *USA Today*, 4/13/92.
7. Until 1998, when the same thing happened to Couples in an early round.
8. *USA Today*, 4/13/92.

9. *New York Times*, 4/13/92.
10. *Golf World*, 4/17/92.
11. *Florida Times Union*, 4/13/92.
12. *Source*: Glenn Greenspan, Augusta National Golf Club.

CHAPTER 15
1. *Golfweek*.
2. *New York Times*, 4/14/92.
3. Ibid.
4. *Sports Illustrated*, 5/25/92.
5. *New York Times*, 6/18/92.

CHAPTER 16
1. November, according to the *New York Times*, 2/10/93; October, according to the same publication, 3/16/93.
2. *Golf Magazine*, April, 1993.
3. Ibid.
4. Andrew Farrell, E-mail.
5. *USA Today*, 2/11/93.
6. *New York Times*, 2/10/93.
7. *USA Today*, 2/11/93.
8. Ibid., 2/23/93.
9. *Golf Magazine*, 4/93.
10. *New York Times*, 3/16/93.
11. *Golf World*, 3/19/93.
12. Ibid.
13. *New York Times*, 3/16/93.
14. Ibid.
15. *USA Today*, 3/17/93.
16. NBC telecast.
17. *USA Today*, 11/10/93.

CHAPTER 17
1. *New York Times*, 1/4/94.
2. Ibid., 1/7/94.
3. Ibid., 1/4/94.
4. Ibid., 2/9/94.
5. Ibid., 6/5/94.
6. Ibid.
7. Ibid.
8. The *New York Times*, 9/13/94, mentioned a live interview that Greg Norman conducted from his home during the 1991 Ryder Cup

matches in which he expressed a desire to have a similar contest for other countries.

9. Ibid.
10. Ibid.
11. *Golf World*, 11/18/98.
12. *Sports Illustrated*, "Golf Plus," November 1994.
13. *Sports Illustrated*, "Golf Plus," November, 1994.

CHAPTER 18

1. This story is included here as a result of conversations at Marge Ryan's 80th birthday party, in Jacksonville, Illinois, between the author's mother and Mrs. Ryan's daughter, Susan Ryan Weeks, who knew the story about Micah Mefford.

CHAPTER 19

1. *New York Times*, 2/22/95.
2. *Golf World*, 2/3/95.
3. Ibid.
4. *New York Times*, 2/22/95.
5. Ibid.
6. *The World of Professional Golf*, 1996, p. 87.
7. *Golf Week*, 9/30/95.
8. A special feature of Oak Hill is that around the 13th green there are oak trees that honor, as club officials explain it, "immortals of golf and the distinguished citizens who have enriched the American way of life." Some of those with their own trees are: President Gerald Ford, President Dwight Eisenhower, Bob Hope, Jack Nicklaus, Arnold Palmer, Gary Player, Bobby Jones, Gene Sarazen, Ben Hogan, Walter Hagen (a Rochester native), Lee Trevino, Curtis Strange, Chick Evans, Roberto De Vicenzo, Billy Casper, Miller Barber, Dr. Cary

Middlecoff, Kathy Whitworth, Babe Zaharias, Francis Ouimet, Horton Smith, Donald Ross, Robert Trent Jones. Others perhaps less well-known to the average fan are Joe Dey, Jr., Richard Tufts, Jim Hand, Bill Campbell, William C. Chapin, Charlie Coe, C. W. Benedict, and Dr. John Williams, Sr.

9. *The World of Professional Golf*, 1996, p. 89.
10. *Golf Week*, 9/30/95.
11. *Golf World*, 11/17/95.
12. *The World of Professional Golf*, 1996, p. 104.
13. Ibid., p. 106.
14. Ibid.
15. Ibid., p. 102.
16. Ibid., p. 305.

CHAPTER 20

1. *Golf World*, 4/5/96.
2. *New York Times*, 6/10/96.

CHAPTER 21

1. *Golf World*, 4/18/97.
2. *New York Times*, 8/19/97.
3. *The World of Professional Golf*, 1998, p. 55.
4. *New York Times*, 8/15/97.
5. *Golf World*, 8/22/97.
6. *Golf World*, 10/3/97.

CHAPTER 22

1. *Golf World*, 4/17/98.
2. Ibid.
3. Reuters, 4/9/98, Internet
4. The Masters, Web site.
5. *Golfweek*, 5/23/98.
6. Ibid.
7. *Golf World*, 6/5/98.

Index